7oC

WITHDRAWN

Hellenistic and Roman Sparta

States and Cities of Ancient Greece

Edited by R F Willetts

Emeritus Professor of Greek, University of Birmingham

Already published

Argos and the Argolid
From the end of the Bronze Age to the Roman occupation
R A Tomlinson

The foundations of palatial Crete
A survey of Crete in the early Bronze Age
K Branigan

Sparta and Lakonia
A regional history 1300–362 BC
P A Cartledge

Mycenaean Greece
J T Hooker

The Dorian Aegean
E M Craik

The Ionians and Hellenism
*A study of the cultural achievement of the early Greek inhabitants of
    Asia Minor*
C J Emlyn-Jones

Thebes in the fifth century
Heracles resurgent
N Demand

Hellenistic and Roman Sparta
A tale of two cities

Paul Cartledge

Lecturer in Ancient History, University of Cambridge

and

Antony Spawforth

Lecturer in Ancient History and Greek Archaeology, University of Newcastle upon Tyne

ROUTLEDGE
London and New York

This book is dedicated to The Ephoreia of Arkadia–Lakonia and The British School at Athens with affection and gratitude.

First published 1989
by Routledge
11 New Fetter Lane, London EC4P 4EE
29 West 35th Street, New York NY10001

Printed in Great Britain by
T.J. Press (Padstow) Ltd, Padstow, Cornwall.

British Library Cataloguing in Publication Data

Cartledge, P.A. (Paul A.)
  Hellenistic and Roman Sparta: a tale of two cities
  1. Greek civilization: Spartan civilization, ancient period
  I. Title   II. Spawforth, A.J.S. (Antony J.S)
  938′.9
  ISBN 0–415–03290–3

Library of Congress Cataloging-in-Publication Data

Cartledge, Paul.
  Hellenistic and Roman Sparta: A tale of two cities
  Bibliography: p.
  Includes index.
  1. Sparta (Ancient city) History.
  I. Spawforth, A.J.S. (Antony J.S.)
  II. Title.
  DF261.S8C373   1989   938'.9   88–32138

Contents

Contents

Preface

The aim of this book is to offer an account of Sparta over the eight centuries or so between her loss of 'great power' status in the second quarter of the fourth century BC and the temporary occupation of the late antique city by the Gothic chieftain Alaric in AD 396. Books on Sparta are hardly rare. One of the chief novelties of this one is that it sets out to give full weight to the Roman phase in Sparta's story, rather than making of it the usual epilogue or (at best) final chapter in a study preoccupied with the earlier periods. We thereby hope to provide a book which will interest, not only students of Sparta *tout court*, but also those concerned with the life of Greece and other Greek-speaking provinces under Roman rule.

Hellenistic Sparta, however, had entered the Roman Empire by no mundane route. In line with her age-old and deeply-entrenched particularism, and indeed by revivifying her esoteric traditions of political and socio-economic organization under the slogan of a return to the 'constitution of Lycurgus', Sparta resisted Roman incorporation right up to the last possible moment. And before Rome, Macedon and the Achaean League had been treated to a similarly defiant denial. For although old Greece ('old' by comparison with the post-Alexander Hellenic diaspora) as a whole was *de facto* subjugated by Macedon in 338 BC, Sparta persisted in ploughing an isolationist and oppositionist furrow, remaining *de jure* independent not just of Macedon but also of all Greek multi-state organizations (not excluding their anti-Macedonian manifestations), until she was formally and forcibly incorporated in the by then Rome-dominated Achaean League in 192 BC. This was the culmination, or nadir, of an extraordinary *pentekontaëtia* during which a succession of Spartan kings (*alias* 'tyrants' to their articulate enemies) sought with surprising success to maintain the traditional freedom and self-determination of the Greek *polis*. This they achieved in spite or because of the most extreme measures of domestic reform, measures that some observers then and now would controversially label 'revolutionary', notwithstanding the ideological appeal to supposedly ancestral 'Lycurgan' precedent and inspiration. Sparta, in short, in the Hellenistic era retains an interest, an importance and a distinctiveness that merit and demand historical enquiry no less insistently than her hitherto more illustrious Archaic and Classical predecessors.

What of the Roman period? The time now seems ripe for taking a fresh look at Roman Sparta. In the last half-century the Greek world under Roman rule has become relatively well-mapped territory, not least as a result of the stupendous scholarship of the late Louis Robert, whose meticulous studies of the post-Classical *polis* through its epigraphy and numismatics to a greater or lesser extent underpin all modern work on the subject, including the Roman section of this volume. The only major study of Roman Sparta to date, that of Chrimes (1949), neglected this larger perspective, adopting instead a retrospective stance and using the evidence for the Roman city merely as 'the starting point for a fresh examination of the evidence about the earlier period'. Her approach was partly a response to that aspect of the Roman city which has most struck modern observers: its tenacious attachment to ancestral tradition – or, in V. Ehrenberg's less flattering formulation, 'the tragi-comedy of Spartan conservatism'. Part Two of the present volume offers, in effect, a reappraisal of the approach of Chrimes. It aims, firstly, to bring Roman Sparta firmly down to earth: to show that the Roman city resembled other provincial Greek communities in its political, cultural and socio-economic organization, displaying the characteristic features of the age from emperor-worship and benefactor-politicians to colonnaded streets and hot baths. As we hope to show, some of the changes arising from Sparta's enforced transition from 'city-state to provincial town' were prefigured by the domestic reforms of Sparta's Hellenistic kings, Nabis in particular; to view Sparta under Roman rule (from 146 BC onwards, that is) without reference to the immediately preceding period would be to lose an essential historical perspective.

Part Two then re-examines Spartan archaism in the Roman era, with a view to showing that this aspect of local civic life likewise had its larger context, that of the archaeomania which, with Roman encouragement, gripped the Greek-speaking provinces during the last century BC and the first three AD; in this period the recreation – or invention – of the past is best viewed as a form of cultural activity in its own right. The likelihood of real 'continuity' is diminished by this acknowledgement of the extent of Greek antiquarianism under Roman rule. On the other hand, the overshadowing of Greek culture in this period by the achievements of the past gave provincial Sparta, home of the widely admired Spartan myth, the opportunity to acquire a new international prominence, above all during the cultural flowering in the second and third centuries sometimes called the Greek renaissance. Part Two aims, finally, to document for the first time Sparta's unforeseen evolution during these two centuries into a touristic, agonistic and even an intellectual centre. Although the Graeco-Roman cultural outlook which permitted this development had its banal side, the development itself is of some interest. It confirms that rumours of the death of Sparta, which buzzed around the corridors of power in antiquity from the late 370s BC onwards and have been too hastily believed in more recent days, are in fact seriously exaggerated. If we stand further back, we can see it as a startling manifestation of the cultural cohesiveness which Greek civilization in its 'Roman summer' drew from the recollection of past glories and which, in turn, contributed to the survival of a unitary Roman state in the east into the Middle Ages in the form of the Byzantine Empire.

*   *   *   *   *   *

As well as modern discussions, we have cited the ancient evidence as fully as we can. For the Roman period some of it is gathered (for the first time) in the four appendices which, it is hoped, will enhance the utility of the book and not merely add to its bulk. Spelling of names has caused even more of a problem than usual in a book that treats both Greek and Roman phases of Sparta's history. To avoid such barbarous hybrids as 'C. Iulius Eurykles', we have, not without some misgivings and inconsistencies, Latinized throughout. Modern work is cited according to the 'Harvard' system, so that most publications cited find their place in the general bibliography at the back of the book.

Many debts have been incurred in the writing of this book. We are grateful to our respective institutions, the Universities of Cambridge and Newcastle upon Tyne, for financial support enabling us to visit Laconia in 1982 and for awards of leave of absence in respectively 1987 and 1988, during which much of the book in its final form was written. Financial support was also forthcoming from Clare College, Cambridge, and from the Leverhulme Research Awards Committee. So far as institutional support is concerned, it remains to thank the staff in the libraries of the Hellenic and Roman Societies, London, and the Faculty of Classics, Cambridge.

The first part of the book (by P.A.C.) continues, both chronologically and thematically, the author's *Sparta and Lakonia. A regional history 1300–362 BC* (1979). That work too appeared in the same 'States and Cities of Ancient Greece' series, and the authors are aware of their debt to Norman Franklin of Routledge and Professor Ron Willetts, general editor of the series, for agreeing to include this companion volume therein. The book's second part (by A.J.S.S.) has as its (completely reworked) kernel the author's Birmingham University PhD thesis, *Studies in the History of Roman Sparta*, examined in 1982 by Martin Goodman and Fergus Millar, from whose comments the present work has sought to profit. Individual chapters in both parts have been read at varying stages of readiness by Ewen Bowie, Riet van Bremen, Simon Hornblower, John Lazenby, Ricardo Martinez-Lacy, Stephen Mitchell, Frank Walbank, Susan Walker and John Wilkes. As a result of their generously offered and unfailingly perceptive criticisms the end-product has been much improved, although its remaining shortcomings are of course entirely the responsibility of the authors. Thanks to the kindness of well over a decade ago of George Steinhauer, formerly Acting Ephor of Arkadia-Lakonia, the book has been written with an awareness of some of the many unpublished inscriptions, mostly of Roman date, in the Sparta Museum. We also wish to thank Nigel Kennell for generously making available the text of his unpublished PhD thesis (Kennell 1985). For other valued help provided in ways too varied to itemize we are grateful to Bob Bridges, Bill Cavanagh, and Graham Shipley. The maps were drawn by Liz Lazenby.

P.A.C.
A.J.S.S.
June 1988

Maps

ROMAN LACONIA

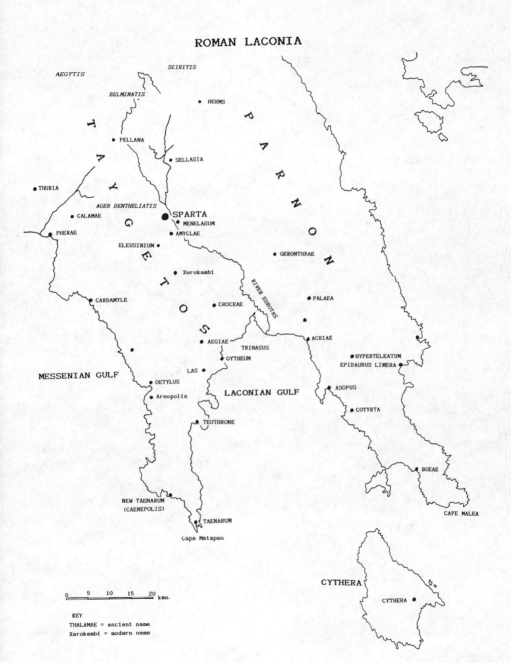

AEGYTIS

SCIRITIS

BELMINATIS

• HERMS

T A Y G

• PELLANA

• SELLASIA

• THURIA

AGER DENTHELIATIS

• CALAMAE

SPARTA
• MENELAEUM

• PHERAE

• AMYCLAE

ELEUSINIUM •

E T O S

• Xerokambi

• GERONTHRAE

• CARDAMYLE

• CROCEAE

RIVER EUROTAS

• PALAEA

P A R N O N

• AEGIAE

TRINASUS

• ACRIAE

MESSENIAN GULF

• GYTHEUM

LAS •

• HYPERTELEATUM
EPIDAURUS LIMERA •

• OETYLUS

LACONIAN GULF

• ASOPUS

• Areopolis

• COTYRTA

• TEUTHRONE

• BOEAE

NEW TAENARUM
(CAENEPOLIS)

• TAENARUM

CAPE MALEA

Cape Matapan

0   5   10   15   20 kms.

CYTHERA

KEY
THALAMAE = ancient name
Xerokambi = modern name

• CYTHERA

xiii

I

Hellenistic Sparta

Chapter one

In the shadow of empire: Mantinea to Chaeronea

History, in the objective sense of 'what actually happened', is a seamless web. All historiographical starting-points must be in some degree arbitrary. Contemporaries as well as modern authors saw 362 BC as signifying something of a historical as well as historiographical caesura.[1] Yet to grasp its full import one must track back almost a decade, to the battle that marked the beginning of the end of Classical Sparta.

In July 371 the Boeotian confederacy under the inspired guidance of the Thebans Epaminondas and Pelopidas soundly trounced the Spartan, allied, and mercenary army led by King Cleombrotus at Leuctra in the territory of Boeotian Thespiae.[2] Opinions differ today, as they did then, regarding the wisdom, legality and competence of Sparta's anti-Theban offensive. But there is no ambiguity, at least in retrospect, about the decisive importance of this historic defeat, the first suffered by Sparta in a major pitched encounter between hoplite infantrymen for some three centuries.[3] For it signalled the declension of Classical Sparta from the status of a great Greek power to that of a second-rate provincial squabbler.

Pausanias, antiquarian travel-writer and commentator of the second century AD, looked back to Leuctra with (for him) uncharacteristic triumphalism as 'the most splendid victory ever, to our knowledge, won by Greek over Greek'.[4] This sentiment would have been cheered to the echo by the many thousands of European and Asiatic Greeks who had experienced the effects of Spartan imperialism since 404, when Sparta with critical Persian aid eventually defeated Athens in the great Peloponnesian War.[5] Indeed, so unpopular had Sparta become by 371 that even some of her inner circle of Peloponnesian League allies 'were not displeased by the way things had gone' at Leuctra and were quick to open negotiations with their Boeotian conquerors.[6]

Prominent among these latter allies, it must be assumed, were men of Arcadia. Towards this ruggedly upland region of central Peloponnese Sparta had long anticipated Rome in the most efficient practice of a policy of divide and rule. As a major result, the Arcadians had not hitherto managed to translate their inchoate pan-Arcadian consciousness into pan-Arcadian political institutions. The Leuctra battle radically altered the geopolitical situation in their favour. Encouraged by the discovery of Spartan military debility and by the disaffection among Sparta's Perioecic subjects situated along their mutual border, Tegea now at last united with her traditional north Arcadian rival Mantinea to forge an (almost) pan-Arcadian political and military federation on democratic lines within a year of Sparta's great defeat. Joining forces next with Elis, another long-dissident former Peloponnesian League ally of Sparta, and with Argos, Sparta's hereditary rival for the hegemony of the Peloponnese, the newly politicized Arcadians conveyed a charged appeal for an invasion of Sparta's home territory to the two most formidable powers of central Greece north of the Isthmus of Corinth, Athens and Thebes.[7]

Athens in 370 led a large and potentially powerful naval alliance, the so-called Second Athenian League. This was a politically more acceptable revival of the fifth-century 'Delian League' that had brought Athens an Aegean empire under cover of an offensive and defensive alliance directed against Persia. The Second League had been formed in 378 against Sparta, yet in 370 it was not a weakened and vulnerable Sparta that most Athenians hated and feared but rather their uncomfortably near neighbours in Thebes.[8]

Ironically, Athens had herself helped liberate Thebes in 379/8 from Spartan military occupation, and Thebes had reciprocated by becoming one of the half-dozen founder members of the Second Athenian League. But the Thebans' overriding strategic and political interests were engaged in central and northern mainland Greece, not the Aegean, and they were quick to refound, on moderately democratic lines, the Boeotian confederacy that Sparta had dismembered in 386 at the behest of King Agesilaus II and under the aegis of the Peace of the Persian Great King Artaxerxes II. This was the confederacy, strengthened (if only negatively) in 373 by the demilitarization of Thespiae and destruction of Athens' ally Plataea, that won Leuctra.[9]

The Athenians therefore rebuffed the Arcadian, Elean and Argive request. The Boeotians at Epaminondas' urging received it warmly and responded to it positively at their earliest convenience. Towards the very end of 370, at the head of the large Boeotian alliance and crucially assisted by Sparta's external and internal Peloponnesian enemies, Epaminondas thus succeeded in invading Sparta's own *polis* territory by land. This unprecedented feat presupposed not only that Sparta's traditional alliance system had collapsed but also that she had lost control of her borderland, a symbolically as well as pragmatically potent space, the crossing of which by a Spartan army required performance of the *diabatēria* ritual. In fact, the Perioecic peoples of both Sciritis and Caryae, whose territories marched with that of Tegea, had revolted to

Epaminondas at the critical moment. So apparently had the Perioeci of the Belminatis area at the headwaters of the Eurotas to the west.[10]

Worse, much worse, was to follow, though not immediately. For the remaining Perioeci of Laconia's eastern and southern coasts stayed loyal, not least those of Gytheum, Sparta's chief port, who withstood a short siege behind their city walls. So too the Laconian segment of the Helots, Sparta's serf-like population of primary agricultural producers, stood firm behind the Spartan colours. Such indeed was their loyalty or indoctrination that in return for a promise of freedom more than 6,000 volunteered to fight as hoplites to compensate for the extreme shrinkage of the Spartiate military effective. The town of Sparta, moreover, remained inviolate, though not because of its artificial defences (which the Spartans still disdained to erect) but because the Eurotas river was seasonally swollen with midwinter snow and Epaminondas had anyway not made its capture his top strategic or political priority.[11]

Yet these bright spots were soon obfuscated by a thick smog of deep gloom for Sparta, as Epaminondas turned to the liberation of the more numerous, more politically motivated, more ethnically self-conscious Helots of the Pamisus valley in neighbouring Messenia. These 'Messenians', as they liked to call themselves in anticipation of their political as well as personal rebirth, had predictably taken advantage of Sparta's immediately local difficulties and of their own remoteness from the masters' central place to rise in revolt as soon as Epaminondas entered Laconia. It was on his return from Gytheum up the Eurotas furrow and along the easiest route into the Pamisus valley *via* the south-west Arcadian plain that the Theban planted the foundations of the new *polis* of Messene. Expatriate Messenians flocked back from points as distant as Sicily and north Africa to stake their claim to land and citizenship in a state whose central space about Mt Ithome was endowed with the finest enceinte walling then known in the entire Greek world.[12]

At a stroke the political geography of the Peloponnese as it had been for some three centuries had been altered dramatically. To make doubly sure that Sparta should not easily rise again to prepotence, Epaminondas also had a hand in a second entirely new Peloponnesian city-foundation. In the south-west Arcadian plain that he had traversed in 370/69 there arose between 369 and 368 'The Great City', known conventionally as Megalopolis. The strategic implications of its very location are transparent. No less significant were its political implications. The double city of Megalopolis was designed both to institutionalize the Arcadians' 'national' consciousness by becoming the capital of the Arcadian federal state and to be a new state in its own right that drew its citizen body from no less than forty existing communities including some former Laconian Perioeci. The post-Peloponnesian War era in Greek history is sometimes labelled 'the crisis of the *polis*'. However much truth there may be in the view that many or most existing *poleis* were undergoing some sort of political, social or economic crisis at this time, these two brand new creations of Messene and Megalopolis must be set boldly on the other side of the ledger. To claim that 'the *polis*' *tout court* was in the grip of a terminal malaise is at best a gross simplification.[13]

In regard to Sparta specifically, however, there can be no question but that 'crisis' is the correct term for her historical experience during the second quarter of the fourth century and probably a lot earlier. By 369 she had been stripped of something like a half of her *polis* territory, including the most fertile soil and some strategically and symbolically sensitive border country. In terms of dependent manpower, she had lost the most important portion of her servile agricultural workforce as well as sizeable numbers of free but politically subject Perioecic soldiers. In 365 what was left of her Peloponnesian League alliance melted into oblivion. Perhaps most serious of all, though, was the catastrophic shrinkage of the Spartiate, full citizen population. Nothing like accurate demographic statistics are available for any Classical Greek city, but it is tolerably clear that in the century or so between the Persian Wars of 480–479 and the Battle of Leuctra the Spartan citizen body (adult male) contracted by more than eighty per cent. No less clearly, this phenomenon lay at the heart of Sparta's decline and fall as a great power.

Why precisely it occurred is and always will be a matter of huge controversy, but that lies outside the scope of the present work. What is relevant and, arguably, correct is Aristotle's laconic judgment that Sparta 'was destroyed through dearth of manpower' (*oliganthrōpia*). It was, that is to say, on account of the dearth of civic military manpower that Sparta was unable to recover from Aristotle's 'single blow', the decisive defeat at Leuctra. That this was indeed a decisive defeat – notwithstanding some territorial retrenchment and possible land- and army-reform in the 360s – was broadcast by the general Hellenic settlement of 362 following the (second) Battle of Mantinea.[14]

This was the largest inter-Greek battle ever fought, involving up to 60,000 men in all. It was an attempt to settle the question of Hellenic hegemony first raised in acute form in the fifth century: could any one Greek state create the military and political framework to exercise a stable control over the pale of Greek settlement around the Aegean basin and up into the Bosporus? The Peloponnesian War had delivered a negative response to Athens, the one postulant with pretensions to a naval hegemony that did not involve co-operation with any external power. Sparta, fundamentally a land-oriented power, had briefly succeeded to Athens' hegemony; but in 386 she abandoned the Greeks of Asia to the Persian Great King, and under the terms of the King's Peace (or Peace of Antalcidas) her suzerainty in mainland Greece and the islands was importantly dependent on that monarch's goodwill. After

Leuctra, and after the assassination of the Thessalian dynast Jason in 370, a Thebes-dominated Boeotia was the greatest Greek power, but in 367 she too sought the Great King's blessing for what was proving an all too labile ascendancy, rather than a stable hegemony, in just mainland Greece. But even Artaxerxes' backing could not bring Thebes' enemies into line. Prolonged engagement on two widely separated fronts, Thessaly and the Peloponnese, not alleviated by a unique naval campaign in the Aegean, exhausted Boeotia's resources and gave heart to Athens and Sparta (allied since early 369) and to the Mantinea-led fraction of the already fissile Arcadian federation. For the fourth time, therefore, in the summer of 362, Epaminondas led an army south across the isthmus of Corinth.

Affairs in Tegea were the immediate and ostensible cause of this intervention. Epaminondas proceeded there post-haste to reassert Boeotian control and issue instructions to Boeotia's Peloponnesian allies to foregather at the appointed battleground of Mantinea. He himself, however, first executed a lightning raid on Sparta by way, as in 370/69, of Caryae. No more than on that occasion did his intentions now include the capture, let alone destruction, of Sparta town. It was enough to demonstrate again the fragility of Sparta's hold over her remaining north Laconian territory and the vulnerability of a wall-less town deprived both of natural protection (in June the Eurotas was no torrent) and of copious manpower. Nevertheless this was the first time on record that the collocation of villages constituting Sparta's 'urban' centre was penetrated by a hostile force; and by his manoeuvre Epaminondas did prevent Sparta from fighting at Mantinea in what had now to count as 'full force', besides gaining time for his allies in Argos and Messene to do so.[15]

As at Leuctra, the issue was decided chiefly by the fighting quality and spirit of the Theban hoplites and cavalry under the inspired generalship of Epaminondas. Only the latter's death, at the hands perhaps of the Spartan Anticrates, robbed the Boeotian victory of its full savour, although it is hard to see how it could have been forcefully exploited in any event. Rather, victors and vanquished met again on the battlefield to swear a general peace. Like the Peace of 386 and its successive renewals, the foundation of the verbal agreement was a pledge mutually to respect the sovereign autonomy and guarantee the independence from external interference of all Greek states both great and small. Like its predecessors, too, the Peace of 362 was supposed to apply to all Greek states, whether or not they had participated directly in the swearing of the oaths. However, in one certainly and perhaps two important respects this Peace broke new ground.

First, this is the first Peace we know for sure to have been actually called a 'Common Peace' (*koinē eirēnē*). The title by itself betrays a yearning for Hellenic unity and a more positive evaluation of peace than

7

as a mere absence of overt martial conflict. Second, this was unquestionably the first of the general peaces concluded since 386 that did not involve foreign, that is non-Greek, dictation or even participation. That point was rammed home by the united Greeks themselves in a document suitably couched in Attic dialect (which was to be the basis of the *koinē* dialect of the Hellenistic Greek world) but found at Dorian Argos. This surely belongs to the immediate post-Mantinea period, when revolted vassals of the Persian Great King were seeking Greek military aid and were politely but firmly rebuffed by the 'sharers in the Peace' who claimed to have no quarrel with the King so long as he 'does not set the Hellenes against each other and does not, in the case of the Peace that we now have, attempt to dissolve it by any device at all or by stratagem'.[16]

One Greek state, however, which had fought at Mantinea, deliberately and ostentatiously excluded itself from this Common Peace. No prizes for guessing that this was Sparta, governed in this decision – as in most matters of policy over the past three decades – by Agesilaus. For Agesilaus, like his son and virtual co-regent Archidamus, could never countenance the loss of that portion of Messenia which now constituted the *polis* of Messene, let alone acknowledge its existence formally, openly, and under oath. The Athenian conservative pamphleteer Isocrates had nicely captured the emotional wellspring of this irredentist passion for Messenia when he made his 'Archidamus' say (in a dramatic context of 366/5): 'the most painful thing is the prospect not of being deprived unjustly of our own territory but of seeing our own slaves become masters of it'. Agesilaus, therefore, unlike the Greeks who rebuffed the satraps, did take up arms against the Persian Great King – in Egypt. His aim was to gain the funds with which to pay the mercenaries Sparta now depended on to fight the good fight for Messenia.[17]

It was on his return from Egypt, amply rewarded, that Agesilaus finally died at the age of about 84. Archidamus, by then in his forties, succeeded his father on the Eurypontid throne, probably early in 359. That happened also to be the year in which a certain Philip son of Amyntas succeeded his brother as *de facto*, and perhaps also *de jure*, king of Macedon. Theopompus of Chios, a dyspeptic historian of oligarchic and so generally pro-Spartan bent, later opined that Europe had never before produced such a man as Philip. The remark was not intended to be altogether flattering, but it does neatly capture Philip's extraordinary impact on the history of, first, northern mainland Greece, and then the whole Aegean Greek world. It was only the chance of an assassination, probably (see the next chapter), that prevented his having a comparable impact on the history of the Middle East, a rôle fulfilled by his son Alexander in his stead.

The history of Sparta during the reign of Archidamus, which forms the subject of the rest of this chapter, has to be written in the interstices and under the cloud of the dominant history of the rise of Macedon. (If I say nothing of Archidamus' Agiad co-king Cleomenes II, who had reigned since 370 and was to continue in post until 309, that is because there is nothing to say.) So too does all Aegean Greek history, in stark contrast to that of the preceding epoch, for which Agesilaus' friend Xenophon was quite justified in taking the histories of Sparta and Thebes as his guiding threads. The lack of good sources for Macedon and of a competent narrative account of Spartan and Greek history between 359 and 338 is therefore lamentable. Diodorus, a Sicilian Greek who wrote a wholly derivative and oddly named 'Library of History' in the first century BC, makes even Xenophon, for all his prejudices and omissions, seem a diligent and competent historian.[18]

It was, however, at least partly due to pro-Spartan prejudice and nostalgia that Xenophon concluded his history on a melancholy note: after Mantinea, he wrote, 'there was more unsettlement and disorder in Hellas than before the battle'. For, looked at in another way, as by the anti-Spartan Demosthenes in 330, that battle had the positively beneficial consequence that the Peloponnese was divided and Sparta could no longer domineer over her neighbours in her accustomed manner. Casting aside all prejudices, Demosthenes' is surely the correct perspective to adopt on Sparta's external history under Archidamus. The way in which Sparta participated, or did not participate at all, in the major enterprises of his day is eloquent supporting testimony. As for Sparta's internal history, we as usual lack the account of an insider, a participant observer who was also a Spartan citizen. But we do possess a very acceptable second-best substitute in the *Politics* of Aristotle. For he and his pupils had conducted what then passed for primary historical research on Spartan institutions, and the philosophic Stagirite brought to his studies the understanding of a properly sociological imagination.[19]

For the first years of Archidamus the annals of Sparta are a virtual blank. But in 356, as is implied by Isocrates' no doubt misplaced appeal to Archidamus to assume the rôle of panhellenic leader against Persia, Sparta was again active on two widely separated fronts, Sicily and central Greece. We shall return briefly to Sicily and the Greek west in connection with the end of Archidamus' career and life. His and Sparta's involvement with Phocis and thereby with the so-called Third Sacred War (356/5–346) was of far greater moment. For it was this prolonged conflict that constituted the introit to Philip's consecration as director of mainland Greek affairs.

The title of the war must not mislead. This was no more a crusade or *jihad* than the Corinthian War of 395–386, which had also arisen from a dispute between Phocians and Locrians fanned by Thebes. Rather, it was a thoroughly secular struggle that found expression through the manipulation, physical occupation and monetarization of the panhellenic sanctuary of Delphi with its oracle and treasures. From of old, the management of this holiest of Greek shrines had lain with an Amphictyony or sacred council, the majority of whose members were provided by Thessalian communities. Tradition had it that control of Delphi had been fought over in the literal sense on two previous occasions, but the first may be a fiction and the second was a brief episode without major ramifications. The Third Sacred War was an altogether larger affair of central significance for all mainland Greek political, military and diplomatic history.[20]

Sparta was an active member of the Delphic Amphictyony with exceedingly ancient, intimate and binding ties to the oracle. Following the earthquake and fire that had wrecked the Temple of Apollo in 373 both individual Spartans (of both sexes) and the Spartan state officially had helped finance and administer its reconstruction. It was partly therefore for reasons of sentiment that Sparta was so quick to get involved in the Third Sacred War. But sentiment was outweighed by yet more pressing pragmatic reasons. First, Thebes had exploited her post-Leuctra predominance to manipulate the Amphictyony into fining Sparta the enormous sum of 500 talents for the sacrilegious seizure and occupation of the acropolis of Thebes in 382. Sparta had not paid, indeed could not afford to pay, but the insult rankled. Second, a major and possibly prolonged war in central Greece was seen by Archidamus as the best chance of halting Theban intervention in Sparta's Peloponnesian sphere on the side of her enemies in Messene, Megalopolis (most recently in 361) and Argos. So when in 356 at the instigation of Thebes the Amphictyony doubled the Spartans' unpaid fine and at the same time inflicted a severe penalty on Phocis for another alleged religious misdemeanour, Archidamus did not need to be bribed to renew the Spartan co-operation with Phocis that had lapsed in 371 and was happy to entrust the Phocian leader Philomelus with fifteen talents.[21]

Diodorus says this transaction was effected 'secretly' and perhaps means that Archidamus had not gone through the formal channels of approval by the Gerousia and Spartan Assembly. But since there is no doubt that they would have consented, the secrecy must have been for the benefit of Philomelus rather than Sparta, unless there is a hint here of the controversial use to which Philomelus put the money. In any case, the form of the Spartan aid is revealing. For even if Archidamus had wanted and been able to give open support, he could not have spared any of Sparta's by now fewer than one thousand citizen hoplites for an extra-Peloponnesian enterprise of doubtful outcome. Money therefore was his only resort, but the Spartan treasury had never been flush at the best of times, not least because the Spartans were reputedly reluctant taxpayers and Sparta anyway was not a very monetized society. For liquid cash it had always depended on sources from outside the economy, like the enormous booty Agesilaus captured in Asia in the 390s or the 'gift' he received from an Egyptian ruler in 360/59. Nor in 356 could Archidamus any longer call on cash contributions from Sparta's allies in the defunct Peloponnesian League. The fifteen talents must therefore have come either from the residue of his father's Egyptian donation or possibly even from his own considerable personal fortune.[22]

Their purpose was to purchase the services of mercenaries, of whom there was a ready supply and on whom most Greek states, not excluding Sparta, had come to depend since the 390s. With his Phocians and mercenaries Philomelus reasserted the Phocians' ancient claim to (geographically Phocian) Delphi in the most tangible way, by seizing and occupying it. The anathema pronounced on this move at the autumn 356 meeting of the Amphictyony formally inaugurated the Sacred War. Philomelus himself was defeated and killed in 354, but his successor Onomarchus proved to have even fewer religious scruples. The real charge of sacrilege against Phocis arose from his decision to monetize the sanctuary's accumulated multinational treasures for the purpose of recruiting yet more mercenaries. This he did to such effect that in 353 he inflicted on the Thessalians' champion Philip of Macedon the only two defeats that monarch suffered in pitched battle during more than twenty years of active campaigning.[23]

By 353 Philip had not merely secured his throne and kingdom from internal and external threats but actually enlarged and enriched the fissile domain he had inherited half a dozen years before, by a subtle combination of more or less veiled bribery and brute force. The rich plains and profitable port facilities of neighbouring Thessaly to his south offered a tempting sphere for expansion as well as a source of legitimate strategic concern. Philip was not the first Macedonian king to involve himself in the politics of this antiquated and not quite Greek region, which only once – under the dynamic Jason in the later 370s – had threatened to become a major power-unit in its own right. But he was the first to dominate them, and the first non-Thessalian to rule the loose-hung Thessalian federation. The military leadership of Thessaly that he had acquired before the Battle of the Crocus Field in 352 was translated after his decisive victory over the Phocians there into formal election as *arkhōn* of the federation. Philip's writ now ran as far south as the pass of Thermopylae. The Phocians, together with their Spartan and Athenian allies, were therefore rightly prompt to occupy it in advance, the Spartans contributing a thousand troops of whom most were of course Perioeci. Philip 'came, saw and retired' (Griffith), but the menace he posed was merely postponed.[24]

In the short breathing-space afforded by this impasse Sparta was active against two of her three main Peloponnesian enemies. In 351 Archidamus and his son Agis (the future Agis III) attacked Megalopolis with 3000 mercenaries provided by Phocis. There was also a campaign against Argos that involved Theban troops. The propagandistic ground for these assaults had been prepared by Archidamus in autumn 353, when he had proposed a far-reaching series of restorations of 'ancestral' territories to their 'legitimate' owners. He had chiefly in mind of course the restitution of Messene to Sparta, together with those northern Laconian Perioecic communities that had been incorporated in Megalopolis. But he couched the proposal in much wider terms with a view to winning the support of Athens, Elis, Phlius, some Boeotian cities hostile to Thebes and some Arcadian ones opposed to the Arcadian federation. The proposal predictably fell flat, though at least Athens stayed neutral rather than fight on the side of Megalopolis as Demosthenes advocated. Hence Sparta's very limited outside succour in 351 and her complete lack of success. The death of the octogenarian Spartiate Hippodamus is notable if only because it reminds us that this campaign came too soon for the crippling loss of 400 Spartiates at Leuctra to have been made good by natural increase. Gastron and Lamius were probably not the only Spartans who now preferred lucrative mercenary service in Egypt to the great patriotic war of irredentist recuperation nearer home.[25]

Non-literary sources cast interesting sidelights on the condition of Sparta at the nadir of her fortunes in the mid-century. First, a proxeny-decree of about 360 BC from the Cycladic island of Ceus (Keos). Among others, men from no less than four Laconian Perioecic communities (Pellana in the northwest, Cyphanta and Epidaurus Limera on the east coast, and one whose name is lost) were honoured with the status of official diplomatic representative of Ceus in their home towns. This must have something to do with Ceus' current disaffection from Athens, which was shared by other members of the Second Athenian League, even if it is hard to see exactly how Pellana and the others could have been of much practical help. For the honorands, on the other hand, it must have been as flattering as it had been for Gnosstas of Oenus (made *proxenos* of Argos a century earlier) to be treated as representatives of autonomous political entities. The influence of Epaminondas is faintly detectable, perhaps, but the political weakness of Sparta is palpable.[26]

Secondly, a perhaps slightly later inscription from the healing shrine of Asclepius at Epidaurus tells on the face of it a heartwarming tale. One Arata, a Spartan female of indeterminate age, was sick of the dropsy, whereupon her mother incubated in the Asclepieum and dreamed an impossible dream in which Asclepius decapitated the daughter and then rejoined the severed head to her neck. Arata, needless to say, was cured when her loving mother returned to Sparta. The growing popularity of Asclepius in the fourth century was by no means peculiar to Sparta, or Spartan women, and dropsy could be fatal. Yet there is something symbolically apt in Spartan women behaving just like any other Greek women for once, rather than as the viragos of laconizing mythology. On the other hand, should Arata have been suffering from dropsy of the womb, there might have been a particular local significance in her mother's incubating at a time of acute Spartan civic *oliganthrōpia*.[27]

However that may be, Sparta's limited manpower was in no position to affect the outcome of the Sacred War, which rested, on appeal from Thebes, in the lap of Philip. The most Archidamus could do was attempt ineffectually to oust the deposed and Philippizing Phocian general Phalaecus from Thermopylae in 347/6 and send a Spartan delegation to the Macedonian capital Pella in early summer 346 when the fates of Phocis and Thebes were in the balance. The reported flare-up between the Spartan and Theban delegations occasions little surprise, especially as Philip in the end made it clear that he had decided for Thebes. With Amphictyonic authorization Philip duly pulverized the Phocians both militarily and politically and then took their place and two votes on the council, the first individual to be so represented. The Philip-dominated Amphictyony imposed a heavy fine on Phocis and appointed him to preside over the Pythian Games of 346. His Hellenic and indeed panhellenic credentials were being securely established with a view, surely, to fulfilling ambitions beyond the bounds of Hellas.[28]

The Delphic Amphictyony, however, prestigious though it was, was not geared to be the choice instrument of power-politics in all Aegean Greece. This fact Philip recognised duly by not pressing for the expulsion of Sparta (who might reasonably have been held guilty of blasphemy by association with Phocis) or for the admission of Sparta's enemies Messene and Megalopolis. On the other hand, since he could not please all Greeks all of the time, he did decide that Sparta, which was anyway very weak, was also the most dispensable state. In 344 he therefore backed up the cash he habitually provided to the leading politicians of cities he wished to woo with mercenary troops for Messene and Argos in their war with Sparta. It was perhaps in this fighting that the seven sons of Iphicratidas and Alexippa fell. Philip's *Geldpolitik* paid off handsomely in 343 when Argos, Messene and Megalopolis allied with him, and Elis was lost by Sparta to Messene and so to Philip. True, none of these fought with him at the definitive Battle of Chaeronea in 338, but at least they did not contribute to the considerable alliance of Greek states mustered against him by Athens and Thebes.[29]

Nor, despite their unappeasable enmity towards Philip, did the Spartans. Indeed, so far removed were they from the centre of political gravity in mainland Greece after the Sacred War that in 342, when Demosthenes was beginning to cobble together a common Greek resistance to Macedon, their only active king preferred to concern himself with the affairs of Lyctus in Crete and Tarentum in southern Italy. Sentiment no doubt had something to do with Archidamus' decision, since Sparta was the real founder of the latter and honorary metropolis of the former city. And it will have flattered Sparta's lingering self-image as a Greek superpower to play the rôle of Hellenic policeman in the West, since her last showing on the wider Greek stage had been a walk-on part in the dynastic squabbles of Syracuse in the mid-350s. Yet more weighty than either of those considerations was Archidamus' need to recoup his own lost prestige and Sparta's depleted finances. The tradition that Archidamus died fighting at Mandonium (? = Manduria, south-east of Tarentum) on the very day of Chaeronea is too true to be good for Sparta's reputation, but it is of a piece with Diodorus' view that his death was divine retribution for sacrilege – an uncomfortable echo of Xenophon's explanation of the Leuctra *débâcle* in which Archidamus had narrowly missed taking part.[30]

The Battle of Chaeronea, as contemporary and subsequent historians have for the most part recognized, sealed and political fate of all Aegean Greece. Philip's allies Messene, Megalopolis and Argos, like most of the Peloponnese, had not taken part in the fighting. But although they had yet to reciprocate Philip's benefactions, they still had more to offer him in propagandistic as well as pragmatic terms. For in face of a notionally independent and irreducibly hostile Sparta they would always need to look to their Macedonian suzerain for reinforcement or protection, while Sparta's very independence could be represented as proving that the union of supposedly free and autonomous states through which Philip intended to rule mainland Greece was voluntary in fact as well as name. (Similar considerations were to guide the Hellenic diplomacy of the Roman T. Quinctius Flamininus a century and a half later: see chapter 5, below.) Hence, late in 338, Philip took to the road in the footsteps of Epaminondas in order to invade Laconia – ostensibly on behalf of his Peloponnesian adherents, in reality in pursuit of his own geopolitical interests. Elis alone is known to have supplied him with troops, but presumably Argos, Arcadia and Messene did too.[31]

This, the third invasion of Laconia within the lifetime of Sparta's new Eurypontid king Agis III, proved definitive in the most literal sense. There were no risings of Helots or Perioeci to assist him, no plots by disaffected 'inferior' Spartans as in 370/69. Nor did Philip capture Sparta itself – because, like Epaminondas, he did not want or need to, not because he could not have done so, let alone because (as the pious and patriotic Epidaurian Isyllus believed) Asclepius prevented him. Yet he was none the less able to effect his sole aim of redrawing the frontiers of the Spartan *polis*. Thus by early 337 he had stripped Sparta of all her former northern Laconian borderlands (Aegytis, Belminatis, Sciritis, Caryatis and Thyreatis), together with the western borderland of Dentheliatis lying between Laconia and Messenia, the east Laconian coastland as far south as Perioecic Prasiae, and the Perioecic communities of the northeast shore of the Messenian Gulf. It is an intriguing possibility that for the finer points of topographical and historical detail he may have utilized Aristotle's work entitled 'Just Claims of the Greek Cities'. It seems certain that the arrangements Philip made on the spot were later ratified by the united Greeks – barring of course Sparta – of what moderns call the 'League of Corinth' (see the next chapter). But, as the Spartans could not but be aware, power not legality was the real arbiter now of their – and indeed all the mainland Greeks' – destiny.[32]

In short, Sparta retained, apart from the Eurotas valley with its invaluable alluvium worked by the Laconian Helots, only the bulk of the Mani peninsula (very unproductive with the exception of the port and territory of Gytheum) and the eastern, Malea peninsula (most important for its iron ores) out of a civic domain formerly more than twice as extensive and populous. So profound was the noiseless social upheaval in Sparta's domestic arrangements consequent upon the loss of Messenia and of chunks of Perioecic land that we now hear for the first time of Spartans turning their own hands perforce to the plough. The dictum attributed to King Cleomenes I (c.520–490) that Homer, not Hesiod, was the poet of the Spartans had acquired a very hollow ring.[33]

Chapter two

Resistance to Macedon:
the revolt of Agis III

Scholars cannot agree whether Philip's son Alexander III the Great was the first Hellenistic king or whether the Hellenistic epoch properly so called began rather with the struggles for supremacy of the 'Successors' after his premature death in June 323. In a sense the dispute is fruitless, since all periodization of the past is more or less arbitrary (as was noted at the start of the last chapter). In a yet more relevant sense, though, this dispute is also beside the point, as the history of Sparta cannot be slotted conveniently into the conventional 'Classical' to 'Hellenistic' transition, wherever the point of transition may be fixed. For as she had done since 362, so under Alexander and his immediate successors Sparta continued to cut a lone furrow in soil that was generally thin and stony. This is why the present chapter does not end with either of the two traditional clausulae of the Greek Classical period, Alexander's death or the defeat of the Greek rebellion of 323–2, but with the decease of the prodigious nonentity Cleomenes II. It focuses, moreover, on Sparta's self-centred war of resistance against Greece's new suzerain as a symbol of her continued exclusion from the mainstream of Greek political, economic and cultural life.[1]

On the other hand, the chapter begins with what most contemporaries would have recognized as a turning-point in their internal and external histories, the foundation by Philip of the organization known to us as the League of Corinth. 'From the impasse of fourth-century politics', it has been well said, 'with the crisis of interstate relations after Mantinea, the revived impact of Macedon, and the social and economic problems of the Greek mainland, sprang Macedonian hegemony, the plan to conquer Persia, and the Hellenistic Age with its new values'. One of those values, though not exactly brand new, was the idea of Hellenic unification on the political as well as the cultural or ethnic plane. To quote Walbank again, 'The idea of a Greek nation is alien to the thought of most Greeks at most periods throughout Greek history . . . Yet . . . we can clearly trace a movement towards integration in larger units . . . possible because ultimately the Greeks felt themselves to be a single people'. *Prima facie,* the League of Corinth as a self-styled 'Hellenic' body qualifies as strong evidence of this movement at the very threshold of the Hellenistic Age. Closer inspection, however, reveals that the evidence should be sought elsewhere, in the rebellion of 323–2. For despite its geographical comprehensiveness, the League of Corinth was a sectarian move in the interests of the few, propertied Greeks and, above all, was merely a means to a larger end in Philip's and Alexander's scheme of things.[2]

Much scholarly ink has been spilt, unnecessarily, over the technical question whether the Greeks who were united under the umbrella of the League were sharers in a Common Peace only or were also members of a military alliance. The distinction is in both senses academic, since the League's first decision in summer 337 was to appoint Philip *hēgemōn* or military leader of an expedition dressed up as a crusade against Persia. Even if the Greeks were not formally subordinate allies of Philip, that was how they were voting to be treated. The relationship between the *sunedrion* (council) of the allies and their Athenian *hēgemōn* in the Second Athenian League may have served Philip as something of a precedent and example; but Philip's League, whose headquarters lay at strategically nodal Corinth, was not in permanent session, and Philip was careful to ensure that Corinth, like Ambracia, Thebes and Chalcis, was equipped with a permanent Macedonian garrison.[3]

Moreover, representatives (not delegates, probably, to use the Burkeian distinction) of the Greek states who constituted the council of the League were virtually hand-picked by Philip. Brief reference was made in the first chapter to Philip's *Geldpolitik*, the way he used his enormous gold and silver reserves to buy adherents in the Greek cities or lubricate existing relations of clientship. These men were non- or anti-democrats of varying hues, members of the propertied classes who believed that, since they contributed most financially and militarily to their states, they should wield political power and that it was actually unjust for the more or less propertyless poor majority of citizens to be in a position to tell them what to do.[4] Once established in control with Philip's backing, they were understandably wholehearted in their support of the Peace-term elements of the League's charter. Two of these may usefully be isolated, since they have a wider bearing on the entire Hellenistic portion (Part One) of the present work.

First, under the by now inescapable 'freedom and autonomy' formula, currently existing constitutions were officially guaranteed against alteration. The majority of Thebans, who until Chaeronea had enjoyed a moderately democratic constitution, will not have been impressed or persuaded by a slogan that legitimated after the fact what they counted as an oligarchic counter-revolution. Nor would the irony of an autonomy that was underwritten by a foreign garrison have been lost on them. The Theban

17

case was extreme, but it was an extreme version of a not untypical *status quo post* Chaeronea.

Secondly, and reinforcing the preceding item, a clause of the Common Peace outlawed the cancellation of debts, redistribution of (expropriated) land, and the liberation of slaves with a view to effecting the sort of political revolution that the two former actions implied. The evidence for the *stasis* (civil strife or outright civil war) that underlay such revolutionary manifestations is much richer for the fourth than for any preceding century, and this is regularly cited by proponents of the view that 'the Greek *polis*' was in terminal crisis at this time. In this instance, if Athens is excepted, the case seems quite sound, although it cannot be determined whether the rich were growing richer at the expense of the poor or the economic 'cake' as a whole was shrinking, with rich and poor maintaining their relative slices but the poor being forced below the margin of decent or assured subsistence. Whatever the explanation of aggravated *stasis*, the marked increase in the pool of men available for mercenary service is clearly a causally related phenomenon. These clauses of the settlement, in short, aimed to freeze the Aegean Greek world in the mould set by Philip's victory at Chaeronea.[5]

Sparta, we saw, had not been defeated at Chaeronea – but only because she had not fought there. Nor had she actually been defeated by Philip during his subsequent invasion of Laconia in winter 338/7 – but only because he chose not to fight or even to bribe the notoriously dorophagous Spartans. For it suited him to leave Sparta alone as the sole Greek 'holdout' from the League of Corinth, which of course duly ratified Philip's frontier-redrawing at Sparta's expense. As such Sparta was living testimony to the ostensibly voluntary character of that organization and a constant cause for concern to her Peloponnesian neigbours and enemies in Messene, Megalopolis and Argos. In this position of inglorious and enfeebled isolation the Spartans were permitted to languish for a further half dozen years. Had they been given to reflection, they could have pondered long the irony of fate and vocabulary that left both them and their old enemies in Thebes 'free and autonomous' under such radically different conditions. Had it not been for the autonomy of Messene, Sparta would have been a far more comfortable member of the strictly reactionary League than Thebes, let alone a still democratic and ungarrisoned Athens.[6]

In other circumstances, too, Sparta, whose oldest citizens knew all about supposed anti-Persian crusades, would have been a natural supporter of Philip's campaign of retribution (for the sacrileges of 480–79) against Artaxerxes IV (murdered 336) and his eventual successor Darius III. Philip himself, though, was not destined to assume the command in Asia. After the advance force under Parmenion had established a beach-head in north-western Anatolia Philip was publicly assassinated at his kingdom's ceremonial capital in what appears to have been a sordid personal vendetta. Those Greek states which took his murder as a sign that the good old days of Macedonian infighting had returned were quickly disabused by Philip's son and heir, the twenty-year-old Alexander.[7]

Sparta made no overt move to join the abortive resistance. It is, however, possible that she put out feelers in that direction. At any rate, surely it was more than a coincidence that the one known occasion on which Cleomenes II crawled out of his shell should have been the immediate aftermath of Philip's assassination, when he both won a victory at the Pythian Games (vicariously, through his chariot-team) and at the autumn Pylaea of 336 joined four of his fellow-countrymen in donating money towards the outstanding cost of rebuilding Apollo's temple at Delphi. What has been written of the ceremonial embassies to Delphi by Athens at this time applies equally, *mutatis mutandis*, to a personal intervention by a Spartan king: 'Such ceremonial embassies maintained the city's position on the Panhellenic stage both in formal and informal ways; besides making an impressive show by their presence, members of the delegation could engage in informal negotiations with envoys from other states and sound out feeling about Macedonian rule'. Since it was through the Delphic Amphictyony that Philip had first emerged as a great power in mainland Greece and within the Greek world at large, and since his Persian campaign had been tricked out in the plumage of Panhellenism, this was the obvious forum in which to challenge Macedonian rule by non-military means.[8]

Non-military, because contrary to expectations the 'boy' Alexander proved to be very much his father's son and compelled his instant election as *hēgemōn* of the League of Corinth's – or rather Philip's – Persian venture. Military resistance would have to wait on his departure from the Greek mainland. In 335, while Alexander was campaigning on his north-western frontiers, rumour reached Greece that he had been killed. This was enough to ignite a more determined and extensive rebellion than the previous year's, but again, not least because Thebes was the ringleader and Sparta's principal Peloponnesian enemies were sympathetic, without Spartan assistance or concurrence. Alexander's response was as ruthless as it was rapid. Formally by vote of the League *sunedrion*, in reality at Alexander's behest, Thebes was annihilated – an object-lesson in terror recalling his father's obliteration of Olynthus in 348. The freedom of the Greeks, plainly, hung by a slender thread which the Macedonian suzerain might sever at his pleasure.

Spartan feelings will have been mixed. Exultation at Thebes' demise can only have been dampened by this demonstration of Macedonian power and tempered still more by the way that Alexander could intervene with impunity in the internal affairs of neighbouring Messene contrary to the League charter by bringing to power the sons of Philiades.[9] Since

Sparta could not bear to co-operate against Macedon with Messene-recognizing Greeks, who anyway apart from Athens were financially and militarily debilitated, she turned to an old friend from her glory days: Achaemenid Persia.

Sixty years earlier, in 394, Agesilaus had been recalled to Greece to face a fearsome combination of Sparta's many Greek enemies. After campaigning in western Asia Minor for two years he had been planning, so his loyal supporters claimed, a new Anabasis into the heart of the Persian Empire with the idea of detaching from the Great King all the nations through which he should pass. Now in 335/4, when Alexander was on the point of putting such an aim into far more realistic operation, Sparta was negotiating with his Persian adversary. Yet this too had a precedent. For in 392 Sparta had begun the negotiations with Persia that were to lead in 387/6 to the pro-Spartan King's Peace, whereby the Greeks of Asia had been consigned to the suzerainty of Persia. It was therefore by no means an outrageous suggestion of Artaxerxes II in 362 that Agesilaus should help him quell his rebellious western viceroys (a suggestion rejected bcause the king had committed the unpardonable sin of recognizing Messene in 367) or of his successor Artaxerxes III in 344 that Sparta should aid his (finally successful) attempt to reconquer Egypt which had been in revolt since 404 (also rejected, because Sparta was then otherwise engaged in the Peloponnese). In the event, renewed co-operation between Sparta and Persia did not materialize before 333.[10]

Darius III or rather his western satraps had by then lost the first of the three major pitched battles Alexander won. This was the Battle of the River Granicus, after which Alexander had deliberately drawn attention for propaganda purposes to Sparta's self-exclusion from the 'Hellenic' crusade. In response to Alexander's southward progress of liberation through Anatolia Darius tardily and less than wholeheartedly embraced the one strategy that might have halted Alexander before his invasion had gathered great momentum. Persian land-forces were detailed to operate in Alexander's rear to hinder communications and prevent supplies and reinforcements reaching him, while a fleet based as ever on Phoenicia (though only recently it had been in revolt) was to cruise through the Aegean and eastern Mediterranean cutting links between Anatolia and the Greek mainland with a view to stirring rebellion again there against Alexander's regent Antipater. Sparta had never been a naval force of any note, although an individual Spartan like Lysander might show surprising aptitude for naval warfare; but her reputation as a land-power, tarnished though it was, and her undimmed yearning for hegemony of the Peloponnese combined to recommend Sparta to Darius' Persian and Greek advisers as potential leader of an anti-Macedonian resistance on the Greek mainland. It was for this reason, so Alexander reportedly was to claim in a bitter letter addressed to Darius himself, that 'You sent . . .

money to the Spartans and some other Greeks, which none of the other cities would accept apart from the Spartans'.[11]

That letter was supposedly sent after the second of Alexander's major set-piece victories over Darius, at Issus in Cilicia in late autumn or early winter 333. By rights it was a battle that Alexander ought to have lost – which presumably is what those many Greeks had calculated who signed up in droves as mercenaries for Darius, as they continued to do in larger numbers than for Alexander right up to the ultimately decisive encounter at Gaugamela. At all events, Issus was certainly a close-run affair, and many of Darius' Greek mercenaries lived to fight another day. Some of them, indeed, were transferred from the direct command of Darius to that of his Spartan lieutenant in the West – King Agis III.[12]

In 335 or 334 Agis had been indirectly involved, we may be sure, in negotiations with Memnon, the Rhodian Greek who commanded Darius' navy. In 333 Sparta's Persian expert Euthycles had been sent as envoy to Darius himself at Susa. Finally, late in 333 or early in 332, after the Issus battle, Agis in person met the successors of the now dead Memnon on the island of Siphnos to co-ordinate Sparta's part in the continuing Persian grand strategy that was aimed 'not only at cutting Alexander's communications but at drawing him off from Asia by threatening Macedonia' (Burn 1952, 83). Thirty silver talents and ten triremes were despatched on Agis' instructions to his brother Agesilaus in Laconia, who was to pay the crews in full and set sail forthwith for Crete. Agesilaus' base was Taenarum at the foot of the Mani peninsula, which here makes the first of its several appearances as a 'huge man-market', that is one of the major mercenary-marts of the eastern Mediterranean. Formerly, Taenarum had been noted chiefly for its sanctuary of Poseidon (Pohoidan in the local dialect), which could serve as an official asylum for fugitive Helot suppliants. The new development of military function is worthy of remark: it 'could not have happened without the co-operation of the Spartan government, and suggests that it found it convenient to have a pool of mercenaries handy to draw on, and also that mercenaries found the place convenient, perhaps because it was easy to get employment locally'.[13]

Agis proceeded as far east as Halicarnassus on the Asiatic coast before joining his brother for the campaigning season of 332 on Crete. Operations here were important as part of the grand strategy outlined above, both because of Crete's location and because it was a ready source of fresh mercenaries. But although Agis is credited with securing the whole island for the Persian interest, this was a minor success compared with the disaster of the defection to Alexander of the Persian fleet which gave him mastery of the sea. Agis therefore returned to the Peloponnese, probably late in 332, and spent the winter of 332/1 in trying to arouse support, especially in Athens, for his projected Greek rising against Macedon.[14]

There is no doubt that Agis was at this moment the protagonist of the anti-Macedonian movement in Greece and that the revolt he led – or, more exactly, the war he initiated, since unlike her Greek allies Sparta was technically not a subject of Macedon – was a serious affair. The sources for it, however, are such that the extensive body of recent scholarship remains divided over fundamental interpretative issues of chronology, purpose and significance. The summary account that follows is necessarily eclectic and opinionated, but the picture it presents is at least consistent with the pattern of Sparta's internal and external history in the earlier part of the fourth century, in so far as that can be reconstructed from fuller and more reliable evidence.[15]

Whether through co-ordination or, more likely, coincidence, Agis began his outbreak in spring or early summer when Antipater was unexpectedly diverted by a domestic revolt in neighbouring Thrace. At this opportune conjuncture Agis attacked and massacred a Macedonian force stationed in the Peloponnese under Corrhagus; a victory dedication to Apollo at Amyclae by an [Agi]s is perhaps to be associated with this success. Next, he turned to what may reasonably be accounted his principal objective, the siege and eventual destruction of Megalopolis. The stages of his campaign cannot be precisely reconstructed, but it is possible that initially Agis had only Laconian troops (Spartan and Perioecic) and mercenaries at his disposal. The mercenaries could have numbered as many as 10,000, as later alleged by an Athenian orator, and included men who had fought with Darius at Issus (though hardly the '8,000' stated by Diodorus). It may then have been the success over Corrhagus which persuaded some members of the League of Corinth to revolt to Agis. For he was still pretty much an unknown quantity, and his state's proven record of aloofness from earlier Greek resistance to Macedon and collaboration with Persia will not have encouraged those Greeks who regarded both Persia and Macedon as equally enemies of Greek freedom. Such Greeks were to be found especially in democratic Athens, which was further constrained from overt anti-Macedonian action by the fact that Alexander was in effect holding hostage up to 4,000 Athenian citizens. In the event, therefore, despite rumours of support from north of the Isthmus, Agis' official Greek allies turned out to be exclusively Peloponnesian. Indeed, *pace* Diodorus, Agis could not muster even the majority of the Peloponnese. In numbers both of states involved and of troops supplied the Peloponnesians who fought with Agis were greatly outweighed by those who fought with Antipater at the decisive Battle of Megalopolis in (I believe) late autumn or early winter 331.[16]

Precise numbers are as usual unknowable. On the most optimistic interpretation (Badian's) of the figures given by the ancient sources Agis commanded somewhat in excess of 30,000 men. Of these, 10,000 may have been mercenaries, 22,000 (at least 20,000 infantry, about 2,000 cavalry) specially selected civic troops supplied by Arcadia (excepting obviously Megalopolis but including, surprisingly, Tegea as well as Mantinea), Achaea (barring Pellene), and Elis as well as Sparta herself. Against these, after much preparation, Antipater could put more than 40,000 soldiers into the field. If the two totals are even approximately correct, this was a massive confrontation, the largest battle on Greek soil since Plataea (479). But no less important than the totals is the composition of the respective forces.

Agis' Laconian complement of Spartiates, inferior Spartans and Perioeci cannot have exceeded 6,000, barely half the number of his mercenary contingent. His Peloponnesian allies therefore numbered at most 16,000 (assuming charitably that Diodorus' 22,000 does not include Dinarchus' 10,000 mercenaries). On Antipater's side the equivalent Greek troops, that is those supplied by the still overtly loyal members of the League of Corinth, amounted to upwards of 23,000 (allowing 12,000 for his Macedonian complement and 5,000 for his Thracians and Illyrians). Regardless, therefore, of generalship, fighting methods or morale, Antipater's crushing victory was virtually assured in advance by sheer disparity of numbers. But the political significance of his victory is greater than the military. Clearly, the Athenians were far from the only Greeks who saw in Agis with his Persian backing merely a deutero-Agesilaus, 'another Spartan monarch who was prepared to sink to any depths to secure domination over Greece'.[17]

Alexander on receiving the news of Megalopolis is said to have dismissed it as a *muomakhia*, a 'battle of mice'. Numerically speaking, this was of course monstrously unfair, but politically it suggests that he saw the affair, rightly, as essentially a struggle between Greeks. Strategically, moreover, he had not allowed Agis' rising to deflect him from his Persian campaign, and by despatching a large fleet and a large sum of money to Antipater he had done all that was possible and necessary to help counter it or prevent a recurrence of Greek resistance. Agis too, perhaps, had done the best he could in unfavourable circumstances, but that, as Alexander seemingly predicted, was not good enough. Besides, whatever one may think of its motives and conduct, the result of his campaign was an unmitigated disaster for his state. If after Leuctra Sparta had been reduced to the status of a second-rank Greek power, after Megalopolis she became simply a third-rate and inconsiderable Peloponnesian community.[18]

The sources agree that 5,300 Laconians and allies, including their commander-in-chief, fell at Megalopolis. The majority of these casualties, if Antipater had learned anything from Epaminondas, will have been Laconians, the great majority of them doubtless Perioeci rather than Spartans. Less than a dozen Perioeci are known to us individually from the latter part of the fourth century, but surface finds of pottery probably indicate continued Perioecic settlement throughout what remained of Sparta's *polis* territory in Laconia after 338/7.[19]

Far more serious were the multiple effects of the defeat on Sparta's citizen population. First, the death of Agis deprived Sparta of her only active and effective king between the Eurypontid Archidamus III (d. 338) and the Agiad Areus (r. 309–265). Second, even though citizen numbers could again have been approaching their pre-Leuctra level of 1,200–1,500 in 331, that small number would still have condemned a Sparta lacking a permanent alliance to the status of a small state even without the further losses sustained at Megalopolis. With these casualties disappeared the prospect of recovering 'great power' status in the foreseeable future. Finally, as at Leuctra, too many Spartan citizen soldiers had not thought it sweet and decorous to die for their fatherland at Megalopolis. Cleomenes II's older son, Acrotatus, who presumably for some reason had not participated in the battle, advocated that the full rigour of Spartan law and custom should be brought to bear on these 'tremblers' (*tresantes*), not excluding their partial disfranchisement. As after Leuctra, and for the same reasons, this iron law was again bent to avoid increasing the number of malcontent 'inferior' Spartans. Yet, if Diodorus is to be believed, the tremblers long harboured deep resentment against the Agiad crown prince.[20]

This was only one of the lastingly dismal legacies of Agis' failure. With due respect for constitutionality Antipater referred the punishment of the rebels to the League council, which imposed a heavy fine on the Achaeans and Elis and somehow chastised the Tegean ringleaders among the Arcadians (Mantinea had possibly withdrawn from the anti-Macedonian axis before the final battle). Sparta, however, was not a member of the League of Corinth; and since Antipater was not prepared to settle the matter himself, Sparta's fate was quite properly – if only after heated debate – referred to Alexander in Asia. But in order to humiliate and hamstring Sparta comprehensively, Antipater did take the precaution of extracting fifty hostages drawn from 'the most distinguished' of the Spartans. Given Spartiate *oliganthrōpia*, this was no small number. It would seem, though the sources are ambiguous, that these men were still in Antipater's possession in July or August 330, and perhaps for long after that. Alternatively, they may have been sent on to Alexander, from whom they would have suffered the same fate of imprisonment (and death?) as the various Spartan ambassadors to Darius whom he captured during 331/0. Either way, Sparta following Megalopolis was temporarily or permanently deprived of a sizeable chunk of her élite citizenry.[21]

In these circumstances of enfeeblement it is almost idle to ask whether Sparta was now at last required to join the League of Corinth and so swear oaths recognizing the legitimate existence of the Messene and

Megalopolis. The poverty of our sources forbids an unequivocal answer, but on balance I am inclined to credit in this case the assertion of the Plutarchan *Instituta Laconica* that Sparta was not ever a member of any Macedon-created League. Support, however, can be brought for both this assertion and for the opposite hypothesis. On the one hand, for example, Sparta did not receive grain from Cyrene in the early 320s, when the still presumably Perioecic island of Cythera did. Since there was an acute dearth of grain throughout mainland Greece, affecting even the breadbasket of Thessaly, Sparta is unlikely to have been untouched, so that a political explanation for Sparta's exclusion seems required. Exemplary punishment of an enemy would fit the bill. On the other hand, there is *prima facie* evidence that Sparta, like the members of the League, received orders (*ta epistalenta*) from Alexander to deify him in 324. However, whether or not Sparta was a member, some special explanation(s) would seem to be necessary to account for Sparta's non-participation in the great revolt against Macedon that had its immediate origins in 324 and culminated in the so-called Lamian War of 323–2 after confirmation of Alexander's death at Babylon in June 323. This abstention was the more glaring for the crucial rôle played in the revolt by the Taenarum mercenary mart, which lay in Spartan territory and had been exploited by Agis for his war. Sparta, moreover, not only did not participate in the revolt but made a conspicuous gesture in support of the return from exile of some Samian refugees – a move ordered by Alexander but resisted by Athens, which had occupied Samos since 365.[22]

One inhibiting factor could have been the hostages, if indeed they were still being held in 323. As these will have included the more warlike supporters of Agis III, their absence will have strengthened the hand of his brother and successor Eudamidas I. He apparently once spoke against war with Macedon in opposition to the wishes of most Spartans (foremost among them, no doubt, being the Megalopolis *tresantes*), and this is the most likely occasion. The joint opposition of the two kings, if we may assume the compliance of the supine Cleomenes II, will have been well-nigh irresistible. The internal decay of Sparta is doubtless also relevant, not least because the increasing gulf between rich and poor Spartans will have inclined the former to favour a Macedonian settlement of Greece that was weighted heavily towards *bien pensant* oligarchs. Finally, there was the fact that the revolt was led by Athens, which had abstained from Agis' war, and supported by Sparta's sworn enemies Messene and Argos. The principle 'my enemy's enemy is my friend', especially when one's enemy was a neighbour, was all too powerful a motive for (in)action in all Greek interstate relations.[23]

Anyway, whatever the reasons, Sparta stood idly by as Athens and her more than twenty Greek allies fought a genuinely 'Hellenic War' against Macedon. For Macedon's character as imperial suzerain had become ever clearer since Alexander cashiered all Greek troops in 330, and its unconcern for the freedom and independence of the Greek cities had prompted orders not only for Alexander's deification but, yet more oppressively illegal, the restoration of all exiles in 324. Even most of the Thessalians joined the revolt, and it was the critical siege of Antipater at Lamia in Thessaly that has given the revolt its name. At the outset the united Greeks had a far better hope of eventual success than Agis. But that siege was lifted, and Macedonian victories by land at Crannon and by sea off Amorgus in 322 made the Lamian War seem in restrospect 'a faltering and self-deluded step on the road to self-destruction'. Athens, stripped once more of her naval power and her democracy, was reduced almost to the level of Sparta *vis-à-vis* Antipater.[24]

He, however, was just one of half a dozen Macedonian warlords contending for the succession to Alexander's ephemeral European and Asiatic empire. Only once, though, in the next half century did it even briefly look as if one of them might actually grab the lot. The debilitating effect of this almost incessant warfare on Macedon and its control of Greece is most strikingly expressed in the irruption from the north of barbarian Gauls. Their most famous feat was to raid Delphi, navel of the earth and symbolic heartland of Hellas. By the same token, however, this intestine inter-Macedonian strife did afford some Greek polities, most notably the federal states of Aetolia and Achaea, the space to develop into much more than pawns in a larger, Macedonian game. Even Sparta, as we shall see in the next chapter, again raised her head sufficiently to claim a place in the Hellenistic sun. But in the first main phase of the Successors' struggles, which ended with the Battle of Ipsus in 301, Sparta was conspicuous by her near-total absence.[25]

The lack of interest taken in Sparta by the rival dynasts was not (*pace* Ehrenberg) a mark of their respect for her ancient reputation but a backhanded acknowledgement of her present triviality. For the demands of neither political nor military strategy required any interest on their part. The nearest Sparta came to involvement in the main action was in or shortly after 319. The League of Corinth had been a dead letter since Alexander's decease, and Sparta was too remote and unimportant to receive a Macedonian garrison, the technique of rule favoured by Antipater's son and successor Cassander. Yet Sparta was sufficiently conscious of her loss of real autonomy to welcome the proclamation by Polyperchon (acting supposedly on behalf of 'Philip III') of freedom and independence for the Greeks. Cassander, it was feared, meditated an attack on Sparta. Hardly surprisingly, this did not materialize (when Cassander did intervene in the Peloponnese in 315, it was to gain control of Messenia, not Laconia). But the threat did provoke the Spartans' first known attempt at fortifying their central place, that is the four villages of Sparta proper as opposed to Amyclae several kilometres distant to the south. This was not a solid, permanent fortification of mudbrick on a stone footing, but a basic ditch-and-palisade affair. All the same, it constituted the first hesitant public recognition by the Spartans that the Spartiate hoplite militia of citizens reared under the Lycurgan *agōgē* no longer provided adequate self-defence. The irony was that such a fortification should have been thrown up in the age of the great Macedonian besiegers, Philip, Alexander and Demetrius 'the Besieger' (son of Antigonus the One-eyed), against whom only enceinte walling like that of Messene offered sure protection.[26]

If Sparta had lost both an empire and all real independence, she yet had one rôle left to play: that of a supplier of mercenaries. Shortly before Alexander's death a certain Thibron, perhaps grandson of a distinguished homonym of the 390s, emerged as friend and mercenary commander of the renegade Macedonian Harpalus, a former treasurer of Alexander, who bolted to Athens with vast treasure in 324 and thereby sowed one of the seeds of the Lamian War. When Harpalus was forced to flee Athens and went to Crete, Thibron killed him, seized his funds and sailed for Cyrene, where his attempt to establish a robber-barony soon led to his own murder.[27]

In 315, when he was at war with Ptolemy of Egypt and Cassander, Antigonus at Tyre emulated Polyperchon's proclamation of Greek freedom. A lieutenant was despatched to the Peloponnese to capitalize on the goodwill that was expected to accrue from the proclamation. He landed in Laconia, presumably at Gytheum, and requested mercenaries from Sparta. At about the same time another request arrived at the same address from three Sicilian Greek cities, not for mercenaries in general but for a single Spartan mercenary commander to lead their struggle against Agathocles of Syracuse. Acrotatus, allegedly still at odds with the Megalopolis tremblers and otherwise motivated in much the same way as the kings Agesilaus and Archidamus before him, answered the call in defiance of the Ephors.[28]

In vigour Acrotatus showed himself the equal of his royal predecessors. But he unfortunately also displayed the old proneness of Spartan commanders abroad to high-handed vindictiveness and cruelty. Forrest has professed to find 'something sympathetic' in the picture of Spartan royals thus earning a livelihood in the only way open to them. But Acrotatus' mission also neatly symbolizes how Sparta had lost her way at home and was unable to find an exit overseas. Expelled from Sicily, Acrotatus returned to Sparta in about 314 but predeceased his father, who finally brought his inglorious life to a suitably inglorious close after a 'reign' of sixty years in 309.[29]

Chapter three

The new Hellenism of Areus I

Periodization, as we have had on more than one occasion to observe, is a bane as well as a boon for the historian. The 'Hellenistic' epoch of Greek history is both dubiously named and chronologically imprecise, its fluctuating limits depending on its contested definitions. Yet some individuating term is required to pick out the era between the reign of Alexander the Great of Macedon (336–323 BC) and the engorging by Rome of a Greek-speaking world that had been hugely expanded by and following Alexander's conquests. 'Hellenistic' will have to do, subject to two major caveats. First, the Greek word *hellēnizō* after which J.G. Droysen coined the modern label in the last century did not carry in its own time the universal cultural significance that Droysen wished to impute to it. Secondly, Droysen's conception of the era as essentially characterized by a fusion of Greek and oriental civilizations is viciously anachronistic – Plutarch poured into a Hegelian mould, in Claire Préaux's apt phrase.[1]

In any case, an alternative conception is needed for the history of a state in Old Greece like Sparta, which was largely immune from oriental contacts let alone deep cultural penetration in the Hellenistic era (here taken to end in 146). An alternative, fortunately, is ready to hand. If the pre-Hellenistic or Classical Greek world was above all the world of the *polis*, the Hellenistic universe was at bottom one of territorial states ruled – at first *de facto*, by 300 *de jure* – by more or less absolute monarchs. Even Sparta, which largely for negative reasons retained the actuality as well as the mentality of an old-style *polis* for longer than almost any other Greek polity, could not altogether escape the forces exerted by the gravitational fields of the major monarchies between which she found herself variously pulled and squeezed. Indeed, in the reign and person of King Areus I (309/8–265) Sparta dropped tantalising hints that, in response to the humiliations of the second and third quarters of the fourth century, she was beginning to exchange her traditionally exceptionalist political profile for one of 'Hellenistic' normality.[2]

The reign of Areus, however, is very poorly documented. Even if technically he acceded to the Agiad throne in 309/8, he cannot be said to have ruled before the late 280s. Nor did he attract the attention of biographers, like his Eurypontid predecessor Agesilaus II, or historians (of sorts) in the way that his Agiad successor Cleomenes III did. The surviving narrative sources for 309–265 are scrappy and jejune, the epigraphical texts few and rarely precise in detail or date, the archaeological record patchy and not unambiguous. In these circumstances the appearance of a new kind of source, coinage, is in itself welcome, however slight its contribution.[3]

For two generations after Alexander's premature death his so-called 'Successors' (Diadochi) and their 'Epigones' slugged it out in a ceaseless struggle for position. The last of the Successors to mount a real challenge for most of Alexander's hypertrophied and evanescent empire was Antigonus Monophthalmus, but he was defeated and killed in battle in his ninth decade at Ipsus in 301 by a combination of Lysimachus and Seleucus. Thereafter it was a question rather of delimiting spheres of power and influence than of monopolizing a single empire, and the next round was terminated more or less at Corupedium, also in Asia Minor, in 281 with the victory of Seleucus over Lysimachus. By 275 Alexander's Graeco-Macedonian and oriental empire was split into three major dynastic blocs: Egypt under the Ptolemies (who for long also laid successful claim to control territories in the Greek Aegean and in the Levant), Asia under the Seleucids (who were later forced to yield part of Asia Minor to the Attalids of Pergamum), and European Greece and Thrace under the Antigonids of Macedon. The latter dynasty by a combination of direct rule (*via* garrisons, the 'Fetters of Greece'), indirect rule through friendly oligarchies or despots, and diplomatic and military alliances exercised a palpable, if far from unchallenged, sway for the better part of the ensuing century.[4]

Sparta's rôle in the first main phase of the post-Alexander struggle was, as we saw in the last chapter, nugatory. Her negligible significance was reconfirmed in 302, when Monophthalmus and his son Demetrius (nicknamed Poliorcetes, 'the Besieger', for his famous though unsuccessful siege of Rhodes in 304) emulated Philip and Alexander in ostentatiously tolerating the refusal of Sparta to join their refounded League of Corinth. By then Areus had nominally occupied the Agiad throne, in succession to his ineffectual grandfather Cleomenes II, for half a dozen years – nominally, since he had been a minor at his accession and even now was barely of age (if that). Earlier Spartan kings had succeeded in their minority, for example the Agiads Pleistoanax and Agesipolis I; and in their cases regents had been entrusted with the supreme command of Spartan and allied armies in major battles. Yet even Regent Pausanias, who eventually paid with his life for his untraditionally egotistical political posturing after his Plataea victory, is not known to have disputed the

Agiad succession. In 309/8, however, Cleonymus, younger brother of Areus' dead father Acrotatus (see end of chapter 2), reckoned he had a better claim to succeed his father Cleomenes II than did his nephew. The Gerousia, which was in effect determining which Agiad to co-opt to the ranks of the supreme governing body of the Spartan state, thought differently and upheld the rule of linear succession. In light of Cleonymus' erratic and ultimately treasonous behaviour in the course of the next four decades, this was probably a wise decision from the standpoint of the Spartan oligarchy. For Areus, although he was to take the Spartan kingship into uncharted ideological waters, did not apparently wish to cut it entirely adrift from its traditional moorings within the framework of the *polis*. For the time being Cleonymus had to be content with the regency.[5]

However, at the earliest opportunity the disappointed Cleonymus, like the disappointed Dorieus a couple of centuries before, left Sparta for greener, western pastures. In 303 Sparta's colony Tarentum again (cf. chapter 2) applied to the mother-city for aid against its hostile non-Greek neighbours in southern Italy. The Spartan authorities typically but reasonably preferred to involve Sparta in this distant but potentially lucrative enterprise rather than have anything to do with Antigonus' anti-Cassander Hellenic League. Thus Cleonymus, unlike Acrotatus a decade earlier, sailed for the west with official blessing, taking with him 5,000 mercenaries bought with Tarentine funds in the still teeming mart at Laconian Taenarum. The venture has been described as 'the only important undertaking of the Spartans during the age of the Diadochi' (Marasco 1980b, 38), but its importance was still rather restricted, both from the narrowly Spartan point of view and in terms of its lasting impact on the broader history of south Italy in the early Hellenistic period. For although Cleonymus did compel the Lucanians to come to terms with Tarentum and may also have had something to do with the treaty of 303 between Tarentum and the Romans (then, it seems, in formal alliance with the Lucanians), he proceeded to act as a true *condottiero* instead of Sparta's obedient servant by seizing Corcyra for his own ends and thoroughly alienating the Tarentines. There is a certain fascination in noting that Cleonymus might have been the first Spartan to fight the Romans, but in the longer run the most lasting result of his western mission would seem to have been the favourable impression he made on King Pyrrhus of Epirus.[6]

More immediately, his behaviour abroad appears to have promoted the career of the Eurypontid king Archidamus IV, who may have succeeded his pacific father Eudamidas I in about 300. Anyway, in 294 he achieved his only recorded public exploit when in preference to Cleonymus (or Areus, if he was of age) he was chosen to lead a Spartan force against the Peloponnesian invasion of Demetrius Poliorcetes. Perhaps also to be connected with this brief emergence from obscurity is the hypothetical restoration to Sparta at about this time of Demaratus son of Gorgion, a Greek from north-west Asia Minor. An agent of Lysimachus, Demaratus was quite properly favoured with an honorific dedication by the Delians in about 295. This was just the sort of thing Greek communities felt regularly obliged to do in the new Hellenistic world of Macedonian dynasts. But Demaratus had mainland Greek as well as Asiatic connections; more specifically, he had Spartan connections, since he was descended, as his name was perhaps intended to recall, from the exiled Eurypontid king Demaratus, who had ended his days in the early fifth century as a pensioner of the Persian Great King. It would therefore have suited the book of Lysimachus, one of the Ipsus victors, if Demaratus had been restored to Sparta soon after the death of Cassander in 298/7. That in turn would have strengthened the Eurypontid cause of Archidamus IV.[7]

However that may be, Archidamus proved an incompetent and unlucky commander in what was Sparta's first real direct involvement in the wars of the Alexandrine succession. Poliorcetes' ultimate objectives were the throne of Macedon and revenge for his defeat at Ipsus; the Peloponnese was merely a stepping-stone. But its control or quiescence was at least a necessary preliminary. At Mantinea he was met by Archidamus. The encounter was a disaster for the latter, who may even have lost his life along with those of (allegedly) as many as 700 Spartans and others. The Besieger pressed on into Laconia itself, where the Spartans anxiously and pathetically refurbished the ditch-and-palisade defence they had first placed around Sparta against Cassander some twenty-three years before. Happily, they were not in the event needed, since Poliorcetes was diverted by more urgent business in the north. Thus after the fourth invasion of Laconia in eighty years Sparta town remained yet inviolate.[8]

Even supposing Archidamus had not been killed at Mantinea, he had certainly been disgraced, and in 293 or 292 Cleonymus was again entrusted with an official command, this time in Boeotia. There is no little irony in Sparta's co-operating with Boeotia against Macedon, given the history of Spartan-Boeotian antagonism since the end of the fifth century. Moreover, Cleonymus' very presence in Boeotia implies co-operation, perhaps even formal alliance, between Sparta and a relatively new force in Greek interstate politics, the Aetolian League. By pursuing a policy of armed neutrality, supporting now one or other Greek state or coalition, now one or another Macedonian dynast, this federal state had become increasingly prominent since the late fourth century. but in 293 or 292 neither Aetolian nor Boeotian support availed Cleonymus against Poliorcetes, and he returned to Sparta empty-handed.[9]

Apart from a handful of straws in the wind, there is little or nothing to clutch at of Sparta's dealings in Laconia or anywhere else between 292 and the very end of the next decade.[10] Then in about 281 Areus made his début, so far as the sources are concerned, at the head not merely of a Spartan and mercenary army but of an army which for the first time since Agis' war of 331 represented something that could be called a Spartan alliance. This has been hailed hyperbolically as a re-creation of the Peloponnesian League alliance that had melted away in the mid-360s. Perhaps that was what Areus intended, but he did not come seriously near achieving such a goal until a decade or more later. Nevertheless, in view of Sparta's near-total impotence for the past half century, this was quite an impressive array.

The immediate background of this minor Spartan renascence was the last major gasp of the Succession wars, in which Seleucus defeated Lysimachus at Corupedium and Ptolemy Ceraunus, a son of the founding Ptolemy I of Egypt, won a naval victory over Antigonus Gonatas, son of the now deceased Besieger. Of all the post-Alexander kingdoms that of Macedon paradoxically had always been the weakest. It had now reached the nadir. Areus therefore sought to exploit Macedon's difficulties like Agis before him, but it was a telltale sign of his own weakness that he chose to confront, not Gonatas himself, but the Aetolians who were now in alliance with the Macedonian throne. Philip II had played the Delphic card from strength (chapter 1). Areus' holy war for the liberation of Delphi from growing Aetolian control was principally a mark of Sparta's and Sparta's allies' decrepitude – though this is not of course to deny Sparta's genuine regard for Delphic autonomy and continued involvement in Delphic administration. Moreover, notwithstanding the support of four Achaean towns (the nucleus of the Achaean League founded in 280), of Boeotia, of Megara, of a large part of Arcadia (excepting, of course, Megalopolis), and of some towns in the Argolid, the major achievement of Areus – as of Cleonymus in 293 or 292 – seems to have been to penetrate central Greece at all in defiance of the Macedonian garrison at Corinth. In the actual fighting the Aetolians inflicted on Sparta a humiliating disaster greater even than that suffered under Archidamus IV. Losses were heavy, as a Spartan *poluandrion* at Delphi indicates, and allied confidence in Spartan leadership was again severely dented. In fact, it was probably only because Macedon had other things on its mind, above all the temporary ousting of Gonatas by Ceraunus in 280 and the famous Gallic incursion of 279 in which Ceraunus was killed, that Sparta's home territory was not once more penetrated.[11]

If Areus did not suffer permanent political eclipse for this defeat in the manner of his co-king Archidamus, he had chiefly his uncle's egregious behaviour to thank. For despite the successful accomplishment of missions in Messenia, Troezen and Crete in the early 270s, Cleonymus in 275 defected to Pyrrhus. The latter in turn used the restoration of his protégé as his pretext for mounting in 272 the fifth invasion of Laconia. In reality, he aimed thereby to shore up his recent seizure of much of Macedon and ensure 'great power' status among the big Hellenistic dynasts. Cleonymus was but a pawn in this greater game.[12]

The true story behind the defection of Cleonymus will never be known. His old connection with the Epirote warlord will have counted for something, and resentment of his nephew's rise to full military command, however disastrous, may have counted for more. But the most relevant precipitating factor seems to have been sexual politics. In the 270s Cleonymus the Agiad, by then in his late fifties, married a young Eurypontid heiress, Chilonis, who, however, responded all too warmly to the attentions of Areus' son Acrotatus (later to be king). Now Sparta was a society in which daughters could inherit property in their own right, even when there was a legitimate male heir available; and in such societies endogamy and other forms of in-marriage are often practised to a high degree 'as a means of restricting diffusion of property outside the kin' (Hodkinson 1986, 404). The near-contemporary marriage of the Eurypontid Eudamidas II to his paternal aunt Agesistrata is a nice case in point. Cleonymus, however, was not marrying within the Agiad patriline but across the line dividing the two royal houses and into the Eurypontid *oikos*. The struggle for wealth and power within the shrinking Spartan élite had now reached such a pitch that the two royal houses were actively competing for eligible, property-bearing heiresses. As for Acrotatus' sexual relations with Cleonymus' young bride, these were surely not the outcome of mere passion but of his father's political calculation.[13]

Pyrrhus in 275 had returned to Greece from Italy after a series of punishing, hence 'Pyrrhic' victories. In 274, with the help of Cleonymus, he had secured a large slice of greater Macedon to add to his ancestral Epirote domain. To consolidate his hold, he invaded Laconia by land with the co-operation of the Aetolians, who clearly now regarded Gonatas as a loser. Pyrrhus' armament was reportedly immense: 25,000 infantry, 2,000 cavalry, and – a typical post-Alexander touch – two dozen elephants. The incursion was unexpected, since Areus was at the time absent in Crete pursuing Sparta's usual policy of headhunting potential mercenaries. And it was facilitated by Sparta's Peloponnesian neighbours in Elis, Megalopolis, and Argos, together probably with some Achaeans. A diplomatically isolated, mentally unprepared and still physically inadequately defended Sparta must have looked an easy prize. Further tactical advantage was gained by his claim, in response to a Spartan embassy that met him at Megalopolis, that he had come to liberate the Greeks from Macedon and by his avowed intention to put his sons through the Spartan *agōgē*, which Pyrrhus at least seems to have believed was still in good working order. Spartan fears were allayed, the edge of their preparedness dulled.[14]

Areus was thus recalled from Crete too late to be able to help defend

Sparta, to which Pyrrhus laid siege after devasting northern Laconia. The account of Plutarch, based as ever on Phylarchus, privileges the heroic rôle in the defence played by the Spartan women led by Archidamia, widow of Eudamidas I and mother of Agesistrata. The contrast with their ancestresses' utter demoralization in 370 is too dramatically complete to carry full conviction; but rich women like Archidamia would certainly have had a great deal to lose from a Pyrrhic victory, and the demonstrable weakness of their once invincible menfolk will have given them their opportunity to intervene publicly at the highest political level. The behaviour of Acrotatus is also painted in glorious colours, but that too may owe as much to literary art as to military reality. For quite clearly what really saved Sparta from occupation by Pyrrhus was the despatch by Gonatas of some of his mercenaries from their garrison at Corinth. As in south Italy so now in south Greece Pyrrhus had displayed his regrettable talent for throwing sworn enemies together at his expense. The Spartans, further reinforced by the return of Areus with 2,000 men, and the Macedonian mercenaries between them deterred Pyrrhus from further action against Sparta town. Dedications to Athena by Spartan men and women perhaps reflect this seemingly miraculous preservation.[15]

Instead, Pyrrhus' forces, like those of Epaminondas in 369, moved on south down the Eurotas valley and into what remained of Sparta's Perioecic domains. It was most likely in this context that Cleonymus overwhelmed Zarax on the east Laconian coast. Against the background of Sparta's many losses of Perioecic dependencies, the loyalty of those in the east Parnon foreland both before and after Argos was awarded the Thyreatis in 338/7 (chapter 2) stands out in high relief. Just three years earlier Tyros too, in dedicating half a hecatomb of bulls at Delphi, had made her dependence on Sparta quite plain. The fine walling of Zarax's inaccessible citadel, which must postdate Cleonymus' sack, is perhaps to be interpreted as Sparta's token of gratitude.[16]

Pyrrhus thereafter beat a tactical retreat to Argos, where both he and Gonatas enjoyed some rival support. But there he was killed in fighting against Gonatas' mercenaries and Areus, who commanded Spartan troops as well as hired Cretans. So this was in a real sense a Spartan victory, demonstrating a resurgence of Spartan military efficiency and renewing Sparta's claim to leadership of free Greece. A competent bronze statuette of an armed Aphrodite dedicated on the Spartan acropolis witnesses at once to the continued skills of Perioecic craftsmen and this regained military *élan*. However, the most strikingly visible effects of Pyrrhus' defeat are to be seen in the self-perception and self-presentation of King Areus, who had taken on and conquered one Hellenistic dynast with the aid of another and was soon to take Sparta into formal alliance with a third.[17]

Historiographically speaking, the year 272 marks an era for Sparta as for Greece generally: the end of the competent history of Hieronymus of Cardia (as preserved through Diodorus), the formal beginning of the greatly inferior account of Phylarchus. It also marks a transformation in Sparta's social and political profile under Areus, the basic documentation for which is not literary but numismatic and epigraphic. Phylarchus' accusation that Areus introduced luxury to Sparta need not be taken too seriously, since this was a time-honoured complaint among Hellenistic writers and Phylarchus was tendentiously concerned to maximize the contrast between his reforming hero Agis IV and his morally lapsed royal predecessors. On the other hand, the fact that Areus sponsored Sparta's first silver coinage, bearing his own image and superscription ('Of King Areus') on the obverse, has to be taken very seriously indeed.[18]

There were many good reasons why Sparta had not coined previously. The metal would have had to be imported, whereas the iron used in Sparta's traditional spit-money was present locally in abundant supply. Spartan social organization and administration did not demand the simplification of economic and fiscal transactions that a universally recognized monetary instrument could bring. Sparta's foreign trade was relatively unimportant and anyway not in Spartan hands. Sparta did not employ mercenaries on any scale before the late fifth century and could in any case use the currency of other states for that purpose. And so on. Moreover, absence of pragmatic requirement had been hallowed by ancient custom and legitimated in terms of a supposedly Lycurgan prohibition (reaffirmed or invented at the end of the fifth century). In short, to strike a coinage of silver tetradrachms was truly breaking one mould in order to create another. Our ignorance of Spartan domestic politics at this juncture is deeply regrettable.

No less interesting than the fact of coinage is Areus' choice of the types of Alexander the Great to represent his image, despite the consistent and pertinacious opposition of Sparta to Macedon. The only plausible explanation of this apparent paradox is that Areus was seeking to present himself as, if not the equal of, then at least the same sort of ruler as Poliorcetes (the first to issue royal coinage after Alexander) and the other Hellenistic dynasts. This, too, is the clue to the function Areus intended for these coins, which were not minted in Sparta and will have had a very limited circulation there. They were meant to sell an image of Areus on the open market of Hellenistic conceptual and dynastic exchange. More precisely, it was at Ptolemy II of Egypt that the message was aimed, with a view to convincing him that Areus was a suitable partner in his anti-Macedonian foreign policy. The 'Chremonides Decree' (below) was the pay-off for an intensive campaign of diplomacy between 272 and 268 in which the coins of Areus played their important rôle of visual propaganda.[19]

Equally impressive in its own way is the Athenian decree passed probably in 268/7 on the proposal of the leading anti-Macedonian politician Chremonides.[20] The following extract suggests by its language no less than its content that under Areus Sparta was experiencing something of a cultural as well as diplomatic transformation:

> Previously the Athenians and Spartans and the allies of each, having established friendship and alliance in common with each other, struggled often and nobly together against those attempting to enslave the cities . . . Now again crises of a similar kind have overtaken all Greece . . . and King Ptolemaeus, in accordance with his ancestors' and his sister's policy, is openly concerned for the common freedom of the Greeks; and the Athenian People, having made an alliance with him, also voted to urge the other Greeks to adopt this policy. Likewise also the Spartans, being friends and allies of King Ptolemaeus, have voted to be allies with the Athenian People together with the Eleans and the Achaeans and the Tegeans and the Mantineans and the Orchomenians and the Phigaleans and the Caphyans and the Cretans, as many as are in the alliance of the Spartans *and of Areus* and of the other allies. . . .

> (my emphasis)

The range of Sparta's allies, far wider than that of 281, is particularly noticeable, even if it still fell well short of the old pre-365 Peloponnesian League. The Athenians might reasonably recall their joint resistance with Sparta to Persia in 480–479 and renew the alliance last concluded between them (in very different circumstances) in 369. Yet more remarkable is the way that on two occasions in the decree, once in the above extract and once elsewhere, Areus is named separately from and in addition to the civic corporation of the Spartan state.

This was not done to make a merely chronological point – in that event both kings' names would have been given in order of priority of accession, as in a Spartan document from Delos of c.400 BC.[21] Nor is Areus' singular prominence to be explained simply in terms of the Spartan law (Hdt. v.75) that only the king might command any one Spartan-led army abroad. Rather, as in the near-contemporary dedications of statues to Areus by Elis, Arcadian Orchomenus, two Cretan communities and – most extraordinarily – Ptolemy II himself, it was Areus' kingship that was being celebrated as a self-sufficient force. In light of such documents it is less surprising to find the Delphians hailing Areus' homonymous grandson as 'son of King Acrotatus and Queen Chilonis' in a text enshrining the grant of a whole barrel of Delphic privileges including proxeny, even though Areus II was not yet ten years of age. Nor, given Areus I's alliance with Ptolemy II, who had strong Levantine interests, is it beyond the bounds of intrinsic probability that Areus should have corresponded, as the author of *I Maccabees* claimed, with the High Priest of the Jerusalem Temple. At any rate, it would have been wholly in character for the Spartan to style himself 'King Areus', and the kinship between the Spartans and the Jews which Areus professed to have been able to authenticate was a characteristically Hellenistic – and indeed later – medium of diplomatic intercourse between Greeks and non-Greeks.[22]

All the same, the so-called 'Chremonidean War' of c.267–262 turned out a disaster for the Spartan–Athenian–Ptolemaic axis. Despite perhaps three attempts, the last of which (in 265?) proved fatal to Areus himself, Sparta's Peloponnesian and Cretan alliance failed to break through the Isthmus dominated by Gonatas' Acrocorinth garrison and link with their Athenian and Egyptian partners.[23] In the light of this dismal performance it is tempting to dismiss the propaganda of Areus as that of a man who was 'something of a megalomaniac' (Will 1979, 107 = 1984, 116). But an alternative, and preferable, view is that it was only through 'Hellenistic bigtalk' of this kind that a mere Spartan king could hope to make the required impact on potential anti-Antigonid allies among the superpowers of the day. Where Areus can be more legitimately faulted, surely, is for failing to undertake structural, especially socio-economic and military, reform at home. The necessity for such reform can only have become more apparent in perhaps 262, when Acrotatus was defeated by Megalopolis alone. For although Sparta remained technically 'free' from direct Antigonid rule, this external freedom was more than overbalanced by mounting social tension within an increasingly polarized and again visibly shrinking citizen body and between citizens and non-citizens within the reduced Spartan *polis* as a whole.[24]

Yet it would be inappropriate to end this chapter on an entirely negative note. In about 270 a Spartan comic actor, Nicon son of Eumathidas, won a prize at the Soteria festival recently established by the Aetolians at Delphi to commemorate their famous repulse of the Gauls in 279. In Sparta's high Classical epoch the very idea of a Spartan professional actor would have been laughable. Several Plutarchan anecdotes illustrate proper Spartan contempt for such a useless calling, and Classical Sparta's 'theatre' was the scene of paramilitary exercises rather than an architecturally elaborated space for the staging of plays. However, at some time in the third century Sparta acquired its first built theatre of normal Hellenistic type. It would not, I think, be entirely fanciful to associate this development with the new Hellenism of Areus I and the influx of funds from his potent ally Ptolemy II. Where actors lead, philosophers follow. Such was the lesson of fifth-century Athens, and such was to be the experience of third-century BC Sparta, lagging a mere two centuries behind the city that Pericles had called, not without justification, 'an education for Hellas'.[25]

Chapter four

Reform – or revolution? Agis IV and Cleomenes III

The lives of Agis IV (Eurypontid, r. *c.*244–1) and Cleomenes III (Agiad, r. *c.* 235–222) are the stuff of novels, ancient as well as modern. After Lycurgus the lawgiver, Leonidas, and Agesilaus II, they are the most famous exemplars of Laconism, bulking largest in the tortuous annals of the 'Spartan mirage'. Their achievements and significance, on the other hand, are the stuff of history. But these will always remain desperately elusive. For against the martyrology of the contemporary historian Phylarchus, prime source of Plutarch's biographical 'novels', we have to pit only the *Memoirs* of Aratus, enemy of Cleomenes, as mediated by Plutarch's life of the Achaean statesman and by Polybius, and of course the latter's *Histories*, itself composed more than a generation later.[1]

The *Histories* is a work of monumental scholarship, no doubt, but the reigns of Agis and Cleomenes fell before Polybius' real starting date of 220 BC and outside the scope of his major theme, the rise of Rome to 'world' dominion. More gravely, the Spartan kings' careers were calculated to arouse two of Polybius' most passionately held personal and historiographical prejudices: a hatred of any socio-economic change that seemed to tilt the balance of power and wealth unduly in the favour of the more or less impoverished Greek masses, and a hatred of Sparta – contemporary, Hellenistic Sparta, that is, as opposed to the 'Lycurgan' Sparta of myth and political theorizing. These twin passions, which in other circumstances need not have coincided, were engendered by Polybius' high birth in about 200 BC into a leading political family of Megalopolis and were nourished by his remarkable exemption of patriotic prejudice from the usual canons of authorial objectivity.[1]

Written, documentary texts that might correct or supplement the opposed tendencies of the two principal literary sources are very thin on the ground. Numismatic and other material testimony tends in this case to illustrate and sometimes illuminate the literary picture rather than form the basis for an alternative account. This is partly because of the selective nature of the data we have. For example, the absence of archaeological corroboration of the literary picture of private affluence cannot be used to overthrow it, given the lack of finds from graves or private dwellings in Sparta. In short, the evidentiary situation is such that too often we cannot say for certain what events actually occurred or in what order, and usually we can only attempt to guess why. The immense modern bibliography on Agis and Cleomenes may suitably reflect the objective and symbolic importance of their reigns but it is inversely proportional to our sure knowledge of them.[2]

It is the objective significance of the reigns for the history of Sparta, of the Peloponnese and of Greece in the second half of the third century that will be this chapter's major theme. But they do also raise, in a peculiarly sharp way, a prime theoretical problem of characterization or definition. It is straightforward enough, perhaps, to dismiss outright such anachronistic modernizing fantasies (or spectres) as Beloch's notion of a struggle between Spartan capitalists and landlords, or von Pöhlmann's view of the two kings as socialists wreaking havoc in the name of the unwashed masses, or Wason's picture of artisans and Helots following the lead given by traders in demanding reforms and of Cleomenes as the champion of the bourgeoisie.[3] It is far harder to decide, as one eventually must, whether Agis and Cleomenes were in any valid ancient or modern sense revolutionaries, as distinct from patriotic reformers and restorers of a presumed *status quo ante* (as they themselves and their propagandists claimed they were).

If properly revolutionary consciousness must necessarily connote the 'idea of a forward-looking, progressive change in the political or social structure' (Finley 1986, 50), and if the achievement of revolution must necessarily entail the initiative or at least the active participation of all or most of the oppressed masses, then it is unquestionably inappropriate and seriously misleading to speak of the 'revolution' of Agis and Cleomenes. If, on the other hand, fundamental change in either the political or the social structure, however it be effected or within whatever framework of ideas or ideology, be a sufficient criterion, then a case can be made, subject to the evidentiary constraints already outlined, that Agis and Cleomenes did, no doubt transiently and inadequately, revolutionize Sparta. That, at all events, was how both adherents and enemies of the kings preferred to view their measures; although it has to be added that the Greeks' political vocabulary (*metabolē, metastasis, neōterismos, neōtera pragmata*) suggests their line between 'innovation' or even 'change' and 'revolution' was much thinner than ours between 'revolution' and 'reform', and that some such apparently self-contradictory construct as 'revolutionary reaction' may be required to capture the full flavour of the projects of Agis and Cleomenes.

On the whole, therefore, it would seem to make better sense of their reigns to see the kings as revolutionaries rather than (merely) reformists. However, the crucial point too often overlooked or blurred in modern discussions is that revolution of the type envisaged or effected by Agis and Cleomenes could not possibly have had the same meaning or consequences in Sparta as the formally identical slogans or measures of 'debt-cancellation' (*khreōn apokopē*) and 'land-redistribution' (*gēs anadasmos, khōras nomē*) had or would have had in other Greek cities of the period. For, notwithstanding the considerable 'normalization' of Sparta's social, economic and political institutions since the later fifth century, the retention of peculiarities like the Helots and Perioeci and, no less determinative, the ideological incubus of the Spartan myth with the Lycurgus legend at its kernel inevitably gave a peculiarly Spartan twist to the kings' superficially 'Hellenistic' programmes.[4]

This does not of course mean, however, that these cannot or should not be viewed within their wider, extra-Laconian context. At its broadest, this wider frame of reference is provided by the continuing balance of power – or weakness – between the big three dynasts of Macedon, Egypt and nearer Asia. Indeed, it was this stalemate and, particularly, the enfeebled suzerainty over Greece of Macedon as represented successively by Antigonus II Gonatas (276–240/39) and Demetrius (c.239–29) that allowed the Aetolian League, the Achaean League, and then Sparta under Cleomenes the space for internal consolidation or transformation and external expansion. Conversely, it was the resurgence of Macedon under Antigonus III Doson in the 220s, ironically precipitated by Cleomenes, that fully exposed the unbreachable limitations of the single Greek city as a power-unit and put paid to Sparta's illusory independence and ephemeral social renewal.[5]

*　　　*　　　*　　　*　　　*　　　*

The Chremonidean War of Greek resistance to Macedon with Ptolemaic aid had ended fruitlessly for Sparta with the death of Areus I near Corinth; yet more depressing were the defeat and death of his son Acrotatus in one more attempt to obliterate the humiliation and strategic blockage constituted by Megalopolis (see chapter 3). About a decade later, perhaps c.250, if Pausanias' account be given any credence, Sparta turned her attention to Mantinea rather than Megalopolis. The attack was led by an Agis, perhaps regent for the future Agis IV (then aged about 15), and is virtually the only recorded event in what has aptly been called the 'dark age' of Spartan history between the late 260s and Agis' accession in c.244.[6]

This expedition, too, was a failure. Sparta's native army was undermanned and demoralized, and the state lacked the funds for an adequate complement of mercenaries. But the expedition commands attention for another reason. To the aid of Mantinea, an ancient state whose destiny had long marched with Sparta's, came not only Megalopolis but the even newer and generically distinct federal state of Achaea. The latter had just begun to feel the ultimately dominating influence of Aratus of Sicyon. Indeed, it was chiefly because in 251/0 Aratus had induced his native Dorian state to join the culturally and politically alien Achaean federation (refounded in 280: chapter 3) that this originally loosely-knit ethnic organization started to acquire more than local political and military significance.[7]

Within Aratus' ambitiously expansionist programme for the unification of the Peloponnese under Achaea Megalopolis was naturally a key objective. But in c.250 it had only recently been liberated, like Sicyon, from a domestic tyranny and was not yet prepared to surrender the external and internal independence, however attenuated, that all Greek cities emotionally prized. Fifteen years later Achaea did acquire Megalopolis as a member-state, since by then it had amply demonstrated its ability to control its own northern Peloponnesian bailiwick. The crucial advance was made in 243. In a surprise manoeuvre more daring even than the *coup* which brought him to power at Sicyon in 251 Aratus relieved Acrocorinth of its Macedonian garrison and Greece of its most potent 'Fetter'. This blow was followed up by an alliance with Ptolemy III Euergetes I, who was tactfully accorded titular *hēgemonia* of the Achaean League. This was most likely also the occasion for Sparta to renew the alignment of 281 and ally with the new-model Achaea.[8]

Achaea, however, had no monopoly on novelty. In the preceding year (probably) the Eurypontid royal house at Sparta had produced its first significant exemplar since the death of Agis III almost eighty years before at (where else?) Megalopolis. Agis IV, eldest son of Eudamidas II, would not have been obliged as heir-apparent to go through the distinctively Spartan educational curriculum known as the *agōgē* even if it had still existed in its full rigour by 250. As it was, that system had apparently lapsed at some point after the late 270s. It was thus a doubly remarkable gesture, an earnest of his future intentions as king, that when still not yet of age he had 'sloughed off and shunned every form of extravagance (*poluteleia*)' and prided himself instead on wearing the traditional but now old-fashioned short cloak, bathing in the Eurotas, taking frugal meals and in general 'assiduously observing the Spartan mode of life' (Plut. *Ag.* 4.2).[9]

No doubt Agis and the writers who endorsed and disseminated his political line, most importantly for us Phylarchus, had the same interest as the Roman emperor Augustus in exaggerating the decay and decrepitude of the old ways so as to heighten the contrast between their degeneracy and his moral rearmament. For instance, differentiation within and between the public messes (*suskania* and other terms) was not after all an innovation of the mid-third century, since already a century earlier Xenophon (*Lac. Pol.* 5.3) had noted that the rich were contributing wheaten bread (*artos*) in preference to the traditional kneaded barley-cake (*maza*). Still, propagandistic embellishment notwith-standing, the sorry picture of Spartan mores in *c*.244 painted by Phylarchus is surely correct in its principal lineaments. The *agōgē*, once the foundation of Sparta's military allure and a condition of the attainment of full Spartan citizenship, had fallen into desuetude. The messes, election to which was the other major condition of becoming a Spartiate, still apparently existed, but more as forums for luxurious display by the sympotic rich than as arenas of political as well as corporeal refreshment and solidarity for the citizenry as a whole. The very meaning of citizenship (*politeia*), in other words, had altered.[10]

The main reason for this decadence, as for the poor military showing at Megalopolis and Mantinea, was the persistent or rather accelerating *Oliganthrōpia*, shortage of citizen military manpower. This in turn was predicated upon an ever more grossly unequal distribution of landed property within the civic territory of Laconia, that is the Spartan plain and Helos basin in the furrow of the River Eurotas. Neither *oliganthrōpia* nor property-concentration was a new, third-century phenomenon. On the contrary, Aristotle had quite rightly laid his finger on these in the 330s to account for Sparta's inability to recover from her defeat at Leuctra in 371. But the problem may have been aggravated by the increased circulation of coined money within Spartan society, due in part at least to lucrative mercenary service by Spartans in Egypt and elsewhere. At all events, by 244 the situation had reached a point at which further advance by the Achaean League might have seemed likely to jeopardize not only Sparta's precarious independence but even her very existence. Aratus' seizure of Acrocorinth prompted one obvious kind of temporizing response from Sparta, an alliance. But it was on radical domestic restructuring that Agis pinned his main hopes for a Spartan political and military renascence, even if he took care to accommodate the expectations of his deeply traditionalistic society to the extent of presenting himself as a Lycurgus *redivivus*.[11]

The exact nature of the social, economic and political crisis that Agis sought to remedy, already obscure by reason of Sparta's admittedly esoteric character, is further obfuscated by the sensationalist literary posturing of our main source. What seems to have been the case is that an adult male citizen body numbering about 1,000 in 370 had shrunk by 244 to a mere 700. Of these one hundred were agro-plutocrats, while the remainder were more or less heavily indebted to the rich landowners and in many cases had had to mortgage even the ancestral lot of land (*klaros*) on which presumably their continued claim to full Spartan citizenship ultimately rested. Below these 700 Spartiates (to use the proper term for the Homoioi or 'Peers' of full status) there lived in Sparta itself a mass of what in the technical parlance of the previous century may helpfully be labelled 'Inferiors' (*Hupomeiones*). Many, perhaps most of these were degraded ex-Spartiates or their descendants, men who had found themselves unable to meet their mess-bills by contributing the prescribed minima of natural produce from their *klaros*. Others had maybe lost their full rights as a penalty for some civic crime or misdemeanour, although these will have been few enough if reports of the total abandonment of the old discipline (*diaita*, *kosmos*) are not wildly exaggerated. Some, finally, owed their inferior status to an accident of birth, having a Helot or other non-Spartan mother. In all, to judge from Agis' projected citizenry of 4,500, there may have been as many as 2,000 of these 'Inferiors', an indigestible and ornery lump three times the size of the citizen estate. They, it would appear, were intended to be the principal group of beneficiaries of Agis' programme.[12]

The constituents of the above-mentioned categories are of course male. Never once to my knowlege does an ancient source for any period or place of Graeco-Roman antiquity attach an absolute figure to any female category of an ancient population. The cautious Aristotle, for example, would commit himself no further than the generalizing assertion that women constituted about half the population of a *polis*. What he was prepared to believe and assert of Spartan women, however, was that in his day almost two fifths of Spartan land – privately-held civic territory, Polybius' *politikē gē* – were in their hands. This specific reference to the economic status of (some of) the feminine half of a Greek *polis* is unique in the *Politics* and eloquent testimony to the widely-perceived importance of women in Spartan political life. Aristotle, in fact, was inclined to speak of gynecocracy or womanly power at Sparta. But whereas there are good reasons for rejecting that biased judgment, there are none for doubting that women were significant owners of landed property at Sparta in the third quarter of the fourth century. By the same token it is reasonable to credit the asseveration of Plutarch (*Ag.* 7.3–4) that by 244 the absolute majority of Spartan private land was owned by women and that Agis' mother (Agesistrata) and grandmother (Archidamia) were not just the richest of their sex but the richest of all Spartans. It was therefore merely prudent of Agis to attempt first to convert the two most important female members of his family to his ideas of communitarian change. In this he succeeded.[13]

Formal politics in Sparta, however, as elsewhere in the Greek world, was an exclusively masculine domain, and in keeping with his constitutionalist pretensions Agis sought to implement his programme through the usual channels of political decision-taking: Ephorate, Gerousia and Ecclesia (Assembly). He thus required supporters in high places, since the Spartan kingship lacked sovereign authority and the political system as a whole is best understood as a peculiar form of oligarchy. Lysander son of Libys, a descendant of the great Lysander, was Agis' chosen instrument, and despite his youth and inexperience Agis was able to see to Lysander's popular election as one of the five Ephors for 243/2 (i.e. October 243 to October 242, roughly speaking). Supported by one Mandroclidas and by Agis' maternal uncle Agesilaus, Lysander duly promulgated a bill (*rhētra*) which, to become law, had first to be predeliberated by the thirty-man Gerousia (twenty-eight elected members, aged sixty or over and of aristocratic birth, together with the two kings *ex officio*) and then put before the Assembly of Peers for final approval. By a majority of one – mathematically impossible, unless there were abstentions or absentees – Lysander's *rhētra* was rejected by the Gerousia and so could not be submitted to the Assembly's vote of acclamation. The kinsmen, clients and supporters of Agis (or his mother) had been outvoted by those of the Agiad king, Leonidas II, who for personal as well as political reasons spearheaded the opposition. To this Agis responded, as Cleomenes I had reacted to the effective opposition of Demaratus in 491, by procuring his fellow-king's deposition – not on the grounds of his illegitimate birth, as in Demaratus' case, but on the grounds of an allegedly illegal marriage (which had not prevented Leonidas' accession in *c.*254). For although Leonidas was a genuine 'descendant of Heracles' (as a grandson of Cleomenes II, and son of Cleonymus), his first wife had been a non-Spartan and possibly non-Greek lady at the court of Seleucus (I?) where Leonidas had spent much of his early adult life as a glorified mercenary.[14]

Again like Cleomenes I, Agis found it necessary to invoke higher than human sanction for the deposition of a fellow-king. But whereas Cleomenes by hook or by crook had been able to call in aid the Delphic Oracle, believed by many to be the *fons et origo* of the entire Spartan polity, Agis relied rather on a putatively antique but not thitherto securely attested skywatching ritual which produced the required unfavourable sign of heavenly displeasure with Leonidas' illegal behaviour. Nor, curiously, had Agis attributed the initiative for his programme to Delphic Apollo. Instead, he had cited the oracular authority of Ino-Pasiphaë at Thalamae (a Perioecic community on the east shore of the Messenian Gulf just inside Laconia's redrawn frontier of 338/7), consultation of which by means of incubation was conducted, like the skywatching, by Ephors. 'The oracles delivered by her ordained that the Spartiates should all be exactly equal in accordance with the original law of Lycurgus' (Plut. *Ag.* 9.3). It cannot be determined whether Agis' choice of Ino-Pasiphaë was conditioned chiefly by Aetolian control of Delphi, a different view of Delphi's role in the foundation of Sparta's constitution, or a desire to promote the Perioeci. Whatever his motivation, the combination of divine backing and a pro-Agis majority on the Spartan Supreme Court that would adjudicate the charge of illegitimacy (Gerousia *plus* Ephors) ensured the deposition and exile of

Leonidas. He was replaced by Cleombrotus, a relative of his both by birth and by marriage (to Leonidas' daughter Chilonis), and Lysander's *rhētra* was finally passed.[15]

Even so, the path to implementation was not yet clear, since the Ephors elected for 242/1 inclined more to the outlook of Leonidas than that of Agis. Unable now to invoke divine authority, Agis cited or invented the doctrine of Conjoint Regal Supremacy. This held that, no matter how restricted were the formal powers of an individual Spartan king at home in Sparta (on campaign they differed markedly), 'the Crown' was not limited. The joint and unanimous will of both kings, it was claimed, overrode all other constitutional forces and had the power even to depose a board of Ephors should they deem it to be obstructing the public good. On this ground was the elected board of 242/1 sacked by Agis and Cleombrotus, who nominated the five replacements. Of these Agis' uncle Agesilaus was obviously intended to carry on where Lysander had left off and implement the *rhētra* in its entirety. But either for personal reasons of perceived self-interest or for prudential political ones he carried into effect only one part of it. To comprehend why that should have been so, regardless of Agesilaus' individual comportment, the package as a whole must be unwrapped.[16]

The top layer was a cancellation of debts. Given that the second layer was a redistribution of land in equal allotments, the debts in question must have been exclusively or chiefly the mortgages taken out by poor Spartiates or ex-Spartiates on what remained of their *klaroi* – hence the term *klaria* for the written mortgage-deeds; hence the burning of those same deeds in the Spartan agora. However, some few of the indebted Spartiates were characters like Agesilaus, men of property whose extensive estates had been mortgaged not for the sake of mere survival as a Spartiate but in order to raise the liquid capital needed for the good life of relative ease and luxury. For such men *klaria* were the combustible equipment of the stone *horoi* that dotted the Attic countryside.

The middle layer of the package was central in more ways than one. The by then unencumbered civic land was to be communally pooled and then redistributed in equal shares, not only to existing Spartiates of full status in order to eliminate the disparity between the super-rich and the more or less poor, nor just to them and to those of the Inferiors who had been degraded solely for lack of sufficient land to pay their mess-contributions, but also to those of the Perioeci who were deemed suitably qualified by education, age and physical fitness, and even to comparably qualified rank outsiders, resident or non-resident non-Laconians (*xenoi*), who were presumably for the most part mercenaries (also called *xenoi*; an issue of Spartan silver tetradrachms has recently been plausibly re-attributed to Agis and would well suit this context). It was calculated that

45

there would be 4,500 such equal *klaroi* in all, so that by this method of *anaplērōsis* or refilling the number of full Spartan citizens would be multiplied some six and a half times.

The fourth and fifth layers of Agis' package comprised respectively the imposition or reimposition of the full rigours of the *agōgē* on the children of the new and old citizens, and for the citizens themselves enforced submission to the old Spartan lifestyle (*diaita*) centred upon communal living within the framework of the military-minded messes. Perhaps with a view to hastening the integration of the new, heterogeneous citizenry and precluding the particularism of the old mess-system Agis' messes were to have some 200 or 400 members apiece, making them many times larger in size and fewer in number than those of the *ancien régime*.[17]

With the confessed exception of the last detail and of the enfranchisement of men of non-Spartan origin, the *rhētra* was inscribed on the banner of Lycurgus in the sense that Agis claimed not to be creating a system *ex novo* but rather reinstating the ancestral *kosmos* credited to that omniprovident lawgiver. This was at least the fourth time since the seventh century that Lycurgus' name had been invoked or taken in vain to help resolve a major political crisis. Most relevantly, he had been at the centre of a debate in the early fourth century that had issued in the composition of written pamphlets including, for the first time, at least one by a Spartan author (the deposed and exiled King Pausanias). Between then and the mid-third century a herd of non-Spartan theorists trumpeted their conflicting and competing versions of Laconism, of which Aristotle's *Politics* preserves a confused echo. Finally, probably some time after 250, Sparta produced in Sosibius her first home-grown antiquary and local historian, thereby emulating Babylon, Egypt and Rome in this truly Hellenistic feat (cf. Hartog 1986, 961). The contribution made by all this learned speculation to Agis' 'Lycurgan' programme cannot be precisely identified, but there is little doubt that Agis was not the only Spartan of his day drenched in an atmosphere of atavistic restoration. One Spartan, indeed, made so bold as to name his son after the lawgiver, little guessing that one day he would become the Eurypontid king (chapter 5). Even Leonidas, who had not passed through even a degenerate *agōgē* and allegedly embodied the anti-Lycurgan corruption Agis set out to rectify, found himself obliged to oppose Agis on his own terms. Perfectly correctly, no doubt, he pointed out that Lycurgus had neither cancelled debts nor admitted *xenoi* to Spartan citizenship.[18]

This pedantry, however, was not what inspired Leonidas to champion and focus the opposition to Agis that was concentrated among the great majority of the richest and many of the older Spartiates. For whatever else was at stake, this was also a class struggle within a class, a *stasis* that divided against themselves the 700 existing citizens, despite the fact that they all ultimately owed their civic status to the exploitation of the largest group within the Laconian population, the Helots. However, opposition to Agis' package was greatly eased by the emergence of Agesilaus as notional leader of the oppressed. Despite Phylarchus' picture of Agesilaus as the evil genius singlehandedly undermining the authority and subverting the idealism of his nephew, Agesilaus was far from alone in desiring a cancellation of debts very much more ardently than a redistribution of land, if the latter meant equal shares for variously alien persons. Once the former measure had been accomplished, probably late in 242, the initial enthusiasm of the younger and poorer of the old Spartiates and of those Inferiors who had been restored thereby to full civic status will palpably have waned. Nor did the antics of Agesilaus, who allegedly displayed very un-Lycurgan leanings towards personal autocracy, help the cause of Agis. But perhaps the greatest blow to the king's prestige and authority occurred outside Sparta, in the summer of 241.[19]

Summoned in accordance with the terms of Sparta's alliance with Achaea, Agis led out to the Isthmus of Corinth a body of his younger, newly re-moralized hoplites to help Aratus resist a threatened Aetolian invasion of the Peloponnese. The threat was real enough, but before it materialized Aratus dismissed the Spartan contingent of allies. The effect on the standing of Agis with his troops and on the Spartans back home was scarcely less drastic than that of the Spartans' dismissal of Cimon and his Athenian hoplites from Ithome in 462. Aratus' motivation, too, may have been similar, namely fear of what seemed to him the excessively revolutionary zeal of Agis' 'Leveller' soldiers. For in spite of its overtly democratic features, the Achaean League was thoroughly dominated by and run in the interests of *bien pensant* landowners like Aratus himself. Indeed, one wonders whether Aratus dismissed Agis precisely to interrupt the momentum for social change which, if established in Sparta, was all too likely to extend to the cities of the Achaean League. However that may be, Agis returned to Sparta to find his cause lost. Leonidas, who (like Latychidas II in the 470s) had gone into exile at neighbouring Tegea, capitalized on the changed mood in Sparta and had himself restored to kingly office with the aid of mercenaries. The other two kings sought sanctuary, Agis in Sparta, Cleombrotus at Taenarum (well placed for overseas flight). New Ephors were installed, and amidst a welter of intrigue and double-dealing Agis was condemned to death illegally by a kangaroo court composed of the Ephors and those members of the Gerousia who toed Leonidas' line. Agis was then summarily executed, together with his mother and grandmother. An unknown but not inconsiderable number of Agis' supporters joined Cleombrotus in exile, including of course Lysander, Agis' brother Archidamus, and Agesilaus' son Hippomedon (we shall return to the last two anon). Sparta thus acquired her first, but by no means last (see chapters 5 and 6), substantial exile-problem.[20]

It was ostensibly to restore the bulk of these exiles that in 240 or 239 the Aetolian League invaded Laconia by way of the territory of the League's friends in Messenia. In reality, Aetolia had other ends in view, economic as well as political. Since their federal state was run on very much the same lines and for the differential benefit of the same social stratum as that of their Achaean rivals, there is no reason to suspect the Aetolians of partiality for Agis' social programme. Their aims, rather, were to forestall what seemed to be Achaea's impending control of the whole Peloponnese and to seize valuable plunder, a peculiarly Aetolian taste. In order, perhaps, to avoid antagonizing the Spartans unduly, they concentrated their attention on the Perioeci of southern Laconia rather than the Spartans' directly held civic territory. Some of these at least were wealthy men, although the figure of 50,000 reported as the number of slaves (*andrapoda*) carried off as booty is doubtless greatly inflated. There is no reason, however, to doubt that the Aetolians characteristically but imprudently despoiled the sanctuary of Pohoidan (Poseidon) at Taenarum. This Perioecic shrine, long an asylum for refugee Helots and in 241 for a fugitive of a very different kind (ex-King Cleombrotus), had been enriched by offerings from the many thousands of mercenaries who congregated here in the expectation of recruitment from the 330s on (chapter 2). Sacking it was not the best way to win anti-Achaean friends among the Perioeci – or indeed the Spartans, who since the massive earthquake of *c*.464 had treated Poseidon the Earth-Shaker with boundless reverence. It is to be noted that one of Sparta's sacred ambassadors of the third century bore the revealing name Taenarius.[21]

Thus the Aetolian raid on Laconia of *c*.239 did little or nothing to profit Aetolia politically or to shake what had become, in default of an adult Eurypontid, the *de facto* monarchy of Leonidas at Sparta. Our ignorance of Spartan domestic politics at this period is well-nigh total, but the one certain fact testifies at once to the importance of women property-holders in Sparta and to the ambition of Leonidas to provide himself with the economic and political means to compete in a world dominated by inordinately wealthy and more or less absolute monarchs. (The example of his cousin Areus I was perhaps his inspiration.) That fact is the theft by Leonidas, not of Agis' political clothes, but of his young widow Agiatis, whom he married illegally to his under-age son Cleomenes. We are told that he did so because Agiatis was heiress (*epiklēros* in Plutarch's Athenian terminology, *patroukhos* in Spartan parlance) to the patrimony of her father Gylippus; and certainly it was an antique prerogative of the Spartan kings to adjudicate the marriage of unbetrothed *patroukhoi* (Hdt. vi.57.4). But by marrying Agiatis to his son, despite his age, Leonidas was both ensuring a sensible increment of wealth for himself and his posterity and at the same time extinguishing Agis' patriline in favour of his own branch of the Agiad house. In the normal way, Agiatis' infant son Eudamidas would have succeeded his father on attaining his majority, his position until then being represented by a regent. As it was, not only is there no mention in the sources of a regent (the obvious candidate, his uncle Archidamus, was in exile in Messene), but Eudamidas' legal guardian (*kurios*) was now the Agiad heir-apparent Cleomenes. The hagiographic tradition on the latter emphasizes the continuity, indeed the identity of ideology between Agis and Cleomenes, mediated romantically by their successively shared wife. Modern scholarship, however, is not wrong to stress also (or rather) the ideology of monarchic absolutism shared between Cleomenes and his father. Put another way, with the judicial murder of Agis there died also the legitimate dual kingship. Cleomenes may have been the last legitimate king of Sparta, in respect of his birth and succession to the Agiad throne, but, as we shall see, the manner of his kingship was scarcely traditional.[22]

The date of his accession was probably 235. He could not have chosen a more pregnant moment. For in that year Aratus achieved the decisive gain for the Achaean League that imperilled Sparta's future in a way that Macedonian suzerainty of Greece so far had not. Megalopolis, led by its now ex-tyrant Lydiadas, threw in its lot with Achaea, whose foreign policy thereby took on a decidedly anti-Spartan flavour. Like all his royal predecessors since Agesilaus II, only more so, Cleomenes had always to keep one eye on Megalopolis no matter how preoccupied he might otherwise be with internal upheaval or other external threats from inside or outside the Peloponnese. Unlike all his predecessors, Cleomenes did not only recover from Megalopolis the perennially disputed borderland of Belminatis but actually destroyed the urban centre of the Great City itself. For this among much else he earned the deathless hatred of Polybius, even though the historian was born in a resurgent Megalopolis twenty years after the king's ignominious death in exile.[23]

Cleomenes' destructive feat of 223 came towards the end of what has always been known, thanks to Aratus, as the 'Cleomenic War', the war *against* Cleomenes as seen from the Achaean standpoint. The weight of the combined prejudice of the two Achaean authors is not, unfortunately, relieved by the opposite prejudice of Phylarchus. Much will necessarily remain unclear about the Cleomenic War of 229/8–222, and the following, inevitably selective account will concentrate on processes, episodes, and events where tolerable agreement as to matters of fact is both conceivable and achievable. Interpretation is of course a different matter altogether.

Aratus' success of 235 was followed six years later, after an obscure passage of Achaean-Aetolian manoeuvring in the Peloponnese, by a second body-blow to Sparta. Argos, Sparta's age-old enemy and for that reason among others hitherto pretty staunchly pro-Macedonian, joined Megalopolis in the Achaean fold – also under the guidance of a self-deposed tyrant, Aristomachus. Soon Phlius, Hermione and Aegina joined too, and Sparta's external situation in the Peloponnese was coming to resemble worryingly that of late 370, when the Boeotians under Epaminondas effected the first-ever hostile incursion of Laconia. On the other hand, by 229 the Aetolians had virtually renounced their lukewarm *entente* with Achaea against Macedon (initiated in the early 230s), and in 229 they allowed Sparta to take over four Arcadian towns, including Mantinea, that earlier they had won away from Achaea. They did not, though, go so far as to commit themselves to direct military aid to Sparta against Achaea (and in practice remained neutral in the Cleomenic War). Elis, however, an Aetolian ally, did make that commitment by allying also with Sparta. As for Messene, another old enemy of Sparta but now a friend of Aetolia, she in 229 was at least not actively hostile towards Sparta and perhaps even somewhat reassured that Sparta entertained no aggressive designs by the presence in her midst of the exiled Archidamus.[24]

So Cleomenes' external situation was not without its brighter spots when, probably early in 228, with characteristic boldness he took the fight to Megalopolis and seized the strategically nodal fort of Athenaeum near the summit of Mt Khelmos in the Belminatis. Aratus countered, unsuccessfully, by attacking Tegea and (Arcadian) Orchomenus by night, a Spartan trick, and the Cleomenic War had begun. In the summer of 228 it was extended by Cleomenes into the Argolis, but both in that year and the following one hostilities were naturally concentrated in Arcadia. Honours remained even, and Cleomenes was having difficulty in overcoming the cautious reluctance of successive boards of Ephors to authorize continued campaigning, until in an encounter at Ladocea near Megalopolis Lydiadas was killed and the Achaeans sustained heavy casualties. This gave Cleomenes the impetus he needed to embark on yet a third campaign in Arcadia in the one season of 227, employing the bulk of his still very few but perhaps now rather better drilled Spartan citizen troops as well as mercenaries. Leaving most of his force, including all the citizen soldiers, on exercises there, Cleomenes himself hastened back to Sparta with a picked band of mercenaries and executed a *coup d'état* of which not even Aratus would have been ashamed (so far as its technical accomplishment was concerned, that is).[25]

The background to the *coup* of autumn 227 is obscure in the extreme, not least because we know nothing of Cleomenes between his accession (when he was aged about 25) and 229. Clearly, though, this radically unconstitutional move could not have been made on the spur of the moment but was rather the fruit of much intense planning and clever exploitation of the unique royal prerogative of military command with a view to establishing himself as a prestigious counterweight to the institutionalized power of the Ephorate. Equally clear is the connection between the *coup* and opposition to his military initiatives by different boards of Ephors. It may therefore be the case that the recall of Archidamus from his Messenian exile in 228, on the death of Agis' still under-age son, signalled Cleomenes' attempt to repeat with Archidamus Agis' manoeuvre with the pliant Cleombrotus against the elected Ephors of 242/1. On the other hand, the almost immediate assassination of Archidamus by persons unknown could also, as Polybius was only too ready to believe, have been ordered by Cleomenes, in that case by Cleomenes the *de facto* monarch and true son of his father. All that is massively controversial.[26]

Whatever the truth about its background, Cleomenes' seizure of the commanding heights of Spartan power could not have been effected without the calculatedly minimal use of violence involved in the killing of four Ephors (the fifth fled) and about ten of their supporters and the exiling of a further eighty. None the less, just like Agis Cleomenes advertised his programme as the restoration of constitutional propriety, a return to the 'ancestral constitution' (*patrios politeia*) of Lycurgus. It is not possible, as already noted, to link Agis positively with any of the many known researchers into that most conveniently plastic of imaginative artefacts. Cleomenes, however, was explicitly said to have been taught in Sparta by the Stoic Sphaerus of Borysthenes (on the northern shore of the Black Sea), and Sphaerus is known to have composed a 'Spartan Polity'. Was Cleomenes, then, a Stoic philosopher-in-arms burning to realize some Stoic principle of politics or morality on Spartan soil? It remains more than a little doubtful, although the confidence with which Cleomenes stood his Lycurgan ground may have owed something to the erudition of Sphaerus.[27]

Of far greater immediate practical significance were the lessons he had learned from Agis' funereal failure. First, power, monarchical power, had to be grasped or rather usurped by force not persuasion: hence his employment of tried mercenaries of foreign nationality who would not be constrained by tender feelings towards fellow-citizens. This lesson he could have absorbed positively from his father, too. Second, merely to depose one obstructive board of Ephors and nominate a replacement panel in the hope that it would prove more amenable was not enough. The Ephorate as such – which, as he did not need Aristotle (*Pol.* 1270b13ff.) to tell him, had to be 'courted' (*dēmagōgein*) by kings – must go. It was merely fortuitous that there also existed a supposed 'Lycurgan' justification in the pseudo-erudite view that the Ephorate was a post-Lycurgan institution. Third, the Gerousia. So quintessentially Lycurgan was this body that it could not possibly be abolished, yet by its very nature it typically carried a built-in majority in favour of the social and political *status quo*. It had therefore to be reformed by attenuating or removing some of its individual powers, especially that of *probouleusis*, and by undermining its overall constitutional authority. The latter

Cleomenes accomplished through the creation of a new annual office of the Patronomos (the title probably means 'Guardian of Ancestral Law and Order') and (probably) by making election to the Gerousia annual rather than for life (a major source of its enormous prestige). The former objective was taken care of by establishing virtually a personal autocracy. The fiction of installing as his co-king his own full brother Euclidas merely made it patently obvious that the days of the ancestral Agiad-Eurypontid dyarchy were over. Polybius (ii.47.3) was not wrong to call Cleomenes a tyrant, although most Spartans did not share his view of Cleomenes' tyranny. Fourth, Agis had erred in allowing his most diehard opponents, the great majority of the richest landowning creditors, to remain physically untouched by the first blast of his zeal for change. The eighty men exiled by Cleomenes were precisely the survivors from those diehards and their heirs. Fifth, and finally, personal example was not enough. After converting his mother (Cratesiclea) to his point of view he married her willy-nilly to an extremely rich and influential man (Megistonous) so as to ensure that his two nearest male relatives could be relied upon implicitly. Leonidas would have understood, even if he might not have approved.[28]

Thus armed, Cleomenes proceeded to implement his socio-political programme, which in essence seems identical to that of Agis and can more assuredly be said to have been prompted ultimately by the desire to restore Sparta's greatness as *hēgemōn* of the Peloponnese. Debts were again cancelled, no doubt mainly because the old creditors had simply redrawn the *klaria* burnt in 242 (perhaps adding in some interest for their trouble). Now at last civic land was pooled and redistributed in equal portions to some 4,000 (as opposed to Agis' projected 4,500) new and old citizens. Eighty of these portions were held in trust against the return (surely not genuinely expected) of the exiles; another 2,500 or so went to the existing full citizens (including some at least of the exiles of 241?) and reinstated Inferiors; the remaining 1,400-odd were allocated to deserving Perioeci and (if this may legitimately be inferred from Agis' proposal) assorted *xenoi*, mainly mercenaries like those who had enabled Cleomenes to effect his *coup*. This is the first, indeed the only recorded instance of an *anadasmos* not confined to the land belonging to opponents defeated in a *stasis*. Membership of a mess was again prescribed for all citizens, and minimum contributions again stipulated. But for the first time the amount of produce the Helots had to surrender to each *klaros*-holder was specified in absolute quantities rather than as a proportion of the annual yield. The citizens' children were required to pass through an *agōgē*, the reconstruction of which was perhaps Sphaerus' major contribution to his former pupil's work. Finally, the adult citizens were to practise anew the old austere *diaita*. In short, only the majority of the Perioeci did not feel Cleomenes' new broom.[29]

As over his supposed philosophical inclination, so there is a question-mark over Cleomenes' social idealism, as there is not to the same degree over that of Agis. It was at any rate entirely consonant with his far more hard-headed approach that, despite the restorationist Lycurgan rhetoric, his genuinely revolutionary package should have been less backward-looking than that of his Eurypontid predecessor. His land-reform was path-breaking. Equally so was the associated military reform. There is an unresolvable debate over the number of mercenaries granted Spartan citizenship in 227 (or later). But those who were will have found themselves in need of a new suit. For Cleomenes decreed that his new-model citizen army should be equipped à la Macédoine. Thus at long last the hoplite spear, the victor of Plataea and many another decisive encounter, yielded place in the ranks to the more than five-metre long *sarissa*, a mere century after the lesson of Chaeronea might have been absorbed. If the hypothesis is correct (as I think it is) that the sixth obe (residential district of Sparta town) of Neopolitae ('New Citizens') attested from late Hellenistic or early Roman Imperial times was also a creation of Cleomenes, his idea may well have been to equate the number of residential units with the number of *morai* ('divisions', the largest army-units). He would thereby have restored the principle of army organization in force at the time of Plataea (though the largest units were then called *lokhoi*), which was altered *c*.450 in response to Spartiate *oliganthrōpia* and heavily increased reliance on Perioeci.[30]

The new-model army performed wonderfully well over the next two campaigning seasons, fighting as only those can who aim for something much more inspiring than mere preservation of the *status quo*. Its success was owed in no small measure to the fact that Cleomenes 'was not only winning battles, he was also everywhere winning hearts' (Freeman 1893, 355). The Cleomenean revolution, that is to say, struck a chord in the cities of Sparta's Achaean opponents, where the sub-hoplite poor citizenry groaned for debt-cancellation and land-redistribution on the Spartan model, which they obviously regarded as exportable. That, however, was a grave misapprehension, both because Sparta's unique socio-political conditions could not simply be reproduced elsewhere and because Cleomenes had no intention of exporting social or economic revolution of any kind. Ideological preference may have had something to do with this refusal, but a more powerful factor was the pragmatic consideration that Spartan hegemony over an association of cities dominated by mass movements of genuinely democratic character was likely to be radically unstable and bound to attract the unwelcome attention of Macedon, which had made its views on popular social movements unequivocally clear from the very outset of its hegemony of Greece (the League of Corinth charter; see further below). If Cleomenes ever formulated a blueprint for a stable Spartan hegemony over the

Peloponnese, it would surely have looked remarkably like the distinctly oligarchic Peloponnesian League of old.[31].

By the beginning of 224 Cleomenes' military-political drive had not only brought Argos (a truly astonishing turn-about) and most of Arcadia within the Spartan camp but had carried his victorious arms into and beyond the original Achaean heartland to the very gates of the Peloponnese at Corinth. The victory in the field at Hecatombaeum in western Achaea in 226 was matched in 225 by the diplomatic triumph of the adhesion of Argos, effected no doubt through collusion between Cleomenes and an opportunist Aristomachus. Even Aratus' own Sicyon trembled before the blast and had its loyalties severely strained, and but for illness it looked at one point as though Cleomenes was going to modulate his military domination of Achaea into some form of political hegemony. A few months into 224, however, the wily and perplexing Aratus, former liberator of Acrocorinth and unifier of much of the Peloponnese on an ostensibly anti-Macedonian ticket, deployed his recently acquired authority as General Plenipotentiary to lead a territorially leaner and socially and politically fissile Achaean League into alliance with none other than the old enemy Macedon.

This historic compromise has been debated assiduously and acidulously ever since, usually in the personal terms of apologia or denigration unfortunately laid down by Aratus and Phylarchus. In sober point of objective fact Aratus and the Achaeans found themselves in a situation of what Thucydides would readily have understood as *anankē*, confronting an unenviable choice between evils. Of course, other things being equal, Aratus would not have wished to summon Macedon to save his and Achaea's bacon on Macedon's rather than their own terms. But compelled as he was to choose between, on one hand, Spartan hegemony with the attendant likelihood of some social upheaval and letting of blood (not excluding his own) and, on the other, a Macedonian suzerainty that on past showing would be exercised fitfully, inefficiently and best of all from afar – in the circumstances his advocacy of the Macedonian option before the Achaean spring assembly of 224 is not altogether incomprehensible. However unexpected this *volte-face* may have been to many of his audience, his face had probably already started to turn as long ago as the winter of 227/6. When, therefore, Ptolemy III of Egypt redirected his subsidy from Aratus to Cleomenes, probably in the winter of 226/5, he was not so much taking out an insurance policy as acting on an insider tip-off. Another Spartan of royal lineage to benefit from Ptolemy's patronage was the exiled Eurypontid Hippomedon who at some time between 240 and 222 was appointed governor of the Hellespont and Thraceward district.[32]

Some of Ptolemy's funding of Cleomenes may have taken the form of his own bronze coins, but the bulk of the subsidy presumably reached

Sparta as silver bullion. Already, it would appear, Cleomenes had followed the example of Areus I and (possibly) Agis in striking a coinage of silver tetradrachms (Group III of Grunauer-von Hoerschelmann). On their obverse he placed his own beardless visage, in the manner of the Seleucids (the influence of his father lingering on?); but on the reverse he had depicted what has been convincingly reinterpreted as the ancient aniconic image of (Artemis) Orthia. This was an astute method of advertising his restoration of the *agōgē*, many of whose religious manifestations were closely associated with the cult of this nature-goddess. However, his second series of coins (Group IV) frankly echoed Ptolemaic symbols. Quite possibly, too, he diverted some of his Egyptian income, together with cash raised from the sale of assorted booty, towards the rebuilding of Orthia's temple (date uncertain); and it is tempting to associate the nearby 'Great Altar' (devoted to the heroized or deified Lycurgus?) with the same propaganda initiative. But the greatest part of his funds was of course spent on preparing his citizen troops and mercenaries for the climactic battle with Macedon that had been on the agenda as soon as Antigonus Doson had himself appointed commander-in-chief of a new, anti-Spartan alliance. That appointment had been made at the autumn 224 synod of the Achaean League, following the defection from Cleomenes of Argos and Corinth in the summer of that year.[33]

A century before, the decisive battle between a still independent Greece and Macedon at Chaeronea had preceded the formation in 338/7 of Philip's Hellenic League, usually known as the League of Corinth (chapter 2). In the 220s the decisive encounter between Macedon and a still technically independent Sparta succceeded the formation of a new Hellenic League conceived on significantly different lines. Not only was Doson's League directed specifically against Sparta and the generalized social revolution she was supposed to stand for, but this was an alliance of federations, not single *poleis*. This reflected alike the increased importance of the federal principle throughout mainland Greece and Doson's political skill in accommodating changed Greek perceptions to his none the less vigorous reassertion of Macedonian suzerainty. When he had assumed power in 229 (as regent: only later was he acclaimed king), Macedon was in desperate straits, threatened with disintegration from within and without. In just over five years he had virtually restored the happy strategic situation under Philip and Alexander. Aratus perhaps had thought to manipulate Doson, but even politically he found himself outmanoeuvred (the political geography of the League was calculated to take care of Aetolia no less than Sparta) and, unlike the Macedonian, the Sicyonian had never been a military man.[34]

The season of 223 passed with credits and debits on both sides. Against Doson's capture of most and garrisoning of part, of Arcadia Cleomenes could set the near-total destruction of Megalopolis, a temporary obliteration of 'the memorial and the pledge of Spartan humiliation' (Freeman 1893, 386). This was achieved after a brilliant feint march worthy of the pastmaster Agesilaus II and realized a huge haul of booty (at least 300 talents in cash, together with various movable loot including, we are told, a *paidiskē*, mistress, to compensate Cleomenes for his recent loss of Agiatis). Even so, Cleomenes was always short of cash. And not only cash: manpower too. In 223/2, therefore, he resorted – *faute de mieux* and not at all from ideological conviction – to the liberation of certain Helots. Unlike the 2,000 or so Helots of the 420s who selected themselves for manumission on the grounds of their contribution to Sparta's war-effort (only to be liquidated shortly thereafter), Cleomenes' manumittees achieved their freedom if they could raise his asking price of five Attic minas (500 drachmas).

Some scholars have professed astonishment at the size of the manumission fee, others doubt that as many as 6,000 Helots (Plut. *Cleom.* 23.1; the even less reliable Macrobius, *Sat.* i.11.34, goes still higher) were reportedly able to pay it, and yet others amazement that Helots had any liquid capital at their disposal whatsoever. But 500 drachmas was within, if at the upper end of, the range of manumission fees attested contemporaneously in relatively infertile central Greece under less stringent conditions of liberation; the Helot population was not subject to the same socio-political or demographic restraints as the master class; and the increasing monetization of the Spartan economy meant that shrewd and industrious Helots, particularly those who had laboured on the *latifundia* of the old rich, might make a tidy profit from the sale of any produce surplus to political or dietary requirements. Two thousand of the ex-Helots were armed in the Macedonian fashion, with a view therefore to their eventual incorporation in the new-style phalanx (just as Neodamodeis had been incorporated, in their own unit, in the regular hoplite phalanx at Mantinea in 418). The remainder – age and fitness permitting – were perhaps equipped as light-armed soldiers for future reference. Various explanations are possible of the fact that only one-third of the Helot manumittees were used to reinforce Cleomenes' principal fighting arm, but the most potent perhaps is the suggestion that he did not wish to spread alarm and despondency among his citizen phalangites (as the arming of, again, 6,000 Helots had done in 370/69). Most Helots, it has to be remembered, were not liberated in 223/2, and these had still – or again – to confront the institutionalized terror of the Crypteia. There could be no sharper illustration of the limits of Cleomenes' – and *a fortiori* Agis' – revolution than his treatment of Helots as the continuing basis of Sparta's entire political, social and military superstructure.[35]

Early in 222 Cleomenes showed his habitual boldness in ravaging

Argolis. But even if it was designed to provoke the Argive masses to revolt, it was a rather hollow gesture. In the high summer of 222, with all the relevant passes occupied in advance, Doson commenced his final descent into Laconia. Cleomenes sensibly determined to resist him at Sellasia. This was the nearest Perioecic community to Sparta, lying some 14 kilometres to the north and on the very fringe of the newly redivided civic land athwart the obvious route of invasion. However, as with almost all ancient and many modern battles, precise details of the battle-site and of the number, disposition and evolutions of the opposed forces are more or less controversial. In one sense this is immaterial. Cleomenes' cause was lost before even battle was joined, and Ptolemy acknowledged that he had become a poor investment by cutting off his subsidy just days in advance of the fighting. But, so far as can be ascertained, the decisive factor in Macedon's victory was superior numbers: Cleomenes was outmanned in a proportion of something like three to two. Thus the magnificent fighting spirit of the 6,000 'Lacedaemonians', their *eupsukhia* (high morale) as Polybius called it, and the efforts of their Perioecic, mercenary and allied fellow-soldiers merely delayed the inevitable outcome. According to Plutarch, all but 200 Spartans perished – an exaggeration, maybe, but if so not one calculated to polish the halo of the most famous Spartan survivor. For once again Cleomenes placed mundane prudence above slavish devotion to the good old 'Lycurgan' laws (under which he ought to have suffered partial disfranchisement as a *tresas*) and fled, by way of Gytheum, Cythera and Aegilia (modern Antikythera), to join his mother as a refugee in Ptolemy's Alexandria and – he vainly hoped – fight again another day. The fate of Echemedes, otherwise unknown to fame, affords an instructive contrast: his austere gravemarker, laconically inscribed 'Echemedes in war', was erected where he fell at Sellasia and eerily echoes the *éclat* of a bygone and now irretrievable era of Spartan history.[36]

Doson next achieved what Philip II had scorned to attempt and Pyrrhus among others had failed to execute, the first ever capture of Sparta town. He remained in Sparta only for a couple of days, but long enough to instal Brachyllas as governor. It was a nice touch to appoint a Theban in return for Sparta's notorious occupation of Thebes between 382 and 379/8. The added humiliation for Sparta of forcible incorporation in – or at any rate alliance to – Doson's Hellenic League is very likely but cannot be proven. Certainly, though, as in 338/7, a major Macedonian victory entailed territorial losses for the Spartan state: Dentheliatis (again?), Belminatis (again), and the east Parnon foreland (probably a repeat performance). As for the internal arrangement of the shrunken polity, Polybius (ii.70.1) ambiguously asserted that Doson restored Sparta's 'ancestral constitution', perhaps meaning only that he restored constitutional legality after the 'tyranny' of Cleomenes. Anyhow, the Cleomenean patronomate and sixth obe were apparently allowed to survive, and it is as likely as not that Doson refrained from interfering with the current, post-Sellasia occupancy of Spartan civic land. For then those few of Cleomenes' new citizens who had survived might feel gratitude to Macedon rather than undying loyalty to the Alexandrian 'government-in-exile' of their former king; and it was perhaps they who publicly hailed Doson – probably after his death in 221 – as 'Saviour and Benefactor'. Alternatively, since the monument in question was found at Perioecic Geronthrae, it could have been erected by disgruntled Perioeci who relished the dethronement of Cleomenes and looked forward to their emancipation from Spartan rule under the aegis of some foreign power. What the eighty old citizens exiled by Cleomenes in 227 did now is not known; perhaps nothing.[37]

As events were soon to show (see chapter 5), a vaguely Cleomenean political tendency at Sparta survived the Battle of Sellasia. But it was a broken-backed affair, and with hindsight the pathetic deaths of Cleomenes and his handful of supporters at Alexandria in spring 219 (in a futile rising against the new Ptolemy, IV Philopator) suggest he ought to have emulated Leonidas I and other kings who went down fighting the real enemy. The legend of Cleomenes, however, was in safe hands. He became one of the small pantheon of heroic examplars offering a constant inducement to invent putatively antique 'traditions', as Sparta accommodated herself to alien worlds which it was beyond her power to control.[38]

Chapter five

Sparta between Achaea and Rome: the rule of Nabis

In late summer or autumn 201 the Greek island-*polis* of Rhodes and the ruler of the Greek kingdom of Pergamum, Attalus I, jointly sent a deputation to Rome. Their request, that the Senate should authorize a second war against Philip V of Macedon, was later echoed by Athens. But it was the two newer eastern Mediterranean powers (the Pergamene kingdom, indeed, had not been carved out of the Seleucid empire until towards the mid-third century) to which Rome's governing body attached most weight. Moreover, Rome herself, thanks to control of Italy and Sicily and defeat of Carthage in the Second Punic War (218–201), was now the greatest Mediterranean power of all. Here, then, was a sea-change in the wider and ultimately determining international framework of Sparta's Hellenistic history. It meant that Nabis, unlike his most successful predecessor in the business of restoring somewhat his state's power and glory (Cleomenes III), had to contend not only with Sparta's neighbours and enemies of the Achaean League, her ambiguous and volatile friends and allies in Aetolia, and the mainland Greeks' notional suzerain in Macedon, but also with the coming of Rome. For by the time of his accession in some capacity to what then passed for power in Sparta, the 'clouds in the west' famously descried by an Aetolian politician a decade earlier had risen above the political horizons of many Greeks and cast a looming shadow over all Greek interstate relations.[1]

Nor would Sparta's domestic situation in 207 have appeared significantly more bright. The heavy loss of life and consequent social disequilibrium inflicted in 222 at Sellasia by Antigonus Doson had been repeated in a minor key at Mantinea in 207 by Macedon's faithful ally, the Achaean League. The interval between these two disastrous defeats had brought Sparta first a sustained bout of *stasis*, involving the usual massacres, exilings and socio-economic upheavals of course, but also repeated changes of government affecting institutions as well as individuals. This had been followed by several long years of exhausted impotence, before an inchoate revival under the umbrella of a tenuous friendship with Aetolia and Rome was cut brutally short on the field of Mantinea. The lure of power, it would appear, never ceases to fascinate. But on any sober estimate the urge to assume direction of Spartan affairs in 207 must be considered the reaction of a wine-sodden gambler. It says much for Nabis, therefore, that he not merely achieved a measure of domestic stability and prosperity but also acquired an international standing which made him briefly the focus of 'big politics' in the entire eastern Mediterranean world.[2]

'Statesman', however, was not the first (or the last) description of Nabis that tripped off the tongue of the politician-turned-historian who, for better or worse, will remain our chief literary guide throughout this and the next chapter. To the Megalopolitan Polybius, as to the Paduan Livy (who in almost all essentials depended on Polybius for the eastern portions of his no less fervently patriotic Roman history and for large tracts of this period gives the only surviving narrative), and other lesser followers, Nabis was a 'tyrant' – and not in the relatively flattering sense in which Aristotle (*Pol.* 1310b26) could say of Pheidon of Argos that he was a king who became a tyrant, but with the wholly denigratory meaning that he was a non-responsible despot and the author of heinous secular and sacrilegious crimes. That Polybian view, not surprisingly, has imposed itself on most modern scholars, since it is the *fons et origo* of the entire ancient literary tradition on Nabis (who sadly lacks his Phylarchus). But there has also been a contrary tendency within modern scholarship which emphasises the easily detectable bias of Polybius the Megalopolitan and Achaean patriot, *bien pensant* spokesman of the Greek propertied class, and privileged and compromised champion of the Roman settlement of Greece, and which therefore dismisses the Polybian portrait as mere caricature. One of the principal aims of this chapter will be to steer a course somewhere between these two exaggerated extremes by using the 'news columns' as it were of Polybius and Livy to check and, where necessary correct, their editorial prejudices. The other major objective will be to provide a perspective on Nabis – a significantly new one, it is believed – which, by exploiting to the full all the available evidence (archaeological, numismatic and epigraphical as well as literary), may show how Nabis' fifteen-year rule (*c.*207–192) laid the foundations of Roman Sparta. Differently put, the thesis of this chapter is that, if Sparta survived incorporation into the Achaean League and conquest by Rome with the social, economic and political potential to become a great deal more than just a museum of her desperately antiquated past, that consummation was owed above all to the success with which Nabis surpassed the irredentist vision of Agis, Cleomenes and their imitators to embrace and realize a truly contemporary conception of Spartan state and society.[3]

*   *   *   *   *   *

Whatever may be thought of Polybius' representation of Nabis, there can be no doubt but that the starting-point of his *Histories*, 220 BC, was most happily chosen. For in 220 Rome, with much of Italy, Sicily, Sardinia and Corsica already under her belt and an interest staked in Illyria to the east, was about to renew her trial by combat with Carthage in the western Mediterranean; while in the eastern sector of the midland sea the thrones of the three major Hellenistic kingdoms were pregnantly occupied by newly acceded incumbents: Philip of Macedon (221–179), Ptolemy IV Philopator (221–204), and Antiochus III of Syria (223–187). Taking a more parochial view (the only sort Sparta was then in a position to adopt), 220 BC also witnesses the outbreak in Greece of the inaptly named Social War (220–217).[4]

That war's immediate background was provided by the 'Cleomenean War' briefly discussed in chapter four. Achaea, guided by Aratus of Sicyon, had felt constrained to look to Macedon for salvation from Cleomenes, and in 224 Doson had skilfully availed himself of the chance both to amputate the renascent power of Sparta and to re-establish Macedon's socially conservative hegemony of Old Greece within the framework of a new-style, federation-based Hellenic League. The forces of the League crushed Cleomenes at Sellasia, and Doson imposed on Sparta what Polybius ambiguously labelled 'the ancestral constitution' but which, as we shall see, combined innovation with tradition in a volatile and explosive mixture. Sparta, however, was not the sole target of the Hellenic League, which simultaneously threw a sanitary cordon around Macedon's irritatingly near neighbours in Aetolia. It was to break this cordon, by severing Achaea practically from Macedon, that early in 219 an Aetolian official visited Sparta and invited the Spartan Assembly to contribute as allies to the war the Aetolians had begun the previous year, by diverting Achaea's attention from north of Acrocorinth (occupied by Macedon since 224) to strictly Peloponnesian matters. The Assembly consented and formally ended Sparta's notional association (probably of alliance rather than membership) with the Hellenic League. But it was an accurate reflection both of Sparta's internal political divisions on the Macedonian issue and of her military debility that she performed her role of Aetolian ally with signal lack of firmness and distinction.[5]

The sources of those divisions and debility are easy to see in outline. Their precise nature eludes us for lack of detailed and unambiguous information, above all regarding the overall size and internal composition of the post-Sellasia Spartan citizen-body. The existence of a 'Cleomenean party', for instance, is purely a modern speculation. Amid all the uncertainty just two facts are tolerably certain. First, the luxury of indulging high passion to the point of repeated assassinations was afforded by the removal by 220 of the Macedonian garrison under Brachyllas, which had been charged with the cleansing of Sparta of the

Cleomenean virus. Secondly, the state thus detoxified was a 'State of the Ephors' (a label sometimes misapplied to Archaic Sparta) in the most literal sense. For after the overthrow of Cleomenes' *de facto* monarchy, neither Doson nor Philip had permitted the restoration of the genuinely ancestral Agiad-Eurypontid dyarchy, and the sanguinary struggles over power and policy centred on the restored Ephorate. Thus in the three succeeding ephoral years of 221/20, 220/19 and 219/18 variously pro-Macedonian, pro-Aetolian and non-aligned Ephors were either butchered or forced into exile. It was partly therefore to take the heat off the office and partly as a response to the genuine attachment to ancestral tradition of many ordinary Spartan citizens (especially, no doubt, the least established and youngest among them) that the (replacement) Ephors of 220/19 sanctioned the restoration of the dyarchy, probably after rather than before news reached Sparta of Cleomenes' death at Alexandria in spring 219.[6]

The situation was of course unprecedented, and in the light of Sparta's recent history it is highly unlikely that the old mechanism for resolving succession disputes (a vote of the Gerousia, probably taken in association with the Ephors and possibly formally ratified by the Assembly) was invoked to decide who should reign, not least because even the post-Cleomenean Gerousia makes almost no noticeable appearance between 227 and the Roman Imperial period (chapter 11). Perhaps the replacement Ephors of 220/19 simply nominated Agesipolis (III) and Lycurgus. Agesipolis was certainly an Agiad (his grandfather was the Cleombrotus who had briefly replaced Leonidas), but he was also unfortunately a minor, which necessitated a regency held by his uncle Cleomenes. This was not a good omen. As for Lycurgus, his name at least could not have been more auspicious; but if Polybius is to be believed, he was no Eurypontid and owed his elevation to bribery (one talent of silver for each Ephor). Polybius, though, is a tainted witness, the bribery story is suspicious, and it is possible to find room for Lycurgus in a collateral branch of the Eurypontids (cf. Latychidas II, plucked from obscurity to replace Demaratus in 491). In any event, legitimate or not, Lycurgus became in spring 219 effectively Sparta's only king and potentially her sole ruler. It was he who commanded Sparta's citizen and mercenary troops inside and outside Laconia during the Social War, and he too who suffered and survived at least one attempted coup and another enforced exile before ridding himself of Agesipolis and bequeathing such power as he retained to his no less propagandistically named son Pelops.[7]

Two military episodes of the Social War merit closer analysis, partly for the light they throw on Sparta's geopolitical situation in south-east Peloponnese and partly because they involved the personal intervention of the young (just 20), energetic and over-ambitious Philip V. In summer

219 Lycurgus launched an offensive into what modern writers habitually miscall 'Argolis' but is more accurately described in geomorphological terms as the east Parnon foreland. Cleomenes had briefly held Argos itself in 225-4, but not only had he failed to retain that city but in losing Sellasia had enabled Argos at last to lay effective hands on the string of formerly Perioecic towns situated on or near the Aegean coast from Prasiae in the north to Zarax. Lycurgus, using the remnants of Cleomenes' defeated army and the three or four newly-adult year-classes of citizens who had passed through the restored *agōgē*, together with a good sprinkling of mercenaries, succeeded in recapturing Polichna (modern Poulithra), Prasiae (Leonidhi Skala), Cyphanta (Kyparissi) and Leucae (?Phoiniki, site of the Hyperteleatum sanctuary), but failed to regain either Glympeis (probably Kosmas) or Zarax (Ieraka). From the east Parnon foreland he retraced his steps to the north Laconian border and underlined the incapacity of Achaea's independent military deterrent by recapturing the vital Athenaeum fort in Belminatis which Doson had returned to Megalopolis and Achaea. Philip had other things on his mind and hands north of the Isthmus, and it well indicates the gravity of the situation that he should have decided to initiate a Peloponnesian offensive in person in midwinter 219/8. This was not his first visit to the Peloponnese or encounter with Spartans, but in 220 he had failed to persuade them to maintain their Hellenic League alignment and was now anxious to show the Macedonian flag. He achieved what seems to have been his limited objective of expelling Lycurgus' garrison from the Athenaeum and firming up Achaea's southern frontier.

Six months later, in response to Lycurgus' invasion of Messenia, Philip embarked on his third spectacular campaign of 218. This time he did not stop at Megalopolis but burst through the north Laconian border, proceeded down the Eurotas valley and on into the Taenarum peninsula as far south as Taenarum itself, then doubled back to conduct the first ever invasion by land of the Malea peninsula, as far south as Boeae (modern Neapolis). the pride of Sparta was humiliated by Philip's capture of the Menelaeum sanctuary area (home of the Dioscuri, who had once symbolized and guraranteed the Agiad-Eurypontid dyarchy) and by his pointed sacrifice at the battle-site of Sellasia. No less hurtful was the economic and political damage caused by Philip's extensive ravaging of the rich Spartan and Helos plains and his unimpeded progress through what remained of Sparta's Perioecic dependencies. If Philip did not capture, or even try to capture, the still largely defenceless town of Sparta, that was both due to shortage of time and in line with considered Macedonian policy and practice since his namesake invaded Laconia in 338/7 (chapter 2).[8]

In the interval between Philip's two anti-Spartan interventions Lycurgus had sustained and temporarily succumbed to an attempted *coup*, the sole evidence for which is a retrospective passage of Polybius (iv.81) reflecting on Sparta's constitutional vicissitudes. The instigator of this temporarily successful manoeuvre was one Chilon, bearer of yet another poignantly 'ancestral' name. In the by now traditional manner he had the Ephors butchered and then apparently sought to legitimize and bolster his claim to regal power (he seems to have been a genuine Eurypontid) by raising the at least superficially Cleomenean slogan of land-redistribution. Lycurgus fled with his private slave-household (*idioi oiketai* – see further below) to Perioecic Pellana to watch developments. Chilon's support was not negligible but insufficient to retain him in power, so he retired to somewhere in Achaea and to oblivion. Much has been inferred from his choice of exile as to his political outlook and connections, but speculation is profitless. Lycurgus, in any event, returned and, somewhat in Cleomenes' manner, sought to rebuild his credibility as leader by attacking Tegea and Messenia in early summer 218. When these attacks proved inconclusive, and Philip's invasion of Laconia devastating, Lycurgus was again driven into exile, this time by the replacement Ephors of 219/18 who accused him of fomenting 'revolution' (*neōterismos*). After a brief sojourn in Aetolia, he returned under the new board of 218/17 and once more invaded Messenia. But this invasion was as ineffectual as his previous one and was in any event overtaken by the conclusion of the Social War. This occurred at the Naupactus conference of summer 217 that produced the 'clouds in the west' allusion already noted. It was perhaps in the wake of the peace treaty between Philip, Aetolia and their respective allies that Lycurgus decided to rid himself of the boy-king Agesipolis. He thereby became the first sole king of Sparta, a natural extension of Cleomenes' *de facto* abolition of the ancestral dyarchy and a suitable comment on the weakness of the supposedly restored 'ancestral constitution'. The next years, almost a decade all told, are an era in Spartan history no less dark than the 250s.

On the international stage, however, Greek history as a whole was marching increasingly in step with developments further west. The Naupactus conference had been conditioned by Hannibal's victory over the Romans at Lake Trasimene in June 217. In 215 Rome's crushing defeat at Cannae (later to be celebrated by the Spartan historian Sosylus) encouraged Philip to hitch his wagon to Hannibal's apparently irresistibly rising star by concluding a treaty of alliance. Three or four years later the Senate was sufficiently alarmed by Philip to conclude a treaty with his principal Greek enemy, Aetolia, though it was careful to disclaim territorial ambitions in Greece: the Romans were to receive all movable booty, but all territorial gains were to be the property of the Aetolians. This was by no means Rome's first venture on the soil of the south Balkan peninsula. In 229–8 she had fought the 'First Illyrian War' chiefly, it seems, to discourage Illyrian piracy directed at Roman or Italian shipping in the Adriatic. But the war had resulted in the establishment of a Roman 'protectorate' over a coastal strip of Illyria. News of this *démarche* was transmitted by Roman ambassadors to various Greek states, including the Corinthians, who returned the diplomatic compliment by bestowing honorary Greek status on the Romans in the form of permission to participate in the panhellenic Isthmian Games of summer 228. This benefit was not forgotten. Almost a decade later, Rome intervened again in Illyria in response to territorial transgressions by Demetrius of Pharus, the Illyrian chief who had been charged with maintaining the protectorate. As a result of this 'Second Illyrian War' Demetrius found refuge with Philip and thereby perhaps implanted in that monarch's mind the seeds of larger and ultimately fatal territorial ambition. Philip's treaty with Hannibal and Rome's with Aetolia thus conform to a comprehensive pattern.[10]

Strengthened by their Roman alliance, the Aetolians sought to reanimate the military alignments of the Social War by involving their Peloponnesian allies in its terms. Polybius, recognizing that here was an important moment of decision, wrote up as a set-piece debate the diplomatic transactions in Sparta in which the Aetolian speaker was opposed by an Acarnanian (ix.28–39). The latter, as reported, advocated a 'panhellenist' line, casting the Romans in the role of 'barbarians' against whom all good Greeks should unite. But whatever the Spartans thought of the Romans (and their first-hand experience of them was presumably nugatory), they were clear that their interest lay in siding with the principal Greek enemy of their own principal enemy (Achaea). So in 210 (probably) they agreed to reactivate their Aetolian alliance and be in Latin parlance 'adscribed' to the Roman-Aetolian treaty of 212 or 211. It would be helpful, to say the least, if we had any certain knowledge of power-relations within Sparta or indeed of Sparta's institutional machinery of decision-making at this time. The Assembly, for instance, is unlikely to have voted the alliance as an exercise in constitutional sovereignty. All we are told, however – in a speech written by Livy after Polybius for T. Quinctius Flamininus to deliver in a debate with Nabis outside Sparta in 195 (see further below) – is that from the Roman point of view the treaty of friendship and alliance was with 'Pelops, the rightful and legitimate king of Sparta' (L. xxxiv.32.1). Pelops' legitimacy may perhaps be allowed, in the limited sense that he was the son of (now dead) Lycurgus. But since Pelops, like the still exiled Agesipolis, was a minor, clearly he was not wielding regal power in his own right. The only known candidate for the role of Sparta's chief executive at this date is Machanidas; but it is only a modern hypothesis that he was Pelops' guardian and regent, and on the extremely tenuous evidence available Machanidas' career as Sparta's military and political leader cannot be documented before 209 at the earliest.[11]

This is very regrettable. For Livy following Polybius pays Machanidas the backhanded compliment of calling him 'tyrant' of Sparta, and there is just enough evidence for his military, religious and perhaps constructional activity to suggest that he deserved to be bracketed thus with the energetic, innovative and effective Cleomenes and Nabis. So far as his building is concerned, there is little enough to go on: just a tantalising reference of the Roman Imperial period to a public structure called 'Machanidai', for which our Machanidas would seem to be the only plausible eponym (App. I, no. 22). The religious evidence is firm, but confined to a single inscription recording a dedication by him to Eleusia, the Spartan version of Eileithyia. Given that divinity's association with childbirth, Machanidas was probably expressing concern either over the continuity of his own *oikos* (and dynasty) or, a perhaps even more attractive hypothesis, over Sparta's endemic *oliganthrōpia* caused not only by losses in battle but also by a recrudescence of the pre-Agis socioeconomic crisis. However that may be, Machanidas certainly wished to pursue an active military policy against Sparta's by now traditional enemies of the Achaean League. The timing was opportune, since Roman forces outdid even the savagery of Philip in their descents upon Achaean positions in the Peloponnese. Thus probably in 208 Machanidas not only recovered the perennially disputed Belminatis but actually captured Tegea, attacked Elis, and in 207 pushed on into the Argolis to threaten Argos. In other circumstances Machanidas might have extended his territorial gains, but in autumn 208 a certain Philopoemen was elected General-in-Chief of the Achaean League and in Philopoemen Machanidas was to meet his superior.[12]

In the 220s Achaea's military condition was ragged, and the rôle attributed to the young Philopoemen (whose lost eulogy was used by Plutarch) probably owes not a little to the exigencies of hagiography. There can be no doubt, however, but that after his return from an actively anti-Spartan decade on Crete (*c.*221–11) and his election first to the Hipparchy (210/9) and then the Generalship of Achaea, he was the moving spirit behind Achaea's long overdue military reform. The army that confronted Machanidas at Mantinea in 207, therefore, was not the same sort of army that Cleomenes had repeatedly beaten in the 220s, and the proximity of the Megalopolis that had risen with difficulty from the ashes of Cleomenes' destruction of 223 was an added source of martial inspiration for Philopoemen and his 20,000 or so re-equipped (in Macedonian style) Achaeans and Cretan mercenaries. The battle, which was fought during an interlude when Rome, Pergamum and even Macedon had withdrawn to the sidelines, has neatly been characterised as 'the last act of the long drama of internal Hellenic warfare' (Freeman 1893, 464–5). Machanidas may not have lost his head during the fray – though his unprecedented and indeed unique deployment of ballistic weapons designed for siegecraft in open battle does smack as much of recklessness as of ingenious invention. But after his army's trenchant defeat (with a reported loss of 4,000 Spartan lives, which must surely include mercenaries and perhaps even Helots) he did literally lose his head after being killed by Philopoemen in person. If even after this victory Achaea was nevertheless still 'little more than a tool in the hands of the great powers' (Errington 1969, 26), Sparta's very existence as a state, let alone her nominal independence, was once again imminently jeopardized. It would be small wonder, therefore, if Sparta had been happy to be included in the separate peace Aetolia was compelled to conclude with Philip in 206. But her inclusion cannot be proved. On the other hand, it is morally certain that Sparta was 'adscribed' to the Peace of Phoenice, by which Rome terminated the First Macedonian War in 205.[13]

The Battle of Mantinea in 207 was obviously a decisive battle, like Sellasia. But whereas Sellasia had been decisive negatively, in that it was followed by the imposition of a foreign garrison and a miserable series of bloody intestine struggles not balanced by significant successes abroad, Mantinea had the positive effect of wiping the slate clean, bringing home to the Spartans the undeniable inefficacy of tried expedients and recommending irresistibly the need for further radical experiment of a novel kind. In terms of personality, the defeat had the effect of opening the door to one of the most remarkable individuals in all Sparta's public history, Nabis son of Demaratus. On the basis really of just one passage in 'his' contribution to the debate with Flamininus already mentioned, Nabis has usually been interpreted as a faithful follower of Agis and Cleomenes marching under the common banner of 'Lycurgan' redintegration. No doubt it would have suited Nabis to represent himself thus before his noble Roman interlocutor, as no less observant than he of his country's *mos maiorum*; and it is easy to believe that in front of Spartan audiences, too, especially those in which the majority were the newest of new citizens created by himself, he would have liked to parade himself as a Lycurgus *redivivus*. The reality, however, as I shall hope to demonstrate, was importantly different from the propaganda. Leaving aside the insoluble problem of what Lycurgus (or another of the same name) may or may not have enacted, there is enough certifiably factual material even in our wildly prejudiced sources to show that Nabis neither emulated nor even imitated his putatively 'Lycurgan' predecessors Agis and Cleomenes. Just where and how his measures differed, and the extent to which his policies were both innovative and fruitful, it will be the purpose of the remainder of this chapter to determine.[14]

Nabis' own name, possibly an abbreviated form or even a Hellenized version of a Semitic original, is a singleton in attested Spartan nomenclature. The name of his father, however, is thoroughly Spartan, indeed regal; and by a plausible chain of inferential reasoning Nabis has been identified as a lineal descendant of the Eurypontid king Demaratus who went into exile as a Persian pensioner in the Troad in 491, by way of the Demaratus son of Gorgion (putatively Nabis' great-grandfather) who was honoured by the Delians in the early third century. It is at all events certain that Nabis drew attention to his connection with the Eurypontids' ultimate progenitor Heracles by having him depicted heroically nude on his coinage. Yet more important than this hypothetical filiation, though, is what it meant to Nabis and the Spartans that he had himself styled 'king' both on his coins and on official title-stamps. Since Nabis was born not later than 240, and perhaps more precisely c.250–45 (an inference from the fact that he had marriageable sons in 198), he was a younger contemporary of Cleomenes. If born a Eurypontid in Sparta, he must either have thrown in his lot openly with Cleomenes or kept his relationship with him to the minimum required to ensure his survival. Either way, he employed the long years of obscurity profitably to ruminate on the failure of Cleomenes, and from the very inception of his rule (whenever and however precisely that was obtained) he was able to set about implementing a coherent package of measures very much as Cleomenes had in 227. But those measures, as his rumination could not but have suggested to him, had to be crucially different, even if sealed with the hallmark of royalty.[15]

Cleomenes had had to abolish the Ephorate and hamstring the Gerousia. By 207 the briefly revived 'State of the Ephors' was again a thing of the past, the Gerousia merely a name and a shadow. Power such as it was had been concentrated in the hands of a sole ruler for as long as most adult Spartans still living in Sparta could recall. It would not, however, have been out of keeping with what we know of Nabis' persona and political profile later on if he had sought and received some public legitimation of his assumption of the title of 'king'. The parallel with Antigonid Macedon of the early 220s, where Doson had ruled first as regent and only after some years been formally acclaimed 'king', may not be wholly far-fetched, especially if Nabis was a genuine Eurypontid. (The allegation that he had Pelops murdered, Diod. xxvii, fr.1, looks like a familiar libel.) However that may be, since Nabis was resolved to do physical violence to considerable numbers of actual or potential opponents, he was careful also to surround himself with a bodyguard composed largely or entirely of mercenaries. Cleomenes, too, had employed mercenaries to effect his coup of 227, but apparently had not thereafter maintained a permanent bodyguard, and indeed strove to present himself publicly as a Spartan king in the old austere *primus inter pares* mode. Nabis, however, not only kept a permanent bodyguard but did not shun the symbolic accoutrements of royalty. Whereas earlier Spartan kings and princesses had kept stables of racehorses (Demaratus, indeed, won an Olympic victory in the four-horse chariot-race) or warhorses (Agesilaus II), Nabis kept a stable of parade-horses, at least one of them white and all no doubt richly caparisoned like Machanidas' charger at Mantinea. Perhaps, too, Nabis, like Machanidas, draped himself in a purple robe. But quite certainly he lived in a palace, an un-Greek kind of edifice not seen in European Greece since the Mycenaean era until the late-fourth-century example at Aegae (Palatitsa) in Macedon. Such symbolic 'distancing' was of course typical of all the Hellenistic Successor kings, and the scholars who have rightly stressed the differences between Nabis and Cleomenes have usually looked in this direction for the source of his regalia. This is not the only possibility. Parallels may also be detected between Nabis and another sort of sole ruler, the wholly Greek 'tyrants' who, starting with Dionysius I of Syracuse (405–367), clothed the power they had usurped in quasi-regal forms that fell well short of oriental absolutism.[16]

At any rate, parallels between Nabis and Dionysius in particular are very striking indeed. Besides the ritual summoning of assemblies, the bodyguard of foreign mercenaries and such symbolic trappings as white parade-horses and (possibly) regal vestments, Nabis resembled Dionysius also in consolidating his rule on dynatic lines. His wife, like that of Leonidas II, was not Spartan; but whereas Leonidas' foreign marriage was made the pretext for his temporary deposition, Nabis' marriage to Apia of Argos (Wilhelm's convincing correction of Polybius' 'Apega') was one of the pillars of his reign. Almost certainly, Apia was niece of the one-time Argive tyrant Aristomachus who had briefly delivered his city to Cleomenes. This cross-*polis* intermarriage, like that of Dionysius, offered Nabis a useful potential source of foreign aid. It also provided him with a line of communication to the heart of a highly important Peloponnesian state ambiguously placed between the Achaean League (of which it was an inconstant member) and Macedon (towards which many Argives felt a sentimental attachment through a presumed tie of kinship). To cement this link, Nabis married one of his and Apia's daughters to Apia's brother Pythagoras, who, like Dionysius' brother-in-law, acted as Nabis' chief of staff.[17]

Nor does that exhaust the line of seeming parallels with Dionysius. Far and away the most controversial of Nabis' many controversial measures, then as now, was his freeing and enfranchisement of many thousands of 'slaves'. Unhappily, Livy's *servi* is as ambiguous as Polybius' *douloi*, and modern scholars are understandably enough in deep disagreement as to whether those whom Nabis liberated were old-style Helots (hereditary serf-like labourers, collectively enslaved to the Spartan state), new-style Helots (descendants of the old Helots but in practice at the free disposal of individual Spartan masters and mistresses), chattel slaves (private slaves bought on the market and/or captured as war-booty), or a combination of all three. There is no reason to doubt that there were chattel slaves at Sparta at the end of the third century, as there had been at least since the early fourth century; Lycurgus' *idioi oiketai* were presumably slaves of this type. But equally there is no good reason for supposing that they were anything but a small minority compared to the hereditary, endogenously self-reproducing Helot population. The question rather is whether Nabis freed and enfranchised all the Helots or just a section of them, and, if so, which in particular. On balance the unsatisfactory evidence does just favour the belief that Helotage in some shape or form did survive the reign of Nabis (as Strabo seems to have said). If, then, one were to pick out a category of Helots whom Nabis might have found it particularly attractive to liberate, one might most readily think of the younger and fitter adult males among those who had worked the extensive estates confiscated from the Spartans 'distinguished for their wealth and lineage' (Plb. xiii.6.3) whom Nabis had allegedly tortured, exiled or killed. For in that case by a single stroke Nabis would have been enabled both to redistribute land to impoverished Spartans, as he did, and to make citizens of those liberated Helots whom he married to the wives and daughters (sometimes landowners in their own right) of the proscribed. That is almost entirely speculative, but the Dionysius comparison may be helpful in one respect at least. He too was said to have liberated and given Syracusan citizenship to 'slaves', and the status of the Kallikyrioi in question was plausibly likened by Aristotle to that of the Helots. In a sense, then, Nabis may have done in Sparta what Epaminondas had done at Messene in 369: restored Helots to ownership of the land of their ancestors and made some ex-Helots citizens.[18]

Whatever the true identity of Nabis' formerly servile enfranchisees, no one can fail to mark the difference between Nabis and Cleomenes in their treatment of Helots. Whereas Cleomenes' liberation of 6,000 Helots was a last-ditch, fund-raising and purely military manoeuvre, Nabis liberated Helots as part of his total package; in this respect, Nabis was about as un-Lycurgan as it was possible to be. No doubt Nabis too had partly military ends in view; a larger citizenry meant a larger citizen army. But the death-blow he dealt to Helotage, a truly archaic form of servitude, was surely much more significant in the longer run. It was all of a piece with what for want of a better word I can only describe as Nabis' concerted 'modernizing' of Spartan society and economy as a whole. Like the boost his policies gave to artisanal and trading activities, it encouraged a more open, flexible, market-oriented social formation. By 189, indeed, Sparta could plausibly be depicted (L. xxxviii.30.7) as economically dependent on the outside world – something almost literally unimaginable before Nabis. No ancient source of course was concerned systematically to collect all the relevant evidence: Nabis' criminality was much more fascinating. So what follows is necessarily a composite picture, indicative rather than probative, made up from scraps of literary, papyrological and archaeological information that are not all certainly dated or datable to Nabis' reign but do all mark or reflect the shock of the new post-Nabian Sparta.

The first scrap of testimony is, paradoxically, negative: the absence of evidence that Nabis cancelled debts in Sparta, as he was said to have done at Argos. Since debt-cancellation was so obviously 'tyrannical', Polybius' failure to cite it against him strongly suggests that he did not in fact carry it out. The reason, I believe, is that Nabis wished to encourage debts – or rather loans, even if (like the Ptolemies) he may have prescribed maximum interest-rates. A passage of one Dioscorides (*FGrHist.* 594F5, not later than the second century BC) details the Spartan procedure for moneylending involving a primitive form of written contract. Far more sophisticated and far less parochial is the bottomry loan recorded on a papyrus of the first half of the second century BC. The loan was negotiated by a Roman (?) broker at Alexandria on behalf of a Greek lender; one of the five shipowners or traders in receipt of the loan was a Spartan, the son of a Lysimachus (good Hellenistic name), and the object of his trade was spice from Punt (modern Somalia on the Red Sea). No Spartan before Nabis' day could conceivably have found himself engaged in such a business. Most Laconian sea-traders, however, then as before, were doubtless Perioeci. By galvanizing the port of Gytheum, mainly but not exclusively for use as a naval arsenal and dockyard, Nabis gave a powerful lift to commercial trading too. The hostile sources present him exclusively as 'king' of the freebooters, friend of Cretan corsairs and organiser of pirate-lairs off the anyway notoriously treacherous Cape Malea. But, as has long been recognized, the handsomely set up honorific inscription from Delos (the major Aegean emporium) which hails Nabis not just as 'king' but as 'benefactor' (so putting him on a par with an Antigonid or Ptolemy) belies the notion that he merely preyed on peaceful commercial shipping rather than encouraging or even participating in it.[19]

Leaving the international scene for the moment, we find that Nabis presided over the first genuine urbanization of the hitherto archetypally non-urban town of Sparta. Probably not all at one go, but by 188 at the very latest, Sparta at last received a complete city-wall of the accepted kind: tile-capped mud-brick on a stone base with towers at regular intervals. This was a truly massive project, since the circuit around Sparta's four sprawling nuclear villages (and now also the new village of the Neopolitae?) measured no less than forty-eight stades and enclosed an area of some 200 hectares. Partly for self-advertisement but also to prevent theft for the very un-Lycurgan adornment of private dwellings, the roofing tiles were stamped officially 'Of King Nabis' (in Doric dialect) or (e.g.) 'Public Property: Of the Pitanatae', Pitana being one of the four or five obes or villages. Another of them, Cynosura, in an inscription of *c*.200, publicly thanked its official water-commissioner (*hydragos*). Such concern for water-supply, like the building of the city-wall, naturally reflected preoccupation with sieges. But like the orientation of farms in north-eastern Laconia along routes leading into the market-centre of Sparta (chapter 11), it also marked the increased density of urban residence and the altered significance of the urban centre. Another economic spin-off of urbanization was an upsurge in artisanal production, especially in the pottery industry located in the southern sector of Sparta. Not only tiles and water-pipes but domestic ceramics (notably the so-called 'Megarian bowl' moulded relief-ware) were fashioned in greatly enlarged quantities and, for the first time in Laconian history, signed by their makers. Nor were potters the sole beneficiaries of the modern movement. A group of monumental Hellenistic tombs excavated in the centre of Sparta, some of whose contents reach back to the first half of the second century, look very un-Lycurgan indeed: elaborate architecture, massive construction, and grave-goods including gold and silver jewellery as well as clay lamps and Megarian bowls. Similarly, Spartan marble sculptors showed that they were in touch with the latest artistic currents flowing from Pergamum and elsewhere, while monumental masons now for the first time began to produce grave reliefs of the usual Greek type, as opposed to the old series of 'hero-reliefs' or the starkly inscribed slabs accorded to the likes of Echemedes (chapter 4).[20]

Not all of these changes occurred overnight, not all in the lifetime of Nabis even. But without the consciously new orientation of Spartan society and economy, the breakdown of the old rigid class- and status-distinctions and the positive encouragement to smash the antiquated, negatively autarkic economic mould, they are unlikely to have happened as fast as they did or have been as decisive as they were for Sparta's future. Cinadon, the failed conspirator of 399, might have looked with envy on at least some aspects of Nabis' achievement. By 204, anyway, after two to three years of innovation and consolidation at home, Nabis felt secure enough to turn his thoughts abroad; and for the next seven years or so, relying heavily on Cretan mercenaries, he engaged in a more or less constant, if at first undeclared, border-war of attrition with the Achaean League. At the same time he was building up Sparta's first considerable fleet since the early fourth century, manned chiefly by Perioeci and based on Gytheum but reinforced by means of his contacts with and perhaps even possessions on Crete. It was the huge cost of this fleet, together with his standing mercenary force, that explains Nabis' unscrupulous search for funds (though the alleged 'iron maiden' torture device in the guise of Apia, on which Polybius expatiates, is best ascribed to the overheated fantasies of embittered exiles). A murky incident of 201, which on the face of it involved Nabis in an unprovoked attack on an ally within the framework of the 205 Peace (Messene), has been variously explained, explained away or denied. What is undeniable is that in the following year, with Philopoemen again *stratēgos* of the Achaean League, Nabis suffered a significant defeat near Tegea and Laconia another destructive incursion (as far south as Sellasia). Still technically an ally of Rome, Nabis for one will not have been sorry when the Senate for its own reasons responded positively to the Rhodian-Pergamene deputation with which this chapter began. For Achaea, the ally of Philip, would now have something to preoccupy it other than himself.[21]

Just what were the Senate's reasons for responding positively and undertaking the Second Macedonian War (200–197) is a subject that has been massively, inconclusively, and not always calmly debated since at least the time of Mommsen – scarcely surprisingly, as the issue is 'one of the most delicate . . . in this crucial epoch of Hellenistic history – and even of all ancient history' (Will 1982, 131). Using Thucydidean terminology, one might isolate three major schools of thought: those who assign the Senate's decision overridingly to either 'fear' (that is, concern for security on the borders of Rome's expanding empire or of what the Senate deemed to be Rome's legitimate sphere of influence or concern), or 'honour' (the need constantly to maintain the image of power that called forth an appeal like that of Rhodes and Pergamum, and specifically to honour its announced commitment to the 'freedom' of Greeks from Philip), or 'profit' (desire for world conquest with a view above all to individual or collective material enrichment). It is beyond the scope of this chapter to adjudicate between the Holleaux, Gruen and Harris 'schools'. What matters is that in 197 and more particularly 195 it was the presence of Roman legions in Greece that crucially affected the standing of Nabis and determined the nature and rôle of Sparta and Laconia thereafter. This is a nice illustration of Freeman's (only slightly exaggerated) generalization (1893, 444): 'From the moment that any independent state became either the friend or the enemy of Rome, from that moment the destiny of that state was fixed'.[22]

Despite Rome's proclamation that Philip should leave all Greek states in freedom, the Roman military presence in Greece met initially with an icy reception outside Aetolia, largely because memories of Roman brutality during the First Macedonian War died hard. However, as Roman military efficiency began to tell in northern Greece and Nabis exploited Philip's difficulties there to renew his anti-Achaean and anti-Megalopolitan offensive, so Philip's Achaean allies were faced with another (cf. Aratus in the 220s) momentous choice between evils. Should they continue to depend on Philip, who at least had a proven record of devastating hostility to Sparta but was increasingly impotent to aid them, or should they revolt into dependence on Rome, a potent but foreign and distant power which had treated them so roughly a decade earlier? The decision at Sicyon in autumn 198 just went in favour of Rome. This was a turning-point in the history of 'free' Greece, but also of Nabian Sparta. For although Achaea as a whole revolted from Philip and allied to Rome, Argos also revolted from Achaea to Philip, who, unable himself either to assure Argive independence from Achaea or to profit from its possession in his war with Rome, offered Argos on trust to the safekeeping of Nabis, with the deal to be sealed by a marriage-alliance. This, clearly, implied the end of the Hellenic League of 224, but controversy afflicts the alleged and implausible condition on which Philip is said to have made this remarkable offer, namely that Nabis should return Argos to Philip when and if he defeated Rome but otherwise keep hold of it. There is no dispute, though, over the consequences of Nabis' acceptance of the gift in early 197. Employing a useful mixture of fraud and family-connections, Nabis – with Apia, Sparta's first real queen – took complete political and military control of Argos, enacted and began to implement far-reaching political, social and economic measures both in Argos itself and in its immediate dependencies such as Mycenae, and greatly enhanced thereby his personal power in Sparta and his influence throughout the Peloponnese. It was from this position of strength that he betrayed Philip and entered into negotiations at Mycenae in late winter or early spring 197 with Rome's representative Flamininus (cos. 198) and his Greek allies, the most prominent of whom was Attalus I of Pergamum.[23]

The most significant upshot of this conference from Sparta's standpoint was that, although she had renewed directly her indirect alliances with Rome of 210 and 205, Nabis personally had now received formal diplomatic recognition from Rome, possibly as king of Sparta, certainly as possessor of Argos. The military aid that Nabis was bound as an ally to provide for Flamininus took the form of a mere token force of 600 Cretan mercenaries. This neither seriously weakened his own military capacity nor made any contribution to Rome's decisive victory over Philip, which was achieved rather with not insignificant Aetolian aid at Cynoscephalae in Thessaly in June 197. Nor, yet more revealingly, was Nabis' rule in Sparta and Argos allowed to hinder Flamininus' almost obligatory but brilliantly stage-managed declaration of Greek 'freedom' at the Isthmian festival of summer 196. Nabis was quite simply not at the top of the proconsul's agenda, or anywhere near it.[24]

However, once the Isthmian hysteria had begun to abate, the horribly sobering question of how precisely the Roman settlement of mainland Greece was to be interpreted in practice presented itself ever more insistently to the major parties concerned: Aetolia, Achaea, the Senatorial commission, and of course Flamininus himself. The latter's consulship of 198 had already been prorogued twice by the Senate and could not be indefinitely prolonged. Moreover, Rome's and his prestige as liberators was at risk so long as Roman garrisons continued to occupy

Philip's three 'Fetters', Demetrias, Chalcis and Acrocorinth. These might be arguments for a swift withdrawal from Greece. On the other side, there was Aetolian and Thessalian unrest to take into account, not to mention the lurking threat of an intervention in Greece by an expansionist Antiochus III of Syria (to whose court Hannibal had retired). These might be arguments for retaining the legions in Greece, but how could that be decently reconciled with Greek 'freedom'? Out of this impasse Nabis offered a convenient exit for Flamininus, and he availed himself of the *carte blanche* and two legions thoughtfully granted him by the Senate to conduct a war of liberation against the Spartan tyrant whose occupation of Argos was a manifest contradiction of the Isthmian proclamation (and whose naval power might threaten Roman supply-ships). Cunningly, though, the formal declaration of war was entrusted by Flamininus to a panhellenic congress at Corinth at which Achaea, Philip, Eumenes II (successor of Attalus) and Rhodes among others voted for Flamininus' proposal and only a resentful Aetolia did not. Thus in the summer of 195 Nabis found himself the exclusive focus of a virtually panhellenic army of invasion spearheaded by Roman legionaries. At some 50,000 strong this was the largest force ever brought into Laconia, and it was further swollen by a bevy of Spartan exiles. In recognition of the importance of Nabis' naval arm, Flamininus also ordered up a Roman, Pergamene and Rhodian fleet against Sparta's maritime Perioecic dependencies.[25]

Militarily speaking, the result was never in doubt. Initially, it is true, Argos stood firm, first under Pythagoras and then under one Timocrates from Perioecic Pellana (a new citizen?); and Nabis, thanks to Argive reinforcements, his new city-defences, some exemplary executions and a consequent absence of treachery from within, did manage defiantly to reject Flamininus' terms at first and barely to preserve Sparta from capture. But Argos soon forced Timocrates to withdraw, Gytheum and the Perioecic dependencies fell to the combined fleet, and, cut off by land and sea, Nabis wisely came to terms quickly with Flamininus to minimize at least his economic losses. It was the failed negotiations outside Sparta preceding the final victory of Rome that Livy chose to highlight in his set-piece debate between Nabis and Flamininus.[26]

Whether or not Nabis in fact had the better arguments (and Livy almost certainly did not think that he had), Flamininus got the better of the argument and imposed the terms he wished in the end. Those terms, as we shall see, were harsh. But in the eyes of Achaea and the Spartan exiles they were not harsh enough, as they left Nabis still in control of an admittedly much pared-down Spartan state and the exiles still in exile. Much has been written on the nature and authenticity of Flamininus' philhellenism, but if there is any truth to the view that it significantly affected his settlement of Greece, it should perhaps be detected in his treatment of Nabis and Sparta between 198 and 192 (see further below) rather than in his Greek policy as a whole. (Is it conceivable that he was introduced to the Spartan *mirage* at Tarentum, Sparta's only true colony, and espoused the notion firmly attested later that Rome and Sparta were linked by kinship?) However that may be, there were undoubtedly also more potent considerations of *Realpolitik* at work in Flamininus' mind. As long as Sparta posed any threat to Achaea, Achaea's loyalty to Rome in face of the impending menace of Aetolia and Antiochus should be secure; and past experience suggested that to restore a large number of influential and embittered exiles would be a recipe for jeopardizing the stability of a satisfyingly tough treaty with Nabis. But the crushing argument in favour of a *Realpolitik* interpretation of the treaty is that, for all the 'panhellenism' of the declaration of war on Nabis, peace was concluded only by Flamininus, Eumenes and Rhodes. Achaea, which had contributed the majority of the Greek troops, was left out in the cold.[27]

These, then, are the terms of the settlement in brief. Nabis was to withdraw from all his extra-Laconian possessions (chiefly Argos but also some Cretan cities) and restore to the rightful owners such movable plunder, animate or inanimate, as could be identified. His extreme socio-economic measures at Argos (debt-cancellation, land-redistribution, seizure of hostages) were to be reversed, and the wives of Spartan exiles now married to ex-Helots were to be allowed to join their husbands in exile should they so wish. He was to surrender his fleet to the control of the relevant maritime Perioeci, whose towns were to be severed from Sparta and placed immediately under the tutelage of Achaea acting on Rome's behalf. Nabis was not to bear arms to recover these Perioecic towns or conduct warfare of any kind or even conclude any external alliance. He was to build no new fortifications either in what was left of his own or in anyone else's territory. He was to hand over five hostages, including his own son Armenas, and, finally, to pay an indemnity of 500 talents, one hundred down and the rest in eight annual instalments of fifty talents. On the other side, however, there were some not trivial concessions and compensations. He was spared the return of the exiles and indeed all interference with his internal socio-political arrangements in Sparta; and he was left remarkably with the Belminatis (minus the Athenaeum), two light cutters (implying an outlet to the sea somewhere – perhaps Cardamyle on the Messenian Gulf?), his city-wall and of course his rule over Sparta. But Sparta was now a state in which the uniquely fructifying identity between 'Sparta' and 'the city of the Lacedaemonians' had been sundered. There, in essence, lay the rub. This treaty was duly ratified by the Senate in the winter of 195/4.[28]

However, despite the apparent finality and totality of Flamininus' settlement, Rome's Spartan war was not yet over, merely interrupted. It broke out anew in 193 within the territory of the former maritime *perioikis* – inevitably so, because the towns here and especially Gytheum were literally vital to Nabis' metamorphosed Sparta. In 195 the *damos* of Gytheum had erected a fulsome honorific dedication to Flamininus, describing him inaccurately as 'consul' and tendentiously as their 'saviour'. It was presumably also Gytheum, the most important town, which united the former Perioecic dependencies into some sort of federated 'League (*koinon*) of the Lacedaemonians' – if indeed 195 is the correct date of its formation. Nabis therefore did not need the alleged encouragement of the Aetolians to begin his war of recovery in 193, exploiting as he hoped the weakness of Achaea and Rome's preoccupation with Antiochus and undeterred by thoughts of his son in Rome. Again, however, as in 207 and 200, Philopoemen was able as Achaean *stratēgos* to upset a Spartan leader's risky calculation. Nabis did defeat Philopoemen at sea and recover Gytheum, but in early spring was himself defeated on land in northern Laconia and shut up behind his now complete city-wall while Philopoemen ravaged the Spartan plain for a month on end. However, before Philopoemen could bring Nabis to terms, Flamininus – who had returned to Greece after a theatrical withdrawal in 194, followed by a spectacular Roman triumph – intervened in person to make a truce with Nabis and so restore the *status quo* of 195, while a Roman and Pergamene fleet simultaneously recaptured Gytheum.[29]

Nabis had now become in the eyes of the Aetolians an unreliable ally for the war in Greece between Antiochus and Rome that they were actively promoting. So it was that Nabis, who had survived all the attacks of his diehard Achaean foes, was ironically felled by a single blow from his notional Aetolian friends under Alexamenus. The Spartans responded to his assassination with a magnificent show of loyalty and solidarity, massacring the thousand or so faithless Aetolians and even appointing as titular king a boy, possibly of royal descent, who had been raised with Nabis' own sons. This time, however, Philopoemen and Achaea were not to be circumvented. With the Romans otherwise occupied with Aetolia and Antiochus until well into 191, Philopoemen by a kind of *coup* worthy of Aratus effected the real capture of Sparta in summer 192. He entered the city with an armed force, secured a vote of confidence from some Spartan body (probably only the wealthiest citizens, possibly even the Gerousia), and thereby realized the Achaean dream of incorporating Sparta in the Achaean League. The terms of incorporation, by comparison with his treatment of Sparta four years later (see below), were quite lenient: no territorial losses (not even Belminatis), no imposition of Achaean-type institutions or any infringement of Sparta's laws and customs (*agōgē*, messes, etc.), and – yet again – no restoration of exiles. For most Spartans, however, incorporation was a shock and a humiliation. In international terms Sparta was now on a par with, say, Achaean Tritaea and in some ways worse off even than her former

Perioecic dependencies. Her independent history was over.[30]

The precise composition of the government of 'best men' that ruled Sparta after the Achaean *Anschluss* is unknown, but it certainly included at least one *xenos* of Philopoemen (Timolaus) and is probably fairly regarded as a Philopoemenist junta. (It was presumably this clique which offered to Philopoemen in person the sum of 120 talents raised from the sale of Nabis' household effects.) It was also, no doubt, an 'extreme oligarchic' régime (Golan 1974, 32), but as such it would by definition have lacked the broad basis of popular support so patently achieved by Nabis. Some time before autumn 191 the junta was therefore expelled to join the army of Spartan exiles, despite an informal demonstration on their behalf by Philopoemen. The new régime in a thoroughly Nabian spirit fired off an embassy to Rome with a twofold request for restitution – of the *perioikis* and of the five hostages surrendered in 195. The latter request, with the notable exclusion of Armenas (a potential resistance leader), was granted, if somewhat tardily. The former, unsurprisingly, was not, and within two years the political and economic problems caused by continued exclusion from the sea and the hostile proximity of exiles reached such a pitch that in autumn 189 the Spartans successfully attacked the exiles based at Las in the Taenarum peninsula. Philopoemen, who had been watching for just such an opportunity for further official intervention in Spartan affairs, demanded the surrender of the Spartans chiefly responsible for this breach of the 195 treaty. The same Spartans replied by murdering thirty pro-Achaeans, seceding from the Achaean League and requesting Roman tutelage. The Senate, however, adopting its usual policy of fostering divisions within the League and using ambiguous replies and veiled threats to keep the Achaeans mutually suspicious and dependent on Rome, responded evasively and did nothing. Philopoemen, on the contrary, did rather a lot. Arriving in northern Laconia with most of the exiles (on whose restoration he was now insisting), he first presided over the massacre at Compasium of at least eighty leading anti-Achaeans, then ordered the demolition of Nabis' city-wall, the withdrawal of all Nabis' mercenaries (whether enfranchised or not), the expulsion or (if they resisted, as 3,000 did) sale into outright slavery of Nabis' ex-Helot citizens, the restoration of Belminatis to Megalopolis, and finally not just the reincorporation of Sparta into the Achaean League but the total abrogation of the existing Spartan constitution and mode of social organisation (*agōgē* and messes above all) in favour of the laws and institutions of Achaea. On these drastic terms the remodelled Spartan citizen-body duly sealed the treaty with oaths.[31]

The critical epitaph of Livy (xxxviii.34.9), who as a Roman could not approve Philopoemen's usurpation of Roman prerogatives, is worth quoting both for its rhetoric and as a testimony to the enduring power of the Spartan myth: 'The Spartan state, unmanned as it were by these measures, was for a long time at the mercy of the Achaeans, but nothing did that people so much harm as the abrogation of the discipline of Lycurgus, to which they had been accustomed for more than 800 years'. In fact, as will be seen in the next chapter, Philopoemen's 188 settlement was no more definitive than that of Flamininus in 195. Although Achaea had by now united the entire Peloponnese within its federation, an irredeemably eccentric Sparta none the less remained perversely central to Achaea's – and Rome's – preoccupation with preserving a solidly oligarchic order of stability. For whether or not Nabis was a principled revolutionary (a question the evidence does not permit us to decide), he had achieved all the points of the revolutionary programme outlawed by Philip II's original Hellenic League and anathematized no less fervently by Achaea and Rome. Indeed, in a sense Nabis had negated not just 'Lycurgan' Sparta (whatever that was) but the very model of the Classical *polis* as such, by accepting as full members slaves, foreigners and at least one woman. All that could not be overturned by a wave of Philopoemen's baton. Moreover, to offset the lingering devotion to that Nabian achievement there was precious little love lost in Sparta for either the Achaean *hēgemōn* or the Roman suzerain.[32]

Chapter six

Sparta from Achaea to Rome (188–146 BC)

Philopoemen's drastic and brutal intervention at Sparta in 188 served among other things to restore the political unity of the Peloponnese that Achaea had at last achieved, with grudging Roman acquiescence, in 191. The original incorporation of Sparta in the Achaean League in 192 was described in the previous chapter as the realization of a dream. In the period currently under review the dream turned into, if not a nightmare, at least a persistent headache and sometimes an acute migraine. Fittingly, it was by way of a final paroxysm of enmity between Achaean federalism and the still stubbornly eccentric *polis* of Sparta that the Achaean League – and so European Greece – was stripped of its remaining tatters of 'freedom' by the fiercely conquering imperial might of Rome. This, then, is a sorry tale, a veritable declension, maybe even a nemesis; and it is not improved either by the theoretical preconceptions, ideological predilections and self-exculpating *arrière-pensée* of our main source, Polybius, or by the truncated condition of the relevant portions of his extant work (scattered through Books xxii–xxxix). Best, therefore, to keep the story as short as decently and comprehensibly possible.[1]

These four decades began as they meant to continue, with an appeal and counter-appeal to the Roman Senate from the governing body of Sparta and the federal authorities of the Achaean League respectively. Within Sparta the properties and reactionary exiles forcibly restored by Philopoemen naturally had their deep ideological and pragmatic differences with the remaining Nabian citizens and with the Nabians' less extreme opponents. But on one issue all the various Spartan fractions and groupings (including of course the Nabians newly exiled by Philopoemen) apparently were in more or less complete concord: that the 'independence' and 'sovereignty' proclaimed by Rome under the slogan of 'the freedom of the Greeks' were incompatible with Sparta's continued membership of the Achaean League, at any rate on Philopoemen's terms. Rome, according to their interpretation, had the duty as well as the power to alter Sparta's status appropriately, and they looked to Rome for 'championship' (*prostasia*: Plb. xxii.3.1) of their cause.[2]

Philopoemen, however, who dominated Achaean counsels until his death in 182, was not only an Achaean but a Megalopolitan. His native state had been founded on an explicitly anti-Spartan basis (chapter 1), and its incorporation in the Achaean League in 235 (chapter 4) had given the League a special preoccupation with Sparta ever since. In the early 180s Philopoemen's as it were hereditary hostility towards Sparta, which thanks to Cleomenes and Nabis had gained wide currency throughout the League at least among the propertied class, was aggravated by two mutually reinforcing circumstances. First, in about 192/1 the Achaeans had been rewarded for their conspicuous loyalty to Rome since 198 (against Philip V of Macedon, the Aetolians and Antiochus III of Syria) with a formally equal treaty of alliance, a *foedus aequum*; it was not therefore for Rome, so the Philopoemenists held, to adjudicate between Sparta and Achaea as if Achaea were Rome's inferior – or, as Polybius' father Lycortas emotively put it in 184 (Livy xxxix.37.9), Rome's slave. Secondly, in 191 (as mentioned above) Achaea had unified the Peloponnese politically; in the Philopoemenists' view the Spartan question was therefore an internal Achaean matter in which Rome had no business to interfere let alone dictate orders.[3]

Unfortunately Livy, whose narrative of Roman annals survives in full only down to 167 and in inadequate epitome thereafter, was not concerned to record senatorial debates in detail.[4] But in light of the *de facto* massive disparity between the two 'equal' allies, it is not hard to conceive the mingled astonishment and irritation that the Philopoemenists' arrogantly autonomist stance will have provoked in many senators. If the Senate nevertheless refrained from unambiguously humiliating Achaea until 167 and from taking up arms against her until 146, and otherwise contented itself with diplomatic notes and veiled oral responses, this was simply because Rome had much plumper fish to fry in the east – not to mention the south and west – than the relatively puny Achaean League.

Thus between 187 and 184 the Senate in Rome and its appointees on the spot in Greece heard complaints against Achaea from a variety of Spartan sources. Conspicuous among these were the so-called 'old exiles', that is, men banished at different times between 227 and, say, 195 and either restored by Philopoemen in 188 or, as was perhaps the case of the 'royalists' Alcibiades and Areus, still in exile. The burden of all complaints seems to have been laid against the abolition of the laws of 'Lycurgus' and, rather incongruously, the destruction of the Nabian city-wall (a manifestly un-Lycurgan structure which had afforded pride as well as physical protection to the by now more urbanized Spartan citizenry). But Areus and Alcibiades at least had a more personal grievance too: they had been condemned to death by an Achaean assembly presided over by Lycortas. The complaints were received with outward shows of sympathy, not least because it suited Rome to have a pretext for underlining Achaea's dependent status. But the practical effect of the Romans' hectoring and tactless admonitions to Achaea and declarations of support for at least some part of the Spartans' case was – apart from the quashing of the death-sentence on Areus and Alcibiades – nil. Not only did many Achaeans bitterly resent the Roman interventions as derogations from their putative equality of status, but Rome had no immediate intention of backing words with direct action.[5]

In adopting this posture the Romans were proved triumphantly correct – if proof were needed – by the extraordinary diplomatic flurry at Rome during the winter of 184/3, a 'regular invasion of envoys' (Werner 1972, 559n.187) from all over Greece. Among them were no less than four rival Spartan deputations. Clearly up till then the Spartans had been manipulating their mutual agreement on hostility to Achaea and the need to restore the wall and 'Lycurgan' laws in order to mask deep political fissures within the post-Nabian and post-188-settlement citizen-body. Now, before a bemused Senate the mask slipped. Given the state of the evidence, it would be rash to claim that we today can formulate a clearer picture than the Senate of the programmes and social composition of the four groups. But two groups of 'old exiles' are discernible, divided pragmatically if not ideologically, and two individual leaders, Serippus and Chaeron (one of the exiles of 188), who cherished different visions of Sparta's status before Philopoemen's second intervention. It would not have been remarkable if the Senate had preferred to leave the Spartan question up in the air – or rather to throw it back, like a dagger into the forum, for the Achaeans and Spartans to cut themselves to pieces on. Instead, the Senate so far shouldered its responsibility to champion and protect Greek 'freedom' as to appoint an arbitral commission of three Greece-experts. Their canny judgment carefully avoided the fraught issue of property-rights within Sparta but did unambiguously recommend the restoration of Sparta's exiles, city-wall and 'Lycurgan' laws. On the other hand, they also recommended that Sparta continue to be a member of the Achaean League on the old basis, except that capital cases involving Spartans should be tried by 'foreign tribunals' rather than Achaean federal courts.[6]

Not altogether surprisingly, this judgment in its entirety pleased none of the interested parties, whether Spartan or Achaean, and remained largely notional. Chaeron's group seems somehow to have been restored in 183, but only at the cost of the renewed banishment of at least some of the 'old exiles' (including perhaps the former boy-king Agesipolis III, who now at last met an ignominious death at the hands of pirates en route to Rome). When in the winter of 183/2 the Senate heard yet further representations from the rival Spartan groupings, it can hardly be blamed for affecting to wash its hands of the whole mess and even hinting that

Sparta's withdrawal from the Achaean League would not be intolerable. That hint, apparently, was taken at Sparta in the summer of 182, perhaps by Chaeron in the absence of the pro-Achaean Serippus, at a time when Achaea was preoccupied with the revolt of Messene. It was in attempting to quell this revolt that Philopoemen lost his life, but his principal successor Lycortas was quick to interpret Rome's non-intervention over Messene as a sign of indifference to Peloponnesian affairs and to restore both Messene and Sparta to the League on his not Rome's terms. What exactly those terms were is unclear, but the gratitude publicly expressed to him at Epidaurus by the self-styled '*polis* of the Lacedaemonians' need not imply that he went all the way or even very far towards implementing the senatorial commission's judgment.[7]

Anyhow, the renewed *sumpoliteia* with Achaea did not heal and may have exacerbated Sparta's internal divisions. A seeming *rapprochement* between Chaeron and Serippus proved ephemeral, and in 181 or 180 the former emulated Nabis – or at least Chilon (chapter 5, n.9) – by announcing a redivision of land. This has prompted the belief that Sparta was again in the grip of a socio-economic crisis of the sort amply attested elsewhere in Greece at this date. But if the previous chapter's analysis was on the right lines, Sparta ought rather to have been garnering the first fruits of her socio-economic transformation. Chaeron, in other words, may simply have been an opportunist seeking to make political capital out of the land newly vacated by the once more banished 'old exiles'. However that may be, political capital seems not to have been the only kind in which he was interested. For an Achaean-sounding board of Spartan auditors (*dokimastēres*) was set up to scrutinize his alleged peculation of public funds. Anticipating an unfavourable verdict, Chaeron had the senior auditor murdered as he left the public baths, but this merely provoked an ominously rapid intervention by the general of the Achaean League and his own condemnation to death. Chaeron's abortive *coup* does, however, seem to have had one positive effect. It concentrated Spartan minds wonderfully on the paramount need for internal harmony and stability in order to preclude for the future such direct Achaean interventions with their unpleasant echoes of 188. No more is heard ever again of *stasis* or even minor civil disturbance in the history of Hellenistic Sparta.[8]

From Sparta's viewpoint, then, the hour to terminate the exile question for good had finally struck. Rome's attitude to the restoration of Spartan exiles was clear in principle, but something or someone more was required to convince Rome that words were no longer sufficient and to persuade the Achaeans to adopt a more flexible, pragmatic and if need be submissive attitude towards Rome's increasingly impatient directives. The man of the hour was Callicrates, who was instrumental in effecting this twofold conversion. Callicrates, however, was the irreconcilable and victorious opponent of Polybius' father Lycortas, and the dominant view of Callicrates that has survived in literary form is that of Lycortas' son (especially Plb. xxiv.10.8: 'the instigator of great miseries for all the Greeks, but in particular for the Achaeans'). Not surprisingly, but still unfortunately, therefore, his epoch-making mission to Rome in 180 and frank admission of Rome's prepotence have usually been branded as the height – or rather the depth – of treachery. On a less committed estimation, Callicrates could be said to have espoused the only mode of approach to Rome that offered Achaea realistic prospects of longer-term co-operation and modest self-determination.[9]

Partly on the strength of his being Rome's acknowledged broker in all her Peloponnesian dealings, Callicrates was elected general of the Achaean League in autumn 180. During his *stratēgia* he finally brought the Spartan exile-problem to a satisfactory and definitive conclusion by restoring those 'old exiles' who were still out in the cold. For this good deed the immediate beneficiaries erected a fulsome thank-offering in the accepted arena for such displays, the panhellenic shrine of the suppliants' patron Zeus at Olympia. It was perhaps also in or soon after 179 that Sparta rebuilt her city-wall, although naturally there was no question of her being allowed by Achaea, let alone Rome, to recover also the sort of military strength mustered by Cleomenes or even Nabis. On the other hand, it was probably not until after 146, with the defeat of Achaea by Rome and the consequent liberation of Sparta from the clutches of the Achaean League, that Sparta was able to restore the *agōgē* (in part), and the distinctive Spartan mode of life as a whole – or rather, some semblance of it: the metaphor of the museum (Shimron 1972, 134) does not seem wholly inapt. All that remained until then of the old Spartan ways were the peculiar mode of clothing and style of hair (Paus. vii.14.2), which constituted both literally and figuratively a mere keeping up of appearances. Only now, belatedly, can Sparta be said to have begun to conform to the 'increasing tendency of the [*sc.* Greek] city to act out a representation of *polis* life for her contemporaries in the Hellenistic world, rather than seek a role in the new configurations of power' (Humphreys 1985, 219).[10]

After 179 Sparta in any case sinks below the horizon of sources concerned only with 'big politics', not to rise again to view until the final cataclysm of the 140s. History, in this sense, 'passed Sparta by' (Shimron 1972, 130), most conspicuously during the epochal Third Macedonian War of 171–168. Polybius crookedly placed the blame for this war on King Perseus of Macedon inasmuch as he had inherited the aggressive designs of his father Philip V. In fact, the seeds of the war had been sown in the mid-180s by the Roman Senate, which treated Philip virtually as a prisoner at its bar and believed too readily the inflated accusations of disloyalty and claims about his menace to Rome's interests. Similarly, it was a charge levelled against Perseus by Eumenes II of Pergamum in winter 173/2 that occasioned Rome's devastatingly effective pre-emptive strike. The Battle of Pydna (168) was as decisive for Macedon's immediate future as had been the Battle of Cynoscephalae in 197. However, so far as the Greeks were concerned, there was a vital difference between the outcomes of the two encounters. Whereas the former had been followed by Flamininus' Isthmian proclamation, 'it is impossible not to agree with Polybius that the Greeks after 168 virtually were subjects of Rome' (Larsen 1935, 206).[11]

Polybius, though, had a peculiarly personal reason for taking this view. Achaea had not sided with Perseus against Rome, but nor had she offered to Rome the kind of unconditional loyalty, respect and assistance she had come to expect and demand. Venting its frustration with the persistent autonomist current in Achaean politics, and with a view to damming it up for good, the Senate vindictively and without legal justification deported to Italy in 167 more than 1,000 leading Achaeans – including the future historian of Rome's rise to 'world' domination. This was an unjust punishment for Achaea. But no less was it an undeserved bonus for Sparta, who, having done nothing for Rome, found herself rid at a stroke of all her principal Achaean enemies. Just one Spartan is known to have made any contribution to the Third Macedonian War, and he (Leonidas, a man of royal descent) had done so on the Macedonian side. Another leading Spartan, Menalcidas, perfectly symbolized his state's general lack of interest in the whole Macedonian episode by serving in a quite different war, the Sixth Syrian War between Antiochus IV and Ptolemy VI in Egypt, where in 168 he was sprung from an Alexandrian prison through the good offices of the powerful C. Popillius Laenas (cos. 172).[12]

In the following winter of 168/7 the victor of Pydna, L. Aemilius Paullus, called in at Sparta in the course of an extended progress through Greece. He is in a sense the first 'grand tourist' on record, since the ostensible purpose of his visit (according to Livy, anyway) was to pay his respects to Sparta's ancestral way of life. But his antiquarianism should not be exaggerated. The progress was chiefly in the nature of a triumphal and goodwill mission, not to mention the opportunity it afforded for some discreet fact-finding and the cementing of patron-client bonds. A comparable mixture of sentiment and pragmatism lay behind the visit to Sparta at about this time of another distinguished and Hellenizing 'barbarian'. But whereas Paullus had come in triumph, Jason the former High Priest of Jerusalem arrived as a refugee from a popular uprising, anxiously parading the fictive kinship-links between the Spartans and the Jews that may have been forged in the time of Areus I and Onias (chapter 3 and n.22).[13]

These two visits are a salutary reminder that, despite her global insignificance, Sparta did not lack all international cachet. The same message is conveyed rather more quietly by a small cluster of epigraphic documents datable to the first half of the second century. These reveal that Spartans were in demand either as arbitrators of foreign disputes or as diplomatic representatives (*proxenoi*) of other Greek communities in Sparta itself. Perhaps the most interesting of these texts is the decree of Arcadian Orchomenus recording the appointment as *proxenos* of Cleoxenus son of Nicolas. Its interest lies not so much in the heap of honour and privileges that accompanied this award (though the right to cut wood is highly unusual) as in the very fact of the appointment. Clearly, their shared membership of the Achaean League was not thought to obviate the need for a diplomatic tie between Sparta and Orchomenus of a kind invented for a bygone era of atomized and jealously independent *poleis*. The limits of Greek federalism are here readily apparent.[14]

Or perhaps one should say, rather, the limitations of Achaea's hold, ideologically as well as practically speaking, over Sparta. For although Sparta did introduce Achaean-type institutions and issue coins of federal type, yet she persisted in displaying an irredentist *polis*-mentality on the fundamental issue of territory. Encouraged no doubt by Rome's hard line with Achaea in 167, Sparta in about 164 sought to re-open at Rome the question of her northern frontier with Megalopolis and perhaps also, if Pausanias (vii.11.1–3) is not merely confused, her north-eastern border with Argos. To recap briefly, Aegytis and Sciritis had been lost to Megalopolis in the 360s, which loss had been confirmed by Philip II in 338/7. So too Belminatis, but this had had a more chequered history thereafter. Recovered briefly by Cleomenes, it had been restored to Megalopolis by Doson in 222. Once more regained for Sparta by Machanidas, it had firmly been returned in 188 by Philopoemen to his home state. Naturally, therefore, ownership and control of Belminatis were on Sparta's Roman agenda in *c*.164, but so too were those of Aegytis, Sciritis and perhaps (see above) some or all of the east Parnon foreland. Rome's response was cleverly contrived. Since the Senate was eager to maintain the Peloponnesian *status quo* of 167 without being seen as overtly snubbing their Spartan friends, its representative in Greece (C. Sulpicius Galus, cos. 166) appointed Callicrates to arbitrate the claim(s), knowing full well that he too would opt for the *status quo* for Achaean as well as personal reasons. The result was a foregone conclusion, but none the less bitterly resented by the Spartans, who resorted to force without success and received the additional humiliation of an Achaean fine.[15]

Foiled here, the Spartans tried another tack, in another place where they had deep interests and sentiments of long standing but where Rome had no *locus standi*. With Delphi Sparta had enjoyed something of a 'special relationship' since the eighth century, which had survived a temporary expulsion from the administering Amphictyony in the mid-fourth century. But from the mid-third century Aetolia had been careful to deny Sparta any prominence therein, and it was not before the demise of Aetolia as a power in 189 that the issue of Delphian management could be profitably reopened. In 168 Paullus had begun his progress through Greece with a symbolic sacrifice to Pythian Apollo at the navel of the earth. In the late 160s Sparta considered the moment opportune to claim a more prominent voice in Delphian affairs. However, it was a fair measure of Spartan impotence that so much energy should have been devoted to achieving a relatively paltry ambition (the right to provide one representative on the Amphictyonic council every other year in alternation with the representative for Dōris, the supposed motherland of the Dorians) – and that the effort failed. For Dōris objected, and the thirty-one Lamians appointed to arbitrate the dispute decided in favour of Dōris. *Sic transit gloria laconica.*[16]

Behind both these initiatives it would not be unreasonable to suspect the hand of Menalcidas, the one considerable Spartan of this era. However, as far as the jejune evidence goes, Menalcidas fades utterly from notice between his inglorious début at Alexandria in 168 and his remarkable election in autumn 151 as probably the first and certainly the last Spartan general of the Achaean League. His election was presumably a token of tolerably good relations between Sparta and Achaea, despite Sparta's territorial disappointments. But in Polybius' partisan terms it epitomized the time of troubles (*tarakhē kai kinēsis*: iii.4.12) between 152/1 and 146/5 that culminated in the Achaean War and ultimate loss of Greek independence, if not the end of Greek history. For Polybius (whose enforced sojourn as a hostage in Italy had ended in 151, but who had preferred to remain outside Achaea in the company of his noble Roman friends until just after the sack of Corinth) placed all the blame for that catastrophe squarely on the shoulders of the increasingly demagogic and irresponsible Achaean leaders like Menalcidas.[17]

Pausanias, too, who was perhaps somehow dependent on Polybius and is unfortunately the only surviving author to offer a connected account of the origins and course of the Achaean War, assigned a decisive part in the causal chain to Menalcidas for his rôle in the Oropus affair. But although major conflagrations have often been ignited by minor sparks, it is hard to see how that obscure episode, so far removed from the direct interests of either Achaea or Sparta, can bear so much explanatory weight. Besides, Pausanias' account as a whole is riddled with contradictions and inconsequentialities. It would seem prudent, therefore, to look elsewhere for the issue that brought Achaea into renewed conflict with Sparta and thereby to final defeat by Rome.[18]

That issue was without doubt Spartan independence from Achaea. Either during or more probably before his generalship Menalcidas had been on a mission to Rome apparently to revive the Belminatis question with a still uninterested Senate. For this among other reasons the ageing Callicrates, who had now to compete for influence with the restored hostages, impeached Menalcidas for treason in 150, on the grounds that he had been agitating for Spartan independence. Menalcidas is said to have secured his acquittal by bribing his successor in the generalship, Diaeus of Megalopolis (probably one of the returned deportees). But the prosecution had inflamed Spartan 'nationalistic' or particularistic sentiments, both because of the disappointed territorial claim that lay behind it and because the trial of a Spartan citizen on a capital charge by an Achaean court seemed an unbearable infringement of Spartan autonomy. When Sparta again sent an embassy to Rome in 149, presumably over the same territorial issue as before, Diaeus treated this as a breach of the federal principle that member-states might not conduct separate missions to Rome. Invading Laconia, he forced into exile twenty-four leading Spartans, including Menalcidas. The double-game allegedly played by a prominent member of the Gerousia and the fact that the motion for the exile of the twenty-four went through the Gerousia suggest that Achaean intervention was having the unintended effect of galvanizing at least one moribund 'Lycurgan' political institution.[19]

The new exiles naturally appealed to Rome. Callicrates set out to state the Achaean case, but died on the way and was replaced as envoy by Diaeus. This was late in 149. Rome at that time was preoccupied with matters of far greater moment in both Macedon (the revolt of Andriscus) and Carthage. It suited the Senate therefore to give a temporizing reply, which Menalcidas and Diaeus could each interpret to his satisfaction. Thus in 140 Sparta seceded from the Achaean League, whose new general Damocritus waged war to coerce her back in, despite the advice of Rome's Macedonian governor to await the arrival of a senatorial commission. Damocritus' campaign dealt Sparta two mortal blows. A battle fought somewhere in northern Laconia allegedly cost Sparta a thousand lives; and the Spartans were now deprived of what would appear to be their last remaining Perioecic dependencies – those that lay 'in a circle round Sparta' in northern Laconia and on the eastern flank of the Eurotas valley. Damocritus also prevented the late autumn/early winter sowing of cereals in what was left of Sparta's nuclear territory in the Spartan basin. He did not, however, press his advantage to the point of attacking Sparta itself and instead made a truce, for which alleged dereliction of duty he was heavily fined by the Achaean authorities, forced into exile and replaced as general by Diaeus.[20]

In 148/7 Diaeus consolidated Damocritus' intrusion into Laconia by garrisoning the newly liberated ex-Perioecic towns. Sparta's – or rather Menalcidas' – reponse in 147 was to recapture one of these (Iasus, perhaps to be located at modern Analipsis) and so break the truce. When the Spartans refused to support him, partly at least because they were experiencing severe hunger, he committed suicide to avoid judicial execution. But his death was not without pathos or irony. For in the summer of 147 a much delayed senatorial commission under L. Aurelius Orestes did at last arrive at Corinth and in effect confirmed Menalcidas' interpretation of his mission to Rome in the winter of 149/8. The Senate had decided that Sparta – together with Corinth, Argos, Aracadian Orchomenus and Oetaean Heraclea – should no longer be part of the Achaean League. Depending on one's view of the character of Roman imperialism in general and the Senate's attitude to Greek affairs in the early 140s in particular, this was either a miscalculatedly over-severe warning to Achaea not to presume on Rome's continued complaisance or an overt expression of Rome's abiding long-term aim of breaking up the League (or at any rate cutting it down to size) by whatever means it saw fit, however morally or legally unjustifiable. There is no ambiguity, however, concerning the Achaean response to Orestes' news. In a frenzied release of pent-up bitterness the Roman delegation was roundly abused, and any Spartans – or suspected Spartans – who had the misfortune to be in Corinth at that moment were lynched.[21]

In the following autumn the arrival of a second Roman mission under the consular Sex. Iulius Caesar coincided with the annual Achaean elections. No matter how emollient Caesar's message was supposed to be, the important point is that he had not been authorized by the Senate to retract Rome's support for the at least partial dissolution of the Achaean League. Critolaus was therefore elected general on the crest of a wave of anti-Roman feeling disguised, displaced or reinforced by hostility towards Sparta. Polybius' condemnation of the Achaean leadership now rises to a crescendo of denunciation in the case of Critolaus. Not only did Critolaus display contempt for the majesty of Rome, but he also committed the heinous crime in Polybius' eyes of inciting anti-Roman enthusiasm among the lower orders of Achaean society. Following Polybius' lead, Critolaus' measures of debt-relief for the poor combined with compulsory financial contributions by the rich have too often been interpreted as primarily expressions of social ideology, when their aim was doubtless to minimize domestic friction with a view to the coming war. It would not be surprising, though, if a by-product of these measures had been a surge of popular resentment directed not only against the Romans' interference in Achaean affairs but also against their partiality for upper-class government. Anyhow, an unprecedentedly high percentage of peasant farmers and small craftsmen attended the fateful Achaean assembly at Corinth in the spring of 146, which appointed Critolaus general plenipotentiary for the war Achaea declared ostensibly on Sparta but in reality on Rome.[22]

If there is room for argument over Rome's motives and methods in its diplomatic dealings with Achaea between 149 and 147, there is no question but that the Achaean decision for war with Rome, magnificent gesture though it may have been, was a vote for collective military and political suicide. The initial attempt to reclaim the revolted Heraclea for the League resulted in the defeat and death of Critolaus near Thermopylae. Despite his successor Diaeus' last-ditch liberation of some 12,000 slaves, Achaea was no match for the amphibious Roman and allied expeditionary force commanded by the consul L. Mummius, who in late summer 146 won a resounding victory at Leucopetra and then made of Corinth an exemplary desert.[23]

Achaea's brave experiment in federalism – 'the first attempt on a large scale to reconcile local independence with national strength' (Freeman 1893, 554) – was thus brutally terminated after a century and a third (280–146). An Achaean federation was probably soon re-formed, perhaps within half a dozen years, but this was confined to Achaea in the geographical sense and shorn of anything but (at most) municipal significance. That was chiefly to suit the administrative convenience of the suzerain. For Rome had decided to convert most of Greece, not into a full-blown province, but into a dependency of the province she had earlier made of Macedonia. Forbidden to possess a city-wall and obligated,if only informally, to satisfy Rome's constitutional and financial demands, the demilitarized and demoralized cities of old Achaea were unlikely to cause Rome a deal of concern. The most that could be said in favour of Rome's settlement from an Achaean point of view – that of the upper classes – was that matters could have been even worse: 'if we had not perished so quickly, we should never have been saved'.[24]

Sparta, of course, fared much better under the new Roman dispensation, since she had played no active part in the Achaean War. Thus she kept the wall rebuilt (probably) in the early 170s and remained 'free' in the Roman sense. It was probably now, as mentioned above, that a limited restoration of 'Lycurgan' institutions occurred, affecting the *agōgē* above all, after more than four decades of Achaean influence. Formally, Sparta was exempt from the burden of tribute. On the other hand, Sparta's political impotence and dependence on Rome the suzerain cannot be gainsaid. The ex-Perioecic communities were not restored to her; twenty-four of them, indeed, were either now organized as 'the *koinon* of the Lacedaemonians' or, if (as suggested in chapter 5) they had been so organized since 195, gained their collective independence from Achaea as well as Sparta. Perhaps Sparta was permitted to recover Belminatis from Megalopolis, but she was quite certainly forbidden by Mummius to reclaim from Messene the disputed frontier-land of Dentheliatis. Since traditionally it was here that the seeds of Sparta's conquest of Messenia and consequent rise to the status of a great Greek power had been planted some six centuries earlier, there was a certain symbolic fittingness in Sparta's renewed claim being rejected by Greece's Roman conqueror.[25]

II

Roman Sparta

Chapter seven

Sparta between sympolity and municipality

Conforming to their larger neglect of the period since Roman domination, writers of Greek history in the Imperial age by and large ceased to interest themselves in events at Sparta after (at the latest) 146 BC, looking instead for stirring historical narrative to the reassurances of the more distant Greek past. Even so, it took the passage of two centuries after 146 BC before we can readily recognize in Sparta Morrou's 'small and peaceful municipality in the unarmed province of Achaia'. In the intervening period local history – for such Sparta's had now become – was anything but tranquil. The Late Republic saw the Spartans drawn willy-nilly, like the rest of Greece, into the drama of the Roman civil wars. The aftermath of Actium then witnessed the unexpected establishment at Sparta of a Roman client-dynasty, that of Eurycles and his descendants, under whose stormy three-generation régime the Spartans experienced for the last time something of the glamour of Hellenistic monarchy[1].

Between 146 BC and the outbreak of the First Mithradatic War in 88 BC, a period during which Greece as a whole enjoyed peace and prosperity, Spartan affairs are largely a blank. As a friendly non-combatant on the side-lines of the Achaean War the city was treated favourably by Mummius and the Roman commissioners. Although the *ager Dentheliatis* remained Messenian, it was probably now that Sparta recovered the Belminatis region on her north-western frontier with Megalopolis (chapter 10). Much more significantly for Sparta's subsequent history, Rome now permitted the restoration of the ancestral Spartan polity, 'as far as was possible after so many misfortunes and such degradations' (Plut. *Philop*.16.9); as a result, the decades after 146 BC were probably a time of intense antiquarian activity at Sparta, concentrated above all on the recreation – after a fashion – of the 'Lycurgan' *agōgē* (chapter 14). The Mummian settlement left the defeated members of the old Achaean League and their allies hovering uncertainly between surveillance by the proconsuls of Macedonia and full provincialization (a Roman governor of Greece is not attested until 46 BC). As a free city, however, Sparta retained full local autonomy and, as a scatter of epigraphic evidence shows, continued to engage in the familiar routines of Hellenistic inter-city diplomacy until well into the first century BC: Spartan *dikastai* were honoured at Delphi *c*.100 BC, (chapter 13); in 81 BC the city was one of the long list of Greek communities recognizing the asylum-rights of the sanctuary of Hecate at Carian Lagina; and Spartan notables continued to cultivate overseas contacts with cities such as Thera – with which Sparta shared a tie of kinship – and Tralles.[2]

The period after 146 BC was also one of intensifying routine contact with Rome, reflected in the construction at Sparta of a special lodging for visiting Roman officials, which, as Kennell saw, must be later than the period of Achaean sympolity, since federal cities were not supposed to conduct independent diplomacy with Rome. The Late Republic was also a time in which Rome's subject-communities in the east became increasingly enmeshed in ties of patronage with the great families of the Roman aristocracy, a development echoes of which can be clearly heard at Sparta. A passage in Suetonius reveals that by 40 BC the Spartans were clients of the powerful patrician clan of the Claudii (below); this tie was at least as old as *c*.100 BC, when the Spartan philosopher Demetrius dedicated a work to a Claudius Nero (chapter 13), and perhaps should be traced back to Ap. Claudius Pulcher (cos. 185 BC), a zealous supporter of the Spartans in their dealings with the Achaean League. Looking ahead somewhat, the importance to Sparta of such patronal ties emerges in the case of Cicero, whose letter of 46 BC recommending the city to the first governor of Greece, Ser. Sulpicius Rufus, still survives. Cicero twice alludes here to his indebtedness to the Spartans, a reference which has baffled commentators; presumably it relates to the trial at Rome in 59 BC of L. Valerius Flaccus, a former governor of Asia, when the Spartans obliged Cicero by sending character-witnesses to appear on his client's behalf. The city's ties with the eminent orator can be traced back to 79–7 BC, when the young Cicero paid a tourist's visit to Sparta in the course of a period of study abroad. The letter reveals that his Spartan ties – conforming to a familiar pattern in this period – were dependent on a personal friendship with an otherwise unknown but no doubt eminent Spartan, one Philippus, at whose request he had undertaken to write the letter and in whose house at Sparta he perhaps had once stayed as a guest.[3]

From 88 BC until 31 BC Sparta found herself the reluctant participant in a succession of Roman wars using Greece as their theatre, the ensuing cost in Spartan lives and resources sounding a sombre note in local history during the last half-century of the Roman Republic. In this period the security of the Eurotas valley once more came under threat; not surprisingly, we now find evidence for repairs to the city's mud-brick fortification wall (App. I, 9). Warfare returned to Greece in 88 BC, when

Pontic fleets appeared in Greek waters seeking allies for the ambitious Mithradates VI of Pontus in his offensive against Rome's eastern ascendancy. Spartan behaviour during the First Mithradatic War is obscure. If the Pontic local historian Memnon can be trusted, Pontic and Spartan troops clashed in battle – presumably following a sea-borne invasion of Laconia – and the Spartans suffered a defeat, after which the city 'came over' to Mithradates. Since there is no suggestion (in the admittedly sparse evidence) of internal *stasis* at Sparta at this juncture of the kind which Mithradates took advantage of at Athens, Deininger's assumption of a formal treaty between Sparta and the king in 88 BC seems unlikely: Sparta did her best to remain loyal to Rome, as is suggested by the fact that the sources give no hint of meaningful Spartan support for Pontus after the city's reverse, although military aid from the Laconian towns is well-documented.[4]

In 49 BC Greece was the chief theatre of war in the struggle between Caesar and Pompey. As with the Greeks generally, for whom Caesar at this time was still an unknown quantity, the Spartans had little choice but to support Pompey, the conqueror of the east, obeying a request for military aid by sending a contingent to Pharsalus in 48 BC. In a curious statement the second-century historian Appian claimed that these Spartan troops fought under the command of 'their own *basileis*'. If this evidence has any weight presumably it means simply that the Spartan contingent was permitted its own commanders: Weil's notion, that Sparta at the time was monarchically governed, is now firmly disproved by the Spartan coinage recently redated to the forties and thirties BC, its legends signifying 'republican' forms of government at this time.[5]

When another round of civil war broke out in 42 BC between Caesar's assassins and the members of the Second Triumvirate, the Spartans showed a spark of their old independence, as they would do again in the Actium campaign, by giving their open support to the triumvirs Octavian and Antony. The decision was a courageous, even a foolhardy, one, taken at a time when Greece was under the authority of M. Brutus, the tyrannicide, whose harsh reaction was to promise Sparta to his soldiery as plunder in the event of victory; in so doing, Brutus revealed the limits of a Roman general's sentimental laconism, which had earlier led him to name parts of his Italian estates after famous Spartan sights. The city's decision was also a costly one: a Spartan contingent of 2,000 foot-soldiers was annihilated at the battle of Philippi – Sparta's worst military disaster since Sellasia in 222 BC (chapter 4). It brought signal benefits for the Spartans, however; as a reward for their support, the triumvirs now took the unusual step of reversing an earlier Roman decision and returned the *ager Dentheliatis* to Sparta (chapter 10). In hindsight, moreover, we can see Philippi as marking the beginning of a warm relationship between Sparta and Octavian, the future emperor Augustus, one given further

95

momentum in 38 BC by Octavian's marriage to Livia: by both birth and her first marriage to Tib. Claudius Nero a member of the patrician Claudii, patrons of Sparta (above), Livia was personally indebted to the city for having given her a temporary asylum in 40 BC in the aftermath of the Perusine War. When civil war broke out nine years later, although Greece had meanwhile fallen to Antony's sphere, Sparta once more made a display of independence by actively backing Octavian – the only city in Greece, along with her old Arcadian ally, Mantinea, to do so. As a result, the Spartans and their leading citizen, Eurycles, were uniquely placed in Greece to benefit from the favour of the victor of Actium, now the first Roman emperor.[6]

Before turning to Sparta's fortunes in the aftermath of Actium, some estimate is required of the cost to local resources of a half-century of Roman warfare. Sparta's exposure to the exploitative practices of Roman imperialism in this period may otherwise have been relatively slight: although the burdensome presence of Roman businessmen on the Laconian coast is well attested, they have left few traces at inland Sparta. The city's heritage of artworks (see chapter 14) did not escape Roman attentions: we hear of a pair of Roman aediles (probably in 56 BC) 'borrowing' a Spartan painting to adorn their games at Rome. But the evidence chiefly concerns Roman demands for war-contributions in the form not only of men but also of supplies and cash – the 'friendly liturgies', as Strabo called them, from which Sparta's free status did not exempt her (chapter 11). The city is unlikely to have escaped the obligation to supply the campaigns of M. Antonius against the pirates in 73–1 BC, when neighbouring Gytheum served as a hard-pressed Roman base, or to have been left unscathed by the demands imposed on Greece during its inclusion in the Balkan *provincia* of L. Calpurnius Piso Caesoninus (58–5 BC), or those of Pompey in 49 BC, specifically said to have included the 'free peoples' of Greece, or those of the Republican admiral L. Staius Murcus, who in 42 BC 'collected as much booty as he could come upon from the Peloponnese'. Coins and an inscription add some precision to this picture. A fragmentary decree of Late Republican date preserves an urgent appeal to the wealthy by Spartan magistrates for help in meeting a series of demands – presumably Roman – for cash. Grunauer-von Hoerschelmann's study of Sparta's coinage has shown that the twenty-nine issues previously dated to the period from 146 to 30 BC all belong to its last two decades, with almost half of them clustering in the thirties. These last included coins which closely resemble in weight the bronze denominations minted by Antony and his subordinates in this period for military purposes. It looks as if the revival of the Spartan mint after the mid-century was largely a response to Roman requests for cash, one of which can be firmly identified: the issue of 39–7 BC bears the portrait of L. Sempronius Atratinus, one of Antony's legates.[7]

Because Sparta by now relied, like other Greek cities, on a system of euergetism to fund extraordinary expenditure (chapter 11), the immediate burden of these demands fell on the well-to-do, in the form either of civic requests for voluntary contributions, as in the decree noted above, or through the generosity of magistrates, as we learn from those Spartan coin-issues of the triumviral age inscribed with the titles of leading boards of civic officials (ephors, *gerontes* and *nomophulakes*) and presumably funded by them collectively. The immediate effect of these Roman demands will have been to divert the resources of the rich away from more routine civic needs, so that – for instance – civic cults would be celebrated on a reduced scale and public buildings might fall into disrepair, as seems to have happened at neighbouring Messene, where a wide-ranging programme of building-restoration was launched under Augustus. But the long-term impact of Roman levies on Greece in this period has perhaps been exaggerated: in Crawford's view, 'their effect on an economy whose basis was subsistence agriculture . . . would have been negligible' (Crawford 1977). In Sparta's case, the resilience of the upper classes (who no doubt managed to pass on most of the burden to their inferiors) is suggested by the case of the future family of the Voluseni: although a triumviral member, Aristocrates son of Damares, was a generous contributor in his city's time of need, funding more than one emission of bronze coinage. His great-grandchildren were to be found among Claudian Sparta's 'first families'.[8]

*   *   *   *   *   *

The remainder of this chapter is devoted to the most absorbing episode in the history of Sparta's first two centuries under Roman domination: the rise – and fall – of the house of Eurycles. Members of this Spartan family are first attested in the triumviral age, a time of unsettled conditions in which provincial protégés of powerful Romans could acquire local prominence in the service of their patrons. Lachares, the father of Eurycles, seems to have been a Caesarian partisan: prominent enough to be courted by the Athenians, who placed his statue on their hallowed Acropolis, he was executed by Antony on a charge of 'piracy'. As Chrimes saw, behind this episode perhaps lay his harassment of Antony's supply-ships from Egypt as they rounded the Peloponnese on the eve of Actium. Eurycles first appears in history as the commander of a warship on Octavian's side at Actium itself. How did a family from land-locked Sparta come to command ships in the triumviral age? The simplest explanation is that Antony's charge against Lachares had some foundation in fact. Laconian waters were notorious for piracy, which saw something of a revival in the eastern Mediterranean during the triumviral age; as Bowersock observed, Lachares and his son perhaps were based on

Cythera, the island which Eurycles later was given by Augustus as a gift (see below).[9]

As we might expect of a privateer, the family origins of Eurycles and his father are veiled in a certain mystery. Like the bluest-blooded of Roman Sparta's 'first families', a Hadrianic descendant – the Spartan senator Eurycles Herculanus – grandly claimed the Dioscuri and (it seems) Heracles as ancestors (chapter 8). Eurycles himself, however, asserted a (by local standards) more *recherché* pedigree, naming a son after the demigod Rhadamanthys, whose mythical connections were with Crete, not Laconia: the impression given is of a social *parvenu*, a Spartan with aristocratic pretensions who did not quite dare, however, to claim one of the lineages deriving from figures of local myth and history with which the Roman city's old aristocracy bristled (chapter 12). Eurycles was an adventurer, for whom the habits of the buccaneer died hard: at Actium, although claiming to be present to avenge his father's execution, he was more interested in capturing one of Antony's treasure-ships.[10]

For Eurycles the reward for his own and his father's loyalty to Caesar was the gift of a personal *dunasteia* over the Spartans, the evidence for which was forcefully restated by Bowersock in 1961. This remarkable development is attested by Spartan coins bearing the legend '(issued) under Eurycles' and by the Augustan geographer Strabo, who referred to his 'rule' (*epistasia*) over the Spartans and his position as their 'leader' (*hēgemōn*). This change from 'republican' to (effectively) monarchical government had occurred by 21 BC, when Eurycles celebrated the visit of Augustus (as Octavian had styled himself since 27 BC) and Livia with coin-issues portraying the Imperial couple; it makes best sense if seen as occurring soon after Actium, when the memory of the Spartan's war-services was fresh in the victor's mind. It is not easy to discern any 'constitutional' basis for the *dunasteia* of Eurycles. As far as is known he bore no official title; and the survival of the outward forms of local 'republican' government is suggested by the fact that in 21 BC Augustus dined in the company of the city's magistrates (chapter 14). Like his Imperial patron, Eurycles seems to have exercised more or less arbitrary power behind a screen of constitutionalism. In doing so he was helped by prominent Spartan collaborators, among whom can be identified the priestly family which presided over the ancient civic cult of the Dioscuri at Phoebaeum and (perhaps) the mysterious Lysixenidas, named on one of his coin-issues. He also used his vast wealth (see below) to curry popular support with a programme of building (notably the theatre: see chapter 10) and shows (chapter 13). The ultimate sanction against any local opposition, however, was his friendship with the emperor, who heaped him with additional gifts: a grant of Roman citizenship, whereafter he became 'C. Iulius Eurycles', and the gift of Cythera – secured, it seems, through the intervention of Livia, whose powerful advocacy of her provincial *clientela* is well attested (could she have been the guest of Lachares during her Spartan visit in 40 BC?) In return, Eurycles made an assiduous display of his loyalty to the Imperial house. He was the founder and (almost certainly) the first priest of Sparta's Imperial cult, the high-priesthood of which was later held by Eurycles Herculanus 'by inheritance'. He also paid court to M. Agrippa, the son-in-law of Augustus, issuing coins in his honour when he visited Sparta in 16 BC during his tour of the east and (probably) instigating a Spartan association of 'Agrippiastae', of which his kinsman, C. Iulius Deximachus, is found as president.[11]

To the obeisance of Eurycles to Rome can perhaps be attributed the local echoes, detectable in the inscriptions, of the Augustan programme of religious restoration. A revival under Eurycles of the outward forms of civic cult is suggested by three series of inscribed catalogues, all of them commencing early in the reign of Augustus. One series recorded the names of the three annual *hierothutai* and the personnel associated with them. These magistrates with priestly functions presided over the city's 'common hearth' and – probably – the building in which it was housed; to judge from their title (literally 'sacrificers'), along with their association with a seer and a ritual 'cook-cum-butcher' (*mageiros*), they were also responsible for performing sacrifices in Sparta's name – a former royal prerogative which had evidently been transferred to civic magistrates after – at the latest – the fall of Nabis. The two other series of lists catalogue annual participants in the sacred banquets of two civic cults, those of the Dioscuri at Phoebaeum (chapter 14) and of Taenarian Poseidon, whose Spartan cult was a 'branch' of the famous sanctuary on Cape Taenarum, once itself under Spartan control. The activities which these catalogues reflect presuppose sizeable outlays on ceremonial and consumption such as would suit a revival of cult following the lean years of the Late Republic. Eurycles was, at the least, involved in this revival: the priest and priestess of Helen and the Dioscuri were his relations and his own sons were among the well-born children who assisted at the ceremonies of the *hierothutai*.[12]

As the only city (with Mantinea) in mainland Greece to have supported Octavian at Actium, Sparta for a while was the cynosure of the newly created (in 27 BC) province of Achaia; for Strabo the city was 'especially favoured' by the Romans. The city's international prestige was augmented when Augustus entrusted it (in the early twenties BC) with the supervision of his victory-games, the quinquennial Actia, established at the newly-founded city of Nicopolis in Epirus, with which the Spartans went on to develop close ties. In this encouraging climate we can detect a last surge of Spartan irredentism in the Peloponnese (see chapter 5), instigated by the new ruler of Sparta, whose Peloponnesian pretensions were advertised in the names 'Laco' and 'Argolicus' borne by a son and grandson respectively. The extensive patronage of Eurycles and his descendants outside Sparta is discussed below: here we concentrate on the vexed question of Sparta's relationship with the Laconian cities at this time. The evidence of late Hellenistic inscriptions for a 'League of the Lacedaemonians', of which Sparta seems not to have been a member, can be taken to show that in 146 BC Rome had sought to ensure the continued separation from Sparta of the Laconian cities, previously guaranteed by the Achaean League, by permitting them a federal structure of their own. At some later date, however, they returned to Spartan control, since Pausanias records that Augustus freed them from their Spartan 'slavery'. Although the accuracy of this passage has been doubted, it is confirmed by inscriptions from Gytheum, which portray Augustus and Tiberius as the restorers of the city's 'ancient freedom' and posthumously hail the former as 'Eleutherius'. In the period after 146 BC Sparta could only have reasserted her old dominion over Laconia with Roman approval. Although Bernhardt proposed that the triumvirs took this remarkable step in 42 BC (above), it makes better sense to associate the return of Sparta's borders to (more or less) their Nabian extent with the *dunasteia* of Eurycles. That Augustus was prepared to favour Sparta to this degree is a measure of the city's strategic potential (in the first century BC it still retained a certain military – and now naval – muscle) in a province the rest of which, to paraphrase Bowersock, had 'entered his empire as a defeated nation'.[13]

The ambitions of Eurycles, however, were not confined to the Peloponnese. Writing under the Flavians, the Jewish historian Josephus preserves a blatantly hostile account of his visit to two fellow client-rulers in the near east, Archelaus of Cappadocia and Herod of Judaea. According to Josephus, Eurycles insinuated himself into the dynastic intrigues of Herod's court and played off different parties against each other, so precipitating the trial and execution of one of Herod's sons, before returning to Greece with a small fortune in royal gifts. But there is little here to indicate – as Pani has suggested – anti-Roman activity. Josephus was probably right in claiming that the Spartan adventurer was motivated by financial opportunism: although clearly wealthy, he was spending heavily on public works at Sparta and – as we shall see – on benefaction in Peloponnesian cities and sanctuaries. In looking eastwards he surely sought to exploit prior connections: Josephus implies a pre-existing tie of friendship between Eurycles and Archelaus; and the kinship between the Spartans and the Jews was by now an accepted fiction (chapter 6), perhaps underlying the benevolence towards Sparta of the philhellene Herod on one of his visits to Greece.[14]

The ultimately fragile basis of Eurycles' *dunasteia* and its complete dependence on Imperial favour is shown by the circumstances of his fall from grace, which Bowersock has convincingly reconstructed in two important articles. A famous passage in Strabo, recently improved with new manuscript-readings, shows that Eurycles was dead by 2 BC or thereabouts, having returned from the east in about 7 BC. In the interim, he had fallen into disgrace: he was twice arraigned before Augustus, who, on the second occasion, deprived him of his *epistasia* and sent him into exile. The full story behind this reversal of fortune is impossible to recover. The allegation of the hostile Josephus, that Eurycles extorted money from the cities of Greece, is not supported by the epigraphic evidence, which presents him, on the contrary, as a benefactor of the Peloponnese (below). Domestic troubles there certainly were: Strabo refers vaguely to *tarakhē* or 'disturbance' at Sparta; and one of his accusers, Plutarch records, was a local aristocrat, a descendant of Brasidas. But the *arriviste* Eurycles had probably always had enemies (as well as friends) among the established Spartan families whose local hegemony his own had displaced. If so, some additional factor seems required to explain the withdrawal of the emperor's friendship. Bowersock has attractively suggested that his real undoing was to pay court too openly to Tiberius, Livia's son, at the time in semi-disgrace on Rhodes and a presence hard for Eurycles to ignore, given his patronal ties with his mother. It would then be the emperor Tiberius, not Augustus, to whom Laco owed the complete rehabilitation of his father's memory and his own installation as ruler of Sparta – both achieved, as a well-known inscription from Gytheum shows, within a year of the new emperor's accession. The fall of Eurycles was probably accompanied by the detachment of the Laconian cities from Sparta's control; in a passage written before 2 BC, Strabo refers to their organization into a new league, that of the Free Laconians or *Eleutherolakōnes*. It may have been now, as compensation for the loss of Gytheum, the best harbour on the Laconian gulf, that Augustus presented the Spartans with the inferior port of Cardamyle, on the Messenian side of Taygetus (chapter 10).[15]

It remains to deal briefly with the history, scarcely less turbulent, of the two successors of Eurycles as client-rulers at Sparta, beginning with his son Laco, who, although ranked by Tacitus among the 'first of the Achaians' (*primores Achaiorum*), for us remains a hazy figure. In the lifetime of Eurycles we hear only of his sons Deximachus and Rhadamanthys; Laco perhaps was a younger half-brother, becoming his father's eventual heir for dynastic reasons impossible now to recover. He makes his earliest appearance in the evidence at Athens, since he can be identified with an otherwise unknown Laco who held the eponymous archonship at the beginning of the first century. At the time he may have been living at Athens, a city with which his family had close ties. The only direct evidence for his eventual succession to his father's position as Sparta's ruler are the coin-issues in his name, although it is tempting to associate him with building activity at the theatre under Tiberius in the form of a monumental arch (?) on which the emperor's name was inscribed in Latin script (App.I, 31). Close ties with the court of Tiberius can be inferred from the marriage of a son, Argolicus, to the daughter of the Mytilenean senator Pompeius Macer, an intimate of the emperor. This connection proved Laco's undoing: when Macer was disgraced in 33, Laco fell with him. Although the language of Tacitus is vague, presumably he now lost his position at Sparta and was forced into exile; and confiscation of property is suggested by the appearance in the Imperial household of one of his slaves. The whole episode is obscure; but it is tempting to suppose that Macer and his connections were caught up in the prolonged witch-hunt which followed the fall in 31 of Seianus, the once all-powerful praetorian prefect.[16]

By the reign of Claudius, Laco, by now well into middle age, had been reinstated at Sparta. For this new twist in the family's stormy relationship with Rome, revealed by coin-issues in which Laco's name as eponym combines with the emperor's portrait, Gaius rather than Claudius may have been responsible, since he too favoured client-dynasties and counted among his intimates one of Laco's hereditary connections, the Jewish prince Herod Agrippa, grandson of Herod, the host of Eurycles. Laco's second term in power was accompanied, it seems, by some clarification of his position, since he now acquired, as a Latin inscription from the Roman colony of Corinth reveals, the title 'procurator of Claudius'. In this text Laco is called 'C. Iulius C.f. Laco' – affiliation by *praenomen* being, of course, no more than normal Latin usage; so Bowersock's attempt to deny that this Laco was the son of C. Iulius Eurycles does not convince. More problematic, however, is the significance of the procuratorial title. Since it attached Laco to the emperor personally, rather than the province, the regular procuratorship of Achaia is not in question; the title can only refer to Laco's rule over the Spartans. Pflaum cites as a close parallel the case of C. Herennius Capito, who administered a private domain in Judaea, inherited by Claudius, as 'procurator of C. Caesar Augustus Germanicus'. But it is difficult to see Sparta, a free city, as the personal property of the emperor in quite the same way. In West's view, the title 'was given to Laco to regularize his position as dynast'; by proclaiming him unequivocally as the emperor's servant, it created a formal tie between Rome and Sparta's ruler which, hitherto, had been conspicuously lacking. Whether, however, its conferment amounted to a 'modification' of Laco's position – as Pflaum maintained – is arguable: by declaring him openly as the emperor's representative, the title is as likely to have strengthened Laco's local authority as to have constrained it.[17]

His family's close ties with Livia and the Claudii suggest that it was Laco who instituted the local worship of Livia, centred on annual games, either after her death in 29 or her official deification in 42 (chapter 14).

The family's increasing romanization – as well as its renewed high standing in the capital – is shown by Claudius's grant of equestrian rank to Laco's son and heir, C. Iulius Spartiaticus, whose public career began with service as an equestrian officer in the Roman army, before he went on to inherit his father's position at Sparta. His succession follows from another Latin inscription from Corinth in which he is described as 'procurator of Caesar and Augusta Agrippina', his title echoing the extraordinary prominence of Nero's mother betwen 54 and 59. As with Laco, this procuratorial title is best seen as designating a position of delegated authority at Sparta, although in the case of Spartiaticus for the first time there is no accompanying coinage. Of his 'reign' we know nothing: only that, like his father and grandfather, he too lost the emperor's favour. His fall seems to have been precipitated by a dynastic squabble, since he can be identified with some probability with one of two brothers, 'the most powerful Greeks of my time', whose extravagant rivalry, Plutarch relates, prompted Imperial intervention resulting in their exile and the confiscation of their property. The episode is not closely dated, but Plutarch's reference to 'the tyrant' would suit the reign of Nero, and Spartiaticus was known as a fellow-exile to the Epicurean philosopher Musonius, disgraced in 65; as we shall see (chapter 8), there are some grounds for placing his fall no later than 61. If an event of the fairly recent past, it might help to explain Nero's boycott of Sparta during his tour of Greece in 67, for which Cassius Dio gives the eccentric (but, admittedly, by no means incredible) explanation that the emperor disapproved of the Lycurgan customs. Once more, the family's fall from favour was of relatively short duration: the descendants of Eurycles were living at Sparta once again under Vespasian and recovered much of their ancestral property, since Eurycles Herculanus, probably the grandson of Spartiaticus, is found, like his Augustan namesake, in possession of Cythera (chapter 8). But the family did not regain its old position as a Roman client-dynasty; henceforth it had to remain content to be the richest and best-connected of Roman Sparta's 'first houses'.[18]

It remains to comment on the extensive patronage within Greece which forms a distinctive feature of this family of local dynasts. It was most marked, not surprisingly, in the neighbouring cities of Laconia. Eurycles was hailed as a benefactor (*euergetēs*) by the coastal towns of Asopus, Boeae and Gytheum; he also protected the interests of Laconia's numerous Roman businessmen. After his death the cities of the Eleutherolaconian League, although nominally independent, were in turn dominated by his son, whom they hailed as their *euergetēs* and the 'guardian' of their 'security and safety'. Further afield, Eurycles was the 'patron and *euergetēs*' of the Asclepieum at Epidaurus, an interest inherited by his grandson; the family also had links with Megalopolis and the adjacent sanctuary of Despoena at Lycosura. Lachares, Eurycles and

Spartiaticus were honoured successively at Athens, where Laco, as we have seen, held the archonship. Beyond Laconia, however, the chief beneficiary of the dynasty's generosity was Corinth, the seat of the proconsul and, as the centre of *Romanitas* in Greece, a city with a strong gravitational pull for the province's magnates. Although it now seems that the Eurycles who constructed public baths at Corinth should be identified with the Hadrianic senator (see chapter 8), both Laco and his son held a succession of colonial offices and liturgies. It was presumably as a citizen of Corinth, rather than Sparta, that Spartiaticus was chosen to be the first high-priest of the Achaean League's Imperial cult. It was argued by Chrimes that Laco's Corinthian career belonged to the period of his disgrace, under Tiberius. But, apart from the fact that he may not have been a wealthy man in those years, having lost the emperor's favour he seems an improbable candidate for high office, including an Imperial priesthood (the flaminate of Augustus), in a Roman colony; these offices are best assigned, as West believed, to the time of his reinstatement under Claudius.[19]

This extensive patronage was only made possible by the family's huge wealth, as is clearly the case at Asopus, where benefaction by Eurycles took the form of a perpetual oil-supply. Some of the sources of this fortune can be identified. Part of it was probably based on his share in the booty at Actium. Presumably he drew revenues from his ownership of Cythera. He was also a large landowner: an estate at Asopus is attested, extensive enough to require management by three stewards, as well as landed property on the Spartan plain, the clay-beds of which were exploited for tile-manufacture (chapter 12).[20]

With the suppression of this flamboyant but troubled dynasty, political power at Sparta reverted into the hands of the local class of *possédants*, a change reflected in Spartan epigraphy by the commencement, under the Flavians, of the long series of catalogues of magistrates inscribed at the theatre. Against this more stable political background, Sparta was set to enjoy a period of renewed prominence in the propitious conditions of the Greek renaissance.

Chapter eight

Sparta in the Greek renaissance

The Euryclid *dunasteia* lasted intermittently for almost a century, a period during which the evidence for internal conditions at Sparta is slight. In the later first century, however, the number of surviving inscriptions rises steeply (e.g. App. IIA, Table), illuminating the Roman city with some clarity for the first time. This epigraphic abundance partly reflects the re-establishment at Sparta of 'republican' government: the practice of inscribing catalogues of civic magistrates in the theatre begins under the Flavians, and to Trajan's reign dates the earliest of the inscribed careers of municipal notables (chapter 11). Since inscriptions required skilled labour and a supply of suitable types of stone, fluctuations in the local attachment to the 'epigraphic habit' also have an economic significance. By the mid-first century, when 'the marks of war and depression [in Achaia] had probably been largely effaced' (Jones 1971b), parts of the province, Sparta included, were enjoying a modest prosperity. Indeed, under the Flavians and Trajan civic life at Sparta displays a distinct vitality, which to some extent was encouraged by the increasing paternalism in the provinces of the central government. Vespasian is attested as the donor of funds for building activity at Sparta's theatre – one of the occasions, perhaps, when he responded to requests for aid from provincial cities damaged by earthquake; and benefaction of some kind by Trajan is suggested by the honorific title of 'saviour' (*sōtēr*) which he received from the Spartans. The Flavian and Trajanic age also saw an increase in the beneficent activities of local notables, whom the suppression of the Euryclid *dunasteia* now left free to acquire prominence as patrons of their community. Their competitive 'love of honour', essential if civic life and institutions were to receive adequate funding, received new encouragement under Trajan with the institution of the so-called contest for best citizen (chapter 11); mostly it took the routine form of discharging the city's liturgical offices in a generous fashion, as with the Flavian gymnasiarch Tib. Claudius Harmonicus, praised by one of the Roman city's tribes, the Cynosureis, for his 'incomparable magnanimity' towards them.[1]

Under Nerva and Trajan a local benefactor on an altogether larger scale emerged in the person of C. Iulius Agesilaus, who held the city's eponymous magistracy, the patronomate, in about 100. In his benefactions Agesilaus associated himself with a certain T. Flavius Charixenus, who seems to have been a younger man, since he held the patronomate well over a decade later. These two Spartans are best seen as close kinsmen – perhaps father-in-law and son-in-law. Together they helped to finance a significant enlargement of Sparta's cycle of agonistic festivals, endowing with prize-money both the Urania, new games founded under Nerva (chapter 13), and the Leonidean games, which were refounded late in the reign of Trajan (chapter 14). Since both these festivals, as we shall see, had associations with the old dual kingship, it is just possible that Agesilaus – as his name might suggest – belonged to a lineage claiming descent from Spartan royalty. Members of the same family-group, now including a Flavius Agesilaus, also contributed to the architectural embellishment of their city with the gift of a building in the Corinthian order, its location and function uncertain, which they loyally dedicated to 'the deified *Sebastoi* and Lacedaemon' (App.I, 29).[2]

Both these agonistic benefactions made conscious reference to Spartan history. Other indicators of the prominent place of tradition in civic life under Trajan are the institution of the 'contest for best citizen', which seems to have been loosely based on the 'Lycurgan' mode of election to the old *gerousia*, and the revival of civic consultations of the oracle of Ino-Pasiphaë at Thalamae (chapter 14). Ephebic dedications from the sanctuary of Artemis Orthia also suggest that before the end of the Flavian age a restructuring had taken place – perhaps over a period of years – in the Roman city's 'Lycurgan' training, reflected in the reappearance late in Nero's reign of *kasen*-status (chapter 11) and the establishment by the reign of Domitian of the post of *boagos* (chapter 14). In the case of the former, Woodward suggested a possible link with the – historically somewhat dubious – tradition of a 'Lycurgan revival' at Neronian Sparta brought on by the visit of the itinerant sage and wonder-worker, Apollonius of Tyana. This tradition is found both in the ancient collection of letters allegedly preserving parts of the sage's correspondence and in the – probably later – 'biography' of Apollonius by the Severan sophist Flavius Philostratus, a work which seems to have been completed after 217. The Philostratean account sets this revival in 61, when Apollonius – so it relates – was invited by Spartan ambassadors to visit their city. Instead, however, the sage wrote a letter to the ephors, condemning the embassy's luxurious dress and effeteness of manner, whereupon these magistrates restored the ancestral practices, so that 'wrestling grounds and exertion once more were popular with the young and the common messes were restored and Sparta became like herself'. Although the historicity of this 'restoration' has found hardly any defenders, the need for caution before dismissing it altogether is suggested by the somewhat more credible picture emerging from recent research of the elusive Damis, allegedly the chief source behind the Philostratean 'life'. In the earlier part of Nero's reign Sparta was ruled by C. Iulius Spartiaticus (chapter 7), whose well-known fondness for luxury, even during his exile, makes him seem an unlikely advocate of 'Lycurgan' austerities at home. It is just possible that the training had been allowed to languish during his régime, to be reinvigorated following his disgrace (no later than 61?) by Sparta's newly reinstalled 'republican' government. Here the influence of a charismatic philosopher-figure obviously cannot be discounted, although equally the developing Apollonius-tradition could have sought to credit its hero with a decisive rôle in a local episode with its own momentum.[3]

Even if there had been a minor revival of the training in the sixties, however, the attendant circumstances were localized in time and cannot be made to account for the pronounced allusions to the past in civic life under the later Flavians and Trajan. It is true that Spartan history and institutions were being written up in this period by Plutarch of Chaeronea, whose connections with contemporary Sparta were close (chapter 13). But it would be simplistic to see this rising mood of local archaism in terms of the stimulus provided by any one individual – whether man of letters or wandering philosopher. It is better linked with the larger cultural and political conditions of the Greek world under the Flavians and Trajan, a time which saw the early stirrings of the great renaissance of cultural activity in the Greek provinces under the principate, for which the peace and prosperity of the Roman Empire provided the necessary preconditions. The lineaments of this movement, which endured until well into the third century, are by now well-established. Its social setting was that of the educated élites which governed the Greek cities on Rome's behalf. In cultural life it produced a flowering of Greek letters and rhetoric, this last cast in the distinctive form of the show-oratory of the Second Sophistic. These activities were informed by a marked archaism or admiration for Greece's pre-Hellenistic past. Archaizing tastes, however, were not simply a matter of the preferences of individuals: since the educated minority who affected them also ran the affairs of their cities, they gave shape to the forms of civic life too. Increasing reference to the civic past from the later first century onwards also had a Roman dimension. It can be seen as an aspect of Rome's evolving relationship with the Greek élites, members of which, from the Flavians and Trajan onwards, were penetrating the Roman aristocracy in increasing numbers as knights and senators – the grandson of Spartiaticus, C. Iulius Eurycles Herculanus, was among the first intake of senators from old Greece (below). This changing political climate altered the historical status of the pasts of the constituent cities of Rome's

Greek-speaking provinces, since they now formed part of the local heritage of a prestigious group of Greeks within the empire's governing class. Rome herself was directly implicated in this change through – above all – the Greek policies of Trajan's successor, the emperor Hadrian.[4]

Having succeeded in 117, Hadrian was to intervene constantly in the Greek provinces as administrator and benefactor. This concern for the Greeks should be seen as part of a fairly systematic Imperial attempt to reinforce the structures of civic life in the Roman east. Among Hadrian's more obvious concerns were the promotion within the Imperial system of old Greece, which hitherto had lagged behind Asia in its political and economic advancement. His well-known benefactions at Athens were echoed, albeit on a smaller scale, throughout the province, with due attention being paid, in accordance with the cultural values of the time, to those cities distinguished – as Hadrian wrote of Delphi – for their 'antiquity and nobility'. Signs of Hadrianic interest in the home of the Spartan myth, although they have not previously been treated in full, are not hard to find. The emperor was the most distinguished and – as far as we know – the first of a succession of foreigners who held the city's eponymous magistracy, the patronomate, the duties of which were closely linked to Roman Sparta's revived 'Lycurgan customs' (chapter 14). The date of his term, previously insecure, has now been assigned to 127/8. Shortly before, in 124/5, Hadrian visited the city personally, as he did again in 128/9 on the second of his two long sojourns in Greece as emperor. These visits may have had their burdensome side: Spartan grain-shortages in this period can perhaps be connected with the strain placed on the local food-supply by the presence of the omnivorous Imperial court (chapter 11). In a provincial city which had not seen a Roman emperor since 21 BC, however, the Imperial presence was also a mark of honour and a cause for official rejoicing; with the first visit can be associated a remarkable dedication *en masse* of small altars (at least twenty-eight are attested), probably signifying the celebration of a special civic festival at which Spartan householders were required to offer sacrifices in the streets on the emperor's behalf.[5]

This civic rejoicing was more than merely dutiful, however, since Hadrian's visits were also the occasion of major benefactions, as is suggested by the laudatory titles of 'saviour', 'founder' (*ktistēs*) and 'benefactor' which the city conferred on him in connection with his first visit. Among these benefactions can be counted grants of territory. In addition to Cythera (below), two other overseas possessions, for which the earliest evidence falls in the 120s, should probably be seen as Hadrianic gifts. One was Caudus, the modern Gavdos, a small island off the south-west coast of Crete, a Spartan *epimelētēs* or 'supervisor' of which is attested precisely in 124/5, the year of Hadrian's first visit. In addition, four Spartans are found in the post of '*epimelētēs* of Coronea', the earliest soon after 125, the latest under the emperor Marcus. Kahrstedt argued unconvincingly that 'Coronea' was an otherwise unknown location within Spartan territory. But it seems preferable to see here, as other scholars have done, a reference to the Messenian city of Corone, in the Imperial period a small but prosperous port with a fertile hinterland. According to Pausanias, the city's correct style had once been 'Coronea'; the archaizing use of this form at Hadrianic Sparta was of a piece with the city's appointment in the 130s of a 'Cytherodices' (below).[6]

As when he presented part of the Ionian island of Cephallenia to Athens, Hadrian's gifts of territory to Sparta were presumably meant to supplement the city's revenues, although there is no evidence to suggest that these were in an especially parlous state at the time. Possibly the extra income was intended in part to contribute towards the cost of maintaining new civic amenities. Hadrianic building-activity at Sparta is suggested by the title of 'founder' (above), which was associated with construction-work in the vocabulary of Greek civic honours; in particular, Hadrian is a strong candidate for identification as the donor of Sparta's long-distance aqueduct – a costly amenity and one requiring regular maintenance over its length of 12 kilometres or so (chapter 10).[7]

Hadrian's standing as a benefactor of Sparta is echoed in a flurry of civic diplomatic activity, including the ceremonial embassy which went to Nicopolis to greet him on one of his provincial arrivals or departures, and the long journey of two Spartan ambassadors to Pannonia in 136/7 to congratulate L. Aelius Caesar on his adoption as Hadrian's heir. A more substantial honour, hitherto overlooked by scholars, was the institution of a civic cult of Zeus Olympius in Hadrian's honour. It is well established that, for political as much as religious reasons, from 128/9 Hadrian associated himself closely with Zeus Olympius, supreme deity of the Greek pantheon. This assimilation is specifically attested at Sparta by an altar dedicated to 'Zeus Soter Olympius'. Pausanias also saw a Spartan temple of Zeus Olympius, a cult the only other clear reference to which comes in the career-inscription of the early Antonine magistrate, C. Iulius Theophrastus. This records the dedication by Theophrastus of statues of the late emperor Hadrian and the Spartan People during a term as priest of Zeus Olympius. Although his priesthood is listed before his agoranomate, which is firmly dated to 124/5, his posts do not seem to be consistently listed in chronological order, since the dedication of one of these statues, with Theophrastus in the rôle of 'supervisor' (*epistatēs*) of the operation, appears to be referred to in a fragmentary inscription from the mid-century. It rather looks as if he held the priesthood in the closing years of his distinguished career, the prestige of the post explaining its position near the head of the text. If this view is correct, nothing stands in the way of assuming that this civic cult, first heard of under Pius, was instituted by the Spartans in Hadrian's honour; the fact that its sanctuary was in a part of the city where Pausanias saw the temple of Sarapis, which he describes as Sparta's 'newest' sanctuary, lends some support to the impression of a recent foundation.[8]

Hadrianic benefaction at Sparta prompted emulation by members of the local élite. The last of the Euryclids, the senator Herculanus, deserves singling out by virtue of the scale of his patronage, which compares not unfavourably with that of the Athenian magnate Herodes Atticus, his younger contemporary and distant connection. Born in about 73, Herculanus entered the Roman Senate probably through the sponsorship of Trajan, climbing the *cursus honorum* at least as high as the praetorian posts. Although somewhat older than Trajan's successor, he had family connections at Hadrian's court through his first cousin, the poetess Iulia Balbilla, a companion of the empress Sabina. Like Herodes, he probably owed some of his wealth to his ties with the Corinthian clan of the Vibullii, the names of one of whom, L. Vibullius Pius, he added to his own following a testamentary adoption. Again like Herodes, Herculanus was the benefactor of Greek cities other than his own, including Mantinea, Corinth and Eleutherolaconian Asopus, in the last of which, as at Corinth, he inherited ancestral ties.[9]

Like many eastern senators, Herculanus retained close links with his native city, where he died and was buried. Recent findings allow more to be said about his euergetistic activity there. He probably funded the revival under Hadrian of Sparta's mint, die-types being employed in the Hadrianic issues which had once been used in the coinage of Eurycles, the senator's ancestor; in a display of genealogical pride characteristic of the Roman city's aristocracy (chapter 12), the choice of types – the mounted Dioscuri and the club of Heracles – made reference to the senator's 'Dioscurid' and 'Heraclid' pedigrees, of which the former is explicitly attested, while the latter can be inferred from the *agnomen* 'Herculanus'.[10]

Other benefactions by Herculanus seem to have been testamentary, following on his death, apparently without leaving a direct male heir, in about 136. On the basis of an important inscription in the Sparta Museum to be published by G. Steinhauer, it now seems clear that the city of Sparta was a major beneficiary of the senator's will, which provided funds – evidently the 'things from Eurycles', a civic administrator of which is attested a year or so after his death – for the endowment of new quinquennial games, the Euryclea. Their first celebration appears in the same year, late under Hadrian, as the emperor's gift to Sparta of Cythera, and the gift seems likewise to have been precipitated by the death of Herculanus, whose ancestor had been given the island by Augustus (chapter 8). That Cythera formed part of the paternal inheritance of Herculanus is suggested by a Cytheran inscription recording the dedication in 116–7 of a statue of Trajan 'in the time of (*epi*) the high-priest of the *Sebastoi* for life, the Emperor-loving and City-loving patron of the city, C. Iulius Eurycles Herculanus L. Vibullius Pius'. The name of the dedicating body is missing, but a reference (ll.9–10) to 'the decree of the civic council' implies, given the stone's provenience, that it was the *polis* of Cythera; similarly the title 'patron (*kēdemōn*) of the city', otherwise unattested at Sparta, is best referred to Cythera. It might be argued that Eurycles appears here as eponym of a Cytheran document in his capacity as Spartan *patronomos*, a post which he held at about this time: Cythera's dependent status, that is, found expression in the use of Spartan *patronomos*-years for the dating of civic documents. But it is surely preferable to see here a reference to the position of Eurycles as hereditary proprietor of the island: his eponymate, that is, does not refer to a specific year, any more than did that of Eurycles and his son on their Spartan coin-issues. As he was in some sense Cythera's overlord, the dedication's fulsome record of the senator's polyonomy and Spartan titles makes sense. The best explanation for Hadrian's gift of Cythera to the Spartans seems to be that he was bequeathed the island by Herculanus, who had followed the common practice among the Roman aristocracy of including the emperor in wills. Perhaps as the testator hoped, Hadrian went on to give Cythera to the Spartans, thereby augmenting his earlier grants of territory to the city. The administration generated by the island's change of status would account for Sparta's revival late under Hadrian, in an antiquarian gesture appropriate to the times, of the title of 'Cytherodices', formerly borne – according to Thucydides – by the Spartan governors of Cythera.[11]

Remaining with Herculanus, it is tempting, in view of his testamentary gift of buildings at Mantinea and his close links with Corinth, to identify him, rather than his Augustan namesake, with the 'Eurycles, a Spartiate' whom Pausanias records as the donor of public baths at Corinth and a gymnasium at Sparta, the site of which is discussed in chapter 10. The gift of a new gymnasium can be coupled with the foundation of the Euryclea, which included athletic contests (chapter 13); as an inducement to foreign athletes, the senator provided funds, not only for the payment of generous cash prizes, but also for the construction of up-to-date training facilities. The scale of his gifts to his native city explains the extraordinary honours conferred on him by the Spartans at his death. His inscribed epitaph shows that he was given a public burial – apparently in the city centre, to judge from the findspot of this and other blocks from his tomb, which are now built into a stretch of the Late Roman fortification-wall to the east of the theatre (App.I, 40). This central location, characteristic of the burials of Greeks worshipped as civic heroes, suggests that Herculanus's posthumous epithet 'hero' was more than just a conventional description for a dead man: the deceased senator seems to have been decreed 'heroic honours', a distinction once reserved by the Spartans for their kings, but one which they could now confer, as did other Greek cities of the time, on a local benefactor of unusual stature.[12]

By means of the benefactions of Hadrian, supplemented by those of a local magnate, Sparta's civic revenues were placed on a firmer footing and her urban amenities enhanced. Similar developments under Hadrian can be observed in other centres in Greece – at Athens, above all, where they took place on a far grander scale, but also – for instance – at Corinth and Argos. Together they can be seen as part of Hadrian's policy of raising the status of Achaia's cities – one pursued at the level, not only of individual cities, but also of collectivities of cities, the so-called *koina* or leagues. To Hadrianic Sparta's involvement with these we turn next.

Hadrianic encouragement of the pre-existing leagues of Greece is well-attested. The institution of the posts of Helladarch in, respectively, the Achaean and Amphictyonic Leagues can perhaps be seen as a Hadrianic initiative arising from a concern to increase the self-regulatory activities of the provincials and lighten the administrative load of Achaia's Roman officials. For historic reasons, the membership of both these leagues was regional rather than panhellenic. Hadrian, however, wished to foster a larger collectivity comparable to the *koina* or *concilia* of other provinces. This Imperial concern is implicit in a long Imperial letter to Delphi in 125, mooting an enlargement of the Amphictyony, on which Sparta had ceased to be represented in the mid-second century BC (chapter 6), by means of a redistribution of votes among 'the Athenians, the Spartans and the other cities, so that the council [of the Amphictyons] may be common to all the Greeks'. Mention of Sparta is significant, since it suggests Hadrian's interest in the creation of a federal structure in Greece which would include major provincial cities at the time unaffiliated with any league. This was certainly true of Sparta at this date, since Kahrstedt's view, that the Roman city belonged to the reconstituted Achaean League, is unacceptable. In view of Sparta's old enmity towards the Achaeans, it seems unthinkable that the Roman city would have renewed its membership of the – reconstituted – league after 146 BC. The tenure of Achaean office by C. Iulius Spartiaticus (chapter 7), on which Kahrstedt based this view, should be seen as deriving from his Corinthian, not his Spartan, citizenship.[13]

In fact, the recommendation in Hadrian's letter seems not to have been acted upon: Pausanias makes clear that in his time Sparta was excluded from the Amphictyony. The explanation with little doubt lies with the subsequent development in Hadrian's thinking in favour of an entirely new organization of Greek cities, the Panhellenion, Spartan membership of which, first attested under Pius and Marcus, should probably be retrojected to the Panhellenion's foundation in 131/2. Among the aims of this remarkable organization, that of promoting 'the ideal of panhellenic concord within the structure of the Roman Empire' is clear both from the scope of its membership, embracing cities from five Greek-speaking provinces, and from its association with the Plataean cult of Greek Concord, for long a symbol of the panhellenic ideal (chapter 14). That its function was not purely ceremonial, however, is suggested by the evidence for its involvement in civic administration. In the nature of the documentation this evidence is slight, but none the less significant in its echoing of other indications (above) of Hadrianic interest in Greek self-regulation. It is also likely that Hadrian saw the Panhellenion as a vehicle for the reassertion of old Greece's cultural primacy, to be achieved not only through the choice of Athens as its seat, but also through the conditions of membership, which required overseas cities to provide proof of their ethnic kinship with the peoples of Greece proper. Although Hadrian confirmed by his choice of capital city for the Panhellenion that this primacy rested above all on Athenian achievements, an inscription from Dorian Cyrene, an alleged Spartan colony at one remove and member-city of the Panhellenion, suggests that he also recognized the prestige of Sparta's distinctive contribution to Greek education in the form of the Lycurgan *agōgē* or training (see chapter 14). In the – now fragmentary – extracts from an Imperial edict or speech to the Cyrenaeans, dating to the 130s, the emperor made reference to things Spartan, including 'Laconian self-discipline (*sōphrosunē*) and training (*askēsis*)'. The context is far from clear, although it has been tentatively referred to Hadrian's legislative activity at Cyrene. The previous section, however, was concerned with local arrangements for the education of the young, which Hadrian had improved. It is tempting to suggest that he then went on to hold up as a model, not Spartan laws but Sparta's renowned *agōgē*, with which, in its (much altered) Roman form, Hadrian himself had been closely connected through his earlier tenure of the patronomate.[14]

Hadrianic initiatives greatly enhanced Sparta's international standing, as is shown by the Antonine city's wide-ranging contacts with the overseas Greek world. Following Hadrian's example, in the three decades or so after 130 a succession of distinguished foreigners associated themselves with the Spartan training by holding the eponymous patronomate. The earliest of these *patronomoi*, in the 130s, was the aged Athenian ex-consul, Tib. Claudius Atticus, whose ties with Sparta had been exceptionally close ever since he spent part of his youth in exile there under Domitian; he had trained as a Spartan ephebe himself and later required his son Herodes, the future sophist, to do the same. Foreign *patronomoi* under Pius included the Pergamene senator C. Claudius Demostratus Titianus; the Ephesian consular and historian, A. Claudius Charax; and a Cyrenaean notable, D. Cascellius Aristoteles. In the 150s and the early 160s Sparta was also invited to send festival-ambassadors (*sunthutai*) to Naples, Puteoli and Rhodes; a Spartan embassy to Tarentum is attested in the 140s; and in the same decade the city exchanged judges with Samos and Alabanda.

Sparta was linked to some of these overseas cities by claims of ethnic kinship. Such a claim emerges clearly in the case of the Phrygian city of Synnada in the hinterland of provincial Asia, which was actively promoting its ties with Hadrianic Greece in the 130s through the agency of a leading citizen, Tib. Claudius Attalus Andragathus. Evidently in connection with Synnada's application to join the Panhellenion, Attalus visited Sparta, where he set up a dedication making explicit reference to his native city's claim to be a Spartan colony. Tarentum, of course, was Archaic Sparta's one genuine colony; through their mother-city of Thera the Cyrenaeans had long claimed a Spartan ancestry; and in the third century the Alabandans also asserted that they were 'Spartans' (below). The Classical Spartans, who enjoyed, we are told, listening to stories about 'the ancient foundations of cities', would no doubt have relished their city's subsequent emergence as one of the most prestigious mother-cities of Greece, with whom not only the Jews (chapter 3) but also a string of cities in Asia Minor now claimed an antique kinship. Although literally interpreted by some as evidence for overseas settlements of Spartans, these claims to a Spartan ancestry are better understood as an aspect of cultural history, reflecting the desirability of Sparta as a mother-city – largely as the result of the fame of the Spartan myth and the recognition accorded to it by Rome – among Hellenised communities anxious to acquire an ethnic Greek pedigree. The vociferous – and competitive – assertion of these claims in the early Antonine age reveals the influence of the Panhellenion, with its requirement that member-cities showed 'proof' of a good Greek ancestry – one which had the effect of confirming Sparta's lately acquired and essentially fictitious status as a leading mother-city of old Greece.[15]

*   *   *   *   *   *

During the peaceful reign of Antoninus Pius the Panhellenion flourished and post-Hadrianic Sparta's overseas diplomacy was at its busiest. Like his adoptive father, Pius was a benefactor of the Spartans, to judge from the mass dedication of altars at Sparta (41 are attested this time) to 'Zeus Eleutherius Antoninus Soter'. The titles 'Eleutherius' and 'Soter' suggest beneficent activity involving an act or acts of 'freeing'; there may be a connection here with the quarrel between Sparta and the Eleutherolacones, in which Pius found in favour of the former; conceivably, if disputed borders were in question, Spartan territory was now enlarged at the expense of her Free Laconian neighbours.[16]

By contrast, under the successor of Pius, the emperor Marcus Aurelius, Rome once more was placed on a war-footing. For appropriately archaizing reasons, the Spartans were directly involved in the earliest of these wars, the Parthian campaigns of 163–6, nominally conducted by the co-emperor L. Verus. Local inscriptions show that Sparta was requested, presumably as a 'friendly service' from a free city (chapter 11), to provide Rome with a contingent of auxiliary soldiers for this war. This levy comprised, or at any rate included, mounted troops, since one participant was described on his Spartan cenotaph as *dekatarkhēs*, the Greek equivalent of *decurio*, the name for the lowest rank of officer in an auxiliary unit of Roman cavalry. The background to this reactivation of Sparta's military tradition still needs elucidation. Arguing that the Spartan contingent included slaves and members of a local *gendarmerie*, von Premerstein claimed that it was levied by Rome in the face of a manpower-shortage, otherwise unknown but anticipating that of the late 160s, when Marcus was driven to recruiting civic police from Asia for his German wars. But the one public slave from Sparta known to have taken part, later claiming 'to have twice campaigned' against the Parthians, could have done so in an attendant capacity rather than as a combatant; and the lightly-armed M. Aurelius Alexys, taken by von Premerstein to be a Spartan *gendarme*, has now been assigned to the Spartan contingent recruited by Caracalla (below). This later contingent was recruited for antiquarian reasons: about to wage war on Parthia, Caracalla levied token forces from both the Macedonians and the Spartans. These were provincial communities especially renowned for their prowess in war against the Persians of old, whose equivalence to the Parthians had been fostered by Rome for propagandistic purposes at least since the time of Augustus (chapter 14); likewise for members of both Spartan contingents the enemy were not Parthians but 'Persians'. In 162, when no other Greek city is known to have provided Rome with troops, the request from Verus for a Spartan contingent should be seen in the same light as Caracalla's: an antiquarian gesture from an emperor attuned to Greek attitudes (Verus was the pupil of the sophist Herodes Atticus), one which acknowledged the patriotic enthusiasm aroused in Greece by the imminent war and which accorded with the enhanced mood of collaboration between Rome and the Greek world in the wake of Hadrian's initiatives. The work on military stratagems by the Macedonian Polyaenus, dedicated to the co-emperors on the occasion of this war, was a product of similar enthusiasm: 'I am a Macedonian', the author boasted in his introduction, 'with an ancestral tradition of military supremacy over the warring Persians'; it was probably no coincidence that Agesilaus – a Spartan general renowned for his invasion of the Persian Empire in the 390s BC – provided 'the central character' for the *exempla* which followed.[17]

After the eastern victories of Verus, the empire entered a more sombre decade. His troops came back carrying plague, to which Sparta would have become vulnerable on the arrival home of her contingent; the doctor hailed by the Spartans as their 'saviour' perhaps earned his civic honours at this time (chapter 13). In 167 the security of the empire was seriously threatened for the first time when German tribes overran the Danube frontier, preparing the way three years later for a raid on Greece by the Costoboci, who penetrated as far south as Eleusis. In the course of the military crisis brought about by these events, cities in Greece, as well as Asia, were called upon to provide Rome with troops. Thespiae sent a contingent of eighty 'volunteers' to Marcus, probably in 169; and a Spartan inscription records service by a veteran of the Parthian war in the campaign of Marcus against Avidius Cassius in 175/6, when the emperor was so hard-pressed for troops that he even accepted barbarian assistance. The economic burden of these wars was for the most part passed on to the provinces, and it is likely that the late 160s and the 170s saw an increase in Roman calls on Sparta for 'friendly services' of a financial kind. Local financial difficulties in this period are suggested by a sudden decrease in the numbers of inscribed catalogues of magistrates from the twenty-nine to thirty-three assignable to the reign of Pius to a mere four to eight under Marcus (App. IIA, Table). The same inference can be drawn from the debasement of metal-content first detectable in Sparta's coinage in issues of the period 172–5.[18]

Economic troubles perhaps provide a context for a mysterious Spartan episode of 'innovations' (neōterismoi) attested in two inscribed careers dated to 168–72. The better preserved of these records that its subject, one C. Iulius Arion, was 'ephor in the year of the innovations' or 'ephor in charge of' them (the Greek word here, epi, admits of both meanings). Oliver, preferring the second sense, saw these 'innovations' as constitutional reforms, which he then associated with the (hypothetical) promotion of the interests of freedmen in Athens and other Greek cities by the emperor L. Verus. But the dating of the 'innovations' does not exactly support this view, since Verus left the east in 165 and was dead by 169. Nor did Oliver give sufficient weight to the negative connotations of the word neōterismoi, which, along with the verb neōterizein, was normally used by Greek writers in the sense of political 'revolution' (see the beginning of chapter 4). A preferable view is to see in these 'innovations' a reference to a local outburst of civil unrest or stasis. This conjectural unrest would be too late to be connected with the supposed revolt in Achaia under Pius, but perhaps reflected socio-economic tensions generated by the city's financial difficulties under Marcus, when the local upper class no doubt would have tried to pass on the impact of increased Roman tax-demands to the lower classes (for instance, by raising rents or interest-rates on loans).[19]

Late in his reign, betwen 177 and 180, Marcus adjudicated a dispute between Sparta and the small Messenian city of Pherae. This dispute probably conccrncd boundaries – with the implication that the *ager Dentheliatis* at the time was Spartan (see chapter 10). If so, it seems permissible to suggest that the Spartans – possibly in recognition of their military services to Rome in this period – had obtained a reversal from Marcus of the Senate's award of the *ager* under Tiberius to Messene. Imperial benefaction of this kind would help to explain the extravagant Spartan honours for Commodus, the emperor's son and heir. Uniquely in the succession of Roman emperors, Commodus was portrayed on Sparta's coinage when still only Caesar or heir-designate (166–77). He was also honoured with an agonistic festival, the Commodean games, which could have been founded any time after 177, when Commodus became co-emperor with his father (chapter 13). His succession as sole emperor in 180 marked the cessation, for the time being, of major wars. The resumption of patterns of civic life familiar from the peaceful days of Hadrian and Pius is reflected in Commodan coin-issues of Smyrna celebrating 'concord' (*homonoia*) simultaneously with Athens and Sparta – a juxtaposition suggesting the overseas perception in this period of a certain symmetry between the two cities and the cultural traditions which they symbolized.[20]

The murder of Commodus in 193 heralded four years of political instability and civil war – in which Greece was not directly implicated – before the founder of a new dynasty, the African P. Septimius Severus, by force of arms established himself securely as emperor. There are some grounds for thinking that Severus and Caracalla, his son and successor, were responsive to the Spartan myth. Caracalla's recruitment of Spartan troops for his Parthian war, treated shortly, points most clearly in this direction; so too, perhaps, does the 'biography' of Apollonius commissioned from the sophist Philostratus by the wife of Severus, the empress Domna, in which Apollonius – an important figure to the Severan family – is portrayed as a zealous admirer of Lycurgan Sparta. Although the militarization of the empire under Severus has been exaggerated, it remains true that the importance of the army to the emperor's rule was now more openly avowed than ever before. The martial brand of Hellenism symbolized by the Spartan tradition may have found more favour with Severus than the tradition of 'high culture' represented by Athens, a city whose privileges he reduced once he became emperor.[21]

At any rate, some such attitude on the new emperor's part would be consistent with the fact that the Spartans were among the most demonstrative supporters of the Severan régime in Achaia. It has recently been established that the local Imperial cult was reorganized under Severus so as to place a new emphasis on the worship of the living emperor and on his descent from earlier *divi* – thus accommodating the dynastic propaganda of Severus, who claimed a fictive adoption into the family of Marcus Aurelius, thereby acquiring an Imperial lineage stretching back to Nerva. Sparta has also yielded the most impressive monument to the Severan family yet to be found in Greece, comprising a massive base (over 7.5 metres long) on which stood statues of Severus, Domna, their elder son Caracalla and other members of the Imperial family. This (by local standards) lavish dedication can be dated to 202–5. Its occasion is unknown, although the local goodwill for the régime which it presupposes is consonant with Imperial benefaction. Either Severus or his son is the most likely candidate for identification with the unknown emperor who promoted a Spartan festival – probably the Commodea – to 'iselastic' rank (chapter 13). It is tempting to see a link between this benefaction and the dedication of 202–5.[22]

In 212–13 the emperor Caracalla, the successor of Severus, enacted the 'Antonine constitution' whereby all free-born provincials became Roman citizens. At Sparta the impact of this measure emerges clearly in the preponderance of (M.) Aurelii in inscriptions of the later Severan period, the city's newly-enfranchised Roman citizens adopting Caracalla's *praenomen* and *nomen*. In the longer term, the value of Roman citizenship as a local status-indicator would now decline: it is perhaps symptomatic of this change that in the middle decades of the third century an honorific dedication for the aristocratic Heraclia, the daughter of Aurelii, no longer bothered to record her *nomen*. In 214, three years after his accession, Caracalla followed the precedent of L. Verus by recruiting Macedonian and Spartan auxiliaries for his offensive against the Parthians. The antiquarian context of these levies is explicit: the emperor, who strove to emulate Alexander the Great, armed the Macedonians in the manner of Alexander's phalanx and organised the Spartan levy into a 'Laconian and Pitanate *lokhos*' – perhaps so named, as Hertzberg suggested, because Caracalla (or rather his more scholarly advisors) wished to refute Thucydides in his disagreement with Herodotus over the existence at Classical Sparta of a 'Pitanate *lokhos*'. The strength of this levy, as a Spartan inscription shows, was 500 – perhaps by no coincidence the same order of magnitude as that of a *lokhos* in the old Spartan army after its reorganization around units called *morai*. The historian Herodian described this Spartan levy as a 'phalanx', implying a force of foot-soldiers. But they were not necessarily heavily-armed – after all, Alexander's phalangites were not heavy infantry in any real sense. The sculptured tombstone of M. Aurelius Alexys, a member of the contingent, who died aged forty 'having campaigned against the Persians', shows a lightly-armed soldier wearing a cap resembling the old Laconian cap or *pilos* and armed with a wooden club. Caracalla's operations against the Parthians were inconclusive and the Spartan contingent may never even have seen action before its presumed discharge in 217, following the emperor's assassination.[23]

With the fall of the Severan dynasty in 235 the Roman Empire moved into a period of rapidly increasing instability termed by some historians the 'third-century crisis'. Until the 250s, however, the Aegean world, unlike some other parts of the empire, remained at peace, its communications and city-life yet to be seriously disrupted by invasion. In the post-Severan period the persistence of familiar civic preoccupations is shown by the continued assertion in Asia Minor of claims to a Spartan ancestry. Under the emperor Maximinus (235–8) Tabae in Caria issued coins celebrating the 'concord of the citizens of Tabae and Lacedaemon', their obverse probably depicting the famous cult-statue of Apollo at Amyclae. Under Decius (249–50) Selge in Pisidia similarly celebrated 'concord' with the Spartans. Behind these agreements, evidently initiated by the minting cities, lay claims to a Spartan *sungeneia*: certain in the case of Selge, whose alleged kinship with Sparta was known to Polybius, and to be surmised in the case of Tabae, since a late tradition, found only in the Byzantine lexicographer Stephanus, records the city's kinship with a neighbouring Spartan 'colony', the city of Cibyra. In the third century other Asian cities used their coinages to advertise, some for the first time, their claims to a Spartan *sungeneia*, including Pisidian Sagalassus under Caracalla and again under Macrinus (217–18), the Carian cities of Amblada and Alabanda under respectively Severus and Philip (244–9) and Synnada under Gordian III. This rash of issues shows that among the cities of Asia a Spartan foundation-legend remained as prestigious in the third century as it had been under Pius, in the heyday of the Panhellenion. In a third-century context, these and other assertions of the Roman world's Greek inheritance, both in Asia and at Rome itself, can perhaps be seen as part of a search for 'a greater, surer past' in the face of the increasing troubles besetting the Roman Empire. To the impact of these troubles on Sparta we turn next.[24]

Chapter nine

Pagans and Christians: Sparta in late antiquity

Under the authoritarian régimes of Diocletian and Constantine I the Roman Empire emerged territorially intact, if institutionally much changed, from the five decades of civil war, invasions and economic chaos which for historians constitute the third-century 'crisis'. Sparta had not been left unscathed by the violence of the times, in 268 enduring invasion for the first time since 88 BC (chapter 7). More seriously, the old vitality of civic life was sapped during this debilitating half-century in the face of increased Roman tax-demands and the administrative machinery developed to implement them. Moreover, although the city was to enjoy a limited economic recovery during the early fourth century, its prestigious position as a bulwark of old-world Hellenism was to be challenged and then marginalized by the progressive Christianization of the Roman world following Constantine's conversion.

We begin, however, by returning to the reigns of Severus and Caracalla, when the city still displayed signs of the prosperity which it enjoyed in the first half of the second century. After a lull in the 170s and 180s, catalogues of magistrates were once more being inscribed, albeit in nothing like the same numbers as under Trajan and Pius (App.IIA, Table). The city's festivals in this period continued to be celebrated and these and other cultural activities still attracted foreign visitors (chapters 13–14). But indications exist too of disturbing social developments. An increasing cleavage between the uppermost and lower ranks of the curial class is suggested by the appearance in Severan inscriptions of a new range of honorific epithets and titles, borne for the most part by members of a small number of leading families: 'the most worthy', 'the all-first', 'the best and from the best', and so on. A dominant interrelated clique of these families can be identified, centred on the descendants of Tib. Claudius Brasidas, a Spartan senator under Marcus Aurelius, and the old family of the Memmii, together with houses of more recent prominence such as the Pomponii and the Aelii. As some of them had done for generations, these families continued to produce civic benefactors, as with C. Pomponius Panthales Diogenes Aristeas, whose unstinting term as *agoranomos* in the early 220s earned him no fewer than twelve honorific statues, or his father-in-law P. Memmius Pratolaus *qui et* Aristocles, lavishly honoured a few years earlier for outstanding service in connection with the patronomate. In this period, however, reluctance to hold office among Spartans of curial rank is also increasingly in evidence; the claim of the ex-*patronomos* Sex. Pompeius Spatalus to have undertaken his second term as gymnasiarch 'voluntarily' implies that compulsion was now in use to propel reluctant candidates into tenure of civic magistracies and liturgies. More remarkable as a pointer to the changing atmosphere of local politics are the repeated patronomates of the god Lycurgus. Having held the patronomate three times between about 140 and 221, this Spartan deity did so no fewer than eight times between 221 and about 240. These 'divine' patronomates were a financial stratagem, enabling the city to fund the expenses of the office in question from the revenues of the cult (chapter 14).[1]

In the Greek-speaking provinces reluctance to hold civic office was not a new phenomenon in the Severan age. But in the early third century it undoubtedly increased as the Roman authorities sought to extract more of the local surplus in order to meet military needs, the added burden falling in the first instance on the shoulders of the curial class. It is surely no coincidence that interventions at Sparta by Roman officialdom, including financial officers, become more noticeable in the early third century (chapter 11). Significantly they included, towards the mid-century, the repair of a bridge across the Eurotas (chapter 10); this Roman interest in the maintenance of communications between the city and the surrounding countryside can perhaps be connected with the increased emphasis in this period on taxation in kind, for the collection and storage of which Sparta may have come to serve as a regional centre. The financial straits of Sparta's curial class as the third century progressed emerge in other ways. It was normal practice in the Roman city for the cost of civic dedications to be funded by the families of the honorands. After about 230, an increasing fashion can be detected for portrait-herms, a cheaper alternative to the free-standing statue. By the mid-century, public inscriptions had become a rarity, whole series of texts disappearing for good: the most recent catalogue of magistrates can be placed no later than 250; likewise the last of the ephebic dedications at the sanctuary of Artemis Orthia, dated by Woodward to 226–40. Under the emperor Gallienus, finally, Sparta's mint produced its last coin-issues. The funding of civic coinages in the Roman east was traditionally reliant on private munificence, as can be seen in Sparta's case by the rôle of Eurycles Herculanus in the revival of the city's mint under Hadrian (chapter 8); their cessation, among a complex of factors, certainly reflects the declining affluence of the curial class.[2]

The withering away of the 'epigraphic habit' also suggests insecurity – a failing in the sense of a future 'audience' without which the laborious carving of texts onto stone becomes a pointless activity. In the 250s and 260s the Aegean world became accustomed perforce to repeated sea-borne raids by barbarian groups from outside the empire's northern frontier. In 268 one such group, a band of Herulian Goths, attacked Thessaly and southern Greece. At Sparta, rumours of imminent danger led to the burying of valuables, as is shown by a hoard of freshly minted coins of Gallienus unearthed on the acropolis. The most notorious achievement of these raiders was the temporary capture of Athens; only one source, the much later Byzantine historian George the Syncellus (*fl*.800), records that they also 'fell upon' Corinth, Argos and Sparta. At Athens the invaders had met with local resistance: 2,000 Athenians, led by the Athenian historian P. Herennius Dexippus, joined with Imperial troops in mounting a successful counter-attack. The new lease of life given to the legend of Spartan military prowess by Rome's recruitment of Spartan troops for her Parthian wars conceivably led to a similar display of resistance to the Heruli by the Eurotas; if so, however, no local Dexippus was at hand to preserve the tale for posterity.[3]

Largely on the basis of the incorporation of ruined buildings of Imperial date into Sparta's Late Roman fortification wall, archaeologists have assumed that the Heruli devastated the city and fired its public buildings. However, now that this defensive work has been dated to the early fifth century (below), little firm evidence at present exists to support this assumption of widespread damage (but cf. App.I, 57). Moreover, the availability for public works undertaken a generation later of architectural fragments from earlier buildings (or *spolia* in archaeological parlance) could as easily reflect the decay of civic amenities through an extended period of neglect as their deliberate destruction: the case of the repaired bridge over the Eurotas (above) shows that even before the Herulian raid, Sparta was experiencing difficulty in the upkeep of civic amenities; and the theatre seems to have known a period of disuse in the third century, probably to be placed in the aftermath of 268. The primary objective of the raiders was booty, and, although some damage no doubt occurred to the city's fabric, how extensive or lasting this was remains at present an open question.[4]

Archaeology to date has been more successful in showing Sparta's participation in the general economic recovery of the provinces by the reigns of Diocletian and Constantine I. Extensive building-activity at the theatre is attested at the turn of the third century, including the erection of a new marble *scaenae frons*, its architrave carrying a dedication to the tetrarchic Caesars Constantine and Maximian (293–305), and the construction of a fountain-house or nymphaeum, richly decorated with marble veneer and sculpture and replacing the Augustan scenery-store in front of the west-*parodos*, whose bricks it reused (App.I, 24). Perhaps as part of the same programme of public works, the theatral area of the sanctuary of Artemis Orthia, focus of the Roman city's revived 'Lycurgan' training (chapter 14), was now given monumental form through the construction of a small amphitheatre (App.I, 38). The building of the nymphaeum indicates that the Roman aqueduct (chapter 10) was still kept in repair; a post-Herulian building-phase has also been detected in the complex identified in chapter 10 as the gymnasium of Eurycles (App.I, 19). Other archaeological evidence for the maintenance of civic amenities includes the recent discovery of a monumental urban thoroughfare flanked by colonnades (App.I, 7; cf.6, 8). For all its reliance on *spolia* in the late-antique manner, a building project such as this suggests that the appearance of their city continued to be a source of pride to the inhabitants of fourth-century Sparta. Alongside new or refurbished civic buildings, the evidence for private luxury at Sparta continues into late antiquity. Most of the finds of impressive figured mosaic-floors belong to the period after the Herulian raid; well-appointed houses continued to have their floors and walls faced with marble; one house had its own water-supply piped into a marble fountain (App.I, 65, 67–9, 73). As a whole, the archaeological evidence for Late Roman Sparta suggests some recovery in urban prosperity after the critical decades of the mid-third century, with the late-antique city continuing to provide a residential centre for a well-to-do class of local landowners (see chapter 12). There is some suggestion too, from the interim findings of the Laconia Survey, that the Spartan countryside saw the intensification of rural activity in the fourth and fifth centuries reported for other parts of Greece, notably the southern Argolid and Boeotia. Given the more optimistic note which has entered modern debate over the health of the Late Roman economy, one might cautiously concur with the archaeologists who have seen in this phenomenon evidence for an 'economic recovery' in Late Roman Greece.[5]

In the fourth century Achaia continued to be governed by senatorial proconsuls, now enjoying a higher rank than they had done under the principate – a gesture by Constantine I, it seems, in recognition of the revival of old Greece's cultural prestige in the previous two centuries. Sparta's diminished local autonomy in this period is reflected in the evidence for proconsular interventions, especially in the field of public works. Substantial benefaction of unknown character by a Constantinian governor, the poet Publilius Optatianus, is indicated by his honorific title of 'benefactor in all things and saviour of Lacedaemon'. A generation later, in 359/60, the proconsul P. Ampelius sponsored building activity in the theatre and perhaps elsewhere, since the Bithynian sophist Himerius – in a well-schooled metaphor turning on the austerity of the ancient Spartans – credited him with having allowed Sparta to 'exchange her filthy locks for blooming braids'. Somewhat later (between 382 and 384?)

the governor Anatolius was responsible for 'rebuilding ruined Sparta' – a reference, perhaps, to proconsular initiatives in the wake of the great earthquake in Greece of 375, when, according to the historian Zosimus, 'many cities were destroyed'.[6]

Turning to cultural life, early fourth-century Sparta continued to enjoy a certain prominence in educated pagan circles as a 'venerable metropolis of the past' and a minor centre of higher studies (chapter 13). In the form of the Roman city's ephebic training the 'Lycurgan customs' continued to play their part in civic life, as is shown by the tetrarchic refurbishment of the sanctuary of Artemis Orthia (above) and the visit of the sophist Libanius of Antioch in 336 or thereabouts to see the 'festival of the whips'. Another famous Spartan sanctuary displaying a certain vitality in this period was that of Apollo at Amyclae, where the priest, in an elegiac inscription which seems to belong to the fourth century, set up the portrait of a local benefactor. His description as a 'donor of prizes' (*athlothetēs*) seems to show that the ancient festival of the Hyacinthia and its accompanying contests (chapter 14) were still celebrated at the time of this text. For the continued existence at Sparta during the fourth century of a highly-educated pagan aristocracy we have the evidence of Libanius, whose broad acquaintance included a number of Spartans, among them the family of the grammarian Nicocles, the teacher of the emperor Julian; one Ausonius, a friend from shared student-days (in Athens?); and the well-travelled Euelpistius, a prominent local figure described by Libanius as the 'leader' of the Spartans. These Spartans, like their Athenian counterparts, belonged to a social stratum which included curial families with a history of local prominence spanning the troubled decades of the third century. A tetrarchic notable claiming to be 'forty-fifth in descent from the Dioscuri' must have belonged to one such lineage; M. Aurelius Stephanus, a Constantinian high-priest of Sparta's Imperial cult, perhaps descended from an earlier homonym, a Spartan *eques* in the Severan age; and it is tempting to recognize a descendant of the *agoranomos* Panthales (above) in the Spartan of the same name mentioned in the rescript of the proconsul P. Ampelius.[7]

The brief reign of the apostate emperor Julian (361–3) saw renewed Imperial support for the pagan Hellenism with which Sparta, like Athens, was now chiefly associated. The city's standing in Achaia, at least in Julian's mind, is shown by its inclusion among those communities in the province to which he wrote for support at the time (361) of his revolt against the emperor Constans II. As emperor, Julian favoured the family of Nicocles, whose brother Sozomenus served as equestrian governor of Lycia in 363. In addition, a letter from Libanius to Euelpistius reveals that the addressee had taken part in Julian's ill-fated Persian expedition in the same year. The presence of a Spartan on an Imperial campaign against Persians at once recalls the Spartan levies of 163–6 and 214–7 (chapter 8): given the antiquarian resonances of Julian's expedition, it seems at least possible that Euelpistius was a member of another such Spartan contingent, raised by Julian for sentimental and propagandistic reasons in the tradition of earlier pagan emperors.[8]

Although a bastion of pagan Hellenism, fourth-century Sparta was far from being isolated from the religious controversies of the age. A Spartan community of Christians had existed at least since the reign of M. Aurelius (chapter 14). In the favourable circumstances of the post-Constantinian era this community can be assumed to have grown in numbers and local influence, although a bishop of Sparta is not attested, as it happens, before 457 (chapter 15). Open tensions between local Christians and the city's pagan population are revealed by a letter from Libanius to his Spartan friend Ausonius, penned in 365 and of some importance for providing 'one of the few instances in Greece where violent conflict between pagans and Christians can be confidently documented'. In this letter the writer raised the topic of the survival of cult-statues at Sparta. He had heard that those of Athena Chalcioecus, Aphrodite Enoplius, the Dioscuri 'and others' were still extant – probably, we can add, because the sanctuaries in question were under the protection of powerful priestly families within the pagan élite, as they are certainly known to have been in the third century. Libanius then alludes, however, to the rumoured destruction of two lesser statues in the sanctuary of Athena Chalcioecus on the acropolis at the instigation of the 'giants' (the author's pseudonym for Christians) acting in collaboration with 'the then rulers'. This last reference – presumably indicating Roman officials rather than local magistrates – suggests an episode which took place some time previously – perhaps under Constantius (337–61), when there is some other evidence for collusion between local clergy and Roman officialdom in attacks on pagan cults.[9]

After well over a hundred years of peace, at the close of the century the Balkans entered once more a prolonged period of insecurity, to which Greece was rudely introduced in 396 by an invasion of Goths led by Alaric, who captured Corinth, Argos and Sparta. Apart from allusions in the poetry of Claudian, of little or no use to the historian, the only account of Sparta's capture is given by the pagan historian Zosimus, writing probably in the later fifth century. According to Zosimus, on this occasion 'there was added to the ranks of captive Greece Sparta, no longer defended by either arms or valorous men; thanks to Roman avarice it had been handed over to magistrates who treasonably and eagerly served the pleasure of the conquerors in everything that looked to the common destruction'. This purplish passage, if at all reliable, suggests that in 396, rather than trying to organize any local resistance, the Spartan authorities attempted to negotiate with the Goths so as to avoid the horrors of a sack. In so doing they may have been influenced by the poor state of Sparta's defences, since, according to Zosimus, almost all the Peloponnesian cities were unwalled at the time. If the view taken below of the date of Sparta's Late Roman fortification wall is correct, Sparta's only protection would have been her old mud-brick city-wall of Hellenistic date (App.I, 9), which, even if still in good repair, the Spartans may no longer have had sufficient manpower to defend.

Clear signs of destruction attributable to the Gothic occupation of Sparta so far are slight. After Alaric's departure, however, the city's defences were rebuilt on new lines. This Late Roman fortification wall, much of it still standing, enclosed only a small central area of the old walled city: the acropolis and a small annexe to the east. Its dating is debatable: the British excavators distinguished an early phase of construction, which they assigned to the post-Herulian period; but it now seems likely, as Gregory has argued, that the whole circuit should be attributed to the early fifth century and associated with an Imperially-sponsored programme of defensive building in Greece, the chief purpose of which was to provide secure centres for local administration in the wake of the Gothic incursions (App.I, 10). The construction of this new defence incorporated on a large scale the remains of civic buildings, including parts of the stage from the theatre and blocks from the Hadrianic mausoleum of Eurycles Herculanus (App.I, 40): the availability of these *spolia* need not reflect Gothic depradations, however, so much as the deliberate dismantling of redundant buildings and monuments. Although the view of Chrimes, that Sparta was 'finally' abandoned after 396, is completely untenable, the construction of this new defence marked a break with the city's classical layout and heralded the beginning of its medievalization – a transformation beyond the scope of this book.[10]

Chapter ten

The Roman city and its territory

Ancient Sparta might be said to resemble ancient Alexandria in that, although literary descriptions of both cities have survived, their urban topography remains difficult to reconstruct. In Sparta's case, the value of the detailed, if partial, account by Pausanias of the early Antonine city is offset by the slow progress of archaeological research, which has yet to locate firmly such cardinal points as the agora, the lines of most of the chief thoroughfares and the city-gates. It is not this chapter's purpose to offer a rehearsal of the evidence and an anthology of modern opinion regarding Spartan topography, present understanding of which remains based on the findings of the campaigns conducted by the British School at Athens before and after the Great War. Instead, it attempts to show what is significant for an archaeological understanding of the Roman city, beginning with a survey, in the light of recent research and personal observation, of the chief monuments of the Roman period, basing itself on the catalogue of sites presented as Appendix I.[1]

Until the time of the Herulian raid at least, the hub of the Roman city remained the agora, the civic centre of Sparta since at least the fifth century BC. By the Antonine period, in a development paralleled elsewhere in old Greece, notably at Athens, this area had acquired the character almost of a museum, crowded with statues of deities and famous Spartans and old tombs and sanctuaries, and dominated by its showpiece, the Persian Stoa, originally built from the spoils of Plataea and famous for the figures of defeated Persians which supported the facade (Paus.iii.11.3). As well as offering attractions for cultural tourists, the agora served as the administrative centre of the Roman city, being flanked by the offices of the chief magistrates, the council-house of the *gerontes* and the so-called Old Ephoreia, the building which seems to have served as the Spartan *prutaneion* in late Hellenistic and Imperial times; nearby probably stood the civic archives or *grammatophulakeion* (App.I,11 and 12). The religious importance of the agora, for long a centre of civic cult, was reinforced by the establishment under Augustus, probably on the initiative of Eurycles, the founder of Sparta's Imperial cult (chapter 7), of shrines (*naoi*) dedicated to Caesar and Augustus – a cultic assemblage of the kind dubbed a *Kaisareion* or *Sebasteion* in neighbouring Gytheum and Messene, although not, as far as we know, at Sparta. The chief public space of the Roman city, the agora provided an obvious setting for honorific monuments: under Gaius or Claudius a portrait-painting of T. Statilius Lamprias was commissioned for display 'in the agora' (*IG* iv² 86.28–9); and the monumental public tomb of the senator Eurycles Herculanus lay in its vicinity (App.I, 40). Although the site of the agora has yet to be located, it probably lay to the east or south-east of the low hill which passed at Sparta for an acropolis in the vicinity of the 'Roman Stoa', a building 'most naturally accounted for in the Agora'.[2]

This stoa (App.I, 18), lying no more than 100 metres to the north of the modern football stadium, is a massive structure of Imperial date, constructed in Roman fashion in rubble concrete faced with brick (*opus testaceum*) and, at the time of writing, the object of renewed archaeological investigation aiming to clarify its date, plan and function. Some 320 metres to its west and on the same alignment lies the theatre (App.I,14), the two linked in antiquity, as excavation has shown, by a thoroughfare running along the southern foot of the acropolis. The archaeological evidence for the theatre reaches no further back than the Hellenistic period, and as yet it remains unclear whether the site was already in use for theatral purposes in Classical times; as Bölte saw, literary references to *theatra* at Classical Sparta may in fact denote theatral settings for religious festivals in the agora and at the Amyclaeum. At any rate, the theatre which Pausanias described as 'worth seeing' (iii.14.1) was essentially a creation of the Augustan age, when the site was completely remodelled, massive earthworks and retaining walls allowing the enlargement on a new axis of the *cavea*, which was now given marble seating, apparently for the first time.[3]

Although the task cannot be undertaken here, the complex history of the stage arrangements requires fresh study in the light of recent doubts cast on the theory of H. Bulle that a wooden sliding-stage was introduced under Augustus; C. Buckler has shown that the grooved blocks identified by Bulle as tracks for the wheels of his hypothetical stage cannot have been used for this purpose; more probably they formed part of the arrangements for storing wooden scenery inside the *skānothēkā*, the brick-built shed erected in front of the west *parodos* as part of the Augustan remodelling. For the time being, we are left with the tentative reconstruction offered by the theatre's excavator, A.M. Woodward, for whom the Augustan period saw the demolition of the Hellenistic proscenium and its replacement with a colonnaded screen in the Doric order. A permanent raised stage (*pulpitum*), its wooden floor resting on a decorated marble facade, is not attested before the third century, although it was built before 268, since rubbish-pits dug behind the facade, apparently after its construction, have been associated with a period of disuse following the Herulian raid (chapter 9). Its predecessor, of which no trace has been found, seems to have been a temporary structure of wood. It has gone unremarked that such an arrangement for much of the principate is also implied by the statement of Lucian (*Anach*.38) that the annual ball-games of the *sphaireis*-teams took place in the theatre, the orchestra presumably being enlarged on these occasions by the dismantling of the wooden stage. As for the successive remodellings of the screen attested by the hundreds of fragments of architectural marbles found on the site, these are problematic to reconstruct and date, although one, it seems, can be assigned to the reign of Vespasian, whom an inscribed epistyle-block from the theatre records as a patron of building (*IG* v.1.691 = *SEG* xi.848), and another to the tetrarchic period (chapter 9).[4]

Substantial remains of a large thermal complex lie in the flat land some 650 metres west of the theatre at the site known locally as Arapissa (App.I,19). The incomplete excavations of the British School uncovered a large area, 155 by 135 metres, featuring rooms with hypocausts, a structure resembling a water-tower, wall-niches for statuary and traces of marble incrustation on floors and walls. The site also produced fragments of an inscribed architrave-block, together with five marble pilasters in the form of hip-herms depicting a bearded Heracles holding his club; these originally formed part of a colonnade, but were reused as building-material in a later remodelling; together with two others from the same series found elsewhere, they have been assigned by O. Palagia, on grounds of style, to the Severan period. The British excavators distinguished a total of three building phases in the (apparently long) history of this complex, placing the latest in the post-Herulian period and the earliest in the late second century, although a provisional re-examination of the brickwork – *opus testaceum* like that of the 'Roman Stoa' – suggests that an original date of construction in the Hadrianic period should not be ruled out.[5]

This possibility invites a refinement to the identification of the complex, the civic character of which is suggested by its size, its expensive finish and its association with what may well have been an inscribed building-dedication. It lay in the area to the west of the theatre in which Pausanias (iii.14.6) saw a group of athletic facilities: the Dromos or race track, and two gymnasia, one of them the gift of 'a Spartiate named Eurycles'. Thermal complexes on the Roman model were a feature of Greek gymnasia constructed or refurbished under the principate. The identification of the Arapissa complex as a gymnasium of this type is suggested by its association with the herms of Heracles, a traditional patron of Greek gymnasia, who was held in special reverence by sportsmen at Roman Sparta, where one of his statues stood in the vicinity of the Dromos, to which the *sphaireis*-teams sacrificed, and another flanked an entrance to the ephebic battle-ground at Platanistas (Paus.iii.14.6, 8). It is suggested here that the Arapissa-complex should be identified with the gymnasium of Eurycles, the donor to be understood as the opulent Eurycles Herculanus, himself allegedly a descendant of Heracles, whose other benefactions at Sparta and elsewhere, most of them posthumous, were discussed in chapter 8. If the gymnasium was also a posthumous gift, construction would have begun at the end of Hadrian's reign.[6]

If correctly identified, the gymnasium of Eurycles must be clearly distinguished from its neighbour, an older establishment presumably to be equated with the gymnasium in which the erection of a bronze portrait-statue was ordered under Gaius or Claudius (*IG* iv^2.86.28–9). This earlier gymnasium was probably at least as old as the Hellenistic period and presumably was the lineal successor to the civic gymnasium destroyed by earthquake in 464 BC (Plut.*Cim*.16.5).[7]

A hundred metres north-west of the acropolis are the remains of some eight piers of an arched aqueduct, noted by earlier investigators but as yet unstudied (App.I,3). Their construction, once more in *opus testaceum*, would suit a second-century date, their orientation suggesting that the aqueduct originally terminated on the summit of the acropolis above the theatre. The full course of this aqueduct has yet to be traced; but it seems to be part of a system, of which further stretches are attested, which brought water from the lower sources of the Eurotas at the copious springs of modern Vivari, some 12 kilometres north-west of the ancient site.

In addition to these structures inscriptions permit the identification of other public works of the Roman period. The inscribed career of C. Iulius Theophrastus, which dates from early in the reign of Pius, contains a unique reference to Spartan *thermai* (App.I,23), which at this date ought to indicate a public bathing establishment organized on the model of the Roman *thermae*. In addition, two inscriptions of Antonine date attest – under the general supervision of the *agoranomos* – a *mukhos*, which here seems to have the sense of 'granary' (App.I, 17); this need not necessarily have been a building of Roman date, but it is tempting to think that it was, since the plentiful evidence for civic organization of the grain supply at Sparta belongs no earlier than the second century (see chapter 11).[8]

The same inscriptions mention a Spartan *makellon* (App.I,16), a Greek loan-word from Latin signifying a *macellum* or alimentary market. This typically Roman amenity, which by the second century had acquired a characteristic architectural form, based on an open court framed by shop-units, is encountered elsewhere in Achaia from the reign of Augustus onwards. That Sparta's *makellon* was somewhat older is implied by the attempt of the Roman antiquary Varro, writing in the mid-first century BC, to link the etymology of the Latin *macellum* with the usage of the Spartans, who in his day – so he claimed – 'still' employed the word *makellon* in the particular sense of a vegetable-market (*Ling.Lat*.v.146–7). This etymology is probably a fantasy, owing much to the larger tendency in Greek and Roman scholarship of the Late Republic to laconize the origins of Roman customs; as van Ruyt saw, the linguistic influence is more likely to have gone in the reverse direction. Varro's story, however, does suggest that the word *makellon* was already applied by the mid-first century BC to an alimentary market at Sparta, although its relationship to the Antonine *makellon* is not entirely clear.[9]

Another amenity inspired by Roman models was the stone bridge (App.I,5) attested by a dedication in honour of a Roman official, the *corrector* Iulius Paulinus, who, towards the mid-third century, sponsored the repair of 'the third arch of the bridge in the direction of the city and the openings (*parapulia*) on both sides, which had fallen into ruin both from the passage of time and the currents of the river and for a long while had been entirely destroyed and collapsed' (lines 14–24). In a lucid study, A. Wilhelm showed that the design of this bridge was Roman, the *parapulia* to be understood as small openings between the arches for flood-waters of the kind first found in the bridges of Late Republican Rome. Hence its date cannot be earlier than the late first century BC, although its attribution by Wilhelm to the age of Eurycles remains no more than a guess, since similar openings continued to be a feature of Roman bridge-building at least as late as the reign of Hadrian. As for the river spanned by this bridge, it can only have been the Eurotas. The sites of two, possibly Roman, bridges across this river have been reported, one just above the modern bridge for the Tripoli road (although this site has also been claimed as mediaeval), another some three miles to the north; presumably the carriage-road for which the bridge was built would have provided the chief link between the Roman city and Spartan territory to the north-east.[10]

The Roman period also saw the construction of new sanctuaries at Sparta. As well as the shrines of the Imperial cult, mentioned earlier, Pausanias saw two sanctuaries in close proximity to each other, one dedicated to the fashionable Egyptian god Sarapis, which the periegete describes as the 'newest' in the city (iii.14.5), the other to Zeus Olympius, whose Spartan cult, it was argued in chapter 8, was founded under Hadrian. That of Sarapis, by implication, would have been yet more recent; the priest of his attested in a mid-Antonine catalogue of *gerontes* (*IG* v.1.109.3–5) conceivably was the first.[11]

The private sphere is considered next. Plutarch implies (*Mor*. 601b) that in his day the choicest residential area at Sparta was the ancient ward of Pitana, firmly located in the north-western angle of the intra-mural area, a neighbourhood little explored archaeologically, although it has produced the remains of a house with a mosaic floor, apparently in use at the time of the Herulian raid (App.I,58). The site of a large house, its earliest building-phase assigned by the excavator to the Augustan period, suggests the presence of another residential agglomeration between the sanctuary of Artemis Orthia and the modern Eurotas bridge (App.I,51), in the presumed vicinity of the ward of Limnae. But most of the evidence for Roman housing comes from the flat land to the west and south of the acropolis and the (probable) site of the agora, an area perhaps embracing another old ward, that of Mesoa. The impression gained by the British archaeologists, from the 'remains of numerous mosaic pavements, and of sculptures such as were used for the adornment of gardens', of a neighbourhood 'covered with houses of some size and comfort', has been amply borne out by the subsequent rescue-excavations of the Greek Archaeological Service in building-plots to the west and east of the football stadium. Although many of the structures discovered date to late antiquity, some six have been assigned to the pre-Herulian period, including a group of four rooms, featuring mosaic floors and walls encrusted with *marmor Lacedaemonium* from Croceae, and parts of four or five luxuriously equipped bath-suites. Although no distinction has been observed by excavators between private and public establishments, the existence of the former is implied in at least one case by the discovery *in situ* of the base for a privately dedicated statue (App.I,52–7 with *IG* v.1.518).[12]

The last two centuries BC have produced the earliest archaeological evidence for substantial built tombs at Sparta. A group of four was excavated to the south of the acropolis, one at least ('Tomb A') featuring an imposing facade of dressed stone crowned with a pediment and, probably, an *akrotērion* (App.I,45). This burial-ground attests the survival as late as the Augustan period of the Spartan custom of burying the dead 'within the *polis*' (Plut.*Lyc*.27.1). Other cemeteries of Roman date, respecting the Roman prohibition of intra-mural burial (Cic. *De Leg*. ii.22.56), are located on the periphery of the Roman city – one to the north of the acropolis, on the left bank of the Mousga torrent; another to its north-east, near the modern Eurotas bridge (presumably to be associated with the ward of Limnae), where an earlier burial-ground remained in use in the Roman period; and possibly a third to the south-east (App.I,46–8). A thorough study of the forms of funerary monument at Roman Sparta cannot be attempted here, but a glance at the material reveals considerable variety of taste and purchasing power, ranging from simple *stēlai*, their epitaphs sometimes invoking passers-by and thereby indicating road-side locations (*IG* v.1.731; 734), to the rock-cut chamber-tombs of the Mousga cemetery, in which the deceased were inhumed in 'troughs' and individually identified by inscribed slabs (cf. *SEG* xi.865) and the statuary and carved sarcophagi fashionable among the wealthy in the second and third centuries, these last either imported from Athenian workshops or manufactured locally to imitate Attic types.[13]

*   *   *   *   *   *

Roman Sparta has been characterized by one of its modern excavators as a 'large and prosperous Roman city'. This description needs some qualification. Although no accurate means exists of estimating the urban population, in the absence of any extenuating factor in what is known of local economy (see chapter 12) it is not easy to believe that it exceeded that of the modern town of Sparti, estimated at a modest 12,000 in 1961, 'well after Greece had been sucked into the orbit of international finance capital'. Compared even with Pompeii, whose urban population in 79 is thought to have been about 15,000, Roman Sparta remained relatively small. Moreover, with the space within the circuit of the Hellenistic city-wall estimated at rather less than 209 hectares (as opposed to Pompeii's 65 hectares), population-density at Roman Sparta must have been relatively low. This inference finds some archaeological support. One of the group of late Hellenistic stone-built tombs (App.I,45), which were sited to the south of the acropolis in the centre of the intra-mural space, did not receive its latest burial before the Augustan period, to judge from the find of a coin of Eurycles. It looks as if the dispersed pattern of settlement in the Classical and Hellenistic periods, based on villages usually identified with the wards of Limnae, Mesoa, Pitana, Cynosura and Neopolitae, persisted into the principate, with burial-grounds placed in the interstices of discrete residential areas. That the Hellenistic wall, its course primarily dictated by defensive considerations, enclosed open land as well as built-up areas is confirmed by the evidence, first noted by Kahrstedt, for the construction of Roman buildings to the south and west of the acropolis – including the complex tentatively identified as the late-Hadrianic gymnasium of Eurycles – on archaeologically virgin soil. The impression is created of an urban habitat in Roman times which continued to comprise, alongside public buildings and private dwellings, a fair amount of vacant plots, perhaps to be imagined as under cultivation in the form of market-gardens, orchards or vineyards.[14]

In terms of public buildings, while it may never have rivalled Corinth or Athens, the chief cities of Achaia, by the late principate Roman Sparta, with its marble theatre, *macellum*, modern gymnasium, thermal establishments both public and private and long-distance aqueduct, had acquired most of the amenities which contemporaries thought of as characterizing urban life; by the standards of provincial Achaia, it was a well-appointed city. To be fair, the monumentalization of Sparta was not a purely Roman phenomenon. Not only was Classical Sparta less devoid of architectural pretensions than Thucydides (cf.i.10.2) would have us believe, but it is clear that the Hellenistic age saw an elaboration, if still relatively modest, of urban amenities. To this period belongs the earliest detected building-phase at the theatre, which included a stone proscenium, although the accompanying seating arrangements have left no trace and were probably temporary; also (probably) the structure known as the Machanidae, its name connecting it with the 'tyrant' Machanidas (chapter 5) and evidently having an athletic or balaneutic function, since, along with the gymnasium and the therms, it was one of the amenities for users of which C. Iulius Theophrastus made provision during his gymnasiarchy (App.I,22). Another Hellenistic construction, hitherto unremarked, can be recognized in the 'stoas in a tetragonal arrangement' which once, but in the time of Pausanias no longer, had been used for the sale of *rōpos* or petty wares (iii.13.6). This complex, to judge by its subsequent change of function, was already long-established when Pausanias saw it. A Hellenistic date is suggested, firstly, by its axial layout, closely resembling the peristylar courts which became common in Greek architecture and town-planning during the third and second centuries BC, and, secondly, by its original purpose, *rōpos* being a term 'particularly associated with the wares of travelling merchants', for whom Sparta became much more accessible with the opening up of local economy in the Hellenistic period (see chapter 5). The later abandonment of this, Sparta's first built market, suggests its replacement by the time of Pausanias with a more modern amenity (one thinks here, for instance, of the 'Roman Stoa' with its alleged shop-units).[15]

Under the principate, however, the pace of monumentalization quickened, with two periods emerging as especially dynamic ones: the Augustan age, when the theatre was rebuilt, and the second century, which saw *inter alia* the construction of the aqueduct and, as was suggested earlier, the gymnasium of Eurycles. The connection in the provincial Greek world, especially Asia Minor, between the upgrading of local water-supply and the construction of thermal amenities is well-established; on Sparta's new aqueduct, in all likelihood, depended the Arapissa-complex and the *thermai* for their water-supply. If, like the Hellenistic aqueduct provided for the ward of Cynosura (App.I,1), the Roman aqueduct supplied water to private users, it may well have stimulated the development into a residential area for the rich of the land to the south and west of the acropolis, of which private bath-suites, as was seen earlier, were a feature.[16]

If the aqueduct emerges as a stimulus to urbanization, establishment of its date is of some importance. Although the issue can be finally resolved only through further field-work, it should be emphasized that long-distance aqueducts of this type were costly engineering projects, beyond the resources of ordinary cities. In Achaia their appearance is associated with the emperor Hadrian, who is known to have funded their construction at Corinth, Athens (where Pius completed the project), Argos and, probably, Thebes. Since the honorific titulature conferred on him by the Spartans is consonant with Imperial gifts of buildings (see chapter 8), it is tempting to identify Hadrian as the donor of the Spartan system as well (one can add that its apparent termination in an elevated reservoir again resembles the Athenian and Argive arrangements).[17]

As for the prosperity of the Roman city, although this need not be doubted (see chapter 12), archaeologically it is suggested more by well-appointed private dwellings than by new public amenities, since, in a city which for cultural reasons attracted foreign benefactors, these cannot always be assumed to have been locally funded. In fact, hard evidence for Spartan citizens as patrons of civic building-activity is modest: two colonnaded structures, both of unknown location; a *peila* (see below for the meaning of this term) in the sanctuary of the Dioscuri at Phoebaeum, and an unlocated stoa, where the benefaction could have been a rebuilding rather than the original construction (App.I, 25, 29, 41). The exception, of course, is the Euryclid family, donors of a new gymnasium and (probably) the remodelled theatre, but it was precisely the unusually large fortune of Eurycles, based, when all is told, on his friendship with Augustus, which gave him and his descendants the means to fund such large-scale projects (see chapter 7).

An important final point arises from this survey of the archaeological evidence for Roman Sparta: it concerns the apparent openness of local society to material – and with it cultural – romanization. Roman methods of construction are attested as early as the reign of Augustus, when fired brick makes its first appearance at the theatre, where it was used for the fabric of the scenery-store; by the mid-second century, mortared rubble faced with brick – and in more costly structures encrusted with marble revetment too – was a staple feature of local architecture; worth noting too is the use in a Trajanic or Hadrianic inscription, apparently in its technical sense, of *peila*, a loan-word from the Latin here describing a partially-submerged structure by the river Eurotas (an embankment?) which had been built following Roman construction-methods. Romanization extended beyond such technical matters, however, to the adoption of types of amenity characteristic of the Roman and Italian, rather than the Hellenistic Greek, way of life; particularly significant here is the appearance at Sparta of thermal installations, whose accompanying hydrotherapeutic practices, as Delorme stressed, heralded a transformation in Greek social customs. Private comfort on Italian lines was also a feature of the Roman city: to the evidence noted earlier in this chapter should be added the examples of typically Roman garden-sculpture in the Sparta Museum, of the sort which once would have adorned well-appointed private dwellings. This embracing of urban living *à la romaine*, in which respect Sparta does not seem to have differed significantly from other parts of the Greek world, underlines the artificiality of the marked archaism whose manifestations in the public life of the Roman city are followed in chapters to come.[18]

*   *   *   *   *   *

The last section of this chapter addresses the rural territory of Roman Sparta, beginning with frontiers. The problems here concern their precise course, where this is important for a proper understanding of the Roman city's resources, and the significance of adjustments to them during the centuries of Roman rule.

Taking the north frontier first, Bölte and Chrimes, the latter independently, claimed that Rome deliberately restored it, at the expense of Megalopolis and Tegea, to its old, fifth-century, course. The only explicit evidence, however, concerns the border-region of Belminatis, where the head-waters of the Eurotas rose; this had belonged to Megalopolis in 189 BC (Liv.xxxviii.34.8), but was Spartan when next heard of under the Antonines (Paus.iii.21.3). This transfer must have happened at a time when Sparta's stock with Rome stood high and that of Megalopolis correspondingly low – hence probably after the Achaean War, in which Megalopolis had fought against Rome. The political status of the Aegytis to the west and the Sciritis to the east is much less clear. The former, a mountainous zone in the north of Taygetus, had been Megalopolitan shortly before 146 BC (SIG^3.665.34). But the comment of Polybius, that Spartan territory (*Lakōnikē*) lay between Messene and Tegea, cannot be confidently used to show its subsequent transfer to Sparta, as Chrimes believed, since, even if Polybius had had the Aegytis in mind, there is no pressing reason for believing that the passage was written after the date of the inscription. It is true that a 'bend' (*kam[pē]*) in Sparta's north-west frontier is epigraphically attested in 78 at a point – in the vicinity of Mt Malevo, to the north of the Langhada pass – which cannot have been far from the ancient Aegytis. But, since it is unknown whether the bend was eastwards or westwards, a bulge in Spartan territory at this point, so as to take in the district in question, is far from certain. As for the Sciritis, it too is last heard of, shortly before 146 BC, in Arcadian (in this case Tegean) hands (SIG^3.665.34) and we simply do not know, in spite of the assumptions of Bölte and Chrimes, to whom it belonged under the principate. In the light of these uncertainties the temptation to speculate about a coherent Roman plan for Sparta's north frontier is best resisted.[19]

In the time of Pausanias the north-easternmost point in Spartan territory lay on the ancient route from Sparta to Argos over Mt Parnon, where the Antonine boundaries of Tegea, Sparta and Argos all met (ii.38.7). As for the eastern frontier, to the north of Eleutherolaconian Geronthrae it lay in the archaeologically little explored Parnon piedmont, a thinly-populated area in modern as probably in ancient times; its course cannot be recovered and may never have had to be precisely defined (Chrimes's unwavering *limes* at this point seems incredible). The frontier to the south-east deserves more attention. *Pace* Chrimes, it certainly embraced the village of Croceae on the right bank of the Eurotas, which, as Pausanias states explicitly, 'belonged to the Spartans'. It is important to establish whether it also took in the district of Helea to the east of the Eurotas estuary, since this, after the Spartan plain, was the most fertile pocket of land in Laconia – its 'finest and largest' territory, according to Polybius (v.19.7). Since in antiquity the modern Helos plain for the most part was either marsh or sea, ancient agriculture was presumably concentrated on the low hills and terraces fringing the plain. In the Classical period the Helea had formed part of Sparta's city-state, as opposed to perioecic, territory. Its marshy coastline probably unable to offer a 'practicable port' in antiquity, the area is not known to have been detached from Sparta in 195 BC, when Flamininus virtually cut Sparta off from the sea (chapter 5); if it had been, we should have to assume that Rome re-assigned it to one or more of the liberated perioecic towns in the immediate vicinity (Gytheum, Geronthrae and Acriae), since its chief settlement, Helos itself, remained a dependent village (Strabo viii, 5, 2, 363). In the second and third centuries, however, there is good evidence for the Helea's close links, ostensibly ones of cult alone, with wealthy Spartan families: a grandson of the Roman senator Brasidas was hereditary priest of Demeter and Core 'in Helos', and this priest's great-niece, Pomponia Callistonice, was hereditary priestess both of Asclepius Schoenatas, also 'in Helos', and of Artemis Patriotis 'in Pleiae'. The obscure Pleiae was a dependent locality, although in whose territory is unclear, since its exact site is disputed, the question partly hingeing on whether Palaea, a village in the territory of Roman Geronthrae (Paus.iii.22.6), was the same place; if not, we are left with Livy's statement implying that Pleiae lay inland, to the east of the Helea, but within sight of coastal Acriae (xxxvi.27.2). The site of Helos, on the other hand, can be located with some certainty on the eastern edge of the marsh. Although the place was said by Pausanias to be in ruins by his day (iii.22.3), plenty of Roman remains have been noted in the vicinity of the ancient site, showing that the neighbourhood was still inhabited and the land (no doubt) under cultivation, although the pattern of settlement was now a dispersed one. The priesthoods just cited indicate the continued maintenance of sanctuaries both there and at Pleiae, a point which Kahrstedt attempted to deny, although in the former's case we have the explicit evidence of Pausanias, who says that on 'stated days' the cult-statue of Core was carried in procession from Helos to the Spartan

Eleusinium some 35 kilometres to the north-west (a sanctuary the priesthood of which also turns up, assuredly by no coincidence, in the family of Brasidas). The hereditary cultic interests of the Spartan élite in this particular corner of Laconia are striking and demand an explanation. In the case of the Artemis sanctuary at Pleiae, Bölte proposed a simple act of benefaction whereby a rich Spartan family took over the financing of a cult in (on his view) Eleutherolaconian territory. But as settlements neither Helos nor Pleiae can be classed with the local urban centres which normally provided the setting and 'audience' for Spartan euergetism elsewhere in Laconia (see chapter 7); nor, moreover, was such euergetism altruistic; Eurycles, for example, benefactor of Asopus, also owned an estate there (chapter 7). It is suggested that the rich families of Brasidas and the Pomponii likewise possessed landed interests in the vicinity of Helos and Pleiae: the wealth of the Helea, that is, in Roman times continued to be exploited from Sparta. It remains an open question whether the region actually lay within the Roman city's borders. The view taken here is that it did. Even if detached in 195 BC, it could have been restored to Sparta at a later date – in 146/5 BC, or else under Augustus.[20]

Roman Sparta's western frontier, much of it passing through the mountains of Taygetus, was conspicuous for its instability, caused largely by the continuing dispute between Sparta and Messene over possession of the *ager Dentheliatis*, a region astride the Langhada pass in the heart of Taygetus. The persistence of this quarrel is in itself remarkable, since the area, although inhabited and not unproductive in the Archaic period, can never have played more than a marginal role in Spartan economy. Although fuelled by religious sentiment, stemming from the presence within the *ager* of a venerable sanctuary of Artemis, with little doubt the dispute turned on the ancient enmity of Messenians and Spartans, which, like the antagonism between Athens and Megara (Philostr. *VS* 529), smouldered on under Roman domination. Thus we find the Messenians, having been confirmed in possession of the *ager* in 146 BC (see chapter 6), pointedly displaying the decision of the Milesian arbitrators at Olympia on the base of the Winged Victory of Paeonius, a monument celebrating a much earlier triumph (this time armed) of Messenians over Spartans in about 421 BC. The history of the dispute after 146 BC is not without problems, one of them hingeing on the *résumé* of the quarrel offered by Tacitus. The reassignment of the *ager* to Sparta 'by the decision of C. Caesar and M. Antonius' provides one crux, the view taken here being that Mommsen and Neubauer were right to link this reversal of an earlier Roman decision with triumviral gratitude for the stand of the 2000 Spartans at Philippi. Under Augustus or Tiberius the dispute was reopened, presumably by the Messenians, and in 25 the Senate confirmed a decision by a provincial governor, the otherwise unknown Atidius Geminus, returning the *ager* to Messene. This ruling comes as something of a surprise, since Laco, Sparta's ruler at the time, was not to lose the favour of Tiberius for another eight years; apparently the Senate's decision rested solely on its considered view of the arguments presented by both sides in 25 through their respective embassies. The permanence of this settlement is open to question. It was still in force in 78, when the boundary between Sparta and Messene along the eastern edge of the *ager*, as we learn from a Messenian inscription and some of the original boundary-stones, was delineated afresh by an Imperial surveyor, no doubt acting on the orders of the governor; perhaps, as Kolbe suggested, he was taking part in a larger review of civic boundaries following Achaia's reversion to provincial status under Vespasian. However, an inscription from Messenian Pherae, sandwiched (along with Thuria) between the *ager* and the eastern frontier of Messene, shows that in 177/8 this town's relations with Sparta became the subject of an Imperial ruling from the co-emperors M. Aurelius and Commodus. The text is too fragmentary to tell us more, but Kolbe is likely to have been right in seeing here a dispute over boundaries, although he does not make the further inference that, for the two cities to have shared a frontier at this date, the *ager Dentheliatis* must once again have been Spartan. The point cannot be pressed, but a successful reopening of the Spartan case under Marcus would help to explain, not only the dispute with Pherae, but also the conspicuous Spartan honours for Commodus noted in chapter 8.[21]

Afer Actium, as a reward to Sparta and a punishment to the Messenians, Augustus had deprived Thuria of its autonomy, giving the city to the Spartans (Paus.iv.31.1), and incorporated Messenian Pherae into *to Lakōnikon* – not a reference to Sparta, as Toynbee thought, but, as Kolbe realised in the light of Pausanias's usage elsewhere, to the Eleutherolacones. By Trajan's reign, as an inscription shows (*IG* v.1.1381), Messenian Thuria had regained its autonomy, although the circumstances are unknown. But the city retained close sentimental ties with Sparta, the first in the surprising form of a fictitious claim, appearing under Trajan and again under Severus, to be a Spartan colony, of a kind familiar in the milieu of Hadrian's Panhellenion (see Chapter 8), and in a Thuriate context presumably to be partly explained as a function of neighbourly rivalry with Messene.[22]

Discussion of Roman Sparta's western frontier raises, finally, the question of the city's access to harbour-facilities. It was proposed earlier, against the usual view, that Spartan territory under the principate still included a strip of coastline to the south, although one bereft of a natural harbour. Gytheum, Classical Sparta's port, had an artificial harbour known to Strabo and, largely as a result, offered the best anchorage on the Laconian gulf; after the fall of Eurycles, however, it once more regained its autonomy from Sparta – this time, so far as we know, for good. It may well have been in compensation for this loss that Augustus gave the Messenian coastal city of Cardamyle, with its small but serviceable harbour, to the Spartans (chapter 7). However, as Kahrstedt saw, it is unlikely that Cardamyle came to supersede Gytheum as Roman Sparta's chief port; the direct overland route between the two, using a pass over Taygetus to the south of Langhada, is impassable in winter and anyway would have been quite impracticable for bulky imports such as grain or marble (see chapter 12); a much easier route to the south, nowadays used by the modern road from Gytheion to Areopolis, does indeed exist, although in Roman times it would have lain in the territory of the Eleutherolacones, Sparta's relations with whom were by no means always cordial (see chapter 8). The natural assumption, as Baladié saw, is that autonomous Gytheum remained the port by which Roman Sparta communicated with the outside world, the relationship between the two resembling, for instance, that of inland Prusa and coastal Apamea in provincial Bithynia. This view gains support from the apparent importance in Imperial times of the overland route between Sparta and Gytheum. It is the only road from Sparta to the south to be marked on the so-called *Peutinger Table*, a mediaeval map ultimately reflecting the roads and posting-stations of the Imperial post in the third or fourth century. If Bölte and others were correct to see it as approaching Sparta from the south-west, having first skirted the western edge of the Spartan plain (where its path in places was engineered, to judge from the Hellenistic or Roman bridge at Xerokambi), we should perhaps see as part of its final stretch the Roman-period colonnaded street, its monumental treatment indicating a major urban thoroughfare, which heads away from the acropolis in a south-westerly direction (App.I,7). There are signs, finally, of continued close ties between Sparta and Gytheum in the post-Augustan period. Thus in 42 the terms of an oil-endowment presented to the citizens of Gytheum by a well-to-do local resident, Phaenia Aromation, stipulated that the Spartan *dēmos* was to hear complaints of negligence against the local magistrates who administered her gift. The Spartan aristocracy also maintained close ties with Gytheum. As well as those of Eurycles and his descendants, touched on in chapter 7, the Spartan Voluseni were related by marriage to a woman given official honours at Gytheum, and the affluent Xenarchidas son of Damippus, who combined tenure of the patronomate with the gymnasiarchy in the mid-second century, held office as senior ephor at Gytheum. It seems possible that commercial interests, based on Gytheum's port, played some part in the formation of these ties (see chapter 12).[23]

From the foregoing survey it can safely be concluded that Roman Sparta, although no longer the territorial colossus of the Classical period, still retained one of the largest territories in provincial Achaia. This apparent advantage, however, was offset by the fact that most of the area comprised either rugged uplands or mountains; as earlier, the rural population of Roman times continued to be concentrated, along with the best of the city's agricultural land, in the Eurotas furrow, above all the Spartan plain itself. The only detailed discussion of Roman Sparta's countryside has been that of Kahrstedt, relying on the partial evidence of Pausanias, who traversed much of it but was chiefly interested in sanctuaries and antiquities, and archaeology (including inscriptions). Since no Spartan rural site of Roman (or indeed earlier) date has ever been excavated, this last category of evidence until recently has had to rely on the more or less unsystematic sightings of surface-remains by topographers and archaeologists. Since 1983, however, Dutch and British teams have been conducting an intensive archaeological survey (the Laconia Survey) of an area of about 90 square kilometres to the immediate east and north-east of Sparta, a project the eventual findings of which may well modify significantly our understanding of the Spartan countryside. In the circumstances, the following comments are limited to a discussion of three interrelated problems only: demographic trends, changes in the pattern of settlement, and the appearance of large estates.[24]

The literary sources have much to say about the general depopulation of Greece in the late Hellenistic and early Imperial periods. Although this theme verged on becoming a *topos* and was doubtless exaggerated by some authors for purely literary reasons, it presumably had a basis in reality at least for some parts of Greece for some of the time. In Sparta's case, however, the picture is less clear-cut than Kahrstedt claimed. Strabo's observation concerning the decline of Laconia's population expressly excludes 'Sparta' and anyway is of questionable value as a demographic insight, since it was based on an apparent reduction in the numbers of Laconian 'small towns' (*polikhnai*) during the Hellenistic period – for which amalgamation as well as depopulation offers an explanation. Pausanias notes the sites of three one-time *poleis*, as he calls them, in the Eurotas furrow; but two of these (Pharis and Bryseae) rested their claims to city-status on entries in the Homeric 'Catalogue of Ships'! Only in the case of Pellana, north-west of Sparta on the way to Megalopolis, could Pausanias have been reacting to a relatively recent depopulation. On the other hand, he notes a series of secondary settlements in Spartan territory, including the 'town' (*polisma*) of Aegiae on the border with Gytheum, the 'villages' (*kōmai*) of Amyclae and Croceae and five places (Alesiae and Therapne on the Spartan plain, Scotites and Caryae in the north-east highlands and Hypsoi to the west of Aegiae) designated by the term *khōrion*, signifying, in Baladié's definition, a 'small dispersed settlement in the middle of a farming area'; no doubt there were other settlements in his day too recent or lacking in noteworthy sights to merit his attention. For the Roman period the Laconia Survey, while admitting the difficulty of dating sites 'because the details of Roman pottery typology are as yet uncertain', provisionally reports that 'many farmsteads and villages of the previous period had been abandoned'. It is debatable, however, to what extent demographic decline was exclusively or even partly responsible for this change. An alternative is to posit a shift of residence from the surrounding countryside into the town during the late Hellenistic and Imperial periods, a process of centralization encouraged by belatedly acquired aspirations (they are scarcely in evidence before the reign of Nabis) to the urban life-style of other Hellenistic cities (chapter 5), a concomitant development of the urban market and the emergence, again in the last two centuries BC, of a town-based system of euergetism which ensured that even the less well-off had access to some of the pleasures and benefits of city-life (see chapter 11).[25]

If the evidence for depopulation as yet remains less than conclusive, the same cannot be said for large estates. In spite of Kahrstedt's imaginative evocation of two 'villas' to the west of the Spartan plain, a villa-site – in the sense of an agricultural work-station at the centre of a landed property, perhaps but not invariably accompanied by a well-appointed residence for the owner (who might sometimes be an absentee) – has yet to be firmly located in Spartan territory. Known instances are multiplying, however, of substantial Roman tombs on the Spartan plain, to be seen as the family-burials of well-to-do landowners. To the one case known to Kahrstedt, a further two can now be added: at modern Psychiko, just to the south-east of the modern town, where a Roman burial has been found within a monumental structure of some kind; and, most spectacularly, at Ktirakia, outside the modern village of Aphyssou, in the vicinity of ancient Therapne. Here a built chamber-tomb was excavated by the Greeks, with a colonnaded facade and a sculpted marble frieze, housing a group of four sarcophagi. The best-preserved of these, with lion's paws at its lower corners and curved fluting on its side, belongs to a class of Attic sarcophagi produced and exported in the first half of the third century. Whether or not this structure had an earlier life as a 'hero-shrine', as its excavator thought, its period of use as a mausoleum should be assigned to the Antonine and Severan age. If the existence of large estates by this time is indisputable, the absence of impressive villa-sites, at any rate on the Spartan plain, tends to bear out the view of the British excavators that the residential area at Sparta to the south and west of the acropolis was 'inhabited probably by the landowners of the surrounding districts'. The labour-force for these estates in part must have been distributed among the secondary settlements noted earlier, which (with the notable exception of Croceae, serving the nearby quarries) presumably were predominantly farming communities. As yet, however, it remains impossible to gauge the numbers of small farms existing alongside these large properties and the extent to which the latter were created at the former's expense.[26]

Chapter eleven

Local government I: machinery and functions

In her book on Sparta Chrimes claimed 'general evidence of continuity' between the 'constitution' of the Roman city and that of earlier times. In doing so she echoed, unwittingly or not, an important facet of the Spartan myth in later antiquity, one which stressed the longevity of Spartan institutions. In 60 BC, for instance, Cicero could claim of the Spartans in a Roman court that 'alone in the whole world they have now lived for more than 700 years with the same customs and unchanged laws'. However opposed the reality, the citizens of Roman Sparta had an interest in maintaining an archaizing veneer to the conduct of their affairs, since the Romans – at least in the Late Republic – were well-known admirers of the pristine Spartan polity, to the extent that the *gerousia* and other alleged institutions of Lycurgus were even claimed as political influences on the early kings of Rome. A cursory glance at the evidence does indeed suggest a certain absence of change: ephors and *gerontes* survived; local government still operated through *rhētrai*; and linguistic archaism lent an antique air to procedural language. The reality, it is argued below, was somewhat different: the reforms of Cleomenes III and Nabis, the abolition of the dual kingship, the legacy of a half-century of *sumpoliteia* with the Achaean League and the indirect but increasingly pervasive influence of Rome, all ensured that institutional continuity was more apparent than real.[1]

The issue of continuity is best approached through an examination of the decision-making machinery of the Roman city as revealed – mostly – through inscriptions; here some discussion of technical problems cannot be avoided. The great bulk of these inscriptions belongs to the period between the Flavians and the later Severans – that is, between the re-establishment of 'republican' government following the fall of Spartiaticus under Nero and the troubles of local government in the third century. The relevant texts fall into essentially four categories: decrees; honorific dedications; lists of magistrates (over 170); and texts which detail the local careers of individual Spartans (altogether some sixty-five persons are commemorated in this way). Pausanias (iii.11.2) provides a thumb-nail sketch of the Antonine city's 'constitution' as he understood it. From the triumviral period local coin-issues with magistrates' names and titles are also of interest.[2]

A start is made with *IG* v.1.4, a Spartan decree dating from the period of the city's union with the Achaean League and of particular importance because it shows the reality behind Sparta's unwilling acceptance of the 'laws and institutions of the Achaeans' in 188 BC. The decree had been passed by the Spartan assembly following an approach made by the honorand himself, not to the *gerousia*, but to a joint-body of chief magistrates calling themselves the *sunarkhiai* (literally 'the joint magistracies'). We have here a clear example of the Hellenistic tendency, in the words of J.K. Davies, for 'the various magisterial boards [of a Greek city] to coalesce into a single college with the power, or in some cases the exclusive right, to carry out probouleutic functions for the assembly'. In Greece itself, this tendency is particularly associated with member-cities of the Achaean League, in which *sunarkhiai* were characteristic institutions with oligarchic overtones, since they lent themselves to the concentration of decision-making power into the hands of the 'persons of standing and substance' who usually held the chief magistracies in this period; as Touloumakos saw, the Spartan *sunarkhiai* were an Achaean-imposed institution. At the time of this decree Sparta must still have possessed a council; the absence of any mention of the *gerousia*, far from proving its suppression in 188 BC, as W. Kolbe, the editor of *IG* v.1, believed, may have resulted simply from compression in the preamble, as in *IG* v.1.5, a decree of the same period, where not even the *sunarkhiai* are mentioned; at any rate, the existence of the *gerontes* at the close of the Achaean period is expressly attested by Pausanias (vii.12.7; see chapter 6).

If we turn to the (invariably incompletely preserved) preambles of surviving Spartan decrees from the period after 146 BC, we find that the *gerontes* are regularly named, but the formulaic expression 'just as the *gerontes* judged as well' suggests that in the passage of these decrees their role was limited to deliberating for submission as preliminary resolutions to the assembly measures put to them on the initiative of others – presumably magistrates present at their meetings. That this power of initiative remained with a body of *sunarkhiai* in the Roman period is strongly suggested by the best-preserved preamble, in a decree of consolation from the reign of Gaius or Claudius. This is sufficiently complete to leave in little doubt that it is echoed precisely by the preamble of a decree passed by the Messenian city of Pherae in the middle decades of the first century BC, of which the first word alone needs restoration: '(?) Decision (*[dogm]a*) of the *sunarkhiai*, just as the *gerontes* judged as well'. Pherae's *sunarkhiai* were a legacy of the city's union with the Achaean League in the period before 146 BC; its claim, like that of neighbouring Thuria (chapter 10), to be a Spartan colony explains its imitation of Sparta's political machinery, including the use of *gerontes*. In the case of the Spartan decree, although only the last three letters of the word 'of the *sunarkhiai*' are preserved, its restoration by Peek therefore seems reasonably assured. It appears, then, that the *sunarkhiai* survived the city's secession from the Achaean League in 146 BC and that the recovery of formal autonomy did nothing to change the oligarchic tenor which they gave to local government.[3]

It remains to identify the magistracies comprising the *sunarkhiai*. In the copious epigraphy of the post-Neronian period the institution does not reappear. Instead there are frequent references to a body of magistrates called the *sunarkhia* or 'joint-magistracy' in the singular. That the *sunarkhia* also comprised the city's chief executive is made more or less certain by two texts in which it appears as the body giving effect to the resolutions of other corporations: in one case the tribe of the Cynosureis, in the other the *gerontes* themselves (*IG* v.1.480; 448). It can be concluded that the terms *sunarkhiai/sunarkhia*, between which no significant difference of meaning can be observed, describe the same joint-board of chief magistrates; conceivably the term *sunarkhiai* was dropped after 146 BC, as in some other former member-cities of the Achaean League, to be replaced at Sparta by the less 'Achaean'-sounding *sunarkhia*; the older form survived, however, in the stylized preambles of decrees.[4]

If the *sunarkhia* comprised the executive magistracies, its composition is left in little doubt. As Bradford observed, the 'sheer volume of lists of *gerontes*, ephors and *nomophulakes* demand that they be considered the three most important offices in Sparta'. This volume can be quantified: respectively fifty-four, forty-nine and forty-eight, whereas the next most often listed board of magistrates, the *bideoi*, has left a mere fourteen catalogues (App.IIA). The inference that ephors and *nomophulakes* comprised the *sunarkhia* is borne out by the way in which their membership is repeatedly listed consecutively on the same stone, indicating close collaboration between the two boards. A close administrative relationship with the *gerontes* is demonstrated, firstly, by the appending of the membership of all three to the Trajanic decree concerning the Leonidea and, secondly, by the relationship of the ephors and *nomophulakes* to the *boulē* of Roman Sparta, its council *par excellence*. Normally this was the body in provincial Greek cities which, together with the executive of annually elected magistrates, provided the real management of affairs. A Spartan council of this type does not emerge clearly in the evidence until the Severan age, when its existence is left in no doubt by the acclamatory title 'mother of piety, the council (*boulē*) and the *dēmos*' borne by a Spartan matron and by the formulation 'chosen by the most brilliant council (*boulē*) and the most sacred *dēmos*', which appears in a dedication of about 221 with reference to the nomination of a Spartan *prokritos* or provincial juror. In the same period – the early third century – the title of 'councillor' (*bouleutēs*) appears for the first time in Spartan epigraphy, in all three cases borne by distinguished foreigners on whom it had been conferred as a mark of honour. Significantly, however, no Spartan is known to have borne this title. Since it seems inconceivable that the council did not exist in some form before the Severan period, this curious silence is best explained on the view that its membership was *ex officio*: the 'councillors' of Roman Sparta, that is, are hidden under the titles of other magistracies.

The simple answer, that these 'councillors' were the *gerontes*, as Bradford believed, is suggested by the fact that the secretary in attendance on the latter body is called the 'secretary of the *boulē*' in post-Neronian texts (formerly he was just styled 'secretary'). But a Hadrianic catalogue of ephors and *nomophulakes*, its significance first seen by Kennell, also closes with the name of the secretary of the *boulē*, who evidently, at least in some circumstances, attended on these two boards of magistrates as well as the *gerontes*. That all three boards and not the *gerontes* alone exercised a deliberative function is confirmed by another Hadrianic text, in which the ephors and *nomophulakes* conjoined to make a dedication to Zeus Bulaeus and Hestia Bulaea. These divine inspirers of good counsel were associated with the council-houses of at least one other Greek city: at Athens the council-house contained a shrine of Zeus Bulaeus, where councillors sacrificed and prayed on entering the building, as well as a 'hearth of the council' (*boulaia hestia*) by which bouleutic oaths were taken. That the ephors and *nomophulakes*, as well as the *gerontes*, performed similar rituals at Roman Sparta is suggested by the attachment to them of groups of youths or young men serving as libation-bearers (*spondophoroi* or *spondopoioi*). From all this the conclusion seems hard to resist that the *boulē* comprised those sessions of the *gerontes* which were joined by the *sunarkhiai/sunarkhia* – the ephors and *nomophulakes*, that is – in the exercise of their probouleutic functions. Not surprisingly, as the Roman city's chief deliberative and legislative body, this composite *boulē* met at fixed times and frequently – in the mid-first century BC more than once a month, to judge from the fragmentary heading of a Spartan decree which, following Kolbe's interpretation, refers to 'decrees of the first session of the council of the month Artemisius' (*IG* v.1.11.4).[5]

The picture which has emerged of the Roman city's political machinery suggests some continuity, but also a marked discontinuity. The *gerontes* were now an annually elected body, a change first attested in the early principate, but usually thought, with reason, to go back to the reforms of Cleomenes III (chapter 4). The probouleutic powers of the old *gerousia* emerge in the Roman period considerably diluted, since now they regularly depended on collaboration with the *sunarkhiai/sunarkhia*, a relatively recent institution of Achaean origin. Hence the statement of Pausanias, that the *gerousia* of his day was the 'sovereign council of the Lacedaemonian polity' (iii.11.2) is misleading: this council in fact was the composite *boulē*, of which the *gerontes* formed only a part (albeit numerically the largest one – see below). As for the ephors, they maintained rather more of their old pre-eminence. In the second and first centuries BC diplomatic correspondence between Sparta and other cities was addressed to them or sent out in their name, a state of affairs hardly showing, as Chrimes asserted, that they had 'sunk to the position of mere secretaries'; rather, as Touloumakos put it, it placed them at the 'summit' of local government, continuing to represent the city in official dealings with the outside world, as they had done in the Classical period. As members of the 'joint-magistracy', however, their probouleutic function was shared with the *nomophulakes*, so that the statement of Pausanias, that they conducted 'all the other important business' apart from the supervision of the ephebic training (iii.11.2) cannot be accepted without some reservation. These *nomophulakes* make their first appearance in the triumviral period on coin-issues of the Spartan mint. The date of their institution is unknown. Chrimes supposed that they were at least as old as their counterparts at Dorian Cyrene, established towards the end of the fourth century BC. In the Classical period, however, the function of 'guarding the laws' (*nomophulakia*) was exercised by the old *gerousia*; if the institution of the *nomophulakes* represents the transfer of this function to another body, they perhaps are better seen as another innovation of Cleomenes III, as part of his systematic weakening of the old *gerousia*. Although their powers no doubt underwent a subsequent evolution, in the Imperial period their literal function as 'guardians of the laws' found an echo in their charge of the *grammatophulakeion* or public archives (App.I, 12), as indicated by their association with the official known as the *grammatophulax*.[6]

It remains to comment further on the oligarchic character of this machinery. The formal involvement of the citizen-assembly, in inscriptions of Roman date simply referred to as 'the people' (*ho dēmos*), is shown by the same decree of consolation from the reign of Gaius and Claudius, technically a 'decision of the people' (line 16). Pausanias knew of a historic building near the agora, the Scias, in which the assembly met in his day; and inscriptions show that it continued to be convened into the third century. A certain deference to its ideal supremacy is suggested by the dedication in the agora (under Pius) of a sculptured personification of the 'Lacedaemonian People', in the name of whom there is one example, from the Neronian period or shortly after, of a Spartan public dedication. But the absence of any tradition of popular politics at Sparta presupposes that the 'democratic' element in the Roman city's decision-making machinery was no less exiguous – and quite possibly more so – than in other provincial Greek cities. The assembly's essentially passive role as merely a ratifying body, echoing that of its Classical predecessor, seems to emerge clearly from the stipulation in the Trajanic dossier concerning the Leonidea that the income from certain fines was to be spent on 'whatever the people wish and' – the text continues – 'the magistrates (*arkhontes*) decide'.

The chief magistracies, on the other hand, comprised a remarkably small number of Spartans. Five complete catalogues of *gerontes*, ranging in date from the reign of Augustus to that of Pius, repeatedly give their numbers, including the president but not the secretary, as twenty-three, evidently their normal strength in the Imperial period. Catalogues of ephors from the Flavian period onwards reveal that they still numbered the traditional five; the *nomophulakes* usually numbered the same, bringing the total strength of the Roman city's composite council to thirty-four (including the secretary). As far as we know it was highly unusual for the council of a provincial Greek city to be so small: typically such bodies numbered from a hundred upwards, with councils of around 500 not uncommon. If the Spartan council were a larger body, the rest of its membership might be expected to have left some trace in the hundreds of inscriptions from the Imperial period; as it is, before the Severan period there is nothing in the evidence of catalogues and careers to suggest the existence of a class of 'ordinary' councillors distinct from the *ex officio* members. Moreover, since Sparta had no tradition of a large council, we might expect the existence of such a body to have caught the attention of an outside observer such as Pausanias; but the literary sources are silent. As it is, the thirty-four 'councillors' represent an increase of only four over the full strength (including the two kings) of the old *gerousia*, Classical Sparta's equivalent of a council (Plut. *Lyc*.6.8).[7]

It is true that this *boulē* seems somewhat more open than its Classical counterpart. But, although election was now annual to all the magistracies involved, and the posts of ephor and *nomophulax* could be held only once, no such restriction attached to that of *gerōn*. As early as the Augustan age a Spartan is known to have served three times in this office; in the second century a second or third term was commonplace, four terms were not rare, and one Spartan under Trajan served six times in as many years. The situation revealed by another Trajanic catalogue, in which two-thirds of the *gerontes* had served at least once, must have been common. In addition, the catalogues of the post-Neronian period reveal a hereditary tendency among the three boards comprising the *boulē*. Appendix III presents the results of a prosopographical analysis of the council's personnel in two years under Trajan when lists of all three component boards happen to have survived, and in one year under Pius from which lists of two of the three (ephors and *gerontes*) are preserved. Taking the three years together, the average number of 'councillors' who may have (the degree of certainty varies) been ancestors, descendants or kinsmen of other 'councillors' works out at between a quarter and a third (27 per cent). The incompleteness of the data makes it likely that the hereditary tendency was even more marked than this figure suggests. It can be stated with some confidence that, although the machinery of government had undergone an evolution, the Roman city was scarcely less an oligarchy than Classical Sparta had been.[8]

       *   *   *   *   *   *

An attempt is made in this second section to characterize the chief preoccupations of local government at Roman Sparta. Before doing so the question of the extent and frequency of Rome's routine interventions in the city's internal politics needs addressing. Once Rome established a permanent administrative presence in Greece, for the first time in 46 BC and regularly from 27 BC, the Roman governor became a figure of great potential influence in Spartan affairs, as the Spartans themselves acknowledged in 46 BC in their attempt, through the good offices of Cicero, to secure the goodwill of Ser. Sulpicius Rufus (chapter 7). It is doubtless only the paucity of our evidence which leaves as the sole attested instance of proconsular intervention at Sparta before the third century the story in Philostratus, if it can be believed, of the anonymous governor who brought to Nero's attention alleged abuses by Sparta of her free status (*VA*.iv.33).

None the less, day-to-day interference was probably less frequent than might be imagined. This follows partly from general considerations concerning the remoteness of Roman provincial administration, but partly from Sparta's privileged standing as a free city. First attested only under Augustus, when it came to be shared with the Eleutherolacones, this status had effectively obtained since 146 BC, when Sparta, as a friendly non-belligerent, had been left by Rome with her newly regained 'independence' intact (chapter 7). Inscriptions show that by the first century BC the privileges of free cities were regulated in considerable detail by Rome through treaties and senatorial decrees; no such formal agreement is attested in Sparta's case, although it remains possible that one was negotiated at some stage in the first century BC. The fiscal and judicial privileges of free status are returned to below; here we need only recall that Sparta would thereby have been excluded from the 'plan' of the province of Achaia and placed outside the routine jurisdiction of the proconsul. Formal scruple over Sparta's status can be detected as late as the reign of Marcus, who in about 174 required a judge hearing Spartan litigants in civil suits to hold court, not at Sparta itself, but in some nearby city – presumably one technically within the province. Such scruple (if only in small matters) was to some extent underpinned by Roman respect for Sparta's past, a factor emerging in Cicero's letter to the governor Sulpicius Rufus and the younger Pliny's to the *corrector* Maximus under Trajan (see below) as the basis for a plea of special forbearance in Rome's administrative dealings with the city.

The routine Roman interference for which there is increasing evidence in the second century was – at least partly – generated by the Spartans themselves. Imperial interventions, although irregular, were now not infrequent, as emerges from the evidence for Spartan embassies to the emperor or his representative. Their business is usually unstated: one certainly, the two-man embassy sent to congratulate L. Caesar in Pannonia following his adoption by Hadrian in 136, was ceremonial; but references to 'successful' embassies, including the one under Pius 'against the Eleutherolacones', show that weightier municipal matters could be in question. These embassies show Sparta fully engaged in the pattern of 'petition-and-response' characteristic of the emperor's routine relations with provincial communities: the initiative for these interventions, that is, by and large would have come from the Spartans themselves, no more able than others to resist the magnet of Imperial powers of arbitration and patronage.[9]

In the course of the third century the administrative distinction between Achaia's free and subject cities to a large extent was eroded away by the repeated dispatch to Greece of high-ranking (usually consular) officials called *correctores* or, in Greek, *epanorthōtai* or *diorthōtai*, with a brief specifically to regulate the affairs of the free cities. In the second century they are attested only sporadically; but inscriptions show that in the third century *correctores* frequently served simultaneously as proconsul. Spartan affairs are known to have been the concern of four *correctores*. The earliest of them, Pliny's correspondent Maximus, seems to be referred to retrospectively in a dedication set up in 116/17 by the city of Cythera, at the time in the possession of the Spartan senator Eurycles Herculanus. The emperor Hadrian and the *corrector* L. Aemilius Iuncus together intervened in the Spartan 'contest for best citizen' (see below) to support the candidacy of a local notable, Tib. Claudius Harmonicus; the larger context is obscure, although it may have been the administrative aftermath to Hadrianic interventions at Sparta which brought Harmonicus to the attention of Roman officialdom; at any rate, Benjamin's attempt to link this episode with Sparta's Imperial cult is unconvincing, since at the time Eurycles Herculanus, not Harmonicus, was the high-priest. The three other instances belong to the third century: in about 221 the *corrector* Egnatius Proculus approved the city's nomination of another notable, P. Memmius Pratolaus *qui et* Aristocles, to jury-service in the Roman governor's court; towards the mid-century

Iulius Paulinus sponsored the repair of a road-bridge over the Eurotas (chapter 10); and a fragmentary letter to the Spartans from an unknown *corrector* dates to the close of the century. These isolated items of evidence shed little light on the aims of the central government in sending *correctores* to Greece, which no doubt varied. But a link with Roman requests for 'services' (*munera*) from the free cities is suggested by the increased presence of *correctores* in the third century, a period which saw levels of Roman exaction in the provinces rise in response to incessant warfare. Since taxes at this time came increasingly to be paid in kind, it is tempting to suppose that in repairing a bridge across the Eurotas the *corrector* Paulinus was mainly concerned to improve communications between rural producers and urban storage-depots.[10]

Roman taxation brings us to the function of local government at Sparta which from the Roman point of view must have been the most essential: the administration of Roman demands. It is true that, as a free city, Sparta was fiscally privileged in the sense that she was exempt from regular payment of tribute; she was also permitted to collect her own customs-dues, as emerges from the Spartan decree concerning the Leonidea, in which the local authorities conferred 'immunity from import-tax' (*ateleia eisagōgimou*) on a group of traders whom they wished to favour. In observing that Sparta 'contributed nothing [to the Romans] but friendly liturgies', however, Strabo shows that the city was excluded from the tiny élite of free cities exempt from irregular liturgies or *munera* as well as regular tribute: presumably Rome considered Spartan resources (relatively ample by Peloponnesian standards) too valuable to be placed completely outside her grasp. As was seen in chapter 7, liturgies imposed on Sparta in the Late Republic included the provision of troops, cash and possibly supplies for Roman wars. Under the principate, at least in peacetime, such demands no doubt eased off, although the evidence for the imposition on Messene between 35 and 44 of a special eight-obol tax warns against the assumption that in such conditions they ceased altogether. In the second and early third centuries Sparta continued on occasion to be asked to supply troops (chapter 8); and financial demands in this period probably underlay the dealings with Sparta of a succession of Roman officials whom the city honoured in gratitude for favourable – or simply fair – treatment: a provincial procurator under Trajan; a Hadrianic scribe attached to the office of the quaestor, the chief finance-officer of the province; and two more procurators in the Severan period. As we might expect, such demands were dealt with in the first instance by the local executive: a Spartan decree from the mid-first century BC reveals the 'magistrates' (*arkhontes*), who – following Touloumakos – can be identified with the *sunarkhiai/sunarkhia*, taking action over arrears in payments to Rome.[11]

There is some evidence to suggest that free cities were responsible for maintaining the public roads (*viae publicae*) in their territories used by the Imperial post. At Sparta, the chief of these – although it can rarely have been very busy – was the route from Megalopolis *via* Sparta, which is marked on the *Peutinger Table* (reflecting original documentation of the third or fourth century) as the site of a lodging-house (*mansio*), to Gytheum and then on to Boeae, the port for Cythera; Roman classification of this as a *via publica*, at any rate in late antiquity, is shown by a milestone recovered in the Helos region, recording repairs under various fourth-century emperors. A Spartan dedication from the late second century expressed the city's gratitude to a wealthy notable of senatorial rank, Tib. Claudius Pratolaus, who had discharged with great generosity the post of '*agoranomos* in charge of the roads'; presumably these were roads in the civic domain requiring repair, the costs of which had been largely met by Pratolaus. One can only speculate, however, as to whether public roads in the Roman sense were in question here.[12]

Leaving aside the administration of cults and festivals and the 'Lycurgan customs' for consideration in chapters 13–14, the two other essential functions of local government, about which the texts permit some comment, were the food-supply and the administration of justice. In the second and third century, to judge from inscriptions, Sparta suffered not infrequently from grain-shortages. Although shortages were not unknown in earlier periods, other factors suggest late Sparta's weakened ability to feed herself. Frontier-changes had effectively reduced the good arable land within the Spartan *polis* to the Eurotas-furrow (chapter 10); the advance of urbanization had enlarged the pool of townsfolk not directly engaged in agricultural production; the Roman city's emergence as a tourist-centre placed a further burden on the food-supply at times of major festivals; and changes in dietary fashion may have enlarged demand in the city for less easily obtainable wheat in place of locally produced barley, the staple cereal of Classical Sparta. Between the Flavian and the Severan periods nine occasions are attested when a failure in the grain-supply obliged the local authorities to appoint a grain-commissioner (*sitōnēs*) to purchase grain by means of what has aptly been named 'search-purchasing': the seeking out of a surplus for sale, either from the private stores of local landowners or from beyond the city's frontiers. Sources of imported grain are discussed in chapter 12; that overseas purchases were not uncommon is shown by the boast of a Hadrianic *sitōnēs* that in none of his three missions had rough seas obliged him to jettison any of his precious cargo.

On two occasions the missions of *sitōnai* are specifically linked to a 'shortage' (*spanis*). The earlier fell between Hadrian's two visits to Sparta in 124/5 and 127/8 and may in part have resulted from the heavy demands on local supplies generated by the presence of the Imperial court; it may have been Hadrian himself on one of these occasions who gave the

Spartans permission to buy wheat from Egypt. Given the endemic nature of ancient food-crises, however, unusual circumstances are not required to explain the crises behind the other attested grain-commissions, which could have been prompted by crop-failure or hoarding by local landowners or a combination of both. The aim of these grain-commissions, of course, was to provide, not free grain, but grain which could be offered for sale below the 'emergency' prices: thus C. Iulius Theophrastus, a Hadrianic *sitōnēs*, bought grain at the 'emergency' price of 40 denarii per measure or *medimnos* and made it available at Sparta at 12 the *medimnos*. Concern for the grain supply in general was motivated less by philanthropy on the part of local government than by civic pride (apropos of visitors) and political expediency (apropos of the local populace, which might riot in times of shortage). By the Antonine period the city had its own granary. There may also have been a public fund to finance grain-purchases, since five grain-commissions, although they appear in career-inscriptions, which usually emphasise financial sacrifices by their subjects on the city's behalf, are not linked to personal munificence. On the other hand, it is clear from the remaining three instances that it was not uncommon for *sitōnai* to make generous personal contributions to the costs of their missions: Theophrastus apart, two later grain-commissioners were publicly honoured for this reason. The case of Theophrastus is of special interest because it suggests the ambiguous rôle of local landowners, who sometimes could profit from, at other times help alleviate, shortage: in addition to his *sitōnia*, he boasted in his career-inscription of 'often' making sales below cost price to the city 'in critical times', where the term used (*paraprasis*) normally refers to sales of either grain or olive oil – in either case, here in all probability coming from the donor's own land.[13]

As a free city, Sparta was entitled to retain her own jurisdiction, both criminal and civil, and, theoretically at least, lay outside that of the Roman governor. An inscription from Thuria strongly suggests that under Augustus capital cases were still heard by local courts. The text is a Thuriate decree in honour of a Spartan notable, Damocharis son of Timoxenus, an Augustan *patronomos* and inheritor of ancestral proxeny-ties with Thuria. At the time of the decree's passage Damocharis was actually resident at Thuria, where he earned the city's gratitude by successfully intervening in an outbreak of civil discord. As Bölte saw, the natural context of this decree is the period after the transfer of Thuria to Sparta (see chapter 10): Damocharis apparently had been sent to Thuria as his city's official representative, the absence of an administrative title showing no more, *pace* Kahrstedt, than that Sparta was exercising her dominion with discretion. The text reveals that under the new régime, understandably, there was much to-ing and fro-ing between Thuria and Sparta. An earlier service by Damocharis had been to use his personal standing in his home city to promote the interests of Thuriate ambassadors and Thuriate citizens with business in Spartan courts, here interceding, if the natural sense of the Greek is allowed, 'even on behalf of murderers'. The inscription, hitherto ignored in scholarly discussion of the problem as to whether free cities retained capital jurisdiction, seems to show that the gift of Thuria to Sparta was accompanied by a transfer of jurisdiction over Thuriate capital cases to Sparta; on this view, the same courts would presumably have been able to pass capital sentences without reference to the Roman governor. Detailed information about the judicial function of Spartan magistrates in Roman times is lacking, although, for what it is worth, Philostratus set the Neronian trial of a well-born Spartan trader before the ephors (chapter 12); in the absence of a tradition of popular courts, however, it is likely that serious cases were heard, as in the Classical period, by the chief magistrates – that is, by some or all of the boards comprising the *boulē*. In addition, the Hellenistic practice of trying cases before a small court of judges sent on request by another city is well attested at Roman Sparta. By the first century BC the city already possessed a special lodging for these visiting judges and was itself the obliging recipient of requests for judges from other Greek cities, including Demetrias, Eretria and Delphi. In the milieu of the Panhellenion, the practice flourished again, with the post of *dikastagōgos*, the official who escorted visiting judges back to Sparta, attested some five times in the inscriptions.[14]

The relationship of local jurisdiction to that of the Roman governor is not entirely clear. In the second and third centuries the city was required to furnish judges for the governor's court, in both attested instances nominating notables with Roman citizenship. But as yet there is no evidence that Sparta was ever the seat of a proconsular assize-court, although free status in itself was no obstacle to acquiring this function, which Greek cities saw as a privilege. Even if the governor, at any rate under the early principate, did not try Spartan cases as a matter of routine, appeals from Spartan to Roman courts were evidently frequent by the second century, since a fragmentary Imperial letter of that date, its authorship uncertain, attempted to limit them by instituting a screening process to be operated by local 'councillors' (*sunedroi*) – presumably the members of the composite *boulē*. Such appeals were encouraged by the gradual increase in the numbers of Spartans with Roman citizenship (chapter 12), a few of them of the highest standing – notables such as the senator Brasidas, an inheritance-dispute between whose family and that of his ex-wife was judged by Marcus Aurelius himself.

Increasing local knowledge of Roman law and of its advantages over Greek law also encouraged this trend, as is suggested by the succession of letters to the Spartans from the three Flavian emperors, which we happen to know about because they were cited by the younger Pliny in his administrative correspondence with Trajan. They all dealt with the same problem, the status of free-born foundlings (*threptoi*) brought up as slaves. Probably they stemmed from disputes in local courts over the payment of compensation for the cost of upbringing in cases where the natural parents asserted the freedom of their offspring against the fosterers. Since Greek custom, which Spartan law probably followed, did not allow for such payments, it seems likely that fosterers familiar with Roman law, which did, were attempting to have the Roman usage applied at Sparta. These Imperial letters on the subject seem to have arisen from appeals to the emperor from local courts. The evidence should be noted, finally, for the frequent appointment in the second century of Spartan *sundikoi* or civic advocates to plead on the city's behalf in disputes with individuals or even other cities; some, perhaps a majority, of these advocates should be imagined as appearing before Roman, not local, courts.[15]

*   *   *   *   *   *

The last section of this chapter considers the question of how the Roman city raised money for civic expenditure, one which, until addressed, leaves obscure the realities of the local political structure. To begin with, there were the 'civic revenues' (*politikoi prosodoi*), as they are described in an inscription from the mid-fourth century. For the early principate, if not for late antiquity, some of the sources of this revenue can be identified. Some of our best evidence comes from the Trajanic dossier concerning the Leonidea, attesting two kinds of indirect tax, customs-dues (*eisagōgimon*) and a licence-fee levied on tradesmen (*pratikē*), along with revenues from certain fines. More unusually, there is mention of a 'bank of exchange' (*ameiptikē trapezē*), which was a public concern, since it was regulated by a 'decree concerning the bank', although its running seems to have been entrusted to private entrepreneurs, referred to as 'those in charge of the bank'. From the city's point of view the function of this bank was to raise revenues: as in the case of the cash-endowment for the Leonidea, it accepted deposits of public funds from which loans were made to private individuals at interest; probably it also enjoyed a monopoly of money-changing operations. The Roman city's bronze coinage played its part here: as well as its symbolic function, as a manifestation of civic pride, its use in local transactions was probably assured by the practice of tariffing items for sale in the city-markets in bronze, rather than silver; customers would then be obliged to exchange their silver for local bronze at the public bank, with the city taking a percentage of the (probably modest) profits of the money-changers. The city also owned land, the administration of some of which formed the subject of part of the Imperial letter mentioned above. Finally, its foreign possessions would have provided some income: Messenian Thuria was presumably tributary to Sparta; and Hadrian's gifts of Caudus and Cythera were chiefly fiscal in purpose (chapter 8).[16]

Whatever the exact scale of its resources, it is clear that the Roman city was crucially dependent on the financial contributions of well-to-do citizens. In the last two centuries BC, that is, we see the emergence at Sparta of the widespread Hellenistic practice of euergetism, whereby the civic community was placed in a position of financial dependence on a small group of citizen-benefactors publicly distanced from their fellows by an increasingly elaborate system of honours. This régime was embedded in the city's system of government, in the sense that magistrates regularly performed liturgies or financial services at their own expense; for this reason the term of Pratolaus as '*agoranomos* in charge of the roads' could be described simultaneously as both a 'magistracy (*arkhē*) and liturgy'. The emergence of a class of politician-benefactors constitutes the other facet of the oligarchic arrangements for government described earlier in this chapter. This development was facilitated by the Roman preference for seeing local government in the hands of the well-to-do and by the absence, at Sparta as universally in the Greek world, of regular income-tax: the burden of financing civic services, in Sparta's case made heavier by the advance of urbanisation in the Hellenistic period, fell largely on the shoulders of the rich, who for the most part were willing to bear it, at least until the third century, as the price to pay for local political predominance.[17]

This dependence first emerges in the evidence with the appeal from the city-magistrates, contained in a decree from the mid-first century BC, for help from 'those [citizens] well supplied with ready money' with payments to Rome. The earliest evidence for the liturgical character of the chief magistracies appears in the triumviral period, when some local coin-issues were funded by the *gerontes*, ephors and *nomophulakes* respectively. But we find the Spartan system of euergetism most clearly revealed in the peaceful and relatively well-documented conditions of the post-Neronian period. To begin with, the practice of inscribing local political careers and the names of annual magistrates requires comment. Over 170 lists of magistrates are attested (App.IIA), some two-thirds of them inscribed under Trajan, Hadrian, and Pius, although the practice began in the first century BC, probably under Augustus, and endured well into the third century. The settings for these lists were places of public resort. Many seem to have been displayed in the vicinity of the agora by the offices of the magistrates whom they record, as with the lists inscribed on free-standing, sometimes double-sided, *stēlai*; also with those apparently inscribed on columns or other parts of public buildings. The other chief setting, where about a third of them were displayed, was the theatre, where they were inscribed on the walls of the east and west *parodoi*, the two chief approaches into the theatre from below the acropolis, and on the covering slabs of the drain which circled the orchestra.

These catalogues were inscribed by official act, as is shown by the abbreviation 'by decree of the *boulē*' which follows two lists of second-century *gerontes*. The career inscriptions (counting each entry individually) number some sixty-five. They first appear under Trajan and are most numerous, once more, in his and the following two reigns, although they are still attested in the later Severan period. Their setting was equally public: notably the theatre, where fifteen were inscribed. As for the purpose of the lists, Chrimes favoured a functional explanation, seeing them as public records, 'making possible the dating of all sorts of legal contracts'. If this was their purpose, however, it would have been sufficient for an interested person to consult the city-archives, without the city having to go to the expense of inscription. Nor does her explanation take account of the fact that the same catalogue could be inscribed in duplicate (nine examples) or even triplicate (five examples; cf. App.IIB). As Beard has emphasized, ancient inscriptions, even when their content seems utilitarian to the modern reader, need not always have served primarily as a 'practical tool of reference'. The chief function of the catalogues – and the career-inscriptions too – was surely honorific and political: they were the visible demonstration of oligarchy. The variation in the frequency with which different magistracies had their membership inscribed may well be connected with the varying degree of personal expense involved. On this view, the fact that catalogues of *gerontes*, ephors and *nomophulakes* – posts whose liturgical character in the Late Republic was noted earlier – predominate so resoundingly (App.IIA) suggests that by the second century, as with provincial Greek city-councils elsewhere, membership of the composite *boulē* regularly carried with it the expectation of 'some *quid pro quo* for the honour of being elected'.[18]

The inscriptions define a further group of four offices, the patronomate, gymnasiarchy, *sitōnia* and agoranomate, incumbents of which were normally expected to subsidize the activities associated with their spheres of competence. Leaving aside the peculiarly Spartan office of *patronomos*, discussed in chapter 14, the other three posts have in common that they were all classified in Roman administrative law as liturgies, exemption from eligibility to them being a privilege conferred sparingly by second- and third-century emperors on favoured provincials only. Two of these three, the *sitōnia* (above) and the agoranomate, were associated with the food supply. The agoranomate is first heard of under Augustus and was probably a magistracy of relatively recent origin instituted in response to the elaboration of the city's market-facilities in the Hellenistic age (chapter 10). Assisted variously by five to eight colleagues, along with a staff of freedmen or slaves, the *agoranomos* in the second century was in charge of the *macellum* and the civic granary. In other cities the liturgical character of the office derived from local expectations that *agoranomoi* would themselves subsidize the cost of staples during times of scarcity. That Spartan *agoranomoi* faced similar expectations is suggested by the case of Pomponius Panthales Diogenes Aristeas, *agoranomos* in the early 220s, who received the unusual honour of no fewer than twelve public statues for 'the unsurpassed generosity of his *agoranomia* and the lavishness of his labours in office and of his entire term'.[19]

The Spartan gymnasiarchy makes its first appearance in the inscriptions under the later Flavian emperors (*IG* v.1.480). That this post too was a relatively recent institution is suggested by the fact that its duties were regulated, not by custom, but by law; as late as the Augustan period, comparable functions may have been discharged, not by a gymnasiarch, but by a 'superintendent' (*epimelētēs*) of the gymnasium and his assistants. The importance of the gymnasiarchy in the life of Roman Sparta is underlined by the fact that more incumbents (nineteen) were honoured with public dedications than any other category of local official (the next most frequently honoured group were the *agoranomoi*, of whom only four are known to have been honoured in this way). This importance reflects the central place of the gymnasia in the social and cultural life of Roman Sparta, their facilities now being used both by local participants in the revived training and also by increasing numbers of foreign athletes (chapters 13–14). Of the administrative duties of the gymnasiarch we know only that he was required to provide a daily supply of anointing-oil for festival contestants. No doubt it was this requirement to supply oil to the gymnasia and training-grounds which was chiefly responsible for the post's liturgical character. The munificent C. Iulius Theophrastus under Hadrian gives an idea of the levels of generosity to which a public-spirited gymnasiarch could aspire: 'having bought at 30 denarii the *hudria*, I placed oil in the gymnasium, in the *thermai* (of the refined sort) and in the Machanidae, and I supplied linen towels (?) to all throughout the year'. This price per *hudria* no doubt was a high one, or else Theophrastus would not have bothered to record it; the probability that the oil in question came from his own olive-trees was noted earlier.[20]

With the provision of funds competing with or even superseding any administrative duties, the endowment of a liturgical post became an alternative to the actual holding of office. This practice was frequent in the later second and third centuries, the donor being rewarded with the right to be styled a 'perpetual' (*aiōnios*) incumbent of the post in question. Offices known to have been endowed in this way were the *sitōnia* (once), the hipparchy, an ephebic post (once), the agoranomate (three times) and the gymnasiarchy (six times) – the last figure confirming the view taken above of the gymnasiarchy's pre-eminence.[21]

In the Roman period it was not unknown for wealthy citizens to confer apparently unsolicited benefaction on the city: in this respect the gifts of

C. Iulius Agesilaus under Trajan and the senator Eurycles Herculanus under Hadrian (chapter 8) stand out by virtue of their impressive scale. But the inscriptions suggest that the practice of euergetism was chiefly aimed at the routine maintenance of public services only. To keep the system going, the local authorities devised a range of honours to reward the more generous and *pour encourager les autres*. Honorific statues and the inscriptions which identified them show how fully the common language of euergetism, visual and written, had been absorbed into civic life by the second century. Honorific titles and epithets conferred by public acclamation included those of 'pious and patriotic', 'noble and just' and 'son of the city and council'. 'Magnanimity' (*megalopsukhia*) and 'zealous ambition' (*philotimia*) expressed through financial generosity were civic virtues repeatedly held up for praise in statue-dedications; the description of a term of office as 'incomparable' (*asunkritos*) invited the emulation of others, as did the claim that one honorand had 'outdone his peers in the zealous ambition of his gymnasiarchy'. Competitive *philotimia* was further encouraged by the foundation under Trajan, within an archaising framework discussed in chapter 14, of the 'contest for best citizen' (*agōn tēs aristopoliteias*). This contest was regulated by a law and victory was formally conferred by the citizen-assembly. Victors received 'honours' (*timai*), among them the title of *aristopoliteutēs* and the right to a public statue. We have no clear evidence for the criteria of victory. But that outstanding public service was gauged largely in financial terms is suggested by the fact that victors can usually be identified as well-to-do notables and by the later appearance of the honorific title 'perpetual *aristopoliteutēs*'. This was taken by Wilhelm to indicate a victor 'whose example stood for all time'. But it seems better understood, on analogy with his own definition of 'eternal' magistracies, as a title conferred in return for the gift of a civic endowment.[22]

The language of the inscriptions conveys an ideal of civic service and does not necessarily reflect the true appetite among the wealthy for the burdens of public office. But it is only in the third century that clear evidence emerges for reluctance to hold office and the introduction of compulsion (chapter 9). Increasing pressure from Roman tax-demands seems to offer at least a partial explanation for these developments, since the burden of payment would have fallen in the first instance on local magistrates. At Athens, perhaps in about 230, the council of 500 was enlarged to 750 members so as to increase the pool of magistrates eligible for liturgies. It is just possible that the epigraphic references to a city-council and city-councillors of the common Greek type which appear at Sparta from about 200 onwards (see above) echo an enlargement for similar ends of the composite council of thirty-four – through the creation, for instance, of a new class of supernumerary councillors.[23]

Chapter twelve

Local government II:
the social and economic base

Among the free population of Sparta, until the Antonine constitution of 212 or 213 the chief formal status-division remained the one between citizen and non-citizen. Given the largely honorific function of Roman Sparta's 'epigraphic habit', the citizens (or *Lakedaimonioi*, as they were officially called) about whom we know most are those whose office-holding is so copiously documented in local inscriptions. That these Spartans formed an economically privileged group within the civic community is implied by the liturgical character of local politics, which, as we have seen (chapter 11), favoured men of property as candidates for office. As well as its pronounced aristocratic element (below), this same group was probably socially privileged in a broader sense, since it is now known from the letter of M. Aurelius to the Athenians that Greek cities in the second century, to guard against infiltration by persons of freedman descent, not uncommonly required proof of three generations of free birth (*trigonia*) from candidates for major magistracies (although at Sparta no less than at Athens, as we shall see, ambitious and well-connected persons of freedman stock were able to evade such restrictions). Under Roman influence Sparta's chief magistrates and their families also came to constitute a legally privileged group. From the reign of Hadrian, Roman law recognized as a status-group with special rights the so-called *honestiores* or 'more honourable', who included not only the Roman aristocracy but also the councillors (*decuriones* in the Latin west, *bouleutai* in the Greek east) of the provincial cities, together with their families. As was seen in chapter 11, the equivalent of a municipal *boulē* at Roman Sparta was the composite council of the *gerontes*, ephors, and *nomophulakes*. Like decurions elsewhere these magistrates enjoyed a special status locally. Under the principate, they possessed the privilege of *sitēsis* or meals at public expense (chapter 14). They also had special seats at civic festivals. That this was so in the sanctuary of Artemis Orthia, where the annual ephebic contests were held (chapter 14), is suggested by the marble bench dedicated in the late first century BC by two Spartans, one of them a former *gerōn*, the other almost certainly an ex-magistrate too: as Dawkins saw, this was an 'official seat', 'a less ostentatious predecessor of the magisterial tribune' built probably on the same spot during the tetrarchic remodelling of the sanctuary. Secondly, excavations in the theatre produced an inscribed *stēlē* (not *in situ*) with the one word '*boulēs*' or 'belonging to the council'; although the text is not firmly dated, its letter-forms would best suit a date no earlier than the second century. Woodward made the attractive suggestion that this *stēlē* served to demarcate a zone of seating within the *cavea* set aside for 'councillors' – to be identified, in that case, with the *gerontes*, ephors and *nomophulakes*; if Woodward is right, it is likely that seating arrangements in the *cavea* as a whole were organised so as to mirror the local status-hierarchy, as in Graeco-Roman theatres elsewhere. In conclusion, given that Sparta's composite council was already marked in the first half of the second century by a strong hereditary element, it seems justified to refer, from this period onwards if no earlier, to a Spartan curial or bouleutic class, comprising the pool of families which provided the city with its ephors, *nomophulakes* and gerontes, together with its chief liturgists.[1]

This curial class should not be thought of as an altogether homogeneous body. A unique reference in the Spartan decree of consolation from the reign of Gaius or Claudius to 'the first houses of the city', to which the deceased T. Statilius Lamprias of Epidaurus was related, shows that, like other provincial Greek cities, Roman Sparta had its 'leading men' (*prōtoi* or *primores viri*), who were distinguished by their prestige from other magistrates. Variations of wealth certainly contributed to such inequalities of personal standing. That a few Spartans were much richer than their compatriots is indicated by the existence of local families (four are firmly attested) of senatorial and equestrian rank, able by definition to meet the census-requirements for those orders of 1,000,000 and 400,000 sesterces respectively. Other well-to-do Spartans can be recognised in C. Iulius Agesilaus, who endowed the Leonidea under Trajan with 10,500 denarii (44,000 sesterces) and the Urania with an unknown, but probably larger, amount and in C. Iulius Theophrastus, the total cost of whose grain-subsidy under Trajan amounted (on one calculation) to 560,000 sesterces. By contrast, C. Iulius Arion, a curial Spartan of the Antonine period, was evidently a man of more modest means, since he took pride in a relatively humble display of euergetism, boasting that he had waived his entitlement to overtime pay from public funds on returning from an embassy to Naples which had lasted longer than planned.[2]

Another highly valued (and unequally distributed) source of personal prestige was noble birth or *eugeneia*, public praise of which emerges as a persistent theme in Roman Sparta's honorific epigraphy. Thus a local notable from the early principate was lauded for 'having confirmed by his own excellence the glory of his descent', a matron of the later Antonine period for having 'served publicly in a manner worthy of the nobility of her house'. Perhaps the most striking testimony to the aristocratic values of local upper-class society comes in the decree of consolation for the Spartan and Epidaurian kin of T. Statilius Lamprias, which includes a six-line paean to his high birth, partly derived from his kinship with one of Sparta's 'first houses', the Voluseni. This inscription and others detail some of the lineages which inspired such praise and show that the Roman city's office-holding families included a hard core claiming descent from the aristocracy of Classical Sparta. Among the pedigrees traced from deities and local heroes the most frequently encountered ancestors are Heracles and the divine twins or Dioscuri, the former the progenitor of the old Spartan royal houses and other families in the Dorian aristocracy of Classical times, the latter intimately linked with the institution of the dual kingship. Other lineages were traced back to historical figures, including unspecified 'kings' and the famous generals Brasidas (chapter 7) and Lysander. Careful maintenance of these genealogies is shown by the inscriptions which enumerate the precise number of generations separating some latter-day 'Heraclid', 'Dioscurid', or 'descendant of Poseidon' from his alleged forefather(s), as by the claim of a Hadrianic magistrate to be 'the most senior of the Heraclid race' (also indicating that the Classical Spartan notion of the Heraclids as a distinct descent-group was still alive under the principate). The generally oligarchic tenor of local government in provincial Greek cities meant that Sparta was by no means unusual in this public parading of noble birth, which the thinking of educated Greek *possédants* now integrated into the moral basis for the claims of their class to local political domination. Genealogical snobbery in the provinces was further stimulated by the attitude of the Roman aristocracy, which was prepared to be impressed by the claims of birth in its personal relations with provincials, as is shown in Sparta's case by the episode involving an anonymous descendant of Brasidas, whom Augustus released from prison on learning of his ancestry (chapter 7).[3]

A third source of personal prestige within Sparta's curial class rested with a family's standing with Rome. The network of personal ties between *bien pensant* Spartans and their Roman counterparts can only rarely be glimpsed, as with Philippus, Cicero's client (chapter 7), or the well-born Tyndares, whose playful *inamorato* was the Vespasianic consular L. Mestrius Florus (chapter 13). Under the principate, the one readily visible pointer to such connections lies with the evidence for viritane grants of Roman citizenship to individual Spartans and their families. Generally speaking these grants, which were in the emperor's gift, were only conferred on provincials in good standing with Rome; usually they seem to have been requested by the recipients themselves, who then assumed the *praenomen* and *nomen* either of the emperor in question or of the influential Roman 'broker' who had interceded at court on their behalves. In Sparta's case, the occasional instance of a family which owed its *civitas* to the emperor's direct interest can be surmised, as with C. Iulius Eurycles, the friend of Augustus, or the athletic family of the (P.) Aelii, quite possibly enfranchised by Hadrian in person on one of his two visits to Sparta. The interventions of 'brokers', however, is indicated by those Roman names of Spartan *cives* which can be shown to derive from known governors of Achaia or other high-ranking Romans, as with the (P.) Memmii, who gained their Roman citizenship from P. Memmius Regulus, governor from 35 to 44. Although increasingly commonplace among the city's 'leading men', in the first half of the second century Roman citizenship was still a distinction within the larger pool of Sparta's curial families, to judge from two complete catalogues of *gerontes* from the reigns of Trajan and Pius, in which no more than 13 per cent and 27 per cent respectively of the twenty-three magistrates were also *cives*.[4]

It should by now be apparent that – broadly speaking – Roman Sparta's social structure followed a pattern widespread in Greek cities under Roman rule. Once the fog of our ignorance begins to clear in the mid-first century BC, we can observe a society scarcely less sharply stratified than in the days before the reforming kings, its upper reaches occupied by a class of property-owners enjoying official Roman support, its apex by a small élite of aristocratic 'first houses'. The citizen-body of Roman times presumably included at least some descendants of those new citizens of Cleomenes III and Nabis who had survived the respective débâcles of 222 and 188 BC with their status and at least some of their property intact (chapters 4–6). But it is difficult to resist the conclusion that the existence of a self-consciously 'old' aristocracy in the Roman period to a large extent reflects the success of the various groups of Spartan exiles in regaining their patrimonies during the early years of Sparta's *sumpoliteia* with the Achaean League. The existence of self-styled 'descendants of Heracles' at Roman Sparta does not in itself, of course, demand this conclusion: pedigrees could be faked. But there are two reasons for thinking that some of these 'old' families were descended from the aristocracy of Classical Sparta (making due allowance for adoption and descent through the female line). Firstly, let us return to the pedigrees themselves, some of which were clearly intended to associate their scions with the heroic age of Greek myth. As Woodward observed, the lineages of different families claiming the same mythic ancestor(s) were not always synchronous. For example, if we allow the usual three generations per century, the pedigrees of P. Memmius Deximachus (Pius) and M. Aurelius Aristocrates (Severan), respectively forty-second and forty-fourth in descent from the Dioscuri, placed their divine progenitors *c.*1250 BC, the other, Heraclid, pedigree of Aristocrates putting this hero four generations earlier, *c.*1400 BC. These pedigrees actually reached back to the Bronze Age, 1250 BC coinciding with the Herodotean date for the Trojan war; they seem to depend on the Greek chronographic tradition and could as easily be Hellenistic or Roman as Classical inventions. But the pedigrees of Eurycles Herculanus (Trajan/Hadrian), thirty-sixth in descent from the Dioscuri, and the anonymous high-priest of Constantinian times, forty-fifth in descent from the same, reached no further back than the eleventh century, placing the divine twins *c*.1100 and *c*.1050 BC respectively. It is possible that these two at least are genuinely preserved lineages, reaching back to (say) the sixth or fifth century BC, since they share with other heroic pedigrees of that period the same curious inability 'to reach back to a plausible date for the Trojan War' – perhaps because their true origins lay in the unsettled conditions of the early 'Dark Ages'.[5]

Secondly, these heroic pedigrees were intimately linked, in a decidedly archaic manner, with priestly functions: out of thirty-four attested civic priesthoods at Roman Sparta, the succession to all but five was hereditary among some seven lineages. Of the cults in question, although some are first attested in the Roman period (in itself no argument against their antiquity, given the paucity of evidence for Classical Spartan religion), others were demonstrably venerable and lay at the heart of the Roman city's official religious life – notably those of Artemis Orthia, Apollo at Amyclae, Helen and the Dioscuri at Phoebaeum and Demeter and Core at the Eleusinium. With cults of this stature, it is hard to believe that their priesthoods were once disposed of by lot or election, becoming hereditary only in later antiquity as a result of some putative 'decline' in traditional piety (nowadays a questionable notion anyway) and consequent melting away of willing candidates for priestly office. On the contrary, the instances of priestly functionaries at Roman Sparta claiming descent from the deities whom they served suggests that these cults were once (no later than the Archaic period?) aristocratic family- or clan-cults which subsequently became absorbed into the civic domain: thus Tib. Claudius Aristocrates, a Flavian member of a leading local family, was a 'priest and descendant of Poseidon'; and the Memmii, the Pomponii and the (Sex.) Pompeii, the aristocratic families which, under the principate, provided the priesthood at Phoebaeum, all claimed the Dioscuri as their ancestors. Aristocratic families of hereditary seers (*manteis*), prophesying at civic religious ceremonies, are also attested at Sparta from the Augustan age to the mid-third century; of the two mantic lineages which can be distinguished, one of them allegedly descended from Apollo *via* the mantic clan of the Elean Iamids, a branch of which had settled at Classical Sparta, their funerary monument still to be seen in the mid-second century. The existence of a priestly aristocracy at Classical Sparta is now recognized, one recalling its counterpart at Athens in the same period. There the survival of hereditary priesthoods into the Imperial age is well attested, notably at Eleusis, where the chief priesthoods were monopolised by leading Athenian families in the 'descent-groups' (*genē*) of the Eumolpids and Ceryces. The most economical explanation of the Spartan evidence is to posit a similar continuity, with any mid-Hellenistic disruption to traditional patterns of hereditary religious authority to a large extent being reversed by the aristocratic 'restoration' of the post-Nabian period.[6]

Moving down the social hierarchy, on the fringes of the Roman city's curial class can be detected a group of citizens pursuing professional careers in Sparta and neighbouring towns, including architects, one of whom served on the magisterial board of *hieromnēmones* in the mid-third century, presumably in his capacity as adviser on sacred building-works; doctors (chapter 13); and sports instructors (chapter 14). Lower on the scale of respectability could be found itinerant Spartan actors (chapter 13), and, not before the Flavian period, a Spartan gladiator, who died at Thessalonice. Inscriptions from the Augustan age attest a still humbler stratum of the citizen-population engaged in artisanal activity, the old ban on which for Spartan citizens is unlikely to have survived the reign of Nabis. At this occupational level, as the same inscriptions make clear, free men mixed with slaves and freedmen. Prosopography brings out clearly the links between this servile population and rich households, as with the Tyndares, Eurybanassa, Ageta and Pantimia attested as Augustan slave-owners, all of whom seem to have belonged to leading local families. The size of this population is likely, therefore, to have been relatively small, although it was swollen by the limited use of slaves and freedmen in the civic services, where they appear under the principate as scribes, cooks (*mageiroi*) and magistrates' attendants. With the disappearance of Helotage (below) and opportunities to capture slaves as war-booty, the Roman city's chief source of supply was presumably the slave-market – a view finding corroboration in a Trajanic inscription which records a slave of Syrian origin, apparently sold into bondage from his home village, the otherwise obscure Thenae; 'Ctesiphon', the name of an Augustan slave, also suggests an oriental origin. A certain amount of home-breeding is perhaps indicated by the two public slaves called Nicocles in the reign of Marcus, one, presumably the other's son, distinguished as 'the younger'.[7]

Some form of Helotage seems to have survived the mass-enfranchisement of Helots by Nabis (chapter 5), since Strabo, living under Augustus, although he wrote of this institution in the past tense, believed that it had survived until the Roman 'domination' (*epikrateia*). From another passage, referring to the loyalty of Helots to Rome when Sparta was 'under a tyranny', Gitti tried to argue that Helotage survived until the time of Eurycles. It is reasonable to doubt, however, whether Strabo would have referred to the emperor's protégé as a 'tyrant' – a term which he scrupulously avoids in those passages where Eurycles is clearly in question (chapter 7): the reference is surely to the 'tyrant' Nabis. If so, by Roman 'domination' Strabo probably had in mind the watershed of 146/5 BC. But it remains questionable whether Helotage was ever formally suppressed, then or later; surviving families of Helot-status working the land as tenant-farmers may simply have slid into much the same status as that of the rural peasantries of Roman Bithynia and Egypt, who, although technically 'free', were without local political rights.[8]

It remains to consider the extent to which Roman Sparta's social structure showed signs of flexibility, allowing promotions in personal status and some replenishment of the curial class from below. Although Sparta under Roman rule was not a cosmopolitan city in the same sense as Corinth or Athens, it seems fairly clear that limited opportunities for social mobility did exist, at any rate in the second century. To begin with, prosopography suggests the infiltration into the curial class and the gymnasium of a trickle of freedmen and their descendants. A handful of magistrates with Roman citizenship can be discerned whose *cognomina* were certainly consonant with, even if they do not prove, servile origins: P. Memmius Melichrus ('Honey-coloured'), a Trajanic *nomophulax*; Iulius Lycus ('Wolf'), an early Antonine *gerōn*; and two late Antonine *sunagoranomoi* (junior colleagues of the *agoranomos*), the Memmii Anthus ('Flower') and Soterichus. All these names occur with varying frequency among the vast servile population of Imperial Rome, one of them, 'Lycus', being firmly attested as a slave's name at Sparta itself; they contrast markedly with the characteristic nomenclature of the Roman city's leading families, in which names with epic ('Eurybanassa'), aristocratic ('Pratolaus', 'Damocratidas'), horsey ('Melesippus', 'Zeuxippus') and royal ('Agesilaus', 'Areus', and 'Cleombrotus') overtones are frequent. The combination of low-status *cognomina* with the possession of Roman citizenship strongly suggests that the magistrates in question owed their Roman status to manumission rather than viritane grants: in particular, the *nomen* 'Memmius' points fairly conclusively towards the slave-household of the aristocratic clan of the Memmii, enfranchised in the second quarter of the first century. The way in which such households could act as breeding-grounds for the socially ambitious slave is perhaps intimated by the dedication, couched in verse so as to display its donor's pretensions to cultivation, of one Aphrodisius, slave of Tib. Claudius Pratolaus, a son of the senator Brasidas. Their ties of clientship with such important families apparently allowed some favoured individuals of freedman stock to go on to overcome the juridical obstacles to their acquisition of local citizenship and candidacy for curial offices. The onomastic difficulties in the way of diagnosing servile origins of other Spartans of this type are demonstrated by the case of one C. Iulius Eurycles, who held the prestigious ephebic office of *boagos* in the early 130s. He is normally taken to be a kinsman of his distinguished older contemporary and namesake, the senator C. Iulius Eurycles Herculanus. If so, however, his existence is at odds with the other evidence that Herculanus died a few years later without leaving a direct male heir. An alternative is to see the younger Eurycles as the descendant of a Euryclid freedman, his *cognomen* a mark of deference to his family's powerful patron; the same onomastic practice has been observed among the clients of important families at second-century Athens.[9]

If the identification of the *boagos* along these lines is correct, it appears that by the second century the Roman city's ephebic training, which one would normally expect to have been the preserve of free-born youths, was open no less than its magistracies to infiltration by well-connected persons of freedman stock. There is other evidence to associate the milieu of the gymnasium with persons of varying social status, their presence partly reflecting civic measures to ensure that levels of recruitment into the showcase of the 'revived' Lycurgan customs – the ephebic training – remained acceptable. Chrimes claimed to distinguish two categories of Spartans for whom access to magistracies depended on passage through the ephebic training. However, one of these, that of the *sunephēboi*, can be set aside. The term *sunephēbos* first makes its appearance in the Flavian period to describe a member of an ephebic band led by a fellow-ephebe or 'herd-leader' (*boagos*); similar teams of 'synephebes' are attested at Roman Athens, there under the charge of an ephebic official called the systremmatarch. Although *boagoi* often (but by no means invariably, as the case of Eurycles suggests) belonged to prominent local families, it is also clear that some 'synephebes' could be well-born: a 'synephebe' of Herodes Atticus, Corinthas son of Nicephorus, served as a Spartan Panhellene, a post for which, at least at Athens and probably in all member-cities, three generations of good birth (*trigonia*) were normally required; and a mid-Antonine 'synephebe', the aristocratic Callicrates, belonged to one of the Roman city's mantic lineages and may have been the hereditary priest of Apollo at Amyclae. If the term 'synephebe' had no juridical connotations, however, it remains possible that some 'synephebes' were helped through the training by the financial generosity of their *boagoi* (see chapter 14).[10]

The second, more problematic, category comprises the forty-seven or so Spartans described as '*kasen* to so-and-so' in inscriptions ranging from the later second or early first century BC down to the years after 230. Although its etymology is obscure, *kasen* is clearly a congener of *kasis* ('brother') and *kasioi* (plural), this last – according to the late lexicographer Hesychius – meaning 'brothers and cousins' in the same ephebic team, apparently referring to Sparta. Prosopography, however, does not support the view that the ties between Spartans of this category and the contemporaries to whom they were *kasen* were ones of kinship. As Chrimes saw, foster-ties seem rather to be in question: persons in the *kasen* category were apparently educated, or at any rate passed through the ephebic training, at the expense of the families to whose sons they were attached; for this reason it was possible for an individual to be *kasen* to two or even three males within the same family. Foster-ties of a comparable kind, as a result of which youths of unequal standing became 'companions in education' (*suntrophoi*), were not uncommon in the Greek world – they can be detected too, for instance, among the ephebes of Roman Athens. At Sparta the archaic-sounding term *kasen*, no doubt retained in the Imperial period in part for its antique resonances, seems to belong to a peculiarly Spartan foster-terminology, along with the earlier terms *mothax* and *mothōn*. However, the absence of strong ties between Spartans of *kasen*-status and the families which 'fostered' them is suggested by the case of M. Antistius Philocrates son of Philocles, a *gerōn* *c*.100. He can almost certainly be identified with Philocrates son of Philocles, *kasen* to Agesilaus son of Neolaus, who made an ephebic dedication in the Flavian period; his son appears to be the 'Damion son of Antistius Philocrates', *kasen* to Agis son of Cleander, who made an ephebic dedication under Trajan. But the two Spartans to whom the father and son stood in the relation of *kasen* cannot be shown to have been closely related (manifestly they were not themselves father and son). As with the 'synephebes', Chrimes held the view that Spartans of this status were juridically barred from certain high offices. She correctly pointed out that no *kasen* is known to have held the patronomate; one can go further, however, and clarify that none of the thirty-five who are attested in public life is known to have held any of the Roman city's chief liturgical magistracies (patronomate, gymnasiarchy and agoranomate), although one, Sosicrates son of Epaphroditus, held the junior tribal liturgy of *diabetēs*. Financial rather than legal disability seems a better explanation of this pattern; from a Roman point of view, magistrates of *kasen*-status perhaps would have fitted into the class of the *inferiores* or decurions of lesser rank. Moreover, as Woodward saw, that at least some Spartans of *kasen*-status were well-born is suggested by their names: 'Charixenus son of Damocratidas', 'Thrasybulus son of Callicrates', 'Xenocles son of Aristocritus' and so on. Apart from one instance dating from the century after 146 BC, all the evidence for this status belongs to the period after 50. Given that the *kasen*-relationship does not appear to have been embedded in the social matrix of the Roman city, it is tempting to suppose that the status was artificially revived in the later first century, essentially as a recruiting device for the ephebic training, this 'fostership' of appropriately archaising type allowing Spartans from less well-off backgrounds to be financially assisted through the training.[11]

* * * * * *

It remains to consider the economic base of the Roman city's propertied class. 'For the city of Sparta the literary tradition and the monuments exclude any thought of a decline in the Imperial period'. Three recent studies only add weight to Kahrstedt's judgement, which prefaced his economic survey of the Roman city and confirmed the briefly-stated impressions of earlier archaeologists. Roman Sparta's mint, producing a series of bronze issues at irregular intervals down to the reign of Gallienus, was one of the four most active in the Peloponnese, along with Corinth, Patrae and Argos. Long ago, Wace inferred from the sarcophagi in the Sparta Museum the existence of 'a considerable wealthy element in Laconia in the Imperial period'; in fact, Sparta can be classed among the only cities in provincial Achaia, along with Corinth, Patrae and Thespiae, from which finds of imported Attic sarcophagi so far exceed ten. The city has also emerged as one of two in the province affluent enough to support two senatorial families. This last figure keeps Sparta in perspective, however, since it somewhat pales behind the comparable figure of six for Pergamum. Levels of wealth at Roman Sparta, although they placed her among the most prosperous cities in Achaia, remained relatively modest when set beside those of the richest cities of Roman Asia.[12]

Although the resources of Roman Sparta were itemized in some detail by Chrimes, to whom the reader is referred, a consensus has yet to emerge as to the basis of the Roman city's prosperity. Kahrstedt saw the 'opening up' of local marble-sources as the great innovation of the Imperial period. The difficulty with this view is that, although the Roman city possessed plentiful supplies of stone for local purposes (below), the only quarries on home territory known to have produced marble for export are those of Croceae, source of *marmor Lacedaemonium*, a dark green 'porphyry' much in vogue in the Imperial period for the revetment of walls and floors. Strabo knew of the private development of these quarries under Augustus (it would be interesting to know by whom) to satisfy 'Roman luxury'; but a relief-dedication from Croceae, its Latin inscription re-edited with new readings in 1961, shows that by the reign of Domitian they were the property of the emperor, administered on the spot by an Imperial slave. It is unknown exactly when or how this change occurred, although it fits into a larger pattern of concentration into Imperial hands of important mineral resources in the provinces. But it is now clear that the period of local exploitation was relatively short-lived.[13]

Quarries, then, cannot be made to bear the weight of explanation placed on them by Kahrstedt. On the other hand, in the belief that Roman Sparta was famous for no one farming product, the same scholar certainly underestimated the contribution of agriculture (and pastoralism) to local prosperity. Land-ownership had always provided the chief source of private wealth at Sparta, as it continued to do in the Middle Ages. For the Imperial period, the link between the two is shown unequivocally by the impressive monument at Ktirakia; on the view taken in chapter 10, the interests of Spartan families in the fertile region of the Helea make the same point. In this period we hear of or can infer cereal-production (wheat and barley), olive-cultivation and horse-raising. None of these unexceptionable strategies of production was new to the Spartan countryside; their profitability in the Roman period will have largely depended on the intensity with which they were pursued and the size of the available market. Regarding the former, we have the isolated notice in an unexpected source, the panegyric for the emperor Majorian (457–61) composed by Sidonius Apollinaris, revealing 'Lacedaemon' as one of the places which exported olive oil to Rome in late antiquity. In spite of its context, there is no need to doubt this evidence for an export-trade in olive oil at Late Roman Sparta. It points to the emergence under Roman influence of specialized olive-growing estates, relying for the necessary capital investment on wealthy individuals. Smaller neighbouring towns – Gytheum in particular – also offered an outlet for the agricultural products of the city controlling the largest and most fertile territory in Laconia. But the chief market was probably the city of Sparta itself. The increasing orientation of Spartan farming, at least within the immediate vicinity, to the needs of the city, is suggested by the observation of the Laconia Survey that 'small farms of Roman date tend to cluster closely at the bottom of the valleys and along natural lines of communication': evidently the Roman period saw a greater emphasis on the transport of agricultural produce to the city. Although its permanent population may have been relatively small, with the city's emergence in the Imperial period (chapters 13–14) as a cultural and agonistic centre the regular influxes of visitors attracted by the cycle of civic festivals provided local producers with an additional market for their surplus, fluctuating but predictable.[14]

Among the products of the land in the larger sense can be included the stocks of wild animals on Taygetus, which in 400 were drawn on for the consular shows given in Milan and Rome by the Roman general Stilicho. On the basis of this (inaccurately reported) item of evidence, Chrimes conjured up an important trade in Spartan wild beasts and animal-skins. But Stilicho had special ties with the Peloponnese, having campaigned there against Alaric in 397, and may have drawn on these links with the area when arranging his games three years later; if his case cannot be regarded as typical, the export of animals from Taygetus may have been far more sporadic than Chrimes imagined. Another resource, easily overlooked, is the plentiful supply of building materials in the Spartan plain and its environs. As Livia's narrow escape from a forest fire in 40 BC emphasizes, parts of the Spartan countryside were still well-wooded in Roman times. The Roman city was also fortunate to possess a plentiful supply of stone suitable, not only for building, but also for inscribing and sculpting. Marble, varying greatly in colour and quality, but including the white variety admired by Pausanias (iii.14.1) at the theatre, was obtained from the eastern side of Taygetus, where ancient workings have been reported; and ancient quarries for limestone building blocks have now been located just to the north of Sparta. Lastly, the Eurotas plain was well supplied with clay-beds for the manufacture of roof-tiles and bricks. Local demand for all these materials increased in the Imperial period, which saw an expansion, not only of public and private building activity, but also of inscriptional and sculptural production; in the case of the last, local workshops now received commissions for honorific statuary, funerary monuments and decorative pieces for public buildings and private homes. Exploitation of these rural resources, however exactly organized, provided income for the owners of the land on which they were located. We catch a glimpse of the owners only in the case of clay-beds. Roof-tiles and bricks commissioned for use in the public domain were normally stamped to discourage theft. For the most part, where these stamps preserve a name other than that of the eponymous official by whom they were dated, it belongs to the manufacturer, his relationship to the actual owner of the clay-source left in the dark. In one case, however, we have what is certainly an owner's name: 'Eurycles'. The dynast can be recognized here, perhaps as the donor of a public building for which he supplied the roof-tiles from his own clay-beds. Other proprietors in Sparta's vicinity, like the senatorial owners of clay-beds around Imperial Rome, probably also profited, if only indirectly, from the exploitation of this resource when available on their land. But Kahrstedt certainly overstated the case when he identified the contractor Callicrates of the Augustan age with the eponymous *patronomos* of the same name and period and claimed a case of profits from brick and tile manufacture 'smoothing the way' to a career in local politics; other considerations apart, this identification is extremely speculative, since the name in question is one of the commonest at Sparta (Bradford lists seventy instances!).[15]

If land-ownership constituted the basis of personal wealth at Roman Sparta, as is here believed to be the case, it remains to consider the ideologically thorny question of the economic rôle of manufacture and trade. It is probable that the Roman city served not only as a consumption centre for local landowners and their households but also as a regional centre of exchange, a function mediated both through permanent markets (see chapter 10) and seasonal fairs: thus, in a linkage of commerce and religion familiar in antiquity, we find the annual festival of the Leonidea accompanied by a fair, at which the city encouraged the presence of travelling merchants by waiving the usual local taxes on imports and sales. The demand for goods and services generted by townsfolk and visitors sustained an urban artisanate: thus an Augustan inscription records among the tradesmen in attendance on a civic festival a sculptor, a gilder, a spinner, a dyer, a baker, a cook, a provisioner, a wreath-seller and a maker of palms. The economic significance in aggregate of such craft-activity at Roman Sparta is hard to gauge; at any rate, although an imitator of the products of others (such as sarcophagi and, at a humbler level, clay lamps), the city was not famous for any manufactured product, once we accept that 'Laconian' was used as a trade-name in the Roman period (and earlier), both of craft-goods and natural products, with no implications for the place of manufacture. In the absence of good evidence to the contrary, the market for the craft-goods of the town is best seen as mainly local and regional (if tourists took away cheap souvenirs, as they seem to have done at Roman Corinth and may have done at Sparta, such a trade is of cultural rather than economic significance).[16]

As for imports, the little evidence which survives relates mostly to exotic objects: oriental slaves; sarcophagi from Athens; and precious marbles for the upper end of the local sculpting and building trades from Proconnesus, Carystus, Larissa and the Docimium quarries at Synnada. But petty wares, as we saw in chapter 10, were reaching the Hellenistic city and continued to do so in the Roman period: among them we can recognise the imports of clay-lamps from Italy, Corinth and Athens which, presumably, gave rise to the attested manufacture of local imitations. The only specific evidence for the importing of staples relates to Egyptian grain under Hadrian (see chapter 11). But the not uncommon grain-shortages of the second century suggest that resort was had to imports on other occasions too; in this respect it may be significant that among the cities with which Sparta enjoyed friendly ties under Antoninus Pius (chapter 8) were Cyrene and Puteoli, the former an exporter of grain, the latter one of the grain-ports of Imperial Rome; and, for what it is worth, the destinations of the Spartan shipowner of Philostratus (below) included Sicily and Carthage, both grain-exporting areas under the principate.[17]

In sum, the impression given by the – admittedly sparse – evidence is that Sparta's trade with the outside world, already marked by the early second century BC (chapter 5), increased in the early empire, a time when levels of trade surged throughout the Mediterranean. Before the third century, however, when Sparta's status as a free city ceased to protect her against frequent Roman tax-demands, it is questionable to what extent fiscal pressure from outside played a part in this development; the stimulus may have come equally from increasing urbanization, the needs of visitors, and the conspicuous consumption, revealed through archaeology, of rich Spartans. In the absence of good evidence to the contrary, the volume of this trade, which was probably dominated, at least in value, by luxury goods, is best seen as relatively modest; nor should the numbers of associated personnel be exaggerated. Although the slight evidence for the presence of Roman businessmen at Sparta (a bilingual epitaph for one D. Livius Zeuxis) should not be overlooked, of the foreigners noted at Roman Sparta by Kahrstedt, the inscription attesting a group of resident *xenoi* at Amyclae has since been shown to be a forgery; and the presence at Sparta of overseas notables such as Flavius Asclepiades of Palestinian Caesarea should be understood in terms of cultural, not economic, activity (see chapter 13). It is none the less possible that commercial activity, at least for a few Spartans, was a significant source of personal wealth. The only Spartan trader of whom we know for certain was one Troilus, whose inscribed epitaph (second or third century) commemorates the devotion of his life to 'labouring across much of man's unchanging earth and striving to sail the unremitting waves of the open sea, in order that sudden fortune might give him something good'. Clearly enough he was a small operator, the sort of person in whose hands seems to have lain immediate responsibility for most movements of merchandise throughout antiquity. But the indirect involvement of high status Spartans, whether as money-lenders or owners of ships, using their slaves or freedmen as middlemen, should not be excluded. It is difficult to know what to make of the tale told by Philostratus in his *Life of Apollonius* of a young Spartan shipowner of noble ancestry, the descendant of 'gymnasiarchs and ephors and *patronomoi*', who himself went on trading voyages to Sicily and Carthage (see above) in contravention of the Lycurgan customs, to be talked to his senses at the last moment by Apollonius during his visit to Sparta in 61. As they do over the *Life* in general, scholars differ as to the historicity of this episode; it was taken as evidence for the existence and status of commercial activity at Roman Sparta by as astute a historian as Victor Ehrenberg; but for Tigerstedt it was a piece of 'free invention'. On the one hand it seems incredible that any provincial Greek city would try a citizen for engaging in commerce; on the other, Philostratus was familiar with Severan Sparta, as the combination of magistracies which he uses to demonstrate the young man's good birth shows, and it is not impossible that he himself concocted this tale, which hinged on the unseemly directness of the young man's involvement in trade, from personal knowledge of Spartan notables with more discreetly managed commercial interests. At any rate, this view is not contradicted by the close ties of certain Spartan families with the port of Gytheum (chapter 10) nor by the evidence, discussed above, for the entry of descendants of freedmen into local politics.[18]

In assessing the resource-base of the Roman city, finally, we need to look beyond her frontiers. Within the south-eastern Peloponnese Sparta seems to have continued to exercise an economic predominance in spite of the nominal autonomy of the Eleutherolacones. The desire to shine on a larger stage attracted benefaction from at least one ambitious notable in a minor nearby town: in the Severan age M. Aurelius Pancratidas, a citizen of New Taenarum (Caenepolis), used his personal fortune, based on the resources of his native community, to display his *philotimia* at Sparta 'in the most serviceable ways' and was rewarded with Spartan citizenship and other honours. As the largest urban centre in the region, Sparta is found supplying specialist skills to neighbouring towns. Thus in the last century BC Gytheum had recourse to the services of a Spartan doctor and arms-trainer; in the next century a Spartan letter-cutter found employment at Cardamyle; and an epitaph from second-century Cythera reveals a local doctor who trained at Sparta (and, more surprisingly, at Eleutherolaconian Boeae). Spartan notables owned estates in adjacent towns, although on what scale is hard to gauge: the clearest case, that of Eurycles in Asopus, may also have been one of the least typical. A second instance is recognizable at Calamae, a village in the territory of Thuria, where the city of Sparta set up a statue-dedication for a (deceased?) member of a resident-family of Spartan citizens. One city's setting up of an official dedication on the territory of another was not uncommon in the Roman period, requiring simply the permission of the civic authority concerned; at Sparta itself the city of Smyrna is found making a dedication under Trajan; hence the text from Calamae need not necessarily, as Kahrstedt asserted, belong to the period of Spartan possession of Thuria in the early principate; its overall tenor, in fact, would sit better in the second century. Its language, praising the honorand for his 'piety towards his parents, his moderation and his education (*paideia*)', shows that he was a youth; probably these qualities had emerged into civic view during service as a Spartan ephebe. As his family was clearly one of standing at Sparta, its residence at rural Calamae is best explained in terms of landed interests there, however acquired (see below). Thirdly, if we allow his identification or close kinship with the 'Tib. Claudius Menalcidas son of Eudamus' honoured at Sparta with a civic dedication early in the second century, another Spartan whose landed base lay outside Sparta can be recognised in the Tib. Claudius Menalcidas, fragments of whose family-tomb, decorated with sculpted reliefs, have been found in the little Eleutherolaconian town of Zarax.[19]

As for the ways in which Spartans acquired property in neighbouring towns, one was through conferment of 'the right to own land and a house', a privilege quite commonly granted to individual Spartans in the second and first centuries BC, to judge from a series of honorific decrees from Arcadian Orchomenus (see chapter 6), Cotyrta, Geronthrae, Gytheum, the Lacedaemonian League and (significantly) Thuria. In Gytheum's case, the Spartans were rewarded for professional services; but the others, including the aristocratic-sounding Pelops son of

Laodamas (Cotyrta) and Damocharis son of Timoxenus, an Augustan *patronomos* (Thuria), were notables who used their standing at home to perform political services for the communities in question. The fact that in two cases the decrees are explicitly said to have been solicited by the honorands (Geronthrae and Cotyrta) suggests that these grants of property-rights were not purely empty honours but were sometimes sought after and subsequently exercised. A second route to land-ownership abroad was through intermarriage between the families of Spartan and foreign notables. Under the principate such unions were not uncommon within the Spartan élite; thus the Voluseni intermarried with the Statilii of Epidaurus and (it seems) a Megalopolitan house; the Memmii were doubly related to the same Statilii and also married into a hierophantic house of Messene; it has been argued that the sister of Herodes Atticus, Claudia Tisamenis, married a Spartan; and a Spartan *patronomos* married into the family of M. Aurelius Pancratidas of New Taenarum. Through dowries and inheritances these inter-family ties brought about a circulation of wealth within the provincial aristocracy: Eurycles Herculanus was a testamentary adoptee of a Corinthian notable, L. Vibullius Pius (in this case no tie of kinship is as yet attested); and it is not unreasonable suppose that through Claudia Tisamenis (one of whose testamentary dispositions, the erection of a family statue-group in her marital home-city, is actually on record) the Spartan relations of Herodes Atticus came to share in some of his family's vast wealth. The possession of Roman citizenship may well, at this social level, have facilitated the institution of heirs in another city, so helping to foster a supra-civic landowning class. A case in point from the mid-first century is the adoption by the Epidaurian T. Statilius Timocrates of his daughter's son, who, although a Spartan, was also a Roman citizen, his father being P. Memmius Pratolaus (III); in this way, the name and property of the Statilii passed to a branch of the Memmian clan.[20]

Chapter thirteen

High culture and agonistic festivals

The cultural sterility of Classical Sparta was notorious in antiquity, as it remains today. Although there is a danger of exaggeration where the decorative arts are concerned, it remains clear that literacy was 'very thinly spread' and that the city as a whole played no part in the intellectual revolution of the fifth and fourth centuries BC. By contrast, there is a large amount of evidence, brought together in this chapter for the first time, to show that the 'normalization' of Spartan society in the course of the Hellenistic period brought with it the city's reabsorption into the mainstream of Greek cultural life. Two major aspects of this process are charted here: firstly, the Roman city's links with contemporary Greek 'high' culture, sufficiently developed by the fourth century for Sparta to emerge as a minor centre of higher studies; and, secondly, the foundation at Sparta by the third century of no fewer than three agonistic festivals of international status, as a consequence of which the city acquired a certain prominence on the Roman Empire's agonistic circuit.[1]

The first clear indication of a change in traditional Spartan attitudes to 'cultivation' (*paideia*) is to be found in the clutch of local authors writing works on Spartan antiquities in the last three centuries BC and under the early principate. The antiquarian bias of Hellenistic scholasticism provides this activity with its larger context; if more of these writers could be dated with any precision, it might be possible to link them with the archaizing movement at Sparta which began in earnest with the 'restoration' of the Lycurgan customs in the period after 146/5 BC (see chapter 14). The best known of them, Sosibius, was active at a somewhat earlier date, however: between the years 250–150 BC, 'and probably closer to the lower date'. He wrote a series of works still consulted in the Byzantine age, their subject-matter including Spartan cults and customs, a rustic form of Laconian mime, and the Archaic lyric poet Alcman. As Jacoby emphasized, to judge from the surviving fragments Sosibius' interest in the past was antiquarian rather than political, so that there is little reason to link him directly with the reinvention of 'Lycurgan' Sparta for statist ends by Cleomenes III (chapter 4). On the contrary, his philological and chronographic interests suggest a tie with intellectual centres abroad, Ptolemaic Alexandria in particular, with which Sparta enjoyed a close association for much of the third century BC (chapters 3–4). Of the other writers, all but one are little more than names in the encyclopaedic work of the third-century sophist Athenaeus or in lexicographical entries (Molpis, Nicocles, Hippasus, Aristocles, Timocrates, Polycrates, Diophantus and Pausanias). The slightly better-known Aristocrates son of Hipparchus wrote a work on Spartan history which Plutarch used in his *Life of Lycurgus*. His name and patronymic suggest an aristocratic Spartan and his assignation by Jacoby to the early principate is confirmed by an unpublished inscription in the Sparta Museum.[2]

These authors show that a local literary tradition had taken firm root at Sparta by the Augustan period. The way to this development was paved by the cultural aspirations of the class of *possédants* reestablished in 188 BC under the aegis of the Achaean League, at least some of whom sought to emulate the '*éducation soignée*' characteristic of their peers in Hellenistic cities elsewhere. The habit among wealthy Spartan families of sending their children abroad for their education was probably first formed in this period. Among the pupils of the famous Stoic philosopher Panaetius of Rhodes, who taught at Athens in the later second century BC, was a certain 'Gorgus the Lacedaemonian'; like many other cultured Greeks in this period and later, Gorgus seems to have been sufficiently enamoured of Athens and its intellectual delights to become a naturalized Athenian citizen, since in all probability he can be recognised in the Gorgus 'of the deme Sphettus' who joined with other foreign students and their teachers to serve on an Athenian festival-commission in about 150 BC. Somewhat later (*c.*100 BC) should be placed 'Demetrius the Laconian', a minor Epicurean philosopher known to Strabo as a student of Protarchus of Bargylia in Caria and now identified with the homonymous author of fragmentary Epicurean writings found at Herculaneum in the villa of the Calpurnii Pisones. An interesting light on the career and outlook of this Demetrius is shed by the dedication of one of his treatises to a Nero, member of the patrician Claudii, hereditary patrons of Sparta (chapter 7): it seems that Demetrius was one of an increasing number of Greek intellectuals in this period who sought patronage in the Hellenized circles of the Roman aristocracy. Three generations later a Spartan named Nicocrates, this time a rhetor, followed a similar path, since it was probably in Rome that his eloquence made a poor impression on the elder Seneca. The case of Nicocrates, although he was clearly a minor figure (more so than Demetrius), is of interest, because it suggests that by the first century BC the rhetorical branch of Greek higher studies, which was to become increasingly dominant under the principate, was now pursued by Spartans no less than other Greeks –

for all that eloquence (at least of the wordy sophistic kind) was so foreign to the Spartan myth. Like Demetrius, Nicocrates presumably trained abroad.[3]

For further evidence concerning educational practice at Roman Sparta we have to wait until the works of Plutarch, to whom we are indebted for a unique glimpse of cultivated society in the Sparta of c.100. Plutarch is as informative as he is in this respect largely because – following an established literary format – he framed his ethical dialogues in social settings taken from contemporary life and peopled with figures drawn from his wide spread of upper-class friends and acquaintances, both Greek and Roman. Familiar with the Sparta of his day, where he had watched the ephebic contests and conducted research in the city-archives (chapter 14), Plutarch also knew a number of prominent Spartan citizens. One of these, the Herculanus to whom he dedicated a treatise on self-praise, can be confidently identified with the Euryclid senator of that name, who is now known to have been a first cousin of another senatorial friend of Plutarch, the Syrian prince C. Iulius Antiochus Philopappus; it may well have been from Herculanus that Plutarch heard the anecdotal material concerning the Augustan Eurycles which he incorporated elsewhere in his work (chapter 7).[4]

In addition, three Spartans feature in Plutarch's dialogues. The best-known, one Cleombrotus, is an interlocutor in the treatise *On the Disappearance of Oracles*, which the author seems to have woven out of real-life discussions which took place under the Flavians during a celebration at Delphi of the Pythian games. If Cleombrotus was dead at the time of this work's composition, which may have fallen under Trajan, Plutarch's somewhat unflattering portrayal of his intellectual powers would appear less impolite. Cleombrotus is depicted as a rich and erudite, if credulous, dilettante, well versed in Greek philosophy, well travelled, and himself preparing a theosophical work. Although the point has been overlooked, epigraphy helps to dispel any doubts over his existence as more than a figment of Plutarch's literary imagination: given the rarity of his name, he can be confidently identified with the homonym to whom a Spartan ephor of Flavian date stood in the relationship of *kasen*.

The epigraphic evidence has similarly been neglected in discussions of Plutarch's other two Spartan friends, Zeuxippus and Tyndares. It shows that they were members of the same aristocratic family: a Zeuxippus son of Tyndares held office as *nomophulax* and *gerōn* under Pius; and, as Chrimes saw, a descendant of his can be recognized in M. Aurelius Zeuxippus *qui et* Cleander, an ephebic *boagos* in the early third century and (hereditary, it seems) priest of the 'daughters of Leucippus' and their mythical husbands, the 'sons of Tyndareus' (the Dioscuri, that is): apparently this Zeuxippus belonged to the Roman city's priestly aristocracy, his family's use of the name 'Tyndares' advertising a claim to descent from the deities whom it served as priests. Plutarch's text further clarifies the inter-relationships of members of this family. He describes the earlier Zeuxippus as his *xenos* (*Mor*.749b), a by now somewhat old-fashioned term describing a form of 'ritualized friendship' between Greek aristocrats with its roots in the Archaic period. In the upper-class circles in which Plutarch moved *xenia*, its reciprocal obligations including the provision of hospitality, retained some of its old force; Zeuxippus is found staying at Chaeronea as Plutarch's guest, and, as Flacelière suggested, he may well have been the Chaeronean's host in Sparta. Their relative ages are of some relevance: that they were more or less coeval is shown by the dialogue *On Love*, the dramatic date of which fell just after Plutarch's marriage (probably in the seventies). Here Plutarch advised Zeuxippus apropos of the married state: 'While at first the feeling is a biting one, dear Zeuxippus, do not fear it as something wounding or painful' (*Mor*.769e). The intimate tenor of this – to a modern western ear somewhat disconcerting – advice points to a close friendship: at the dramatic date of the dialogue it seems that both were young men of marrying age, but, whereas Plutarch had taken the plunge (as evidently he saw it), Zeuxippus had yet to do so.

Tyndares, by contrast, belonged to a younger generation. In the *Table-Talk* Plutarch depicts him as his guest at Chaeronea, celebrating Plato's birthday in the company of – among others – L. Mestrius Florus, the Vespasianic consular, and Autobulus, one of Plutarch's sons, whose presence suggests a dramatic date not much before the nineties, when Florus was 'enjoying a sprightly old age in Greece'. That Tyndares was much younger than both Florus and his host is suggested by the fact that the former, presumably attracted by his boyish charms, liked to play at being his lover (*Mor*.719a). Drawing the literary and epigraphic evidence together, Tyndares can now be identified as the son of Plutarch's Spartan *xenos* and the father of the Antonine magistrate Zeuxippus, who was named after his paternal grandfather according to widespread Greek onomastic practice.

Plutarch sheds some light on the education of these three Spartans. Like Cleombrotus, Zeuxippus and Tyndares are depicted as highly cultivated men: Zeuxippus is portrayed as an admirer of Euripides and in philosophy inclined towards Epicureanism, Tyndares as something of a Platonist (but perhaps no more so than any well-educated Greek of his time). The tie of *xenia* between Plutarch and his father, if it was not hereditary, might well have been initiated during shared student-days at Neronian Athens, where Plutarch was taught by the Alexandrian philosopher Ammonius. The presence of the youthful Tyndares in the house of the by then middle-aged Plutarch suggests that at the time he was attending the private 'academy' which Plutarch had established at Chaeronea, its students were drawn from among the sons of his relations and friends. As for Cleombrotus, the fact that Plutarch calls him 'sainted' (*hieros*) implies that he was a good age at the dramatic date of the dialogue in question; if so, he was probably among those interlocutors who had studied in the thirties with the famous rhetor Aemilianus of Nicaea (*Mor*.410a, 419b). In all three, Plutarch portrays upper-class Spartans who were at ease in highly cultivated company without themselves being culturally distinguished in any way (if Cleombrotus ever completed his theosophical work we know nothing of it): typical products, in fact, of the expensive 'gentleman's education' enjoyed by sons of leading provincial Greek families.[5]

Some two and a half centuries later, in the lifetime of Libanius, Sparta had developed into a minor centre of higher studies. The seeds of this somewhat unexpected development lay in the larger cultural rôle assumed by Sparta in the favourable milieu of the Greek renaissance (chapter 8). By the later second and early third centuries, with its tourism, its cycle of new festivals and its small circle of highly cultivated local families, Sparta offered foreigners a congenial setting for the pursuit of philosophy and rhetoric. Symptomatic of this changing atmosphere is the appearance of Spartan philosophers-in-residence. One, Iulius Phileratidas son of Hippodamus, is named in a list of *gerontes* from between 165 and 170 as an *ensitos* or recipient of honorific dining-rights at the public meals of these magistrates. Like (probably) the first, the second, Q. Aufidenus Quintus, was a Spartan of curial rank, honoured with a public statue in – to judge from the letter-forms – the early Severan period, in recognition of his 'magnanimity (*megalophrosūnē*) in public affairs'. Although his *nomen* is rare, his family had been settled at Sparta for at least two generations, to judge from the *cognomen* of his father, 'Sidectas' – a good Spartan name. His philosophical interests were inherited, since his uncle, Q. Aufidenus Sextus, is styled 'the most philosophical'; possibly he had been named after the celebrated philosopher Sextus, Plutarch's nephew and teacher of the future emperor M. Aurelius. As philosophers, both Phileratidas and Quintus were minor figures, unattested elsewhere: 'big fish in a small pond', one might be tempted to say of their continued residence as adults in their home-city. But the evidence considered next shows that by the early third century professional teachers at Sparta could expect to attract an increasingly international clientele – as well, probably, as the local ephebes – to their lectures.[6]

This evidence comprises a group of four inscribed dedications set up by the city of Sparta which have in common that the honorands, high-ranking provincial Greeks, were all lauded for their 'cultivation' (*paideia*). One honorand, a citizen of Trapezus on the Black Sea, was a certain Tib. Claudius Montanus *qui et* Hesychius, the son of a Eupator; his name suggests kinship with Tib. Claudia Eupatoris Mandane Atticilla, a woman of consular rank honoured at Tralles. The name 'Eupator' recurs in the Mithradatid dynasty of Pontus, the rare Median name 'Mandane' in the Persian Achaemenid dynasty, from which the Mithradatids claimed descent; Montanus and Mandane may both have belonged to an old Pontic family with a royal pedigree. As for date, the Spartan notable who paid for the dedication, P. Ulpius Pyrrhus, had served as an Imperial high-priest under the Severi. A second honorand, one Flavius Asclepiades *qui et* Alexander, a Syrian Greek from Caesarea, likewise had his dedication paid for by an ex-Imperial high-priest, who this time was a grandson of the senator Brasidas, the early Severan Tib. Claudius Spartiaticus; he claimed Asclepiades as his 'friend' (*philos*). M. Aurelius Cleanor son of Rufus, who funded the dedication for a third honorand, Aelius Metrophanes, should probably be identified as the father of a mid-third century *hieromnēmōn*, M. Aurelius Cleanor son of Cleanor. In this case, the absence of an ethnic could be taken to show that Metrophanes was a native Spartan; if so, however, it is odd that the costs of his dedication were not defrayed by his family, the normal Spartan practice in this period, but by an apparently unrelated notable; like the previous two, Metrophanes, whose *cognomen* is otherwise unattested at Roman Sparta, was probably a foreigner. The fourth honorand, M. Ulpius Genealis, was honoured by a Spartan decree inscribed in his home town, the Hellenized Thracian city of Augusta Traiana in the province of Moesia. The date of this text fell after 161, to judge from the Aurelian citizenship of the compatriot who supervised erection of the monument; in all probability he had been enfranchised by the Antonine constitution of 212–3.

The motives for these honours are not made explicit by the texts themselves. Seure saw them as 'diplômes de fin d'études, délivrés par l'Université spartiate'; but the notion of a 'university' in the modern sense is anachronistic in this period, at Sparta or anywhere else. But it does seem possible that Montanus and Metrophanes, at any rate, were youths or young men when they received their Spartan honours. Montanus was praised for his 'moderation' (*sōphrosunē*) and cultivation', the former a quality particularly associated with women and youngsters; both qualities recur in the Spartan eulogy for the seventeen-year-old T. Statilius Lamprias of Epidaurus. Metrophanes, who 'outshone his fellows (*hēlikes*) in philosophic *ēthos*, in cultivation and in eloquence (*logoi*)', also sounds like a young man. One explanation would be to see both as furnishing the proofs of their cultivation – perhaps by declaiming in public – while pursuing rhetorical studies at Sparta; it then becomes tempting to identify Metrophanes with one of the two third-century sophists of that name, one from Eucarpia in Phrygia, the other a Boeotian from Lebadea; the Spartan dedication might be seen as a testimony to early promise. With the other two, their age is more in doubt. It is true that Spartiaticus, the friend of Asclepiades, had already held the Imperial high-priesthood

181

twice and won the 'contest for best citizen'; as the son of a Roman senator, however, these civic honours may have come to him early in life. Genealis was praised for his 'zeal for cultivation and eloquence (*logoi*)' and thanked for his 'goodwill' (*eunoia*) towards Sparta; as Apostolides suggested, he might have been a practising rhetor or sophist, although perhaps not an established one, as the text gives him no professional title. This 'goodwill' suggests benefaction, possibly aimed at some appropriately 'cultural' institution, such as the Spartan ephebic training; Herodes Atticus, a benefactor of the Athenian ephebate, was likewise praised – this time by the emperor M. Aurelius – for his 'renowned zeal for cultivation'. Some act of euergetism by Genealis would also provide an understandable context for the long-range diplomacy which Sparta was prepared to conduct in his honour.[7]

In sum, although these honours cannot all be explained in the same way, in a general sense they demonstrate clearly enough the cultural attractions of early third-century Sparta for rich provincials from the Greek diaspora; in two cases at least the honorands perhaps should be seen as foreign students. Against this background, it is not entirely surprising to find that Sparta went on to produce sophists and philosophers of some eminence in the later third and the fourth centuries. At least two members of a Spartan family using the name 'Apsines' taught at Athens in this period. The younger of these was involved in an academic *cause célèbre* in early fourth-century Greece when faction-fighting between his own pupils and those of another celebrated sophist teaching at Athens led to a trial before the proconsul. A series of confused entries in the Byzantine lexicon, the *Suda*, can be unravelled to identify this Apsines as the son of Onasimus, another Spartan sophist living under Constantine, and the grandson of the elder Apsines, who is confused by the lexicon with a famous but somewhat earlier homonym, Valerius Apsines of Gadara, a Syrian Greek sophist teaching at Athens under the later Severi. Given that the name 'Apsines' is otherwise unknown at Sparta, a connection between the Spartan family and the Gadarene – presumably formed in Athens – seems not unlikely: the father of the Spartan Onasimus could have been born in the second quarter of the third century and named after Valerius Apsines either as an act of academic homage or because the two families were related by blood; on either view, this would not be the only case of personal ties in this period between the *pepaideumenoi* of Sparta and Syria, as is shown by the friendship between Spartiaticus and Asclepiades. A century later, Roman Sparta produced its most famous man of learning, the grammarian Nicocles, who was teaching in Constantinople in the years around 340, when the future emperor Julian was among his pupils (chapter 9). At the close of the century another Spartan, the pagan philosopher Epigonus, was one of the 'successors' to another former teacher of Julian, the eminent neoplatonist Chrysanthius of Sardis.[8]

Although none of these later Spartans is known to have taught at Sparta, it is quite possible that some had done so before going on to establish or develop their reputations in intellectual centres elsewhere. That Sparta was now a recognized home of higher studies is shown by the plaintive observation of Julian, in a eulogy of the empress Eusebia composed in the 350s, that, along with Athens and Corinth, it was among the cities in old Greece which 'philosophy had not yet abandoned'. Libanius, writing in 364 to a Spartan correspondent, implies much the same when he refers (no doubt with the intention to flatter) to 'Sparta the wise', a place 'full of much good instruction'. The city's intellectual prominence in this period should undoubtedly be attributed in large part to its – almost inevitable – position as a bastion of late-antique paganism: with its famous Classical past, ancient cults and priestly families Sparta, like Athens, was an old-world city well placed to accommodate the alliance in this period between Greek philosophy and pagan belief. In a Spartan context, the convergence of these two approaches to the ordering of human experience is nicely illustrated in the middle decades of the third century by inscriptions recording a learned and aristocratic family sprung from one of the city's mantic lineages: the 'oracular' Tisamenus, his wife Aurelia Oppia, and their daughter Heraclia, the last said to belong 'to the race of Heracles, Apollo and the Iamidae'. All three are described as 'most philosophical', indicating their pursuit of philosophical interests; in the case of Heraclia, her pagan piety earned her the honour of a portrait-statue set beside the cult-image of 'the most holy Orthia Artemis'. These texts provide further evidence for the close association in this period between pagan oracular activity and late Greek philosophy.[9]

Before finishing with high culture, 'the old nexus between philosophy, oratory and medicine' requires us to consider the neglected evidence for Spartan doctors. The earliest is met with in an inscription from Gytheum, dated to about 70 BC, recording the city's grant of proxeny to a Spartan citizen called Damiadas, who practised as a doctor free of charge when Gytheum was gripped by a financial crisis and was praised as a 'man of culture' (anēr. . .pepaideumenos). Damiadas suggests the existence by his day of Spartan public doctors (dēmosioi iatroi) of the widespread Hellenistic kind – in contrast to Classical times, when Sparta had relied on the services of foreign doctors. We know of two local doctors in the second and third centuries, one of them an anonymous bearer of the titles arkhiatros, granted in this period to a class of civic doctors distinguished for their wealth and access to high local office, and 'saviour of the city', the last suggesting valued services at a time of epidemic. The impression that Sparta had developed by now into a regional medical centre is confirmed by an inscription from second-century Cythera, recording an islander who had trained at Sparta as a doctor. This local tradition of medicine evidently developed in the Hellenistic period and conceivably was encouraged by Spartan links with Ptolemaic Alexandria, the great medical centre of the time. In the Roman period it could claim a distinguished recruit to the international world of medicine in the person of Claudius Agathinus, a Spartan doctor who acquired fame as the founder of a Roman medical sect, the Eclectics. His reputation was made, not locally, but in the highly competitive medical circles of Imperial Rome, where he studied as a young man and remained to teach and practise under the Flavians. His social origins are unclear; his Roman citizenship permits him to have been the freedman of a leading Spartan family (such as the subsequently senatorial Tib. Claudii); alternatively he may have owed it to a viritane grant from Nero in recognition of his professional standing.[10]

*   *   *   *   *   *

Until well into the third century, periodic games for itinerant (and local) athletes, musicians, actors and an ever greater variety of other types of performer formed one of the most vigorous and distinctive aspects of the culture of the Greek cities. Although by the Severan age games on the Greek model were celebrated as far afield as Damascus, Carthage and Rome, provincial Achaia maintained a privileged position in the agonistic world, a status deriving chiefly from the continuing renown of the ancient Olympic, Pythian, Isthmian and Nemean games, but enhanced by the emergence of new agonistic centres at Athens and Sparta. Although Sparta's importance in this respect has been recognised before, this chapter brings together the relevant evidence for the first time.[11]

In the last three centuries BC Spartan citizens are found competing in both athletic and dramatic contests abroad. Perhaps in part as a result of a lingering xenophobia, however, foreign *agōnistai* do not seem to have competed at Sparta on a regular basis before the Augustan age. To this period, almost certainly, belongs the foundation of Sparta's Caesarean games. These are first mentioned in an inscription of Flavian date from Iasus in Asia Minor, which records the victory of a local athlete, T. Flavius Metrobius, at 'the *Kaisarēa* in Lacedaemon' (App.IV, 1). But the 'Caesar' whom they commemorated was presumably Augustus, since it is inconceivable that the Sparta of Eurycles would have lagged behind the rash of other Achaian cities which founded new festivals or augmented the activities of existing ones in honour of the first *princeps*. As the construction of *naoi* of Caesar and Augustus shows (chapter 10), the reign of Augustus saw the establishment of a Spartan cult in honour of the ruling family. The foundation of the Caesarea belongs to this same local initiative, the festival, which would have incorporated civic sacrifices on the emperor's behalf as well as games, providing the new cult with its ceremonial focus. On other grounds Eurycles has been identified as the founder of Sparta's Imperial cult (chapter 7); that he instituted the Caesarea as well is suggested, as Moretti saw, by their association in the post-Hadrianic period, apparently as part of a single, prolonged, episode of festival, with the Euryclean games, which were founded and endowed by the dynast's descendant, the senator Herculanus (below). Although only athletic contests are certainly attested for the new festival, the costly refurbishment under Augustus of the civic theatre (chapter 10) suggests a new beginning, of a kind consonant with the institution for the first time of regular dramatic contests. These are not attested for Hellenistic Sparta, although the way for them was paved by the development of a local taste for theatrical spectacle, reflected in the initial phase of construction at the theatre (perhaps under Areus: see chapter 3) and in the iconography, apparently inspired by Athenian drama, of a Spartan mosaic floor dated to about 100 BC (App.I, 50). As we saw in chapter 10, Eurycles has also been identified as the donor of the new theatre.[12]

Although the Caesarea continued to be celebrated into the third century, by then they had long been overshadowed in importance by a succession of more recent foundations, which, to judge from the surviving evidence, were much more successful at attracting foreign competition (see App.IV, where the evidence for foreign *agōnistai* is gathered together). In chronological order of foundation these were the Uranian, Euryclean and Olympian Commodean games, which taken together point to a sustained effort by the Spartans to establish their city as a rival to the traditional agonistic centres of old Greece. Motivation probably lay partly in the realms of civic pride, partly in that of profit: games prestigious enough to attract champion-class contestants – as these did – also brought in the crowds, whose beneficial impact on urban economy was not lost on contemporary observers (see Dio Chrys. *or*.xxxv.15–16).

The Uranian games were founded in 97 or 98 with the financial help of a local notable, C. Iulius Agesilaus (chapter 8). Strictly speaking, they formed only an element (albeit the dominant one) in a festival (*panēguris*) founded in honour of Zeus Uranius, whose cult seems to have been revived for this purpose (chapter 14). Something is known of their organization. Like all games of any importance, they were celebrated quinquennially, festival-years being computed (in ultimate imitation of the famous 'Olympiads' and 'Pythiads') by a local era of 'Uraniads'. The games were presided over by a civic official, the *agōnothetēs*, the festival as a whole by another magistrate, the panegyriarch. As for the programme, part of it may be preserved on a document discussed below. Even if this refers to the Euryclea, the list of known victors in the Urania is sufficient to show that contests in athletics, music and drama were included, presumably staged in either the stadium (App.I, 21) or the theatre. One of these victors, the Hadrianic P. Aelius Aristomachus, a champion-wrestler from Magnesia-on-the-Maeander, boasted in a poem commemorating his achievements in the ring of how 'in venerable Sparta, by the tower of Lacedaemon, I was crowned with the illustrious prize at the Urania' (App.IV, 6). Apart from its reference to this unidentifiable 'tower' (conceivably a purely poetic conceit inspired by Alcman's 'well-towered Therapne'), the text is interesting for showing that victors at the Urania were crowned with a symbolic prize, the wreath, as well as receiving a cash prize – paid for (presumably) by an endowment given by Agesilaus, the original *athlothetēs*. Technically, then, the Urania fell into the agonistic category of 'sacred crown-games' (*agōnes hieroi kai stephaneitai*) or, more precisely, 'crowned prize-games' (*themateitai stephaneitai agōnes*); they can presumably be identified with the anonymous 'sacred' festival at Sparta which conferred a Hadrianic victory on a Cilician wrestler (App.IV, 7). The generous size of the prizes no doubt lay behind the success of the Urania in attracting foreign competition, as revealed by the home cities of known victors, who include – in addition to Aristomachus – athletes from Corinth, Phocaea and Seleucia-on-the-Calycadnus (in Pisidia), a cithara-player from Thessalonice and a flautist from Gortyn (App.IV, 2–10).[13]

In 136/7, just over a generation later, the Euryclean games were celebrated at Sparta for the first time, as we learn from an important inscription in the Sparta Museum to be published by G. Steinhauer. This text clarifies that the Euryclea were named after, not the Augustan dynast, but the Hadrianic senator, Eurycles Herculanus, who died at about this time (chapter 8). Since the senator posthumously received heroic honours from the Spartans, it is possible that the Euryclean games had heroic overtones, providing the ceremonial focus for a civic hero-cult in much the same way as the periodic games founded privately a generation or so later by Herodes Atticus in memory of his heroized foster-son, Vibullius Polydeucio.

Since they did not commemorate a deity, the Euryclea fell technically into the less prestigious category of 'prize-games' (*agōnes themateitai* or *talantaioi*), as we learn from an inscription of early Severan date from Rome, recording the victory in the *pankration*-contest of M. Aurelius Asclepiades of Alexandria (App.IV, 12). As it happens, the only other firmly attested victors were also athletes: an Alexandrian wrestler of the same name but earlier in date (M. Aurelius) and the celebrated pancratiast and boxer, M. Aurelius Demostratus Damas of Sardis (App.IV, 10). These three show that the Euryclea, like the Urania, successfully established themselves as games of international stature; their prestige is suggested too by the fact that a leading Corinthian, L. Gellius Areto, probably identical with a homonym who held high office in the Achaean League in 138, is found among the six attested *agōnothetai*. Four of these presided over the combined 'Caesarea and Euryclea': it seems that by the mid-second century the two sets of games were usually celebrated successively in the same year, the Imperial festival naturally taking precedence. Since the *agōnothetēs* received 'agonothetic monies' from the city for both festivals, the reasons for this association may have been financial – perhaps so as to allow the more recent endowment bequeathed by Herculanus to subsidize the (by now depleted?) funds given by his ancestor for the older festival. It is clear, however, since foreign victors name the Euyclea alone, that the two programmes remained distinct.[14]

The third and (so far as we know) the last of Roman Sparta's major new games were the Olympia Commodea, the scattered inscriptional evidence for which has recently been recalled from near oblivion and requires only a brief summary here. Their titulature shows that they were founded as an Imperial festival in honour of Commodus, presumably including sacrifices on his behalf as well as a programme of contests. This extravagant gesture suggests local gratitude for some Imperial benefaction – conceivably the return of the *ager Dentheliatis* by the emperor Marcus, the father of Commodus (chapters 8, 10). Two inscriptions from respectively Delphi and Pisidian Adada, both from the Severan age, show that by then the festival was classed as 'sacred', or, more specifically, as 'sacred and iselastic', a highly prized status in the emperor's gift alone and limited to an élite-group of agonistic festivals. Its distinguishing mark was that victors were entitled to highly honorific and lucrative prizes from their home cities (as well as any that the host city might confer), including the right to a triumphal procession (hence the term 'iselastic', from the Greek verb *eiselaunein*, 'to enter in triumph'), a cash pension, and immunity from civic liturgies; because these honours (especially the last) represented a potentially heavy burden on civic resources, it was in the Imperial interest not to be over-generous with new grants of 'iselastic' status, which in Greece are otherwise attested only in one other case, that of the Panathenaea. It appears that the Commodea were not founded as 'iselastic' games, however, since they can probably be identified with the unnamed Spartan festival whose promotion to this rank by either Severus or Caracalla is recorded in an inscription from Sardis (for Sparta's favourable relations with both these emperors see chapter 8). It was probably on this occasion that the festival received the epithet 'Olympic' and was reorganized, like many agonistic festivals under the principate, on the fashionable model of the famous Olympics; of this reorganization we only know that a local era of 'Olympiads' was now instituted, showing that the 'iselastic' festival was celebrated quinquennially. The international character of the Olympia Commodea is revealed by the three known victors: a poet from Argos, an athlete from Adada, and (probably) the Sardian celebrity, Demostratus Damas (App.IV, 14–16).[15]

That Roman Sparta provided an appreciative audience for poetry-readings is shown by the Spartan citizenship of another itinerant poet, one Claudius Avidienus of Nicopolis, who lived at the turn of the first century and perhaps had competed in an otherwise unattested poetry-contest at the Urania (App.IV, 5). The variety of cultural activities placed before spectators at these new festivals is perhaps brought out most vividly by an important inscription on bronze, unfortunately incomplete, recording the accounts (*logismos*) of a Spartan *agōnothetēs*. The text can be dated more precisely than it was by Woodward, since the winner of the men's pentathlon, the Olympic champion Aelius Granianus of Sicyon, in spite of Moretti's doubts is surely the same as the Sicyonian 'Cranaus' listed by the third-century chronographer Africanus as victor in the men's stade-race at Olympia in 145; his victory at Sparta, and the date of the text, would then belong in about 143–8. Although the name of the games is not preserved, their international stature is shown by the home cities of the victors, including citizens from Tarsus, Sidon and Damascus (App.IV, 17–23), and by the scale of the prizes, which add up to a total value (although the list of victors is incomplete) of HS 87,760; at this date, only the Urania or the Euryclea can be in question. As for the programme itself, it included not only contests for athletes, musicians, and tragic actors, but also ones for trumpeters, painters, and even rhetors. One is left with the impression of a determinedly up-to-date agonistic entertainment, attempting to cater for as many tastes as possible.[16]

At Sparta as elsewhere in this period, the extent to which agonistic contests provided truly popular entertainment is arguable. Certainly the musical, literary and rhetorical contests would have appealed most to a cultivated audience. Partly because they were associated with the socially-exclusive milieu of the gymnasium, athletics continued to have aristocratic associations in this period, as is clearly demonstrated in Sparta's case by the champion-runners P. Aelius Damocratidas and his son P. Aelius Alcandridas, twice an Olympic victor in the 220s, who both held high local office and were related to the family of the senator Brasidas; a number of other Spartan magistrates also bear agonistic titles obtained (probably) through athletic success, such as 'Victor in the Nemean Games' (*Nemeonikēs*), 'Sacred Victor' (*hieronikēs*), 'Victor in Very Many Contests' (*pleistonikēs*) and 'Astounding' (*paradoxos*). But theatrical spectacle seems to have had a wider appeal in this period; significantly, in the accounts just discussed, the highest prize (HS 12,000) went to a tragic actor. In the second century proletarian tastes were being catered for in other ways. Agonistic festivals now tended to attract all kinds of unscheduled acts by performing mountebanks, one of whom can be recognised in the Carthaginian muscleman (*iskhuropaiktēs*) whose performance earned him a grant of Spartan citizenship (a measure, incidentally, of the declining prestige of this once highly prized commodity). Sparta also provided an eager audience for the pantomime, a 'solo performance by one masked mimetic dancer with a singing chorus providing musical interludes'. In a lost piece of show-oratory the mid-second century sophist, Aelius Aristides, berated the Spartans for this 'immoral' and 'un-Lycurgan' enthusiasm. Whether his work was ever delivered before a Spartan audience is unknown; but if it was, it had no lasting effect, as we learn from an Ephesian dedication for a celebrated pantomime artist from the end of the century, Tib. Iulius Apolaustus, whose performance at Sparta in the course of an Achaian tour earned him an honorific statue.[17]

As a final point it is worth underlining Sparta's links in the second and third centuries with the officialdom of professional athletics. A lost inscription, possibly a statue-dedication originally set up in one of the city's gymnasia, commemorates the champion-wrestler M. Ulpius Domesticus of Ephesus, a leading dignitary in the ecumenical federation of athletes based at Rome. In the second century we also encounter at Sparta the post of xystarch, 'an athlete nominated for life by the emperor to supervise the conduct of the athletes in a festival or in all the festivals of a city or region'. The known incumbents were both foreigners: a wrestler from Seleucia-on-the-Calycadnus, appointed – apparently by Hadrian – to the post of 'xystarch of the games in Lacedaemon'; and (once more) the champion boxer Demostratus Damas of Sardis, who received from either M. Aurelius or his successor the xystarchy of the Euryclea. The internationalism of athletic officialdom at Sparta is perhaps best captured by an early third-century epitaph commemorating a Greek from Alexandria who died at Tarentum after serving at Sparta as clerk of the city's *xustos* or athletic association, where he received a grant of local citizenship for his services.[18]

Chapter fourteen

The image of tradition

The preceding chapters have attempted to show how the profound political, social, and economic changes undergone by Sparta in the last three centuries BC had the effect of levelling much of the city's old distinctiveness. In the Roman Empire's heyday, under the Antonines and the Severi, Sparta emerges as in many ways a typical provincial Greek city, with its comfortable urban amenities, its up-to-date entertainments and its society dominated by a wealthy educated élite but not impervious to one of the characteristic figures of the Imperial age, the successful parvenu of freedman stock. On first sight this picture seems at odds with perhaps the best known aspect of Roman Sparta today: the maintenance, until as late as the fourth century, of an archaizing 'Lycurgan' facade to civic life. In fact, the 'Lycurgan customs' of Classical Sparta (as they were remembered or reconstructed in the Roman age) formed only one element in a set of local traditions informing and shaping a wide range of civic activities. Moreover, modern perceptions of archaism at Roman Sparta have been distorted by a tendency to see it in isolation, without reference to its links with the political and cultural preoccupations of the larger Roman world in which Sparta was now embedded. In Rome's Greek-speaking provinces, where 'ancient tradition was the touchstone of civic life', archaism of one sort or another was a widespread civic phenomenon, above all in the age of the Greek renaissance, when it was encouraged by the Greek policies of Roman emperors such as Hadrian (chapter 8). From this larger provincial perspective Sparta is chiefly interesting because – for reasons to which we shall return – the dialogue between past and present was louder and more persistent there than in many other cities. This chapter explores three 'themes' in this dialogue, two major and one minor: the rôle of Sparta in the Persian wars on the one hand, on the other ancestral religion and the Lycurgan customs. An attempt will then be made to analyse, in Sparta's particular case, the dynamics of local archaism.[1]

The recollection of the Persian wars at Roman Sparta has a particular interest, firstly, because it provides a clear example of an episode in the

Classical city's history which remained to the fore of civic consciousness throughout the principate (and possibly until later) and, secondly, because here the broad link between local archaism and Imperial initiatives cannot be in doubt. Although the battles of Marathon, Thermopylae and Plataea were commonplace *topoi* in the Greek and Roman schools of rhetoric, an often quoted passage in Plutarch shows that the memory of Greece's glorious repulse of the Persians between 490 and 479 BC still held a strong patriotic appeal for Greeks living under Roman domination. Complicating the resonances of the wars in the Imperial age, however, was the fact that Roman emperors from Augustus to Gordian III, recognizing their potency as national myth, followed Philip and Alexander in exploiting them for propagandistic purposes when representing Roman struggles against oriental 'barbarians' (now in the form of the Parthian and Sassanian Persian Empires) to a Greek audience. These larger attitudes help to explain the prominent part played by recollection of the Persian wars in those cities in Achaia which traditionally claimed decisive rôles in the repulse of the Persians and its commemoration: Athens and Sparta, but also Plataea, a city which, since the mid-third century BC, justified its existence largely through the hosting of cults and festivals celebrating the victory of 479 BC. In Sparta's case, the inhabitants of the Roman city were confronted in no uncertain terms with the ghosts of Thermopylae and Plataea when – for propagandistic as well as sentimental reasons – they were required by a succession of Roman emperors (L. Verus in 161, Caracalla in 214 and – quite possibly – Julian in 363) to send armed contingents on Imperial campaigns in the east (chapters 8–9). In a more peaceful vein, Roman Sparta played a prominent part in the four-yearly 'Freedom' festival or Eleutheria at Plataea, along with Athens being party to a ceremonial dispute over which city was to lead the procession, enacted as a recurrent contest in declamation between orators representing the two sides. This curious tradition, probably invented in the late second century BC, was evidently intended as a deliberate echo of the alleged quarrel between Athens and Sparta in 479 BC over the so-called meed of valour. In the second and third centuries, when the recreation of the past through the medium of rhetoric was a feature of the show-oratory of the Second Sophistic, the rhetorical 'duel' at Plataea became well known among educated Greeks and even formed the subject of a Greek rhetorical treatise.[2]

In this same period the Spartans were cultivating the claims of their own city as a 'shrine' to the Persian wars. In the mid-second century the city's tourist-itinerary embraced a group of civic monuments evoking Sparta's part in the wars, including the tomb of Eurybiadas, the Spartan admiral-in-chief at Salamis, the memorials for Leonidas, Pausanias, and the Spartan dead at Thermopylae, and the Persian Stoa in the agora. The second-century city also had its own commemorative ceremonies. Two of these formed part of the ritual at the annual ephebic festival for Artemis Orthia: the 'procession of the Lydians' and the so-called contest of endurance (below), both of which, according to Plutarch (our sole source for this tradition), were said to commemorate an incident on the eve of Plataea when the Spartan king Pausanias was set upon by a band of Lydians as he performed a sacrifice. The allegedly commemorative function of these rites hints strongly of more recently invented tradition, however, especially in the case of the endurance-contest, the true precursor of which seems to have been a ritual game in the Classical sanctuary of Orthia centred around the theft of cheeses.[3]

The Roman city also celebrated an annual festival, the Leonidea, in memory of Leonidas and Pausanias, the Spartan heroes of Thermopylae and Plataea respectively. It was known to Pausanias, who mentions declamations in memory of the dead and games in which only Spartans could compete. It was also the subject of a long and fragmentary inscription which once formed part of an honorific monument set up near the memorials for the two kings opposite the theatre. The text lays down detailed regulations for the conduct of the festival and clearly reflects its complete reorganization. In fact there is no earlier evidence for this festival, in spite of which its origin is usually attributed to the fifth century BC. Bulle's hypothesis of a sliding stage at the Spartan theatre depended on the assumption that the Leonidea were celebrated under Augustus; now that his theory has been placed in doubt on archaeological grounds, however, the accompanying premiss cannot be said to retain much weight. The only indication of the festival's existence earlier in the Roman period derives from the fact that on the occasion of its reorganisation the previous value of the cash prizes was said to have been 'doubled', the new endowment for the festival apparently totalling HS 120,000, just over a third of which (HS 42,000) had been given (or rather promised) by C. Iulius Agesilaus so as to provide or increase the prize-money in specified events. As to date, the inscription belonged to a year in which the *gerontes* included one Nicippus son of Nicippus, *kasen* to Eurycles Herculanus, who was born in about 73. From this it follows that the minimum age for *gerontes* in the Imperial age can no longer have been sixty, as in the old *gerousia*, since the text cannot possibly be dated as late as 133; indeed, the fact that Agesilaus had been *athlothetēs* of the Urania in 97/8 seems an obstacle to placing it much later than the end of Trajan's reign. On the assumption that a minimum age as low as thirty must be excluded, if only because it seems too young for a body calling itself (literally) 'the old men', we are left with forty as perhaps the most likely age-threshold in the Roman period, placing the inscription late in the reign of Trajan. This dating, if correct, is of some interest, since it would consign the 'renewal' of the festival to the period (113–117) of

Trajan's great eastern campaigns, in the preparations for which the Peloponnese had been actively involved. It is at least possible that the two events were connected: at a time when Greek memories of the Persian wars – not least in southern Greece – were being fanned by a major Roman initiative against the Parthians, Sparta chose to place on a firmer footing the old festival commemorating the city's famous exploits against the Persians at Thermopylae six centuries earlier.[4]

*   *   *   *   *   *

An excellent study has done much to lay to rest the view of older scholarship that Greek paganism was in decline or 'crisis' during the first two and a half centuries AD; on the contrary, civic cults based around the Homeric and Hesiodic pantheon, as well as novelties of more exotic origin, were the object in this period of a 'lasting traditional "religious-ness"', in which respect for ancestral practice loomed large. An ancient community such as Roman Athens, where an array of venerable deities continued to be the object of rites and festivals, struck visitors as particularly pious (cf. Paus.iii.24.3). The impression that Sparta, a city well-known for its religiosity in Classical times, provided another focus of old-world piety in the Imperial age emerges clearly from the same author, who listed for the city an impressive array of twenty-one hero-tombs and as many as sixty-four temples or sanctuaries. The Roman city was open to newer ways of approaching the divine: we have already noted the Imperial cult, established under Augustus, and that of Sarapis, a second-century innovation (chapter 10); by the reign of Marcus the city was also host to a community of Christians in the pastoral care of the bishop of Corinth. The emphasis here, however, is on the evidence for the continued prominence of traditional cults in civic life, which a brief discussion of those of Apollo, the Eleusinians and the Dioscuri will hope to exemplify.[5]

The worship of Apollo, a deity particularly associated with the Dorian Greeks, lay at the heart of Classical Sparta's three principal religious festivals: the Hyacinthia, the Carnea and the Gymnopaediae, all three of which were still celebrated in the Imperial age. The Carnea – as it happens – are only attested for the Augustan period, when their local prestige was such that a victor in the accompanying games or 'Carneonices' enjoyed, like an Olympic victor, the privilege of *sitēsis* or public maintenance. The other two are best attested in the Antonine and Severan ages, when they are mentioned by several contemporary Greek authors, including Pausanias, according to whom the Gymnopaediae were the most zealously maintained of Sparta's traditional festivals, and Philostratus, who implies that, together with the ephebic festival of Artemis Orthia (below), these were the three religious gatherings at

Sparta attracting the most foreign visitors in Imperial times. In the mid-second century the Gymnopaediae took place in a specially designated part of the agora, where ephebic choirs sang in Apollo's honour; Lucian adds that there were traditional dances too. Rather less is known of the specifically Roman content of the Hyacinthia, which were celebrated at the Amyclaeum. A fragmentary dedication for an 'instructor' (*didaskalos*) suggests the maintenance of the old songs and dances of the Spartan youth; if organised on agonistic lines these activities perhaps constituted the Hyacinthian 'games' to which two Antonine inscriptions refer, although hippic or athletic contests, for which there is evidence from an earlier period, may also be in question. As for the Amyclaeum itself, its famous cult-statue appeared on the Roman city's coinage, and, in part thanks to this and its other works of Archaic Greek art, it formed the chief tourist-attraction at Roman Sparta outside the urban centre. It is one of the few civic sanctuaries the continued existence of which is attested into the fourth century (chapter 9).[6]

The worship of Demeter and Core at the sanctuary of the Eleusinium, some seven kilometres south-west of the city on the edge of the Spartan plain, was certainly as old as the fifth century BC, when the goddesses, as a well-known inscription records, were honoured with chariot-games. The flourishing state of this sanctuary in the Imperial period is brought out by a series of inscribed dedications found either near the ancient site or at the modern village of Amyklai (formerly Sklavokhori), to which they had been removed as building-material in more recent times. Like many Demeter-cults elsewhere, the Spartan Eleusinium was essentially a women's sanctuary, as is shown by the striking fact that these inscriptions are all dedications by or for females, the bulk of them recording the setting-up of statues of well-born Spartan matrons in the name of the city. In the Imperial age, to judge from repeated references to a female official called the 'mistress of the banquet' (*thoinarmostria*), the ritual (and social) focus of the cult was an annual feast, at which perhaps only women were present. The dependence of the cult on the generosity of individuals, in this case well-to-do women, is shown by the descriptions of the posts of *thoinarmostria* and *pōlos* as 'liturgies' and the scope for their incumbents to hold office 'magnificently' (*megaloprepōs*) or 'with high-minded generosity' (*megalopsukhōs*). For its more impressive dedications the sanctuary likewise relied on the piety of leading families, as with the two elaborate reliefs now in the British Museum, one of them given in the last decades of the second century by Claudia Ageta, a granddaughter of the senator Brasidas.[7]

In myth the Dioscuri were natives of Sparta and in the Classical age had enjoyed a special relationship to the dual kingship. In the Roman period, the continuing reverence in which these demigods were held is shown by the frequency with which they or their symbols were depicted on local coin-issues; as the numerous instances of 'Dioscurid' pedigrees suggest, the cult retained aristocratic, if no longer royal, overtones. Since the time of Herodotus the chief Spartan sanctuary of the Dioscuri lay to the south-east of the city at the cult-centre of Phoebaeum on the right bank of the Eurotas, below the bluff on which stood the sanctuary of Helen and Menelaus. Inscriptions point to the vigorous life of this sanctuary, where the Dioscuri had their temple or shrine (*naos*), until as late as the mid-third century. Sacred banquets are attested under Augustus by a series of inscribed *stēlai* which show the integration of the cult into civic life, since they record the participation of the senior members (*presbeis*) of the boards of *bideoi*, *gerontes*, ephors, and *nomophulakes*, along with the *gunaikonomos*. These *stēlai* are decorated with reliefs depicting the Dioscuri in the company of Helen. This iconography suggests that by the reign of Augustus the cult had been enlarged to include the worship of the sister of the Dioscuri, a development perhaps to be associated with the cessation of cult at the nearby sanctuary of Menelaus and Helen, which excavation dates to the late second or the first century BC. Although the site was now abandoned, it seems likely that the age-old worship of Helen was not, being merely transferred to the more accessible sanctuary on the plain below. By the mid-third century the sanctuary also celebrated games, grandly called the 'Great Dioscurea', although no foreign victors are attested and they perhaps were a local event only. From the reign of Augustus until the mid-third century a dual priesthood of Helen and the Dioscuri can be traced as a hereditary perquisite within an inter-related group of leading local families, whose financial support did much to contribute to the cult's outward vitality: under Trajan or Hadrian P. Memmius Pratolaus and his priestly partner and kinswoman, Volusene Olympiche, funded building activity at the sanctuary; and the fact that in the mid-third century the hereditary priest was also hereditary president (*agōnothetēs*) of the Dioscurea suggests that a priestly ancestor had endowed the games earlier in the Roman period, their presidency then devolving by hereditary right to his descendants.[8]

The revival or re-invention of ancestral practice was another feature of Greek civic religion in the Roman period of which examples can be detected at Sparta. The festival of the Urania, founded in 97/8 (chapter 13), was celebrated in honour of Zeus Uranius, whose priesthood was one of two which the former Spartan kings held by hereditary right. In the Roman period the priesthood only emerges into view after the foundation of the Urania, now no longer a hereditary post but one to which the city made appointments for a fixed term. Its more or less complete dependence on the festival is shown by the fact that one incumbent (under Hadrian) served simultaneously as panegyriarch and that another (under Trajan) was baldly styled 'priest of the Urania'. It seems at least possible that this civic priesthood of Zeus Uranius was no older than the foundation of the games, the cult having been allowed to lapse following the demise of the dual kingship three centuries or so earlier, to be revived under Nerva as little more than a venerable-looking vehicle for the new festival. Ancestral piety would be one explanation for such a revival, but perhaps an insufficient one: those Spartans most closely involved in founding the new festival (including no doubt the *athlothetēs* C. Iulius Agesilaus) may have felt that its association with a historic (indeed a royal) cult would enhance the international prestige on which depended its agonistic success. It should be added that the initial titulature of the games, the 'Greatest Augustan Nervan Uranian Games', shows that the festival was also intended to honour the emperor, whose association with the worship of 'Heavenly Zeus' is attested elsewhere by this date.[9]

A second episode of revival concerns the oracular shrine of Ino-Pasiphaë in the formerly perioecic town of Thalamae on the western side of Taygetus. In the Hellenistic period this oracle used to be consulted by the ephors on Sparta's behalf (chapter 4). The practice seems to have lapsed by the time of Cicero, who writes of it in the past tense; the oracle may have ceased to speak; or Spartan access perhaps became problematic after the 'liberation' of the perioecic towns in 192 BC. But two inscriptions from the sanctuary, dating to the earlier second century, reflect once more a recurrent Spartan presence at Thalamae. One of them records three groups of Spartan visitors under Trajan, Hadrian and Pius respectively. Their size and make-up seem to have varied, but the first included representatives of the chief Spartan magistracies, the second four out of the five ephors in the year 127/8. The official, civic, character of these visits was understood by Bölte, who did not go on, however, to make the connection with oracular consultation. With little doubt this inscription is a record of embassies of civic magistrates sent, as in the Hellenistic period, to consult Ino-Pasiphaë; the lapse of time between the date of each is well suited to an irregular pattern of consultation, taking place as the need arose; and the inclusion of a choral element recalls the choirs of boys and girls accompanying embassies sent from other Greek cities to the oracle at Clarus in this period. It is probably no coincidence that the evidence for this apparent renewal of ancestral Spartan practice coincides in date with the larger revival of oracular activity in the Roman east, in which the oracle at Thalamae evidently shared; when the sanctuary was visited by Pausanias, he found the cult-statue almost obscured under its weight of festive wreaths.[10]

Lastly, Sparta and Delphi. In Classical times Sparta 'placed a premium on maintaining a special relationship' with the sanctuary of Apollo. The force of tradition emerges strikingly in the inscriptional evidence for the perpetuation of these ties into the early third century. After 146 BC

Sparta was no longer represented on the Amphictyonic Council (chapters 6 and 8). But the maintenance of cordial relations with the citizens of Delphi is shown by the despatch of Spartan judges to hear Delphian lawsuits in about 100 BC and by mutual grants of proxeny-privileges in the early principate. Those conferred by Sparta on a Delphian notable in about 29 BC were partly prompted by his services for Spartan visitors to Delphi. A Spartan who received this same honour from the Delphians in about 23, Alcimus son of Soclidas, bears the same rare name as a Spartan *naopoios* at Delphi in 360 BC, suggesting his membership of an old family with hereditary Delphian ties. After a silence of almost two centuries, Spartan interest in Delphi resurfaces in the Severan age, when Tib. Claudius Spartiaticus, grandson of the senator Brasidas and a leading figure in his city, received an honorific statue from the Delphians, installed within the sanctuary. More remarkably, to this period probably belongs the latest evidence for Spartan consultation of Apollo's oracle. The oracular ambassador (*theopropos*) despatched by Sparta on this occasion, one M. Aurelius Euamerus, was assigned by Bourguet to the mid-second century on prosopographical grounds which are less than compelling. It seems more likely that his Roman citizenship, like that of most Spartan M. Aurelii, derived from the Antonine constitution of 212 or 213. His mission would then provide the latest evidence for a relationship kept up over some eight centuries.[11]

*   *   *   *   *   *

Since at least the time of Herodotus the Spartans had attributed their distinctive form of polity to the prescriptions of Lycurgus, their semi-mythical lawgiver. From the first century BC until late antiquity we have good evidence for the restored position of Lycurgus at Sparta as the 'good genius' of civic life. Coin-issues of the triumviral age present us for the first time with an (imaginary, of course) portrait of Lycurgus, which was probably based on some sculpted prototype, now lost: he appears as a majestic, Zeus-like figure, wreathed and bearded. As at Classical Sparta, he was worshipped in the Roman city as a god. The focus of this cult was a sanctuary on the right bank of the Eurotas not far from that of Artemis Orthia; its enormous masonry altar, showing signs of Roman-period repairs, has been tentatively identified by excavation (App.I, 37). In the Antonine and Severan ages, to judge from the god's repeated patronomates (chapter 9), his sanctuary was a wealthy one. As late as the fourth century, the Spartans could confer no higher honour on benefactors of the city than to set their portrait-statues beside one of Lycurgus which stood (it seems) in the vicinity of the theatre – a juxtaposition intended to convey a flattering 'equality' between the '*ēthos* and deeds' of the honorands and those of the great sage.[12]

In the second and early third centuries, civic magistrates could claim to have discharged their duties 'according to the ancient customs' or were publicly praised for their 'protection of the Lycurgan customs': civic life in the Imperial age, that is, still claimed in some sense to be shaped by the lawgiver's prescriptions. Before assessing the content of these 'Lycurgan customs', however, the problem of the disputed date of their 'restoration' needs addressing. According to Livy, the Lycurgan institutions of the Hellenistic city had been suppressed by the Achaean League in 188 BC. They were then 'revived' under Roman patronage at a date left vague by Pausanias ('later'), but which Plutarch by implication assigns to the Roman settlement of 146/5 BC, since he explicitly couples the restoration of the 'ancestral polity' with Sparta's final secession from the Achaean League. Notwithstanding this last item of evidence, the 'Lycurgan' restoration is usually placed before 167 BC on the basis of another passage in Livy, who glossed the sight-seeing visit to Sparta of L. Aemilius Paullus in 167 BC (chapter 6) with the remark that the city was 'famous, not for the magnificence of its public works, but for its *disciplina* and its institutions'. A few scholars have rightly seen that Livy here is merely echoing the conventional Roman perception of Sparta: the passage cannot safely be used to show that by 167 BC the 'Lycurgan customs' had been restored – a reversal incompatible with Sparta's full sympolity at the time with the Achaeans. The point is an important one, since the later date leaves a gap of well over a generation between the suppression and the revival of the customs, increasing the likely rôle in this revival of antiquarian tradition over first-hand recollection.[13]

The extent and limits of this 'restoration' can now be assessed. The long-standing custom, whereby the ephors each year read the work of Dicaearchus of Messene on the Spartan constitution to the city's youth seems best referred to the Hellenistic, not the Roman, period. In fact, as was seen in chapter 11, local government at Roman Sparta, for all that its outward forms recalled famous features of the 'ancestral constitution' (*gerontes*, ephors and so on), in its day-to-day workings was shaped by far more recent influences (Cleomenean, Achaean and Roman). Nonetheless, there is some indication that the ancestral polity continued to supply at least a frame of reference for innovations in the administration of the Roman city, as with the institution of the 'contest for best citizen' (*agōn tēs aristopoliteias*). An apparently identical contest is found at Roman Messene, the one probably copying the other, since no comparable civic institution is found outside this particular corner of the Greek world (conferment by cities elsewhere of the honorific title of 'best citizen' does not amount to the same thing). The Spartans seem to have taken the first step, since an inscription presents the establishment of their contest between about 110 and 120 as a 'renewal' of an older institution, although nothing is known in their more recent past which could be plausibly claimed as a model for this contest. Given that other Greek cities at this time employed the same idea of 'renewal' (*ananeōsis*) to allude to the distant, even mythical, past, Chrimes may well have been correct in proposing that the Spartan contest modelled itself on the method (allegedly instituted by Lycurgus) by which the Classical city elected *gerontes* from the citizen-body: according to Plutarch, success went to the candidate judged by the assembly to be 'best' (*aristos*) in respect of personal excellence, who was then crowned with a wreath like an agonistic victor: this last practice is not actually recorded for Roman Sparta, but the 'best citizen's wreath' was a feature of neighbouring Messene's contest; the involvement of the Roman city's *dēmos* in the selection of the winner, however, is well attested. On this view, the 'contest for best citizen' was an antiquarian creation, giving a traditional guise to a newly invented institution which redefined the 'Lycurgan' ideal of civic virtue in contemporary, euergetistic, terms.[14]

The 'Lycurgan' resonance of one further feature of the Roman city's political life requires mention here, since it offers an indication of the limits of the post-146 BC 'restoration'. When Augustus visited Sparta in 21 BC he was said by Cassius Dio to have 'honoured the Spartans by messing together with them': 'paying homage to Lycurgan Sparta', the *princeps* apparently took a meal in a setting represented to him and his entourage as an approximation of the famous common messes (*suskania*), participation in which had been compulsory for full citizens of the Classical age. There is no other evidence to suggest that this old Spartan institution, 'so clearly . . . military in ethos and function', survived into the Imperial age; on the other hand, from the early principate onwards the entitlement of certain boards of magistrates to meals at public expense (*sitēsis*) is well attested. The evidence concerns the *gerontes*, ephors and *nomophulakes*, the *hierothutai* (see chapter 7) and the *agoranomos* and his colleagues. It comes chiefly in the form of references to cooks (*mageiroi*) or dining guests (*ensitoi* or *sussitoi*) attached to these different groups of magistrates; in addition the ephors and *nomophulakes* are once described (*IG* v.1.51) as 'those who enjoyed public maintenance' (*hoi sitēthentes*); and in the mid-second century the junior colleagues of the *agoranomos* included an official called the 'president of the common mess' (*phidition*). The public meals of these magistrates, along with those of other citizens on the list of those entitled to *sitēsis*, probably took place in Roman Sparta's equivalent of a civic *prutaneion* or *hôtel de ville*; this, as Kennell has argued, can be recognized in the so-called Old Ephoreia in the agora. Public maintenance of magistrates during their terms of office was a common feature of Greek civic life; at Sparta it is first attested (with reference to the ephors) under Cleomenes III. In the Imperial age, the chief executive and bouleutic magistrates shared the privilege with the *hierothutai*, whose duties included the provision of civic hospitality, and the *agoranomos*, whose responsibility for supervising Sparta's markets may have extended to the victualling of the public dining-rooms. When Augustus 'messed' with the Spartans, in fact he probably dined with the city's magistrates. The fact that his participation at Sparta in a routine feature of Greek civic life was considered remarkable suggests that the meals of the magistrates were thought of as somehow special – perhaps because foreigners were encouraged to assimilate them to the famous 'Lycurgan' institution which they (superficially) resembled.[15]

Other characteristic aspects of the 'Lycurgan' social organization are conspicuous at Roman Sparta by their absence. It was noted earlier (chapter 10) that in the Imperial age the inhabitants of Sparta enjoyed or aspired to the level of material comfort widespread among the urban communities of the time: no sign here of the well-known austerities of Classical Sparta. 'Lycurgan' eccentricities of personal appearance are difficult to document in the Imperial age. Plutarch, it is true, refers to the banning of moustaches by the ephors when they took office each year, but his use of the 'timeless' present tense here seems insufficient grounds for assuming a reference to the Sparta of his own day. Elsewhere he preserves an anecdote about a Spartan woman on visiting terms with the wife of a Galatian dynast in the first century BC, each of whom appalled the other by her smell – the Spartan reeking, not of perfume, but of butter! If anything, this passage may suggest that the rusticity of Spartan dress still observable in 148 BC (chapter 6) lingered on into the first century BC. However, although little weight can perhaps be put on the sartorial attachment to 'Sybaris' for which the Philostratean Apollonius berated a Spartan embassy under Nero, the draped statues of the senator Brasidas and his daughter Damosthenia suggest that the local upper classes – at least by the Antonine age – wore the usual dress of Greek provincials of their rank.[16]

Nor does the women's sphere at Roman Sparta display any of the licence for which it was notorious in Classical times. In honorific dedications for Spartan matrons from the second and third centuries the repetitive praise of their 'moderation' (*sōphrosunē*), 'husband-love' (*philandria*), 'dignity' (*semnotēs*) and 'decorum' (*kosmiotēs*) shows that local society, at least in its upper reaches, 'valued the same domestic virtues in women as those held up for praise by Plutarch of Chaeronea, in this period Greece's fullest surviving spokesman on the themes of love, women and marriage'. To judge from the evidence, the role of women in public life was largely confined to religious cult, where the matrons of leading families, society ladies such as Memmia Xenocratia in the mid-second century or Claudia Damosthenia a generation later, could obtain a genuine civic prominence through their pious (and generous) discharge of a range of priestly offices reserved for their sex. That the public deportment of free-born women was now the object of civic surveillance is shown by the existence of a *gunaikonomos*, a type of magistrate widespread in the Greek world by the first century BC. At Sparta the post is attested from the Augustan until the later Severan age, its duties sufficiently weighty, it seems, to require the assistance of (usually) five junior colleagues (*sungunaikonomoi*). The survival of the post throughout the principate may well reflect the importance which the Roman city attached to the decorous celebration of its traditional festivals, in which the wives and daughters of citizens played a prominent part, no doubt subject to strict regulations as to dress and behaviour.[17]

The literary and epigraphic evidence leaves in little doubt that the chief concern of the Spartans who guided the post-146 BC 'revival' was to reconstitute the most famous feature of their ancestral régime: the *agōgē* or public 'rearing' of Spartan boys and girls, from which, as we shall see, the ephebic training of the Roman city claimed direct descent. Like its Classical precursor, this training was a civic institution, supervised by annual magistrates. The best documented of these were the so-called *bideoi* ('overseers'), numbered five by Pausanias, although inscriptions place their normal strength at six. According to Pausanias they organised the ephebic contests, especially the one at Platanistas (below); inscriptions associate them too with the ball-tournament of the *sphaireis*-teams and with an athletic contest (the 'Dionysiades': see below) for girls. The magistracy is first attested in the Augustan period and its antiquity, in spite of its archaic-sounding name, must be in doubt, since in the Classical age the *agōgē* was under the overall supervision of the ephors, aided by a specially appointed official, the *paidonomos*: conceivably the *bideoi* were another constitutional innovation of Cleomenes III, belonging to his larger assault on the powers of Sparta's traditional magistracies (chapter 4). Whatever the case, Tod was surely wrong to see the *bideoi* as officials 'of small importance' – a view which underestimates the role of the ephebic training in the public life of the Roman city. After the *gerontes*, ephors and *nomophulakes*, they were the magistrates most frequently commemorated by catalogues, of which fourteen are attested, the most recent belonging to the later Severan period (App.IIA); in the Augustan age, along with these other three boards and the *gunaikonomos*, they were represented at the sacred banquets at Phoebaeum, the *bideos* actually taking precedence over the other civic magistrates present.[18]

The importance of the training in civic life is further underlined by its association – largely unnoticed so far – with the Roman city's most honorific magistracy, the eponymous patronomate. The nature of this office, established by Cleomenes III (chapter 4), has been misunderstood by some scholars, at least as far as the Imperial age is concerned. An inscription from the reign of Marcus leaves in no doubt that at that date the patronomate was a singular office, the incumbent giving his name to the year and discharging his duties with the help of six junior colleagues (*sunarkhoi* or *sunpatronomoi*) and a secretariat of two. Chrimes argued that the *patronomos* played an important part in local government, although the surviving evidence, as Schaefer and Bradford independently concluded, suggests the contrary. That its organisational duties cannot have been burdensome is shown by the occasions in the second and third centuries when the post was conferred on foreign notables or the god Lycurgus. On the other hand, they were not entirely negligible, to judge from the presence of junior colleagues and secretariat, and required a physical presence, since incumbents were replaced with a substitute (*huperpatronomos*) if for some reason they were unable to discharge the duties of the post, or, in the case of the god Lycurgus, by a 'supervisor (*epimelētēs*) of the patronomate'. Whatever evidence we have connects the post with the local gymnasia and the ephebic training. On five occasions, none earlier than the reign of Trajan, the post is found combined with that of gymnasiarch; and a Severan *patronomos*, P. Memmius Pratolaus *qui et* Aristocles, was honoured with public dedications 'for his protection of the Lycurgan customs', one of which was paid for by ephebic instructors and athletic trainers. Above all, the financial stratagem of conferring the post on the god Lycurgus (chapter 9), the mythical founder of the old *agōgē*, suggests – given Greek scruple about the sanctity of sacred property – some close relationship between the 'Lycurgan customs' and the patronomate's sphere of competence. In the absence of evidence it is hard to be more precise about the duties of the post, although its founder, Cleomenes III, may from the outset have intended the 'guardianship of law and order' implicit in its title to extend to the training, which he had revived after an earlier period of decline (chapter 4). By the second century, in a typically Roman development, the office had acquired a liturgical character: this emerges clearly from the practice of conferring it on Lycurgus, as from the praise of an Antonine incumbent for his 'goodwill and *philotimia* towards his fatherland'. It is likely, then, that in the Imperial age the annual *patronomos* assumed some of the expenses associated with the ephebic training: in the case of Pratolaus, since the ephebic instructors were public employees whose salaries could be threatened in times of financial stringency, his 'protection of the Lycurgan customs' may have taken the form (for instance) of paying them their arrears.[19]

Broadly speaking, this 'revived' training can be said to have comprised instruction in song, dance, and athletic and military exercises, prowess in which was tested in a series of contests attached to the Roman city's cycle of religious festivals. As such, the training resembled in a number of respects – and in its activities were probably influenced by – the institution of the *ephēbia*, the civic training for adolescents widespread in the Greek world in Hellenistic and Roman times. Exploration of both similarities and differences will help to define the distinctive, 'Lycurgan', aspects of Roman Sparta's training.[20]

For the age-range of participants in the training the most detailed evidence is provided by the long series of ephebic dedications from the sanctuary of Artemis Orthia, which resume in the later second or first century BC and continue until well into the third century AD. These dedications, marking victories in the ephebic contests celebrated annually in honour of the goddess, show that the 'revived' training continued to be organised around age-sets, the archaic-sounding names of five of which are preserved (the *mikikhizomenoi, pratopampaides, hatropampaides, melleirenes* and *eirenes*). These five partially correspond with the schemata for Spartan age-sets preserved in the glosses of ancient or Byzantine scholars on passages in Herodotus and Strabo, comparison with which indicates that they covered successively the six years from fourteen to nineteen. Participation in the revived training, that is, spanned the transitional years between two universally recognised, if loosely defined, Greek age-categories: those of the ephebes and the young men (*neoi*). Although these adolescent ephebes could refer to themselves as 'boys' (*paides*), just as the Greek agonistic age-class of the 'boys' embraced contestants from the age of fourteen to seventeen, there is no evidence to suggest that the 'revived' training still embraced small children: Greek writers of the Imperial age invariably describe participants as ephebes, or, in the case of the *sphaireis*-teams, 'those about to pass from the ephebes into the men'. In this respect the 'revived' training differed significantly from the old *agōgē*, which began to recruit at the age of seven: it looks as if this aspect of ancestral practice was dropped after 146 BC – a lapse conforming to the larger decline of Greek interest in public primary education during the Roman period. On the other hand, in the Roman age, when ephebic training normally lasted no longer than a year, it is striking that at Sparta youths could take part in the 'revived' training for a period of up to six years. This unusual state of affairs, reflecting the special claims of this training, will be returned to below.[21]

As for the internal organisation of the 'revived' training, we know that it was based around the Roman city's citizen-tribes, named after the city-wards of Mesoa, Pitana, Limnae, Cynosura and the Neopolitae. In the old *agōgē*, the age-sets were divided into 'herds' (*agelai*) under the leadership of older youths. In the period after 146 BC, a team-structure is not attested before the later first century, from when until the early third century the inscriptions indicate the division of the age-sets into bands led by a *boagos* or 'herd-leader', a youth of the same age as his charges, who described themselves as his 'fellow-ephebes' (*sunephēboi*). This post of *boagos* is attested no earlier than the Domitianic age, *boagoi* or their 'synephebes' then going on to account for thirty-five of the fifty ephebic dedications which Woodward assigned to the period *c.*80–240. As he saw, the appearance of the post seems to mark a change in the organization of the training, which he understood as involving the transfer of leadership of the teams from older youths to 'boys the same age as their fellow-members'. If the team-structure already existed, however, it is difficult to see why this change (departing, after all, from the 'Lycurgan' dispensation) should have been felt necessary at this particular date. The inscriptions make clear, moreover, that this team-structure gave continuing shape to the public life of ex-ephebes: that team-membership created a lasting sense of companionship is shown, for instance, by the boast of a board of *nomophulakes* of about 100 that it comprised an ex-*boagos* and four of his old 'synephebes'; and the fact that ex-*boagoi* retained their title into adult life shows that the position was thought of as highly honorific.

The evidently intense experience which team-membership constituted, however, has left no mark at all on the epigraphic material from the first century BC and the Julio-Claudian age – another reason for doubting whether a team structure existed earlier in the period of the 'revived' training. If a recreation of the Flavian age, its purpose may not have been solely antiquarian: at Roman Athens the ephebes were likewise divided into bands of 'synephebes' under the charge of one of their number, who was responsible for certain ephebic expenses. Were the post of *boagos* similarly a quasi-liturgy, this would help to explain both its honorific character and the marked tendency of incumbents to belong to established curial families: perhaps they helped with the training expenses of their team. If so, the institution of the post (and perhaps the concoction of an appropriately pastoral-sounding neologism, that of *boagos*, for its title) may be seen as part of a larger reorganization of the training in the later first century, aimed partly at placing recruitment on a firmer financial and numerical footing; *kasen*-status also reappears in the epigraphic evidence in the second half of the first century (late in Nero's reign); likewise it seems best understood as a device (in archaizing guise) for helping the sons of less well-off families to pass through the training (chapter 12). At first it may seem odd, if these views are accepted, that the reorganization did not assign leadership of the teams to older youths – in line with ancestral practice – but to coevals. An explanation can perhaps be found in the fact that in the first century, at least where the sons of prominent families were concerned, the training had to compete with the demands of a conventional higher education abroad (see chapter 13). Higher studies in this period tended to begin precisely in the mid-teens – a fact which may help to explain why nineteen of the twenty-six ephebic dedications which record the age-sets of *boagoi* or 'synephebes' pertain to sixteen-year-olds (*mikikhizomenoi*).[22]

Those activities of the ephebes and young men constituting the 'revived training' are briefly considered next. The inclusion of conventional gymnastic training and military drill is shown by the presence of athletic trainers (*aleiptai*) and drill-masters (*hoplomakhoi*) among the ephebic instructors and by the victories of a (?) Hadrianic ephebe in wrestling contests in local religious festivals. Intellectual training of the usual kind is not firmly attested, although its inclusion by the later second century can perhaps be inferred from the development of philosophical and rhetorical studies at Sparta in that period (chapter 13). Not least because they were of much greater interest to our literary sources, we hear rather more of the 'traditional' activities of the ephebes. Prominent among these were performances of old songs and dances, for which the Spartans of their time were well-known to Lucian and Athenaeus: the chief stages for such performances seem to have been the Gymnopaediae and the Hyacinthia (above) and the annual ephebic festival of Artemis Orthia, which included archaic-sounding contests in singing (*mōa* and *keloia*) and dancing (*kaththēratorion* – some sort of hunting dance?).[23]

The 'revived' training also included three sporting activities which conformed less readily, and in one case scarcely at all, to conventional Greek gymnastic categories. One was the 'no holds barred' battle between two ephebic companies on an artificial island called Platanistas. As Patrucco noted, the description by Pausanias suggests a form of rough combat not unlike the widely-practised *pankration*, an 'all-in' contest in wrestling and boxing. The second, held in the theatre, was an annual tournament between five teams of twenty-year-old ball-players or *sphaireis*, each team being fourteen-strong, to judge from one fully-preserved catalogue of a victorious team. No parallel in Greek sport can be found for this ball-game, which was also rough, according to Lucian; Woodward's analogy with American football cannot be too wide of the mark. The third event was the 'contest of endurance' (*agōn tēs karterias*). Its exact nature is debated, since, although it was frequently referred to by contemporary writers, none of them has left a satisfactory account of what actually happened. It took place at the annual festival of Artemis Orthia and was undoubtedly a violent event, in which fatalities seem not to have been uncommon; Chrimes was right to stress, however, that it does indeed seem to have taken the form of a proper contest, with ephebes having 'to make some sort of attack upon the altar, which was defended by whip-bearers'; the Augustan writer Hyginus adds that the ephebe who endured the longest was declared the winner, receiving the title of 'altar-victor' or *bōmonikēs*, which is epigraphically attested under the Antonines and Severi.[24]

A small scatter of evidence, not previously gathered together, shows that the Roman city organized contests for girls as well as youths. In the second century the traditional dances of Spartan girls at the sanctuary of Artemis at Caryae, on Sparta's north-east frontier, were well-known to contemporary Greek writers. Female athletes took part in the Livian games, instituted under Tiberius or Claudius (chapter 7); and in the second century a ritual race between girls called 'Dionysiades' formed part of the civic cult of Dionysus. That some girls received a training in wrestling is suggested by a scholiast's anecdote of a wrestling-match between a Spartan *virgo* and a Neronian senator, M. Palfurius Sura; as Moretti saw, this episode probably took place at the Neronia in Rome, the Greek-style games founded by Nero, which evidently included contests for girls (one of them apparently hijacked by Sura). That the training of the girls was a civic concern at Roman Sparta is shown by the fact that the 'Dionysiades' fell under the supervision of the *bideoi*; and civic promotion of feminine athletic prowess is reflected in the honour of a public statue conferred on the sole attested victrix at the Livia. It needs to be stressed, however, that if Roman Sparta encouraged athletics for girls, these were anyway no longer uncommon in the Graeco-Roman world: a text from Delphi, for instance, shows that in the first century girls' races (including one in armour) were staged at the Pythian and Isthmian games and in festivals at Athens, Sicyon and Epidaurus. Because such contests were no longer especially shocking, their existence at Roman Sparta need not imply that local attitudes to women were out of step with the times; as we saw earlier, other evidence suggests the contrary.[25]

The inclusion of contests for girls in the 'revived' training was certainly a deliberate allusion to a well-known feature of the 'Lycurgan' *agōgē*. It is equally clear that the whole ephebic system of Roman Sparta asserted continuity with this 'ancestral' régime – and never more so than in the archaizing age of the Greek renaissance. The foundation of both the 'endurance-contest' and the battle at Platanistas was attributed to Lycurgus; in the early third century the ephebic instructors apparently included 'teachers of the Lycurgan customs'; and an ephebe in the same period was praised for his 'moderation and manliness, together with his courage and obedience to the ancestral Lycurgan customs'. As we have seen, an archaic-sounding terminology was employed to describe the activities and organisation of the training; to the examples already cited can be added the formulaic expression whereby the victorious teams of ball-players were said to have 'defeated the *ōbai*' – a reference to the old sub-divisions of Sparta's citizen-body, by the Imperial age assimilated to *phulai* or tribes of the usual Greek civic type. In the Hadrianic age, at a time when linguistic archaism was fashionable among Greek litterati, Spartan ephebes suddenly adopted – and continued to use intermittently into the third century – a 'hyper-Doricizing' dialect in their dedications to Artemis Orthia, a piece of antiquarianism presumably intended to reinforce the claims of the training to represent ancestral practice.[26]

The justice of these claims, however, is another matter. In a view which has not passed without challenge, Chrimes argued for a strong element of real continuity between the old *agōgē* and the 'revived' training of Roman times. But the old *agōgē* had already undergone one revival under Cleomenes III, about which nothing is known, although the possible involvement of the Stoic philosopher Sphaerus should warn us against assuming a straightforward return to old ways on this occasion (chapter 4). The artificiality of the second 'revival' – after 146 BC – is suggested by the fact that it took place after a period of over forty years during which Sparta's ephebic training had been – perforce – organized on the Achaean model; the lingering influence of this interlude can perhaps be detected in the more conventional activities of the Roman city's ephebes. This 'revival' fell, moreover, in a period of intense antiquarian activity by local writers (see chapter 13), whose influence should not be underestimated, especially since their interests are known to have extended to sport, as is suggested by the lost work on 'ball-playing' (*peri sphairistikēs*) attributed to one Timocrates. The antiquity of the more distinctive sports of the revived training is more easily asserted than proved. The battle at Platanistas is first attested in Cicero's day; and the earliest evidence for the ball-tournament is dated to 70–75. A Classical precursor can be identified with some confidence only in the case of the 'endurance-contest', the idea of which seems to have been based on the Xenophontic cheese-ritual around the altar of Orthia. Scholars are also agreed, however, that the contest in its Roman form was a recent reinvention (could it have been the Stoic Sphaerus who first turned the old ritual with the cheeses into a test of physical endurance?). The revived training, moreover, as well as being an artificial construct when it was first recreated in the years after 146 BC, underwent further episodes of reinvention in the Roman period, as is indicated by the innovations of the Flavian period identified above. Given such multi-layered archaism, it seems prudent to accept that any kernel of ancient practice around which the Roman training was built up is irretrievably concealed by a much more recent archaising husk.[27]

*   *   *   *   *   *

In order to understand the prominence in civic life of this artificially-revived training we need to realize the extraordinary degree of outside interest which it generated. There can be no doubt, to begin with, that this training was the chief attraction of Roman Sparta's thriving cultural tourism, for which there is evidence from the first century BC to the fourth AD. Such tourism was a recognized cultural activity in the Hellenistic and Imperial ages, generating its own periegetic literature. Perhaps the first clear sign that Sparta had become a focus for visitors with antiquarian interests is the lost work on Spartan votive offerings composed by Polemo of Ilium (fl. *c*.190 BC), evidently on the basis of autopsy. The fullest spokesman for Spartan tourism, of course, is Pausanias, who found so much to see in the city and its environs that he was compelled, as at Athens, to restrict himself, in the guide-book to Greece which he went on to write, to 'the most memorable things'. Contrary to the famous dictum of Thucydides, Sparta by now was crammed with ancient sanctuaries, historic monuments and archaic works of art. However, judging from Livy's remark, quoted above, the tourist of his day would not have come to Sparta primarily to see *objets d'art*. In fact, it is clear that visitors to the Roman city came chiefly to witness those civic activities which could be identified as vestiges of the 'Lycurgan customs': apart from the visit of Augustus to the magistrates' messes, foreign spectators are attested at the ball-tournament of the *sphaireis*, the battle at Platanistas, and the festivals of Artemis Orthia, the Gymnopaediae and the Hyacinthia. Pausanias himself drew attention to at least six different displays by the Antonine city's youth, although it is unclear whether he himself was a spectator at any of them. This evidence shows, moreover, that the 'endurance contest' was by no means the 'star' attraction for tourists: according to Philostratus, Greeks 'flocked' to the Hyacinthia and the Gymnopaediae just as much as they did to the sanctuary of Artemis Orthia.[28]

At the risk of over-schematization, two distinct phases in this tourism can be detected. Down to the Augustan age the evidence concerns Romans only, present in Greece either on official business (as perhaps with the Augustan consular Laelius) or, as with Cicero, while studying at Athens, a popular centre of higher studies for well-born Romans in the first century BC. The second phase, for which the evidence by contrast concerns Greeks, can be linked to the great revival of Greek cultural life in the second and early third centuries, which brought with it a new Greek interest in Spartan antiquities. This development was encouraged by the emperor Hadrian, who held up 'Laconian moderation and training' as a model to the Cyrenaeans and served as eponymous *patronomos* (chapter 8). His tenure of this post went some way to establishing it for a generation as a rival in prestige to the Athenian archonship, as is shown by the succession of rich and distinguished overseas *patronomoi* holding office in the emperor's wake (chapter 8). Unlike the archonship, however, the patronomate could not claim a venerable origin: the attraction of the post for cultured foreigners like the historian A. Claudius Charax presumably lay in its association with the ephebic training, to the expenses of which he and these other foreign incumbents – along with Hadrian himself – no doubt made generous contributions.

In this second phase, Spartan tourism has as its most typical representative Pausanias, a citizen of Magnesia-ad-Sipylum in Asia Minor, who visited Sparta probably under Pius. The background to his touristic activity was misunderstood by Habicht, who saw him as a 'loner':

undoubtedly he should rather be viewed as part of an upsurge of visitors from overseas (Asia especially) drawn to Greece in the wake of Hadrianic initiatives and providing Pausanias with his envisaged readership. Lucian of Samosata was probably another early Antonine visitor during one of his visits to Greece, since his familiarity with the displays of Roman Sparta's ephebes and *parthenoi* is most economically understood as deriving from autopsy. Spartan tourism continued to thrive in the Severan age, when the antiquarian enquiries of cultured visitors were probably the chief *raison d'être* of a uniquely attested civic official called the 'expounder (*exēgētēs*) of the Lycurgan customs'. As well as the overseas visitors in this period discussed in chapter 13, another Severan tourist can probably be recognised in the sophist Flavius Philostratus, an Athenian citizen and resident, whose *Life of Apollonius* shows familiarity with Roman Sparta, including its ephebic spectacles – in particular, alone of all surviving writers, Philostratus knew the 'endurance contest' by its official title, as attested in a Trajanic inscription. Given that the historicity of the Philostratean Apollonius is open to doubt, this familiarity is perhaps best understood as reflecting the personal experience of the author himself.[29]

Although the scale of this tourism is impossible to quantify, it was clearly more akin to that of the Grand Tour of eighteenth-century Europe than the mass-tourims of today: when individual sightseers can be identified, they almost invariably belong to the Roman and Greek upper classes, who alone enjoyed the leisure and wealth to travel for pleasure. Cultural tourism of this kind was best undertaken on the basis of an educated interest, moreover: the ephebic performances of traditional Spartan songs and dances seem unlikely to have appealed much to popular taste, although with the more violent sports of the ephebes, which are likely to have had a wider appeal, the Roman city may consciously have 'played to the gallery'. Broadly speaking, however, this tourism bears witness to the enduring interest aroused by Spartan history and customs among the educated classes of the Graeco-Roman world – a topic exhaustively examined by Tigerstedt. After the second century BC this interest focuscd more and more on Sparta's renowned contribution to Greek educational theory and practice – the 'Lycurgan' *agōgē*, with its distinctive emphasis on physical rather than intellectual training, an emphasis which the violent games of the Roman city's ephebes were clearly intended to evoke. The austerities of this training held a certain appeal for educated Romans in the Late Republic, as is suggested by the attitude of Cicero. In the age of the Greek renaissance, the Spartan tradition was seen as an aspect of that old-world Hellenism which educated Greeks laid hold of as their common cultural property. Writers such as Lucian and Philostratus produced debates on the merits of the 'Lycurgan' system of education, and the archaizing fantasies which the idea of Sparta now conjured up are echoed in the travels of the

Philostratean Apollonius, who 'after crossing Taygetus . . . saw Sparta hard at work and the ancestral practices of Lycurgus thriving', or in the rhetorical claim of the Hadrianic sophist Favorinus to be worthy of a public statue at Sparta because he 'loved gymnastic exercises'. Like other guardians of the Greek cultural tradition, such as the Athenians or the Rhodians, the Spartans were open to literary or rhetorical castigation if they seemed to fail in their trust: hence the polemic of Aelius Aristides against the contemporary Spartan taste for the pantomime (chapter 13) and the alleged censure of Spartan effeminacy by the Philostratean Apollonius. In such a hot-house atmosphere, it is not surprising that Spartan archaism blossomed: to the age of the Greek renaissance belong the 'hyper-Doricizing' dialect of the ephebes, all the epigraphic references to the 'Lycurgan customs' and the elevation of ephebic athletics instructors to the status of civic celebrities, as in the case of one C. Rubrius Vianor (a foreigner?), who received a public statue 'for the sake of his seriousness concerning the Laconian *ēthos* and his excellence in the gymnasia'. In an age when the re-creation of the past was itself a valid form of cultural activity, any definition of Roman Sparta's place in the cultural life of the Greek renaissance must take account, not only of her newly-founded *agōnes* and her philosophical and rhetorical studies, but also of the shows provided by her ephebes and *parthenoi* and the audiences which they attracted.[30]

Not only the respect for ancestral practice which marked all Greek civic life but also the fame of the 'Lycurgan customs' in particular explain the tenacity with which Sparta maintained its archaizing facade. The prestige of the 'revived' training and the tourism which it generated helped this otherwise fairly typical provincial Greek city to maintain a place in the world and allowed the Spartans to feel that they were still 'special'. In these circumstances it is perhaps easier to comprehend the whole-hearted attitude of both participants and their watching families in the 'endurance-contest': for all the irony of a Lucian (who satirized other objects of contemporary reverence too) we should assume that many visitors went away impressed with what they saw on such occasions. That an awareness of the benefits of this tourism to local economy, although no doubt a factor in Spartan archaism, was not the chief one, is suggested by the dependence of the ephebic training on the moral and financial support of established curial families, whose vital role in maintaining the Roman city's ancestral cults has already been noted. That the training was financed largely through euergetism is suggested by the liturgical character of the patronomate, the post of *boagos* (as proposed above), and two other posts, those of *diabetēs* and hipparch. The former was a tribal liturgy which helped to fund each tribe's *sphaireis*-team; in the Antonine period a *diabetēs* of the Neopolitae boasted of having served 'of his own free will'. The duties of the latter, a post likewise linked with the training, are unknown, but their liturgical character is shown by the Severan evidence for an 'eternal hipparch', who evidently had given the office a cash-endowment. The patriotic attitude to the training of the Roman city's aristocracy is best demonstrated by the well-documented case of the Memmian clan, which is known to have produced – over a period of some two centuries – five *boagoi* and eleven *patronomoi*, including P. Memmius Pratolaus *qui et* Aristocles, 'champion' of the Lycurgan customs. Because the ephebic training was the source of such great civic prestige, in Sparta's case it was something more than simply a 'kind of university training for the sons of the well-to-do'. The unusual length of the training helps to explain civic efforts to encourage the recruitment of boys from less well-off families – the larger purpose, it was suggested earlier, of the reorganization of the Flavian period. That a certain tension at times developed between the maintenance of traditional status-distinctions within local society and the need to provide sufficient manpower for the ephebic training is suggested by the presence of two slaves and a freedman in *sphaireis*-teams from the early Flavian and Trajanic periods. For the local upper class at least, however, the expense and administrative burden of the training were clearly outweighed by an enhanced sense of civic pride. In the Antonine and Severan heyday of the Greek renaissance the Spartan aristocracy, like its Athenian counterpart, had the satisfying sense of living in a prestigious centre of Greek cultural activity, partly as a result of which civic service continued to provide a meaningful outlet for its wealth and political ambition.[31]

Chapter fifteen

Epilogue: Sparta from late antiquity to the Middle Ages

In the fifth century the pagan, classical, Sparta with which this book is concerned drops out of sight. In his apologetic work *The Cure of Hellenic Maladies*, composed early in the century, the Christian bishop Theodoret triumphantly referred to the complete demise of the Lycurgan regime at Sparta. Whether this text should be taken *au pied de la lettre* to prove the final disappearance of all vestiges of Roman Sparta's archaizing laconism is perhaps arguable. However, in spite of recent claims for 'the survival of paganism [in Greece] well into the Byzantine period', it is not easy to believe that a fully civic institution such as the Roman city's ephebic training, with its cycle of contests organized around pagan sanctuaries and festivals, could have long survived the law of Theodosius I, promulgated in 391 and upheld by later emperors, which banned pagan rites and closed temples for public use[1].

In the period after 400 the evidence for Christianity at Sparta also becomes more marked. The city's first attested bishop, one Hosius, appears in 457. Although local epigraphy has so far produced only a meagre crop of Christian epitaphs, the Christianization of Sparta can now be documented in archaeology far more clearly as a result of Greek excavations over the last half-century. An Early Christian cemetery and two buildings identified with varying degrees of confidence as Early Christian basilicas have been discovered in the area to the south and south-east of the acropolis (App.I, 42–3, 49). In addition, the large and well-built basilica on the acropolis itself is now assigned a date no later than the seventh century (App.I, 44). In a development paralleled at Athens, it looks as if the earliest Christian building-activity took place well away from the old civic centre with its strong pagan links. By the seventh century, however, local paganism was so weakened that a major church (the episcopal seat?) could be built only metres away from the old sanctuary of Athena Chalcioecus, patron deity of Classical Sparta. The Spartan myth was now well on its way to becoming no more than a learned memory, although in Byzantine circles it would continue to provoke speculation and debate, as it does today.[2]

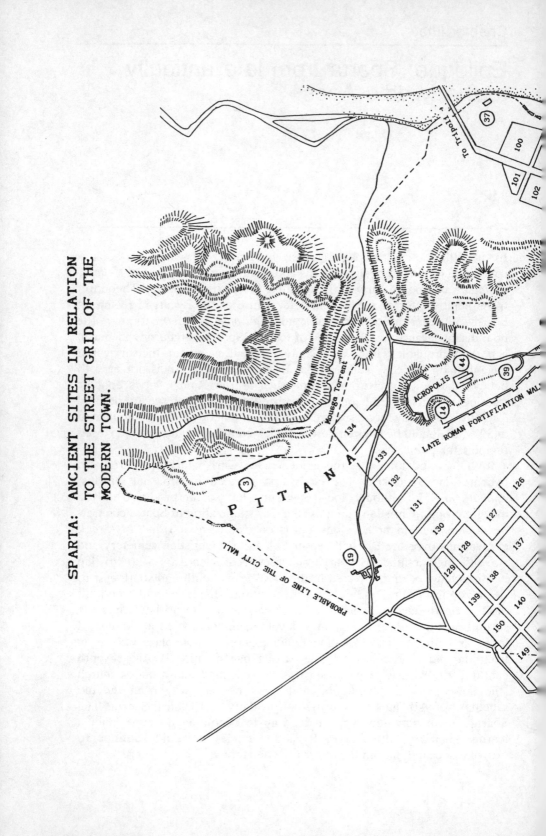

SPARTA: ANCIENT SITES IN RELATION
TO THE STREET GRID OF THE
MODERN TOWN.

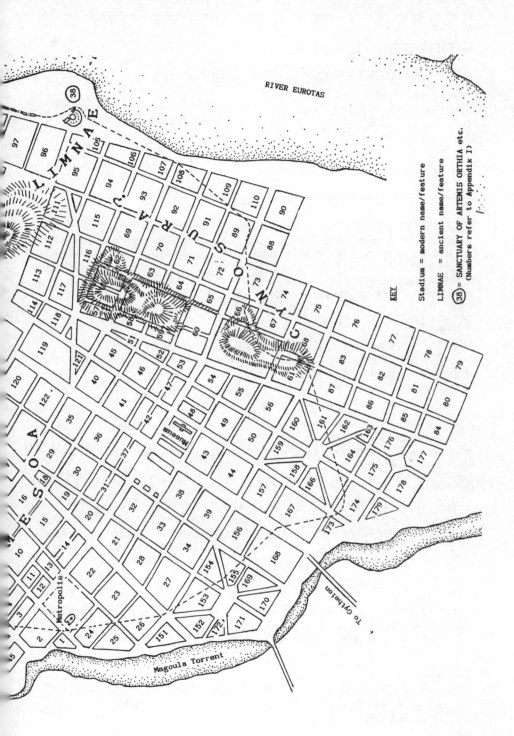

RIVER EUROTAS

Museum

Metropolis

Magoula Torrent

To Gytheion

215

Appendix I
The monuments of Roman Sparta

The following catalogue briefly lists the principal archaeologically and epigraphically attested monuments of Roman Sparta, with some Hellenistic or earlier sites included, usually only where they retained their importance into the Roman period. Where possible a location is given by reference either to the British School (hereafter BSA) plan in *ABSA* 13, 1906–7, pl.1 or to this book's Map 1, showing the blocks of the modern town's municipal grid.

1. Aqueduct

Peek 1974, 295–303. Location unknown. Existence implied by a dedication set up by the ward of Cynosura in honour of a civic magistrate who 'brought down the water'. Date: third century BC.

2. Aqueduct

Le Roy 1974, 229–38. Location: unknown. Attested in a dedication by a residential group calling itself 'those who live under the aqueduct'. To be distinguished from No.1 (so Le Roy; Peek *contra*). Date: about 200 BC?.

3. Aqueduct

Blouet 1833, 46, 'LL'; Loring 1895, 43–4; *ABSA* 12, 1905–6, 425; A. Adamantiou, *PAE* 1931, 92. Location: remains of approach to acropolis marked on BSA plan, 11J-K and 9H-J; cf. Map 1. The brickwork of the piers nearest the acropolis are of a size and type commensurate with a Hadrianic date (pers.comm. S.Walker). See chapter 10.

4. Vault

ABSA 12, 1905–6, 423. Location: Tower 'E' of the Late Roman fortification wall (below, No.10); BSA plan, K13. Vaulted chamber, constructed in *opus testaceum*, its original function unclear; later built into the line of the fortification wall.

5. Bridge

IG v.1.138 = Wilhelm 1913, 858–63; Spawforth 1984, 274–7. See chapter 10. Sites of two possible candidates for identification with this bridge: *ABSA* 12, 1905–6, 437 and 13, 1906–7, 9; Loring 1895, 42.

6. Thoroughfare

AD 28, 1973 (1977), B1 Chronika 172. Location: Map 1, Square 124. Unpaved road running north towards the acropolis. Date: tentatively placed around 300.

7. Thoroughfare

AD 30, 1975 (1983), B1 Chronika 74–5. Location: Map 1, Square 126. Broad (5.50m.) surfaced (but not paved) street flanked by colonnades and running NE towards the acropolis. Date: tentatively placed after 268.

8. Thoroughfare

AD 28–9, 1973 (1977), B1 Chronika 164–6 with figs.1–2. Location: NE of acropolis, junction of the Tripoli and Kastori roads. Unpaved road, 5.50m. wide, running towards the acropolis. Date: 'fourth century'.

9. City-wall

ABSA 12, 1905–6, 284–8; 1906–7, 5–16. Location: Map 1. Tiled mud-brick on a masonry socle. Evidence from tile-stamps for repairs in the first century BC: Kahrstedt 1954, 195. For Roman repairs in a stretch on the right bank of the Eurotas: *ABSA* 12, 1905–6, 300–301. Date: after 184 BC.

10. Late Roman Fortification Wall

ABSA 12, 1905–6, 417–29; Gregory 1982, 20–21. Location: Map 1. See chapter 9. Date: early fifth century.

11. 'Old Ephoreia'

Kennell (1987). To this building may have belonged two architectural blocks of similar marble and dimensions, reused in the SE stretch of the Late Roman wall, inscribed with Augustan catalogues of *hierothutai*, the magistrates who tended the civic hearth and oversaw official hospitality (chapter 7): *IG* v.1.141–2; *ABSA* 12, 1905–6, 433; Spawforth 1985, 195.

12. Public Archives

IG v.1.20a.3–4. Trajanic decree referring to a *grammatophulakeion*. Presumably identical to the Spartan archives (*Lakōnikai anagraphai*) personally inspected by Plutarch (*Ages*.19.10).

13. Sunodos

IG v.1.882–3; Woodward 1928–30, 236. Location: unknown. Evidently a roofed assembly-building, possibly to be identified with the Scias, meeting-place of the citizen-assembly (Paus.iii.12.10).

14. Theatre

Paus.iii.14.1; Luc. *Anach*.38; *ABSA* 12, 1905–6, 175–209; 26, 1923–5, 119–58; 27, 1925–6, 175–209, including (pp.204–5) a summary of Woodward's view of the theatre's history; 28, 1926–7, 3–36; 30, 1928–30, 151–240; Bulle 1937, 5–49; Buckler 1986, 431–6. Location: Map 1. See chapters 9, 10 and 13.

15. Lodgings of the Romans and Dicasts

IG v.1.7. 5–6; 869. Location: unknown. Date: second or first century BC.

16. Makellon

Vitr.*Ling.Lat.*v.146–7; *IG* v.1.149 (*SEG* xi.600) and 151 (*SEG* xi.598); de Ruyt 1983, 192, where the post of *epi tou makellou*, signifying a slave-overseer, is mistaken for that of a 'marchand'; and, *pace* de Ruyt, the *mageiros* of 149.8 is a separate functionary, ministering to the dining mess of the *agoranomos*. See chapter 10.

17. Granary

IG v.1. 149 (*SEG* xi.600) and 151 (*SEG* xi.598). See chapter 14.

18. 'Roman Stoa'

Traquair 1905–6, 414–20; *AA* 1942, 155–8. Location: Map 1. The Augustan date for this building given by H.Dodge in Macready/Thompson 1987, 107 seems too early (and is unsupported by the reference which she cites at n.10); the measurements of the brickwork are close to those of the Arapissa-complex (Susan Walker, pers. comm.). At the time of writing (June 1988) the stoa is the object of renewed archaeological investigation by the Institute of Archaeology, London, under the supervision of J.J. Wilkes.

19. Gymnasium of Eurycles

ABSA 12, 1905–6, 407–14; Palagia, forthcoming. Location: Map 1. See chapter 10.

20. Gymnasium

Paus.iii.14.6; *IG* iv^2.86, dated to 38–48 by Spawforth 1985, 254; *IG* v.1.20a.3 (Trajanic); 493 (Antonine); 529.9–12 (Severan); *SEG* xi.492.10–11 (reign of Pius). The older of Sparta's two gymnasia. See chapter 10.

21. Stadium

IG v.1.20.7. Trajanic dossier stipulating the provision of oil 'in the *st[adion]*' during the days of the athletic contests of the annual Leonidea. Location and date unknown. For the dubious evidence of early antiquaries for an ancient stadium on the right bank of the Eurotas see *ABSA* 12, 1905–6, 306–8 with earlier refs.

22. Machanidai

SEG xi.492.11–12 with Woodward 1925–6, 232.

23. Thermai

SEG xi.492.11. See chapter 10. Conceivably to be sought at the partly excavated therms featuring two apsidal rooms of 'massive construction' in rubble-concrete faced with brick and stone, some 45m. south of the theatre: *ABSA* 12, 1905–6, 405–6; 26, 1923–5, 118. Location: BSA plan, K12.

24. Nymphaeum

Woodward 1926–7, 6–14 and 32–6; S. Walker, *The Architectural Development of Roman Nymphaea in Greece* (unpublished dissertation, London 1979) 211–17. Location: BSA plan, K12. Fountain-house, presumably fed by the Roman aqueduct, immediately in front of the west-*parodos* wall of the theatre, built with re-used bricks from the demolished scenery-store and other *spolia* and veneered with marble. Date: almost certainly after 268, since it re-uses a dedication set up in about 240: Spawforth 1985, 239–43; probably part of the building-programme at the theatre around 300.

25. Public Portico

Woodward 1928–30, 235–6; *SEG* xi.881. Finds of tiles for a pastas indicate a location near the theatre.

26. Public Stoa

IG v.1.692. Location unknown. Built (or merely repaired?) by the ex-*boagos* M. Aurelius [——] son of Callicrates, not before 161.

27. Portico

IG v.1.884. Roof-tile stamped 'Of the pastas in Alpeion'. For the location see Paus.iii.18.2 with Bölte 1929, col.1362.

28. Colonnaded Structure

Woodward 1928–30, 188 no.14 and 215–7 no.6 (*SEG* xi.847); Spawforth 1985, 198–9. Inscribed fragment from the entablature of a colonnaded structure, connected with the family of the Memmii. Date: first century?

29. Colonnaded Structure

IG v.1.378. Incomplete inscription, now lost, copied by Cyriacus of Ancona in 1437; the original drawing is lost, but a copy is preserved in a sketchbook of the Florentine architect Giuliano di Sangallo ('Giamberti') now in the Vatican (Vaticanus Barberinus latinus 4424, folio 29r), illustrated by Kleiner 1983, pl.xxxv. Copied 'in Lacedaemonia ad ingentia et ornamentissima columnarum epistilia (*sic*)', according to Sangallo, who represents the inscription on three epistyle-blocks supported by three pairs of columns and superimposed on each other in an architectural conceit, although presumably preserving something (epistyle-blocks on a Corinthian colonnade?) of Cyriacus' original drawing of an ancient ruin still standing as late as M. Fourmont's visit (1729–30). Could the columns be the two 'outside' the Late Roman fortification wall in front of the theatre seen by Le Roy, *Les Ruines des plus beaux monuments de la Grèce*, Paris 1770, p.33 pl.xiii? Bulle 1937, 40–42 argued that it formed part of the Flavian remodelling of the theatre, on grounds, however, which now seem unconvincing in the light of criticisms of his reconstruction of the theatre's history (chapter 10).

30. Public Building

Ergon 1964 (1965) 102–12. Location: BSA map, K13. Large masonry building associated with late Hellenistic stamped tiles; deliberately buried statue of the empress Fulvia Plautilla (?) found inside: Spawforth 1986, 326.

31. Monument

ABSA 28, 1926–7, 46–7. Fragments of an unpublished Latin inscription in monumental lettering apparently naming the emperor Tiberius. Found on the acropolis above the theatre; part of a massive base or conceivably a gateway.

32. Corinthian Building

ABSA 12, 1905–6, 426. Remains incorporated into the north line of the Late Roman fortification wall.

33. Public Buildings?

AD 17, 1961–2 (1963) B1 Chronika 83–4. Location: BSA plan, L14. Remains of two large buildings, one of ashlar masonry. Associated with a list of *gerontes* from the patronomate of P. Memmius Eudamus, Spawforth 1985, 212–3, and roof-tiles stamped 'Belonging to the public lodgings'.

34. Public Building?

AD 20, 1965 (1966), Chronika B1 174–6; 1969 (1970), B1 Chronika 137–8. Location: east of the acropolis, Sparta-Tripoli road. Basilica-like building destroyed by fire or earthquake. Date: 'early fourth century'.

35. Public Building

AD 28, 1973 (1977) B1 Chronika 168–70. Location: Map 1, Square 31. Large building with two apsidal rooms, a geometric floor-mosaic and producing fragments of columns and Corinthian and other capitals. Date: 'Late Roman'.

36. Public Building?

AD 29, 1973–4 (1979), B2 Chronika 285. Location: Map 1, Square 138. Large apsidal building perhaps featuring a colonnade. Date: 'last years of antiquity'.

37. Altar

ABSA 12, 1905–6, 295–302. Location: Map 1. Massive altar of ashlar masonry, 23.60m. (length) × 6.60m. (width) × 1.90m. (height), remodelled in the Roman period. Quite possibly the altar of Lycurgus, whose sanctuary stood in this general area (Paus.iii.16.1) and whose cult is well-attested as late as the third century. Date: Hellenistic?

38. Sanctuary of Artemis Orthia

Dawkins 1929. Location: Map 1. In the Roman period the sanctuary's chief features were: (a) a Hellenistic, non-peripteral Doric temple *in antis*, replacing a late Archaic temple on the same site; (b) a masonry altar, rebuilt once and possibly twice in the Roman period on the foundations of a late Archaic predecessor; (c) a theatral area, first attested in the Augustan period, when its front row(s) included stone seating (*IG* v.1.254), and remodelled on a monumental scale probably around 300, when a quasi-amphitheatre was built of rubble-concrete faced (probably) with marble, with a tribune for privileged spectators; (d) dedications, notably the ephebic *stēlai*, and honorific monuments, one a portrait-statue set up in the mid-third century beside the cult-statue: *IG* v.1.599; Woodward in Dawkins 1929, ch. 10.

39. 'Round Building'

Frazer 1898, iii.325–7 (with earlier refs.); *Ergon* 1964 (1965), 102–12. Location: BSA plan, L13. Semi-circular ashlar wall of (?) Classical date retaining a level platform repaired and paved in the Roman period, when a massive statue-base was probably installed near the centre, perhaps supporting a colossal marble statue of which a thumb was found nearby, identified by N.E. Crosby, *AJA* 8, 1893, 342, 9, 1894, 212–3 (C. Waldstein, *AJA* 9, 1894, *contra*) with the 'large statue' of the Spartan *Dēmos* in the agora (Paus.iii.11.9), probably in turn to be identified with the dedication of C. Iulius Theophrastus when priest of Olympian Zeus under Pius (*SEG* xi.492.4–5; see chapter 8 for date).

40. Heroön of Eurycles Herculanus

Spawforth 1978, 249–51. See chapter 8.

41. Colonnaded Structure

Woodward 1928–30, 188 no.13 and 217 no. 7 (*SEG* xi.846). Inscribed block from the entablature of a colonnaded structure, probably once within a sanctuary, dedicated by the priest Polydamas son of Phoebidas. Date: first century BC?

42. Basilica?

AD 29, 1973–4 (1979) B2 Chronika 287–9. Location: Map 1, Square 117. Basilica-like building on an eastern orientation featuring a vast room (7.60 × 18m.) with a mosaic-floor with animal scenes. Date: 'sixth century'.

43. Basilica

AD 24, 1969 (1970), B1 Chronika 138. Location: north of the Xenia Hotel. Date: 'Early Christian'.

44. Basilica

P. Vokotopoulos, *Peloponnesiaka* suppl.vi.2, 1975, 270–85 with earlier refs. Location: acropolis, BSA plan, 12K-L and 13K-L. Date: most probably seventh century.

45. Cemetery

ABSA 13, 1906–7, 155–68. Location: BSA plan, K14–15. Four built chamber-tombs of dressed stone. Earliest burial dated to 200–150 BC, the latest, from a coin of Eurycles, to the Augustan age.

46. Cemetery

PAE 1931, 91–6; 1934, 123–9. Location: north of the acropolis, on the banks of the Mousga torrent. Cemetery of about ten rock-cut chamber-tombs, yielding about eighty inhumations set into the floor. Painted plaster walls, one depicting Apollo and the Nine Muses. One inscribed epitaph survived for a 12-year-old girl, Philumene. Date: first two centuries AD.

47. Cemetery

AD 27, 1972 (1976), B1 Chronika 242–6. Location: Tripoli road, immediately SW of the modern bridge. Roman tomb associated with a Geometric and Archaic cemetery.

48. Cemetery?

Tod/Wace 1906, 235 no.549 and 240 no.685. Location: BSA plan, O18. Two Roman tombs.

49. Cemetery

AD 24, 1969 (1970), B1 Chronika 135–7. Location: Map 1, Square 31. Date: 'Early Christian'.

50. House

AD 4, 1918 (1921), 171–6; 19, 1964 (1965), B1 Chronika 136–7; Loukas 1983. Location: Magoula. House with mosaic floor depicting Triton framed by Dionysiac scene. Date: late second century BC.

51. House

AD 27, 1972 (1976), B1 Chronika 242–6. Location: Sparta-Tripoli road, SW of the modern bridge. Three rooms of a large house with plastered and painted walls. Date: 'Augustan period'.

52. Baths

AD 20, 1965 (1966), B1 Chronika 173–4 and pl.155; 28, 1973 (1977), B1 Chronika 170–71. Location: Map 1, Square 126. Bath-complex of brick and concrete construction with floor mosaics and marble paving. Date: 'most probably third century'.

53. Building

AD 29, 1973–4 (1979), B2 Chronika 290–91. Location: 59 Kon.Palaiologou St.

Building of brick and concrete construction with two apsidal rooms and heating pipes in the walls. Date: 'probably third century'.

54. House(s)?

AD 29, 1973–4(1979), B2 Chronika 283–5. Location: Map 1, Square 137. Complex of rooms, three with hypocausts, two with geometric mosaics. Date: 'late second or early third century'.

55. Baths

ABSA 12, 1905–6, 435. Location: BSA plan, J15. Quatrefoil building with plastered walls and a hypocaust; finds included a marble statue of Asclepius ('second century') and an apparently private statue-dedication set up by Claudius Apo[——] for his daughter Callistonice (*IG* v.1.518). Date: second century.

56. House?

ABSA 45, 1950, 282–9; Waywell 1979, 303 no.50. Location: BSA plan, L14–15. Complex featuring four rooms with geometric mosaics and fragments of wall-revetment in *marmor Lacedaemonium*. Date: late second or early third century.

57. Building(s)

AD 19, 1964 (1965), B1 Chronika 144–5. Location: Paraskevopoulos plot, 500m. south of the theatre. Walls associated with storage-jars containing charred seeds and a *cache* of 200 Corinthian lamps. Date: first half of the third century. Traces of destruction by fire, tentatively linked by the excavator with the Herulian raid.

58. Buildings

AD 27, 1972 (1976), B1 Chronika 248–51. Location: Magoula. Building with a mosaic floor. Date: first half of the third century (coin of Gallienus). Later fourth-century building on same site.

59. Houses

ABSA 28, 1926–7, 46, Location: BSA plan, K12. Complex of houses, including a 'small, domestic, bath' incorporating a coin of Gordian III. Date: late third century?

60. Baths

Blouet 1833, 65 and pl.45, 'E', pl. 48, fig.3. Location: about 600 m. south-west of the sanctuary of Artemis Orthia.

61. Building

AD 29, 1973–4 (1979), B2 Chronika 285–6. Location: Map 1, Square 125. Date: 'Roman'.

62. Workshop

ABSA 28, 1926–7, 47. Location: south slope of the acropolis. Finds of 'terracotta figurines and votive limbs, and a few moulds for their manufacture – apparently indicating a factory and shop for the supply of votive offerings in terracotta to those about to visit the shrines of the Acropolis'. Date: Roman.

63. Buildings

AD 16, 1960 (1962), B1 Chronika 102. Location: Map 1, Squares 112–4. Plentiful remains, mainly 'private houses', two producing mosaics. Date: 'Roman'.

64. 'Villa'

ABSA 26, 1923–5, 117–8. Location: east of the acropolis. 'Extensive Roman villa, with an elaborate system of hypocausts'.

65. Bath?

ABSA 12, 1905–6, 435. Location: south slope of the acropolis: 'a . . . house, or possibly a bath-building, with a well-preserved mosaic pavement exhibiting a polychrome design of geometric type, alongside which was a cement-built water-conduit with several pipes, apparently of Late Roman date'.

66. Buildings

AD 28, 1973 (1977), B1 Chronika 170–1. Location: Map 1, Square 119. (a) Large apsidal building, later incorporated into a Byzantine church. (b) A complex of four rooms with geometric mosaics. Date: 'Late Roman'.

67. House

AD 30, 1975 (1983), B1 Chronika 74–6. Location: Map 1, Square 126. House with a large central apartment (10 × 5.50 m.), with an internal marble fountain, a dining (?) apse, and a mosaic floor depicting Helius and Selene. Date: after 350 (coin-evidence).

68. House

AD 19, 1964 (1965), B1 Chronika 136; 30, 1975 (1983), B1 Chronika 76–7; Waywell 1979, 302–3. Location: Moustakakis plot, Brasidas St. House-complex with a polychrome mosaic floor overlying an earlier hypocaust. Date: early fourth century?

69. House

AD 29, 1973–4 (1979), B2 Chronika 285–6. Location: Map 1, Square 125. Building featuring a room with marble flooring and wall-revetment. Date: 'perhaps fourth century'.

70. House

Waywell 1979, 302 no.46 with earlier refs. House with two figured mosaic floors

(Orpheus and the Abduction of Europa). Date: late third or early fourth century (grounds of style).

71. House

Waywell 1979, 302–3 no.48 with earlier refs. Several rooms, producing three figured mosaics as well as geometric ones, the former including the Surrender of Briseïs to Agamemnon. Date: 'late third century?' (grounds of style).

72. House?

Waywell 1979, 303 no.49 with earlier refs. Mosaic floor depicting the Nine Muses and portraits of famous poets and Alcibiades. Date: 'late third or early fourth century' (grounds of style).

73. House (?) and other remains

AD 20, 1965 (1966), B1 Chronika 170–3; Waywell 1979, 302 no.47. Location: Paraskevopoulos plot, 500 m. south of the theatre. 'Villa' with five rooms. Walls with polychrome painted plaster and marble revetment. Four polychrome marble floors, one depicting Dionysus in a theatrical scene. Date: 250–300 (grounds of style).

74. Bath?

AD 20, 1965 (1966), B1 Chronika 176–7; 22, 1967 (1968), B1 Chronika 200; 24, 1969 (1970), B1 Chronika 137. Location: Map 1, Square 100. Complex with a (?) colonnaded courtyard and a mosaic floor with marine imagery. Date: 'third century'.

75. Building

AD 28, 1973 (1977), B1 Chronika 168. Location: Map 1, Square 117. Date: fourth century (coin-evidence).

76. Building

AD 29, 1973–4 (1979), B2 Chronika 289–90. Location: Map 1, Square 117. Courtyard building. Date: 'fifth century'.

77. 'Farm'

AD 27, 1972 (1976), B1 Chronika 246–8. Location: east of acropolis, building site of the Organismos Ergatikis Katoikias. Courtyard building producing a wine-press and storage-jars. Date: 'sixth century'.

Appendix II
Catalogues of magistrates

A. Chronological summary.

Chronological Key: A = Augustus; A/T = Augustus/Tiberius; F = Flavians; F/T = Flavians/Trajan; T = Trajan; T/H = Trajan/Hadrian; H = Hadrian; H/P = Hadrian/Pius; P = Pius; P/M = Pius/Marcus; M = Marcus; C = Commodus; C/S = Commodus/Severus; LS = Later Severi; PS = Post-Severan.

References: numbers refer to *IG* v.1 or (when prefixed by Roman numerals) to *SEG*.

Gerontes:

A: 50? (xi.505);92; 93; 95; 96?
A/T: 94
F/T: 162 (xi.580); xi.570; xi.558–60
T: 97 (xi.564b); 98; 99 (xi.566);100 (xi.571): 103 (xi.568); 117 (xi.573); 121 (xi.574); 163?; 191 (xi.567); 193? (xi.637); xi.561; xi.563–5; xi.569; 572?
T/H: 101
H: 60; 61 (xi.547); xi.102 (xi.579); 104 + 166 = xi.580; 114 (xi.576); xi.575; xxxi.340
H/P: 107; 112 (xi.577); xi.578
P: 105 + 106 = xi.582; 108–9; 110 (xi.587); 111 (xi.584); 115 (xi.592); 120 (xi.583); 180?; 182 (xi.586); xi.585
P/M: 162 (xi.580)
M: 116 (xi.590); Spawforth 1985, 212–3
Second century: 118; 119 (xi.589); 122

Ephors and *Nomophulakes:*

F/T: 72; xi.557b
T: 51 (xi.506); 52 (xi.506); 57 (xi.509); xi.557a
T/H: 83?
H: 59 (xi.521; 548); 62
H/P: 91; xi.557c
P: 64–6; 68 (xi.525); 71a; 71b.1–39; 90 (xi.552)
C/S: 75 + 78 + 81 = xi.554; 89 (xi.556)

Ephors:

A: 49
F: 79; xi.510–12
T: 158? (xi.631); xi.506; 513; 514?; 515–17; 533?
T/H: xi.518
H: xi.521b
P: 53; 55; 65; 66.13–19; 67; 70; 71b.40–59; 73; 157 (xi.547); xi.528–9
M: xi.530
Second century: 76?; 77

Nomophulakes:

F: 79; xi.539
F/T: 80; xi.534
T: 148 (xi.537b); xi.535–6; 537–8; 540–43; 546a-b
T/H: xi.544
H: 61 (xi.547a); 82 (xi.543); 157 + 187 (xi. 547c); 547b
P: 69; 71b.iii.23–39; 85; 87 (xi.551); 88 (xi.553); xi.550; 554
P/M: 84?

Patronomos **and colleagues:**

A: 48
P: 74 (xi.527); 115? (xi.592)
C/S: xi.503
LS: xi.504?
Second century: 137 (xi.612)

Bideoi:

A: 136
F: xi.605; 608–9
F/T: xi.611
T: 137 (xi.612); 152 (xi.604); xi.606?; 607; xi.610
H: 139 (xi.614)
P: 113; 138 (xi.615)
LS: 140 (xi.616a)

Gunaikonomos **and colleagues:**

F/T: xi.628?
T: xi.626
M: xi.627
LS: 170

Agoranomos **and colleagues:**

A: 124–7
P: 128 (xi.597)
P/M: 151 (xi.598); 155 (xi.599)
C/S: 129 (xi.602); 150 (xi.601)
LS: 130 (xi.603)

Epimelētēs **and colleagues:**

A: 133–5

Hieromnēmones:

PS: 168 + 603 = Spawforth 1984, 285–8

Hierothutai:

A: 141–2

Pedianomos:

A: 123?

Summary

	A	A/T	F	F/T	T	T/H	H	H/P	P	P/M	M	C	C/S	LS	PS	TOTAL
Gerontes:	5	1		5	16	1	7	3	10	1	2					51 (54)
Ephors/ *Nomophulakes*:			2	4	1	2	2	7					2			20
Ephors:	1		4		8	1	1		11		1					27 (29)
Nomophulakes:			2	2	11	1	4		7	1						28
Patronomos:	1								2				1	1		5(6)
Bideoi:	1		3	1	5		1		2					1		14
Gunaikonomos:				1	1						1			1		4
Agoranomos:	4								1	2			2	1		10
Epimelētēs:	3															3
Hieromnēmones:															1	1
Hierothutai:	2															2
Pedianomos:	1															1

B. Catalogues inscribed in duplicate and triplicate:

Duplicates:

Nomophulakes:

79 and xi.539 (late Flavian)
148 (xi.537b) and 537a (Trajan)
xi.546a-b (Trajan)
65 and xi.549 (Pius)

Ephors:

59 (xi.521a) and xi.521b (Hadrian)
66–7 (Pius)
65 and xi.523 (Pius)

Gerontes:

97 and xi.564 (Trajan)
182 (xi.586) and xi.585 (Pius)

Triplicates:

Nomophulakes:

61 (xi.547), 157 (xi.522; 547) and xi.547b (Hadrian)
69.30–35, 71b.23–39 and xi.554 (Pius)

Ephors:

69.23–9, 70 and 71b.23–39 (Pius)

Ephors and *Nomophulakes:*
51 (xi.506), 52 (xi.506), xi.506 and 538 (Trajan)

Appendix III
Hereditary tendencies in the Curial Class

Three groups of documents, representing (with a varying degree of completeness) the composition of the Spartan *boulē* as defined in chapter 11 in three different years, are analysed here for signs of hereditary tendencies in the curial class.

A. *Nomophulakes*, **ephors and** *gerontes* **in the year of the** *patronomos* **C. Iulius Philoclidas (Trajanic):** *IG* **v.1.51–2; 97;** *SEG* **xi.538; 564–5.**

Ephors:

Euclidas son of Dinacon:? ancestor of Damion son of Bellon, *nomophulax* and *agoranomos* (*IG* v.1.99;129)

Gerontes:

Aristomenes son of Epictetus: father of Aristomenes son of Aristomenes son of Epictetus, *sunagoranomos* and ephor (*IG* v.1.66 [*SEG* xi.524]; 128 [*SEG* xi.597])
Tib. Claudius Harmonicus: probably father of the Tib. Claudii Plistoxenus and Xenophanes, *sussitoi*, latter a *nomophulax* (*IG* v.1.79; *SEG* xi.546)
Soander son of Tryphon: probably father of Soander son of Soander, *nomophulax* (*IG* v.1.57)
Agiadas son of Damocratidas: for the family see Woodward 1948, 215
Aristocles son of Callicrates and Aristocles son of Callicrates 'the younger': for the family see Spawforth 1985, 197
Damocles *qui et* Philocrates son of Damocles: for the family see Spawforth 1986, 324

Grammateus Boulēs:

Agippus son of Pollio:? son of Pollio son of Rufus (Bradford 1977, s.v.)

Summary: out of a total of 34 magistrates, nine (26%) can be shown to have been definite or likely ancestors/descendants of other magistrates.

B. *Nomophulakes*, **ephors and** *gerontes* **under the** *patronomos* **L. Volusenus Aristocrates (Trajanic):** *SEG* **xi.516; 542(?); 569.**

Nomophulakes:

Sipompus son of Cleon: father of Cleon son of Sipompus, *nomophulax* (*IG* v.1.62)

Ephors:

Agippus son of Pollio: see above

Gerontes:

Melesippus son of Eucletus: father of Eucletus son of Melesippus, ephor (*IG* v.1.20b)
Soander son of Tryphon: above
Agiadas son of Damocratidas: above
C. Iulius Damares: for the family see Spawforth 1980, 214–8
Pasicles son of Mnason: father of Mnason son of Pasicles, *agōnothetēs* (*IG* v.1.667) and *nomophulax* (*SEG* xi.534); grandfather of Lysippus son of Mnason, *patronomos* 129/30 (Bradford 1986a for the date and refs.); great-grandfather of Mnason son of Lysippus, *gerōn* (*SEG* xi.528)
Onesiphorus son of Theon: father of Theon son of Onesiphorus, *nomophulax* (*IG* v.1.20b)
Callicratidas son of Agesinicus: probably descended from Agesinicus son of Call[——], *gerōn* (*IG* v.1.95)
T. Trebellenus Philostratus: uncle of T. Trebellenus Menecles, ephor (*SEG* xi.511)
Socratidas son of Eudamidas: father of Eudamidas son of Socratidas, *agoranomos* (*IG* v.1.128)

Summary: out of a total of 29 magistrates, nine (31%) are known (definitely/possibly) to have been ancestors/descendants of other magistrates.

C. Ephors and *gerontes* under the *patronomos* C. Avidius Biadas (Pius): *SEG* xi.528; 553.

Ephors:

Tib. Claudius Aristoteles: for these Claudii see Spawforth 1985, 224–44

Gerontes:

Philonidas son of Eucrines: father of Eucrines son of Philonidas, *sunagoranomos* (*IG* v.1.155)
Nicippidas son of Menemachus: probably son of Menemachus son of Menemachus, *nomophulax* and *gerōn* (*SEG* xi.582; 543)
Antonius Ophelion, son of C. Antonius Ophelion son of Aglaus, *nomophulax* (*SEG* xi.546)
Marcus son of Nicephorus, son of Nicephorus son of Marcus, *nomophulax* and *protensiteuōn* (*IG* v.1.59 [*SEG* xi.548]; 1313)
Mnason son of Lysippus: for the family see above
Philonidas son of Agion: father of Agion son of Philonidas, *sunpatronomos* (*SEG* xi.503)

Grammateus Boulēs:

P. Memmius Damares: for the family see Spawforth 1985, 193–215

Summary: out of a total of 29 magistrates, eight (28%) definitely/probably were ancestors/descendants of other magistrates.

Appendix IV
Foreign *agōnistai* at Sparta

A. The Caesarea:

1. T. Flavius Metrobius of Iasus. Runner. Victor shortly before 86. Moretti 1953, no.66.

B. The Urania:

2. T. Flavius Attinas of Phocaea. Wrestler. Victor in the first celebration of 97/8. *IG* v.1.667.
3. C. Heius Magio of Corinth. Wrestler. Victor in the third celebration of 109/10. *IG* v.1.659 (*SEG* xi.835).
4. C. Iulius Iulianus of Smyrna. Tragic actor. Victor in the third celebration of 109/10. *IG* v.1.662.
5. Claudius Avidienus of Nicopolis. Poet and Spartan citizen. About 100. A victor at the Urania (see chapter 13)? *FD* iii.1.no.542.
6. P. Aelius Aristomachus of Magnesia-on-the Maeander. Pancratiast. Victor in about 120. Moretti 1953, no.71.
7. P. Aelius Heliodorus of Seleucia-on-the-Calycadnus. Wrestler. Victor under Hadrian. Robert 1966, 100–105.
8. M. Ulpius Heliodorus of Thessalonice. Cithara-player. Victor in the Antonine period. *IG* iv[1] 591 with W. Vollgraff, *Mnemosyne* ser.2 47, 1919, 259–60.
9. Tib. Scandalianus Zosimus of Gortyn. Flautist. Twice victor in the second century. *CIG* i.1719 with G. Daux, *BCH* 68–9, 1944–5, 123–5.
10. M. Aurelius Demostratus Damas of Sardis. Pancratiast and boxer. Three times victor. Late Antonine/early Severan. Moretti 1953, no.84 with Spawforth 1986, 331–2.

C. The Euryclea:

11. M. Aurelius Asclepiades of Alexandria. Wrestler. Victor in the reign of (?) Marcus. *IG* v.1.666 with *SEG* xi.836, xv.217.
12. M. Aurelius Asclepiades of Alexandria. Pancratiast. Victor in about 200. Moretti 1953, no.79.
13. M. Aurelius Demostratus Damas of Sardis. See no.10.

D. Olympia Commodea:

14. M. Aurelius Ptolemaeus of Argos. Poet. First victor in the contest for poets under (?) Severus. *FD* iii.1. no.89.
15. M. Aurelius Abas of Adada. Runner. Victor possibly in the 220s or 230s. Moretti 1953, no.75; Spawforth 1986, 328–9.
16. M. Aurelius Demostratus Damas of Sardis. See no. 10.

E. Urania or Euryclea:

17. Socrates son of Migon of Thyateira. Herald. Victor about 143–8. *SEG* xi. 838.
18. Theodotus son of Theodotus of Sidon. Tragic actor. Victor about 143–8. *SEG* xi.838.
19. Anonymous of Tarsus. Victor in about 143–8. *SEG* xi.838.
20. Apollonius son of Apollonius of Ni[——]. Victor in about 143–8. *SEG* xi.838.
21. T. Cornelius Dionysius of Sardis. Runner. Victor in about 143–8. *SEG* xi.838.
22. Aelius Granianus of Sicyon. Runner. Victor in about 143–8. *SEG* xi.838; see chapter 13.
23. [—]onion son of [--]onion of Epidaurus. Runner. Victor in about 143–48. *SEG* xi.838.

F. Unknown:

24. SE[—]VATUS of Damascus. Encomiast and Spartan citizen. *FD* iii.4 no.118.
25. C. Antonius Septimius Publius of Pergamum. Cithara-player. Victor under Severus. *IGRR* iv.1432.
26. M. Aurelius [. . ...]lon of Ancyra. Flautist and Spartan citizen. About 200. *FD* iii.4. no.476.
27. [——] Polycrates of Cibyra. Runner and Spartan citizen. Reign of Severus. Moretti 1953, no.82.
28. [—]us Glycon of Hypaepa. Pancratiast. Honoured (or buried?) at Sparta. Second or third century. *IG* v.1.670.
29. Metrophianus *qui et* Sosinicus son of Metrophianus of Selge. Spartan citizen. Probably an *agōnistēs*. Antonines/early Severans. *SEG* xi.832.
30. [——] son of [——]ates of Athens. Honoured at Sparta. Probably an *agōnistēs*. Third century? *SEG* xi.833.
31. M. Aurelius Lucius of Smyrna. Athlete and Spartan citizen. Antonine period. L. Robert, *Hellenica* 7, 1949, 105–12.
32. L. Cornelius Corinthus of Corinth. Twice victor. Reign of Pius or slightly later. Clement 1974, 36–9.
33. Tib. Claudius Protogenes of Cypriote Salamis. Flautist. Buried at Sparta. Second or third century. *IG* v.1.758.
34. C. [——] Inventus of Smyrna. Wrestler and Spartan citizen. Second or third century. *CIG* ii.2935 with Ph. Le Bas/W.H. Waddington, *Voyage archéologique en Grèce et en Asie Mineure* iii (1870 repr. Hildesheim 1972) no.598.

Notes

Chapter 1 In the shadow of empire: Mantinea to Chaeronea

1 Most conspicuously Xenophon; cf. n.18, below. Among modern historians, see, e.g., Bengtson *et al.* 1969, 280.
2 Cartledge 1987, Index s.v. 'Leuktra'; date: ibid., 'Chronological Table'.
3 Since the Battle of Hysiae (Argolis), trad. 669 BC: Cartledge 1979, 126, 134, 136, 140.
4 Paus. ix.6.4, with Habicht 1985, 113–14.
5 Spartan imperialism: Cartledge 1987, ch. 6. Sparta and Persia: ibid., ch. 11.
6 Xen. *Hell.* vi.4.15,24. Peloponnesian League: Cartledge 1987, ch. 13.
7 Arcadia: Cartledge 1979, Index, s.v., especially 152; 1987, 257–62. Elis: ibid., 248–53. Argos: Tomlinson 1972; Cartledge 1987, especially 309.
8 Second Athenian League: Cargill 1981; cf. Cartledge 1987, 301–2.
9 Thebes and reformed Boeotian confederacy: Buckler 1980; cf. Cartledge 1987, ch. 14.
10 *Diabatēria* sacrifice: Cartledge 1977, 17 and n.53. Sciritis and Caryae: Xen. *Hell.* vi.5.25–6 (misunderstood by Chrimes 1949, 378). Routes into Laconia: Loring 1895; Cartledge 1979, 187ff. Perioeci in general: Cartledge 1979, 178ff.; 1987, Index s.v. 'Perioikoi'.
11 Gytheum: Cartledge 1987, 47,178,385. Defence of Sparta: ibid., 232–5.
12 Messenian Helots: Cartledge 1979, 1987, Index s.v. 'Helots . . . Messenian'. Foundation of (New) Messene: Roebuck 1941. Walls: Adam 1982, 171–5.
13 Arcadian federation: Larsen 1968, 180–95; Cartledge 1987, 261–2. Megalopolis: Bury 1898; the results of a recent B.S.A. survey are forthcoming. Crisis of 'the *polis*': e.g. Rostovtzeff 1941, 90–125, especially 94,104; Welskopf 1974; but see e.g. Browning 1976.
14 Spartan crisis in general: G. Bockisch in Welskopf 1974, I.199–230; David 1981, ch. 2; Cartledge 1987, *passim*, especially ch. 21. Spartan land-lots in Messenia: Figueira 1984 (speculative). *Oliganthrōpia* as topos: Gallo 1980; as Spartan reality (variously explained): Figueira 1986; Hodkinson 1986; Cartledge 1987, Index s.v. 'Sparta/Spartans . . . citizenship'. Possible post-Leuctra land-reform (alleged '*rhētra* of Epitadeus'): Marasco 1980a; *contra* Cartledge 1979, 167–8; 1987, 167,169,401. Army-reform (?): Anderson 1970, 229–51.
15 Battle of Mantinea: Lazenby 1985, 168. Theban 'hegemony': Buckler 1980, *passim*. Invasion of Laconia: Cartledge 1987, 235–6.
16 Anticrates: Plut. *Ages.* 35; but see Poralla/Bradford 1985, no.99. 'Common Peace' in general: Ryder 1965. Peace of 362: *SV* II.292. Reply to Satraps: *IG* IV.556 = Harding 1985, no.57.
17 Isoc. vi.28; cf. Buckler 1980, 314n.28. Early career of Archidamus: Hamilton

234

1982a. Agesilaus as mercenary: Cartledge 1987, ch. 15, esp. 327–9.

18 Philip: best modern account is G.T. Griffith's in Hammond and Griffith 1979, Pt. II (hereafter 'Griffith 1979'), with a useful chronological table at 722–6; see also Ellis 1976. Theopompus (*FGrHist.* 115): Lane Fox 1986b. Diodorus: Hornblower 1981; cf. Cartledge 1987, 67–8. Xenophon: Cartledge 1987, ch. 5, *passim* (with bibliography). The most reliable and compendious modern narrative of Spartan history remains Ehrenberg 1929 (full references to ancient sources). Archidamus: Hamilton 1982b.

19 Xen. *Hell.* vii.5.27. Dem. xviii.231. Aristotle on Sparta: most recently David 1982–3; cf. Cartledge 1987, especially 403–4.

20 Isoc. *Ep.* ix (incomplete, authenticity disputed). Isocrates in general: Baynes 1955, 144–67; cf. Cartledge 1987, 67, 401–2. Third Sacred War: Kennedy 1908, 258–310. Delphic Amphictyony: Ellis 1976, 132–3 (table); Griffith 1979, 450–6.

21 Sparta and Amphictyony: Zeilhofer 1959; Daux 1957. Spartan *naopoioi* (building commissioners) and donors: Poralla/Bradford 1985, svv. Agias, Alcimus, Andocus, Antileon, Gorgopas, Diaecles, Erasis, Echeteles, Cleosimenes, Megyllias, Polypeithes, Philolaus, Philostratis (female, the earliest of series, 364/3). Amphictyonic fine: Diod. xvi.29.2–3. Sparta and Phocis in 370s: Cartledge 1987, 304ff. Alleged bribery of Archidamus and Deinicha: Paus. ii.10.3 (after Theop.); rightly doubted by Noethlichs 1987, 152–3, no.27.

22 Archidamus & Philomelus: Diod. xvi.24.2. Spartan public finance: Arist. *Pol.* 1271b10–17, with Rawson 1969, 76; David 1982–3, 91 and n.93; cf. Cartledge 1987, 49.

23 Sparta and mercenaries: Cartledge 1987, ch. 15. Seizure of Delphic sanctuary and treasure: Bury/Meiggs 1975, 424 (action defended).

24 Philip and Thessaly: Griffith 1979, chs VI.1, VII, XVI; quotation, ibid., 279. Archidamus at Thermopylae: Diod. xvi.37.2–3.

25 Agis (later III), Hippodamus, Gastron, Lamius: Poralla/Bradford 1985, svv. 'Ancestral' restitutions: Dem. xvi.4,11,16; cf. Hamilton 1982b, 65 and n.16. Campaigns of 351: Diod. xvi.39.4–7; Paus. iv.28.2.

26 *IG* XII.5(i).542.18,20,21,22 = Poralla/Bradford 1985, nos 799–802. Gnosstas: Cartledge 1979, 215–16. Ceus and Athens: Cargill 1981, especially 134–40.

27 *IG* IV.952.1–6. Asclepius cult: Pollitt 1972, 166. Spartan women: Kunstler 1983 (seeking to modify Cartledge 1981).

28 Weakness of Sparta: Isoc. v.49–50. Archidamus and Phalaecus: Diod. xvi.59.1; Aesch. ii.133–4. Flare-up at Pella: Aesch. ii.136. Ambitions of Philip: Ellis 1976, 92.

29 Despite Paus. x.8.2, Sparta probably was not expelled from Amphictyony: Ehrenberg 1929, 1416; Ellis 1976, 272n.157; or only briefly: Daux 1957, 107. Philip's *Geldpolitik*: Dem. xviii. 295; Plb. xviii.14; cf. Cargill 1985, 83–4. Mercenaries: Griffith 1979, 476–9. Iphicratidas, Alexippa and seven sons: *Anth. Pal.* VII.435. Battle of Chaeronea: Griffith 1979, 596–603.

30 Archidamus in Crete and southern Italy: Theop. 115F232; Diod. xvi.62–3; Strabo vi.280; Plut. *Ag.* 3; Paus. iii.10.5; and ?Stephanus' *Philolacon*, with Rawson 1969, 36n.3. Sparta and Syracuse, 356–5: Poralla/Bradford 1985, nos.180,718. Xen. on Leuctra: v.4.1.

31 Spartan exceptionalism: Arr. *Anab.* i.16.7; Just. ix.5.3; cf. Ellis 1976, 205 and nn.125,128; Hamilton 1982b, 83. Elis: Paus. v.4.9; cf. Griffith 1979, 617n.4.

32 Invasion: Griffith 1979, 616–19. Isyllus (*IG* IV².1.57ff.): Griffith 1979, 616–17; Marasco 1980b, 58–60 (unpersuasive attempt to redate Isyllus' hymn to c.280). Frontier-demarcations: Roebuck 1948; Ellis 1976, 204, 297nn.113,115–19.

33 Spartans as would-be farmers: Arist. *Pol.* 1264a9–10; contrast Plut. *Mor.* 223a (Cleom.).

Chapter 2 Resistance to Macedon: the revolt of Agis III

1 'Hellenismus' as concept: Bichler 1983 (includes discussion of periodization in general). Cleomenes II: Jones 1967, 148 (a slight exaggeration; see now Podlecki 1985, 237 and n.58, for two Theophrastan mentions, one referring to a trial of the otherwise unattested Cleolas, who should therefore be added to either Bradford 1977 or Poralla/Bradford 1985).

2 League of Corinth: Ryder 1965, 102–9,150–62; Griffith 1979, 623–46. Quotation from Walbank 1985, 17–18 (originally 1951).

3 Crusade (idea already exploited by Philip in Third Sacred War: ch. 1): Hornblower 1983, 255. Garrisons (later called 'Fetters of Greece'): Griffith 1979, 611–13.

4 Aristotle's *Politics* for all its flaws is easily our best source for oligarchic and other Greek political thought: e.g. Mulgan 1977.

5 Peace-clauses: Ps.-Dem. xvii.8,15. Fourth-century *stasis* (methods for forestalling which occupy the central books of the *Politics*): Huxley 1979, 40–50; Ste. Croix 1981, 283–300; Lintott 1982, chs 6-7; Gehrke 1985. Mercenaries: Parke 1933; Griffith 1935; cf. Ste. Croix 1981, 295; Cartledge 1987, ch. 15. On the 'social question' as oligarchically filtered by Isocrates and Plato: Fuks 1984, 52–79, 80–171. 'Crisis of the *polis*': ch. 1 and n.13, above.

6 Frontier-ratification: Plb. ix.33.12; Just. ix.5.1–3; cf. Walbank 1967, 172–3; Griffith 1979, 618 and n.2. Philip's calculatedly different treatment of respectively Athens and Thebes: Griffith 1979, 613.

7 Alexander: perhaps the best short summary in English is Hornblower 1983, ch. 18 (261–93, 314–22). Apart from documents and archaeology, Arrian is no doubt the most reliable source, but see Bosworth 1980; Brunt 1983, App. XXVIII ('The date and character of Arrian's work').

8 Cleomenes: Poralla/Bradford 1985, p.182. Spartan envoys: Poralla/Bradford 1985, nos 178,532,697,754 (as cited in ibid., App. I). Athenian embassies: Humphreys 1985, 211. Delphic Amphictyony as (later) anti-Macedonian focus: Marchetti 1977.

9 Revolt of Thebes: Arr. i.7–9; cf. Brunt 1976 and Bosworth 1980, *ad loc.* Olynthus destruction: Griffith 1979, 324–8. Messene: Ps.-Dem. xvii.4.

10 Sparta and Persia in the time of Agesilaus II: Cartledge 1987, ch. 11; in 344: Diod. xvi.44.1–2; cf. Griffith 1979, 484. Persia and Egypt: Ray 1987.

11 Post-Granicus propaganda: Arr. i.16.7. Persian amphibious strategy, 334–2: Burn 1952, 81–4; Brunt 1976, App. II. Lysander: Cartledge 1987, ch. 6. Alexander's letter: Arr. ii.14.6.

12 Issus battle: e.g. Brunt 1976, App. III. Mercenaries: Diod. xvii.48.1, but see text and n.16, below.

13 Memnon (and all matters prosopographical): Berve 1926, no.497. Euthycles: Mosley 1972. Taenarum as 'man-market': Will 1984, 30; as Helot asylum: Cartledge 1979, Index s.v. 'Pohoidan . . . cults'; new military development: Jones 1967, 148–9 (quotation).

14 Agis on Crete, 332: Potter 1984 (speculative but plausible relocation of *IG* ii² 399).

15 Agis as anti-Macedonian protagonist: Ehrenberg 1929, 1418. Revolt (or War) of Agis: Niese 1893, 102–7; Badian 1967 (excessively pro-Agis); Cawkwell 1969 (dating); Lock 1972 (answering Cawkwell); Ste. Croix 1972, 164–6, 376–8 (opposing Badian on significance; open-minded on date); Bosworth 1975 (date of outbreak); Brunt 1976, App. VI; McQueen 1978 (absentees and participants, settlement, *tresantes*); Atkinson 1980, 482–5 (mainly chronological). Sources: especially Aesch. iii.165; Din. i.34; Diod. xvii.62–3; Q.

Curt. vi.1.1–21 (incompletely extant); admirably discussed by Lock 1972.
16 Amyclae victory-dedication: Poralla/Bradford 1985, no.27a. 10,000 mercenaries: Din. i.34. 8,000 ex-Issus: Diod. xvii.48.1; rightly rejected by Parke 1933, 199. Career of Agis: Poralla/Bradford 1985, no.27; Berve 1926, no.15. Date of Megalopolis battle: Badian 1967; Brunt 1976, 483–4.
17 Agis' numbers: Ste. Croix 1972, 164–6. Athenian view of Agis: Potter 1984, 234; cf. Ste. Croix 1972, 166n.202 (reading 'Antipater' for 'Antigonus' in Plut. *Mor.* 219ab).
18 'Battle of Mice': Plut. *Ages.* 15.4. Alexander's support: Bosworth 1975. Sparta's situation post-331, as reflected in her foreign policy: Cloché 1945, 219–22; cf. Ehrenberg 1929, 1421.
19 Perioecic settlement: Cartledge 1979, App. I; now confirmed by B.S.A./ University of Amsterdam Laconia Survey (unpublished; information kindly supplied by Dr W.G. Cavanagh).
20 *Tresantes* in 331: Diod. xix.70.5; cf. McQueen 1978, 59; in 371: Plut. *Ages.* 30.6, with Cartledge 1987, 241,411–12; as legal status: Ehrenberg 1937; MacDowell 1986, 44.
21 Hostages: McQueen 1978, 53–6,60–4 (but these are unlikely to have been *paides*, as in the unreliable anecdote Plut. *Mor.* 235b(54) – Diod. xvii.73.5 has just 'the most distinguished of the Spartiates').
22 Sparta never in any Macedonian League: Plut. *Mor.* 240ab. Grain from Cyrene: Tod 196 = Harding 1985, no.116 (Cythera at lines 48, 52); cf. Kingsley 1986 (political interpretation). Sparta ordered to deify Alexander: Plut. *Mor.* 219e (Damis); cf. Aelian *Var. hist.* ii.19, with Balsdon 1950; Badian 1981. Sparta's non-participation in Lamian War: Ehrenberg 1929, 1419–20. Taenarum: Lepore 1955, 163,176,180; Badian 1961, 25–8. Sparta's pro-Samian gesture (one-day fast): Ps.-Arist. *Oec.* ii,1347b 16–20; cf. Shipley 1987, 168. Refusal of help to Athens: Habicht 1975a.
23 Apophthegm attributed to Eudamidas I: Plut. *Mor.* 220f (4); rightly dated to his reign by Griffith 1979, 617n.3. Powers of Spartan (dual) kingship: Cartledge 1987, ch. 7. 'My enemy's enemy . . .' principle: Hornblower 1983, ch. 2.
24 Lamian War: Will 1979, 29–33 (summary, sources and modern bibliography – as ever in this indispensable work); cf. Walbank 1985, 12. Quotation from Miller 1982, 100.
25 Succession down to Ipsus: Will 1984, 23–61; from Ipsus to re-establishment of Gonatas in Macedon (276): Will 1984, 101–17. Gauls at Delphi: Will 1984, 115. Aetolia and Achaea: bibliography in *CAH* VII².1, 542–3; cf. chs.3–6 in this volume.
26 Polyperchon's proclamation: Diod. xviii.56; cf. Hornblower 1981 (on Diod.'s main source for the Successors). Sparta fortification (317?): Diod. xviii.75.2, xix.35.1; Just. xiv.5.5–7; cf. Ehrenberg 1929, 1421–2; Oliva 1971, 201; Piper 1986, 175. Siege-warfare in general: Garlan 1974.
27 The mercenary option: Piper 1986, 2. Thibron: Poralla/Bradford 1985, no.376 (possibly occasioning Ptolemy I's interventions in Cyrene). Harpalus: Badian 1961.
28 Proclamation of Antigonus: Hope Simpson 1959, esp. 389–93. Mission of Antigonus' lieutenant (Aristodemus): Diod. xix.60. Acrotatus: Diod. xix.70–1; cf. David 1981, 117–19; Meister 1984, 391.
29 Quotation: Forrest 1968, 141. Length of Cleomenes II's reign: McQueen 1978, 60n.73 (with bibliography).

Chapter 3 The new Hellenism of Areus I

1 'Hellenismus': ch. 2, n.1, above; cf. Hornblower, *CR* 34 (1984), 245–7. Droysen: Momigliano 1977, 307–23 (stressing D.'s vision of the era as a *praeparatio evangelica* for the rise and dissemination of Christianity); Préaux 1965; cf. Préaux 1978, I.5–9, II.680–3; Walbank 1981, 60–78. Useful brief conspectuses: Badian 1962; Jones 1964a; Ehrenberg 1974, 64–106.

2 Monarchy and monarchic ideology: Walbank 1984, 62–100; cf. Gruen 1985 (stressing that Monophthalmus set rather than followed a precedent, in which he was aped by Ptolemy I, Seleucus I, Lysimachus and Cassander, by assuming the title 'King').

3 On all political and military matters relating to Areus and Spartan history of this epoch: Marasco 1980b; but for a less optimistic and more realistic assessment of Spartan foreign policy: Cloché 1945–46 (summary: 1946, 59–61). Sources for Hellenistic history: Walbank 1981, 13–28; 1984, 1–22 (coinage: 18–21).

4 Hellenistic political history: Will 1979–82; in English summary for 323–276: Will 1984. Tarn 1928 is still worth reading. Antigonids and Greek states: Briscoe 1978; Buraselis 1982.

5 Hellenic League of Monophthalmus and Poliorcetes, 302: *SV* III.446 (from Epidaurus). Accession of Areus: Diod. xx.29.1; Paus. iii.6.2; cf. Marasco 1980b, 31–8 (arguing that Cleonymus was officially designated Regent). Role of Gerousia: Cartledge 1987, 111–12. Age of Areus: Oliva 1971, 206n (rightly rejecting Beloch's birthdate of *c*.312; I would set it *c*.320).

6 Western venture of Cleonymus: Diod. xx.104–5; Duris, *FGrHist*. 76F18; Livy x.2.1; Trog. *Prol*. 15; cf. Cloché 1945, 221–2; Meloni 1950; Marasco 1980b, 38–48; David 1981, 120–1; Meister 1984, 406; Piper 1986, 193n.30 (Cleonymus might have fought Romans); Brauer 1986, ch. 5 (Cleonymus' coinage of gold).

7 Archidamus IV: Bradford 1977, s.v. Demaratus: *SIG*³ 381; Bradford 1977, s.v.; see further ch. 5 in this volume (ancestry of Nabis). 'Friends' of Hellenistic rulers: Herman 1980/1.

8 Invasion of Poliorcetes: Plut. *Demetr*. 35–6; Polyaen. iv.7.9–10; cf. Cloché 1945, 223–5; Marasco 1980b, 48–60. Perhaps the occasion of *IG* V.1,704 ('Nicahicles in war'): Bradford 1977, 291.

9 Cleonymus in Boeotia: Plut. *Demetr*. 39; cf. Cloché 1945, 225–7; Marasco 1980b, 51–5 (over-optimistic). Aetolian League: briefly Walbank 1984, 232–6; see further chs. 4–5 in this volume.

10 Spartan embassy to Poliorcetes, ??289: Plut. *Demetr*. 42.2–4, *Mor*. 233e; cf. Marasco 1980b, 55 and n.91. Exile of Cleonymus' son (future Leonidas II) to court of Seleucus (I?): Plut. *Ag*. 3.9; cf. Marasco 1980b, 55–6 (after 275). Gonatas' alleged control of Sparta, 285/4: Eusebius *Chron*. II, p.118; rightly rejected by Marasco 1980b, 57n.97.

11 Gonatas in Aegean: Buraselis 1982, 152ff. Areus in Phocis: Plb. ii.41ff.; Paus. viii.6.3; Just. xxiv.1.1–7; cf. Ehrenberg 1929, 1422–3 (exaggerated); Cloché 1945, 227–33; Marasco 1980b, 63–73 (*poluandrion*: 72n.28). Old Peloponnesian League: Cartledge 1987, ch. 13. Spartans at Delphi: Bradford 1977, svv. Aristoclidas, Cleosimenes (*naopoioi*), Phabennas (*hieromnēmōn*), Ce(rc)id(as), Pratonicus. Achaean League: Urban 1979; Walbank 1984, 243–52. Gallic incursion: Walbank 1957, 51; Will 1984, 114–16.

12 Cleonymus in Messenia: Paus. iv.28.3; Marasco 1980b, 74–5 (?? recovered Dentheliatis); Habicht 1985, 106; at Troezen: Front. iii.6.7; Polyaen. ii.2.9; Cloché 1945, 239–40; Marasco 1980b, 77–9; on Crete: *SV* III.471; cf. Marasco 1980b, 84–5. Defection of Cleonymus: Plut. *Pyrrh*. 26.20ff., *Mor*. 219f;

Polyaen. vi.6.2, viii.49; cf. Ehrenberg 1929, 1423–4; Marasco 1980b, 93–100. Invasion of Pyrrhus: n.14, below.

13 Spartan sexual politics: Cartledge 1981; Hodkinson 1986, especially 402–3 (Eudamidas and Agesistrata: Table, p. 402). Cleonymus, Chilonis and Acrotatus: Plut. *Pyrrh*. 26.16ff.,27.10 (after Phylarchus, *FGrHist*. 81F48); cf. Piper 1979, 7; Bradford 1986b, 14.

14 Pyrrhus: generally Lévêque 1957; Garoufalias 1979. Pyrrhus in Macedon (with Cleonymus): Polyaen. ii.29.2; cf. Oliva 1971, 204. Pyrrhus in Greece: Plb. v.19.4ff.; Plut. *Pyrrh*. 26.8–29; Paus. i.13.6–8, iv.29.6; Just. xxv.4.6–10; cf. Ehrenberg 1929, 1424–5; Cloché 1946, 29–42; Will 1979, 214–16; Marasco 1980b, 100–19. Areus in Crete: Plut. *Pyrrh*. 27.2. *Agōgē*: possibly relevant is Amphiares' wrestling victory at the 296 Olympics; Bradford 1977, s.v.; see further ch. 4 in this volume.

15 Archidamia: Plut. *Pyrrh*. 27. Acrotatus: Plut. *Pyrrh*. 28 (there is no need to identify him with the 'Akrotatos kalos' celebrated in a graffito recently discovered at the Nemea Stadium). Dedications to Athena (sometimes 'Chalcioecus'): Bradford 1977, svv. Damar(is), (De?)xagoris, Etymocles, (Eury)stheneia, (Euth)ymia.

16 Cleonymus at Zarax: Paus. iii.24.1; cf. Cartledge 1979, 314; Marasco 1980b, 20n.10. Walling: Wace/Hasluck 1907/8, 67ff. Tyros dedication: *SIG*³ 407; cf. Ehrenberg 1929, 1424.

17 Bronze statuette: Dickens 1907/8, 145–6; Piper 1986, 184 (citing Paus. iii.17.5 for cult of Aphrodite Areia).

18 Hieronymus: Hornblower 1981. Phylarchus (*FGrHist*. 81): Gabba 1957; Africa 1961. 'Luxury' of Areus: Phyl. F44; as Hellenistic commonplace: Marasco 1980b, 42. Coinage of Areus: Bellinger 1963, 89–90; Kraay 1966, 345, no.520; Grunauer-von Hoerschelmann 1978, ch. 1; Marasco 1980b, 124–7. Spartan coinage debate, 404: Cartledge 1987, 88–90.

19 Ptolemaic coins later buried in Sparta: below, ch. 4 and n.33, ch. 5, n.2.

20 Chremonides Decree: *SIG*³ 434/6 (*SV* III.476) = Burstein 1985, no.56; cf. Ehrenberg 1929, 1426; Cloché 1946, 46–7; Will 1979, 223–4; Marasco 1980b, 119–23; Habicht 1985, 86 (cf. ibid., 86n.76 for decree for Chremonides' brother Glaucon at Plataea with reference to a '*koinon* of the Greeks').

21 *IDélos* 87; cf. Cartledge 1987, 94.

22 Dedications to Areus: Paus. vi.12.5 (Elis, at Olympia); *ISE* I.54 (Orchomenus); *SIG*³ 433 = Oliva 1971, fig. 54 (Ptol. II, at Olympia). Delphic honours for Areus II: *SIG*³ 430, as interpreted by Tarn 1913, 303n.84; cf. Cloché 1946, 43n.1, 54n.4; Marasco 1980b, 96–7; Marek 1984, 129, 336. Letter of Areus to Jews: *I Macc*. 12.7,19–23; cf. Cardauns 1967 (with bibliography, mostly condemning as forgery, at 317–18n.1); Janni 1984, 49–51. For authenticity: Ginsburg 1934; Forrest 1968, 142; Bernal 1987, 109–10 (though he wrongly retains Biblical misspelling 'Areios'). Kinship as 'ticket of admission to European culture': Bickerman 1962, 154; cf. Davies 1984, 258, 305; in age of Paus.: Habicht 1985, 127; ch. 8 in this volume.

23 Chremonidean War: Paus. i.1.1,7.3, iii.6.4–6; Just. xxvi.2.1–9; Trog. *Prol*. 26; Plut. *Ag*. 3.7; cf. Cloché 1946, 51–6; Heinen 1972, 199ff.; Will 1979, 224–8; Marasco 1980b, 139–53; David 1981, 132–9; Walbank 1984, 236–43.

24 Acrotatus at Megalopolis: Plut. *Ag*. 3.7; Paus. viii.27.11,30.7; cf. Marasco 1980b, 153–6. Perhaps now (again? see above, n.12) Sparta had to cede Dentheliatis to Messene: Tac. *Ann*. iv.43.4; cf. Walbank 1957, 288. See further chs. 4–6 in this volume.

25 Nicon: Bradford 1977, s.v.; cf. Loukas 1984 (*SEG* XXXIV.320). Soteria:

Walbank 1981, 70, 147. Anecdote: Plut. *Mor.* 212f. Spartan theatre: pre-Hellenistic – Hdt. vi.67.3; Plut. *Ages.* 29.2; Hellenistic – Dilke 1950, 48–51; Piper 1986, 185, 223n.20. (Plut. *Cleom.* 12.3 perhaps illustrates the 'traditionalist' reaction against Areus.) Hellenistic theatrical performance in general: Davies 1984, 319.

Chapter 4 Reform – or revolution? Agis IV and Cleomenes III

1 Plut. *Ag.* and *Cleom.* (treated as a single work in the MSS) as novels: Bux 1925; comm.: Marasco 1981, with Martinez-Lacy 1985. Agis, Cleomenes and the 'mirage': Ollier 1943, Rawson 1969, and Tigerstedt 1974, svv. Plut.'s *Aratus*: Porter 1937, with Aymard 1967, 46–50. Phylarchus: Gabba 1957; Africa 1961; Shimron 1966b; David 1981, 145–8. Polybius (ii.56–63, anti-Phylarchus; xvi.14.6, xxxviii.4.2, patriotism): Walbank 1957–67–79; 1972. 'Non-Phylarchean tradition' (Teles fr. 3 Hense; ?Plb. iv.81.12–14; Cic. *Off.* ii.78–80): Fuks 1962b. Mitchison 1931 is a superb historical novel of the 'New Times' of Cleomenes.
2 Archaeology and literature, lack of fit: Siebert 1978, 88. Modern accounts of *c*.244–222 in general: Niese 1899, 296–324; Tarn 1928, especially 739–44, 752–4; Will 1979, 315–401, especially 333–5, 371–401; Walbank 1984, especially 252–5, 458–9, 467–73. Agis, Cleomenes and Sparta: Ehrenberg 1929, 1427–35; Oliva 1971, 208–68; Shimron 1972, 9–52; Marasco 1981, 70–127; Piper 1986, 25–74.
3 Against Beloch and von Pöhlmann: Kazarow 1907. Against Wason (1947, 195, 197): Ste. Croix 1981, 41 (general critique).
4 Revolution as general concept: Porter/Teich 1986; cf. Martinez-Lacy 1985, 289–92. Revolution in Hellenistic Greece, especially the Sparta of Agis and Cleomenes: Fustel de Coulanges 1864, Book IV; Tarn 1923, especially 128–38; Ehrenberg 1929, 1428; Shimron 1972 ('revolution' in subtitle, but 'revolution' and 'reform' indiscriminately in text); Fuks 1974 = 1984, ch. 1, especially 29–34; Heuss 1973, especially 11–12,37–46; Meier 1984, 1986, 509; Finley 1986, especially 59n.18; Martinez-Lacy 1988, especially 71–105.
5 Macedonian viewpoint: Briscoe 1978. Greek (federal) viewpoint: Freeman 1893; Larsen 1968. All matters of detail: Will 1979. Limitations of single city: Davies 1984, 291.
6 Mantinea expedition: Paus. viii.10.5–10; cf. Walbank 1984, 247n.68 (disbelieved); Jones 1967, 151 (accepted); Will 1979, 320 and Habicht 1985, 101–2 (agnostic). 'Dark Age': Ehrenberg 1929, 1429. Honours for Areus II at Delphi (ch. 3 and n.22) and service of Xanthippus with Carthage (below, n.11) belong to this obscure era.
7 Plut. *Arat.* (n.1, above); cf. Walbank 1933.
8 Alliance: Plut. *Ag.* 13.5. (Perhaps the fragmentary *IG* v.1,3 is the record of this.) Character of Achaean League: below, n.20.
9 Exemption from *agōgē* of heir-apparent: Cartledge 1987, 23–4. Lapse of *agōgē* post-late 270s: inference from Pyrrhus' offer (ch. 3 and n.14, above); also from Xanthippus' 'having participated in the Spartan *agōgē*' (Plb. i.32.1).
10 Augustan exaggeration: Beard/Crawford 1985, 28–9. *Artos* contributed to mess by rich Spartans in early C4: Cartledge 1987, 131,178,410; noted for C3 by Persaeus, *FGrHist.* 584F2 (adding that in this respect the messes were a sort of microcosm of the polity as a whole); cf. Sphaerus, *FGrHist.* 585F2; and on Spartan decadence generally Phyl., *FGrHist.* 81F44; Plut. *Mor.* 240ab; *Cleom.* 16.7.

11 Aristotle on *oliganthrōpia*: Cartledge 1979, 307–17 *passim*; 1987, 409–10. Spartan mercenaries: Tarn 1923, 129–30 (exaggerated); Bradford 1977, svv. Aristaeus, Aristei(das), Aristocles (6), Asclapiadas, Aphrodisius, Cleometus, Tetartidas (?), and most famously Xanthippus (especially Plb. i.32–36.4; 255 BC); generally Griffith 1935, 93–8. Invention of 'traditions' in conservative societies: Humphreys 1978, 249 (cf. Roman manipulation of 'mos maiorum').

12 Citizen and sub-citizen numbers in *c*.244; Plut. *Ag.* 5, as interpreted by Fuks 1962c = 1984, 230, 246–8 (Fuks, however, considers the '*rhētra* of Epitadeus' genuine; *contra* ch. 1, n.14). Number of 'Lycurgan' *klaroi*: Cartledge 1979, 169–70 (invention); *contra* Marasco 1978, followed by Figueira 1986. *Hupomeiones* in C4: Cartledge 1987, Index s.v. 'Sparta/Spartans . . . citizenship', especially 170 (Xen. *Hell.* iii.3.6 – sole attested use of term).

13 Sexual politics: ch. 3,n.13. Women of Agis' family: Bradford 1977, svv. Agesistrata, Archidamia; Piper 1979, 7. Women, cult (Hyacinthia) and literacy: Edmonson 1959. *Politikē gē*: Plb. vi.45.3; cf. Walbank 1957, 728–31; Cartledge 1979, 166–7; wrongly situated (on the basis of Plut. *Ag.* 8) by Chrimes 1949, 5, 286–7, 429–30.

14 Decision-taking: Cartledge 1987, ch. 8. Kingship: Cartledge 1987, ch. 7. (Will 1979, 334, following Beloch, cannot envisage Agis as other than a supporter of the faction of Agesilaus.) *Rhētra* of Lysander (?model for Epitadeus): Plut. *Ag.* 8. Named individuals: Bradford 1977, svv. Agesilaus (2), Lysandros (1), Mandrocleidas, Leonidas (1). Other alleged 'intimates' of Agis (*Ag.* 18.7): Bradford 1977, svv. Amphares, Arcesilaus, Damochares. Leonidas and Seleucus (?I): ch. 3, n.10; cf. Bernini 1978, 48n.82.

15 Cleomenes I and Demaratus: Noethlichs 1987, 155–6, no.30. Skywatching: Plut. *Ag.* 11.3; cf. Parke 1945; Cartledge 1987, 95. Ino-Pasiphaë: Plut. *Ag.* 9.2–3 (citing Phyl. F32), *Cleom.* 7.2; *IG* v.1, 1317 (C4); Sosib., *FGrHist.* 595F46, with Jacoby 1955 (Comm.), 665–7; also Cartledge 1975, 53–4, no.54 (site); see further ch. 14 in this volume. Comparable oracular manipulations in C16–17 England: Thomas 1971, ch. 13. Chilonis (not to be confused with homonym of ch. 3, n.13, above): Bradford 1977, s.v. Chilonis (2); ?dedicatrix of Dawkins 1929, 372–4, nos 61–3, 65.

16 Spartan 'Crown': Adcock 1953, 166.

17 Agis' programme in general: Fuks 1962a = 1984, ch. 12; 1962b = 1984, ch. 13; 1962c = 1984, ch. 11; cf. David 1981, 148–62 (Spartan social structure). Debts as 'mortgages' only: Ehrenberg 1929, 1429. Attic *horoi*: Finley 1985 (new introduction by P. Millett; 'mortgage' is technically inaccurate, but it is hard to find an alternative). Tetradrachms of Agis (?): Furtwängler 1985, 639 (redating Grunauer-von Hoerschelmann 1978, Group IX.1–15).

18 Early C4 pamphleteering (especially King Pausanias, *FGrHist.* 582): David 1979; Cartledge 1987, 163. Authors of a *Lac. Pol.* or other work on Sparta: (a) *Local* – *FGrHist.* 586–90, 595 (Sosibius, on whom see also Marasco 1978, 124n.35; Boring 1979, 55–8, 81–2; and further ch. 13 in this volume); (b) *Foreign* – Persaeus of Citium (*FGrHist.* 584: Stoic, commander of garrison of Acrocorinth surprised by Aratus, 243); Dioscorides (*FGrHist.* 594). Lycurgus (later king): Chrimes 1949, 23. Rejoinder of Leonidas: Plut. *Ag.* 10.

19 Helots as basis: below, n.35. Varieties of support for Agis: Cloché 1943, 53–70.

20 Corinth expedition: Plut. *Ag.* 13.10,14–15; *Arat.* 31–2; Paus. ii.8.5. Cimon at Ithome: Cartledge 1979, 220–1. Aratus' motivation: Forrest 1968, 146; Will 1979, 336. Character of Achaean League: Aymard 1938, especially 32–3; Urban 1979; O'Neil 1984–1986, 33–44, 55–7. Hellenistic 'democracy' in

general: Jones 1940, 168. Downfall of Agis: Cic. *Off.* ii.80. Exiles: Fuks 1962c = 1984, 233 (numbers); Shimron 1972, 27n.43 (nature).

21 Aetolian raid: Plb. iv.34.9, ix.34.9; Plut. *Cleom.* 18.3. Aetolia and Messenia: *SV* III.472; cf. Tarn 1928, 733; Walbank 1984, 250. Nature of Aetolian League: Tarn 1928, 208–11; Oliva 1984, 7; Mendels 1984–1986; O'Neil 1984–1986, 45–54, 57–61. Agis and Perioeci: Plut. *Ag.* 8.2 (dubious). Mercenaries at Taenarum: Launey 1949, 105 and n.1; Walbank 1957, 568. Poseidon and earthquake of *c.*464: Cartledge 1979, 96, 214. Taenarius: Bradford 1977, s.v.

22 Leonidas' monarchy: Bernini 1978; cf. Tarn 1928, 742 (defending Leonidas). Marriage of Agiatis: Bradford 1986b, 16. *Patroukhoi*: Cartledge 1981. Agis' infant son: Paus. ii.9.1, iii.10.5 (Eurydamidas probably a mistake for Eudamidas: Oliva 1971, 240 and n.5). Continuity between Leonidas and Cleomenes: Bernini 1978.

23 Accession of Cleomenes: Plut. *Cleom.* 3.1,38.1. Lydiadas and Achaea: Plut. *Arat.* 30.4, *Mor.* 552b; cf. Walbank 1957, 238. (The Thearidas who was willing to come to terms with Cleom. in 223 – Plb. ii.56.8; Plut. *Cleom.* 24.2ff. – was probably Plb.'s grandfather: Walbank 1957, 259.)

24 'Cleomenic War': Plb. ii.37–70; cf. Fine 1940; Walbank 1957, 215–16; 1979, 740–1; Oliva 1968. Chronology (pegged to year of Sellasia battle, almost certainly 222): Walbank 1957, 272; 1967, 634; 1979, 763. Aristomachus: Plut. *Arat.* 27–29, 35.1ff.; cf. Walbank 1957, 238. Aetolia and four Arcadian towns: Plb. ii.46.2–3, 57.1–2; Plut. *Cleom.* 5.1, 14.5. Aetolian neutrality: Larsen 1966.

25 Athenaeum: Plb. ii.46.5; Plut. *Cleom.* 4.1–2; cf. Loring 1895, 38–41, 47, 71–4, figs.2–3, pl. 1; Walbank 1957, 243–4 (but note correction, 1979, 762); Cartledge 1975, 61–2, no.70. Ladocea: Plut. *Cleom.* 6.3ff.; *Arat.* 36.4–37.5; Plb. ii.51.3. Mercenaries: Plut. *Cleom.* 7.5.

26 Cleomenes and Archidamus: Plb. v.37.2, viii.35.3–5, followed by e.g. Bernini 1981–82 (Cleomenes guilty); Plut. *Cleom.* 5.2–3, followed by e.g. Oliva 1971, 235–43 (not guilty).

27 Sphaerus (*FGrHist.* 585) in general: Boring 1979, 68–70; and *agōgē*: Plut. *Cleom.* 11.1–4. Influence (?) on Cleomenes: Ollier 1936; doubted by Rostovtzeff 1941, 1367n.34; Boren 1961, 368–9n.25; Oliva 1971, 232; David 1981, 166–8; Shaw 1985, 28; also Vatai 1984, 124, 126.

28 Ephorate: Plut. *Cleom.* 8–10; cf. Chrimes 1949, 9–10, 19–20, 405–6; Cartledge 1987, 125–6. Gerousia: Paus. ii.9.1; cf. Shebelew *ap.* Kazarow 1907, 51 (annual election?); Chrimes 1949, 19, 143–8 (Patronomos; cf. Andreotti 1935; Shimron 1965; but see also ch. 14 in this volume); Ste. Croix 1981, 527. Agiad dyarchy: Tod in Tod/Wace 1906, no.145. Cleomenes as 'tyrant' (in addition to Plb. ii.47.3): Plb. iv.81.14, ix.23.3, xxiii.11.4; Plut. *Cleom.* 7.1; Paus. ii.9.1; Livy xxxiv.26.14; cf. Boren 1961; Pozzi 1968; Shimron 1972, 44; Heuss 1973, 43–4; Walbank 1979, 224; Marasco 1980b, 28. (Note that, according to Xen. *Lak. Pol.* 15.9, 'Lycurgus' aimed to prevent 'tyrannical ambition' in kings.) 80 exiles: Plut. *Cleom.* 10.1 (proscribed), 11.1. Megistonous: Bradford 1977, s.v.

29 *Anadasmos*: Plut. *Cleom.* 11.1; cf. Pozzi 1968, 398 and n.18; Cartledge 1987, 167–74. Shimron (1972, 43,151–5) argues for the creation of 5,000 citizens by Cleomenes: cf. Marasco 1979, 61 (next note). *Diaita*: Poralla/Bradford 1985, 177, s.v. Gnosippus (of whom an example was made).

30 'Lycurgan' rhetoric: Marasco 1980b, especially 7–23. Mercenaries and citizenship: Marasco 1979, 61 (unconvincing argument for 2,000 ex-mercenary citizens, making 6,000 citizens in all). Mercenaries typically equipped as

peltasts: Griffith 1935, 95. Military reform (going Macedonian): Launey 1949,361–2. Neopolitae *IG* v.1, 680: cf. Oliva 1971, 88 and n.6, 245n.3. Army-organization (N.B. Plb. fr. 60 B.-W. for size of *mora* in ?? Cleomenes' army): Cartledge 1987, 427–31 (on 'obal' army); 1979, 254–7 ('moral' army).

31 Fighting for more than *status quo*: the point is made forcefully in George Orwell's *Homage to Catalonia* (1938). Achaean socio-economic tensions: Walbank 1984, 253–4. Cleomenes' revolution 'not for export': Gabba 1957, 22; cf. Shimron 1966b, 459. Old, pre-Peloponnesian War Pel. League: Cartledge 1987, 9–13; post-Peloponnesian War: Cartledge 1987, ch. 13.

32 Hecatombaeum: Plut. *Cleom.* 14, *Arat.* 39.1; Plb. ii.51.3. Argos: Plut. *Cleom.* 17.5ff., *Arat.* 39.4–5; Plb. ii.52.1–2, 55.8–9,60.6. *Volte-face* of Aratus: Freeman 1893, 359–61; Will 1979, 382–5. Ptolemy III and Cleomenes: Plb. ii.51.2; Plut. *Cleom.* 22.9; *IvO* 309 (dedication by Ptolemy in honour of Cleomenes at Olympia; cf. *SIG*³ 433, cited above ch. 3,n.22: Ptolemy II in honour of Areus). Hippomedon: *IG* xii.8.156 = *SIG*³ 502, discussed fully (with L. Robert's new readings) by Gauthier 1979; cf. Herman 1987, 85, 86.

33 Ptolemaic coinage (bronze): Walbank 1984, 464n.44. Cleomenes' silver: Grunauer-von Hoerschelmann 1978, Group III (on Orthia statue: see also Pipili 1987, 97–8n.438), Groups IV–V (Ptolemaic models). Orthia temple: Grunauer-von Hoerschelmann 1978, 14–16. 'Great Altar': this volume, ch. 14 and App. I. Defection of Argos: Plb. ii.52.5ff.; Plut. *Cleom.* 20–1, *Arat.* 44.

34 Doson's Hellenic League: Walbank 1957, 256; 1981, 97. 'Triumph of federalism': Tarn 1928, 747–51; cf. Walbank 1976/7; Will 1979, 389–90. The League and social revolution: Tarn 1923, 128. Doson's accession: Will 1975, 389.

35 Destruction of Megalopolis: Plb. ii.54–5, 61–2 (booty: 62.1, with Rostovtzeff 1941, 205–6, 750–3, 1366n.31, 1507n.20, 1606–7n.85), 64, ix.18ff.; Plut. *Cleom.* 23–26, *Arat.* 45, *Philop.* 5; Paus. viii.8.11, 27.15, 49.4. Helots: Oliva 1971, 259–60 (too sceptical); Welwei 1974, 162–8; Noethlichs 1987, 167n.193 (in general discussion of money at Sparta, 165–9); cf. *IG* v.1, 1340 (1 mina of silver paid, but not certainly Helot manumission and possibly of Nabian date). Manumission fees elsewhere: Hopkins 1978a, 158–63; but cf. Duncan-Jones 1984. Helots as basis: Ehrenberg 1929, 1429; Oliva 1971, 229; Cartledge 1987, 13. Continued status-difference: Sosib. *FGrHist.* 595F4 (taking 'those from the country' as Helots, not Perioeci); Plut. *Cleom.* 28.4–5 (Crypteia commanded at Sellasia by Damoteles).

36 Ptolemy ends subsidy: Plb. ii.63.1; Plut. *Cleom.* 22.9, 27. Battle: Plb. ii.65–9 (based on lost account of Philopoemen, a participant); Plut. *Cleom.* 28 (after Phyl.); *Philop.* 6; cf. Walbank 1957, 272–87 (date, sources, numbers, arms); Pritchett 1965, ch. 4 (site); Oliva 1971, 262–3; Will 1979, 396–401; Lazenby 1985, 172; Noethlichs 1987, 153–4 (alleged bribery of Damoteles). *Tresantes*: ch. 2, n.20, above. Echemedes: Papanikolaou 1976–1977. Victory-dedication (Delos): *SIG*³ 518; cf. Aymard 1967, 109.

37 Doson at Sparta: Plb. ii.70.1 (meaning of *patrion politeuma* disputed – Walbank 1966 preferable to Shimron 1972, 53–63; cf. Welwei 1974, 168–9; Mendels 1981, 1982); Plut. *Cleom.* 30.1. Sparta's incorporation in Hellenic League (?): Plb. especially iv.24.4; cf. Walbank 1957, 470 (probable); Cartledge 1979, 321 (dogmatic); *contra* Shimron 1972, 66–8 (alliance only). Garrison: Plb. iv.22.4ff., xx.5.12; cf. Launey 1949, 155–6. Denthaliatis: Plb. iv.24.7–8; cf. Pozzi 1970, 391 and n.17. Belminatis: Walbank 1957, 247 (*ad* ii.48.1). East Parnon foreland: Chrimes 1949, 21–2; Walbank 1957, 485; see further ch. 5 in this volume. Doson as 'Saviour and Benefactor': Plb. v.9.9–10;

cf. Walbank 1957, 290. Geronthrae inscription (*IG* v.1,1122): Pozzi 1970, 392–3n.24. (Note, however, Will 1979, 397–8: Doson's treatment of Sparta *not* mild.) Exiles of 227: Shimron 1972, 62 and n.23, 136 (no return).
38 Death of Ptolemy III (late 222): Walbank 1979, 763. Deaths of Cleomenes and co.: Plb. ii.69.10–11, v.35–9; Plut. *Cleom.* 29–37; Just. xxviii.4; cf. Shimron 1972, 64–6; and the brilliantly fictionalized account in Mitchison 1931. Legend: above, n.1.

Chapter 5 Sparta between Achaea and Rome: the rule of Nabis

1 Rhodian-Pergamene embassy: Plb. xvi.24.3; L(ivy) xxxi.2.1; cf. Holleaux 1957, 339–45; Badian 1964, 113; Walbank 1967, 530–1; Briscoe 1973, 55–6, 1978, 156–7; Will 1982, 13, 128–30. Athens' support: Will 1982, 129–30; Habicht 1985, 92–4, 99n.14, fig.30 (Cephisodorus). Rome's rise to empire: Errington 1971; Walbank 1981, 227–51; also below, n.22. 'Clouds in the west' (Plb. v.104.10): Freeman 1893, 435–8; Colin, 1905, 50–1, 78; Walbank 1940, 66; Errington 1969, 24–5; Will 1982, 76.
2 Battle of Mantinea (207): below, n.13. Period between Sellasia and Nabis: Pozzi 1970; Shimron 1972, 53–78; Toneatto 1974/5; Texier 1975, 7–14; Martinez-Lacy 1983. Indicative of unsettled conditions is coin-hoard buried in Sparta *c.*220: Hackens 1968, 72–3; Davies 1984, 279. 'Big politics': Ehrenberg 1929, 1438 = 1935, 1475; cf. Gruen 1984, 437.
3 Chief literary sources for Nabis: Plb. xiii.6–8, xvi.13; L. xxxiv.31–2; Diod. xxvii, fr. 1; Plut. *Flam.* 13, *Mor.* 809e. Polybius: see ch. 4, n.1; add Mendels 1979, especially 330–3, 1982, 93–5; Walbank 1985, 280–97. Plb. as source of entire literary tradition on Nabis: Mundt 1903; cf. Shimron 1974, 40 and n.1; Mendels 1979. Livy: Walbank 1940, 282–3; 1971; Briscoe 1973, especially 1–12,17–22, 1981; Taïphakos 1984. Comparison of Livy and Polybius, distinguishing Livy's debts respectively to Polybius (especially L. xxxiii.10.10) and the Latin annalists: Nissen 1863. Chief modern work on Nabis: Mundt 1903 (revisionist); Ehrenberg 1929, 1437–40; Hadas 1932, 74–6; Passerini 1933, 315–18; Ehrenberg 1935; Aymard 1938, 33–46,184–255,294–324; Chrimes 1949, 27–42; Mossé 1964; Jones 1967, 157–63; Mossé 1969, 179–92; Oliva 1971, 274–98; Shimron 1972, 79–100,118–28; Taïphakos 1972; Texier 1975; Bradford 1977. s.v..; Fontana 1968; Forrest 1968, 148–50; Piper 1986, 95–116. See also relevant passages in general studies of period: Freeman 1893; Niese 1899, especially Bk. 10; Holleaux 1957; Will 1982.
4 Polybius' starting-point: Walbank 1940, 23; Will 1982, 70. Social War: Plb. iv.3–37,57–87, v.1–30,91–106; cf. Freeman 1893, 395–438; Holleaux 1926, 201–7; Tarn 1928, 763–8; Walbank 1940, 24–67, 1984, 473–81; Will 1982, 71–7.
5 Spartan-Aetolian alliance: Plb. iv.34–35.5,ix.30.6,31.3,36.8; cf. Freeman 1893, 411,450–3; Walbank 1967, 169.
6 'Cleomenean party' or 'faction': alleged by (e.g.) Walbank 1957, 469; Shimron 1972, 69–78; denied by Martinez-Lacy 1983. Citizen-body 219/8: Shimron 1972, 153–4 (guesswork). Withdrawal of Brachyllas: Ehrenberg 1929, 1435. Murders of Ephors: Plb. iv.22.3–24.9,34.3–7. Restoration of dyarchy: Plb. iv.2.9,35.10ff.,xxiii.6.1; cf. Walbank 1957, 484; Oliva 1971, 268 and n.5.
7 Succession-disputes under *ancien régime*: Cartledge 1987, 111–12. Post-227 Gerousia: ch. 4 and nn.28,37; Plb. iv.35.5 (Gyridas, a *gerōn*, murdered 220). Agesipolis III: Bradford 1977, s.v. Lycurgus' alleged bribery: Plb. iv.35.14–15,

81.1; doubted by Noethlichs 1987, 162–3, no.86. Lycurgus as Eurypontid: Poralla/Bradford 1985, 163.

8 Lycurgus in east Parnon foreland: Plb. iv.36.5; cf. Chrimes 1949, 22,24; Walbank 1957, 485; Cartledge 1975, nos. 83 (Prasiae), 86 (Glympeis), 87A (Polichna), 88 (Cyphanta), 89 (Zarax), 99 (Hyperteleatum). Athenaeum: Plb. iv.37.6,60.3; cf. ch. 4, n.25. Philip in Peloponnese, w.219/8: Plb. iv.81.11; cf. Walbank 1940, 42–4. Lycurgus in Messenia, s.218: Plb. v.1.4,17.1–2. Philip's invasion of Laconia, s. 218: Plb. v.18–24; *IG* iv².1,590A (Epidaurus); ?*Anth. Pal.* vii.723; cf. Walbank 1940, 57–8, 1957, 553–8.

9 Chilon's *coup*: Plb. iv.81.1–10; cf. Ehrenberg 1929, 1436. Lycurgus' *idioi oiketai*: Plb. v.29.8–9; cf. Ehrenberg 1929, 1436; Piper 1984–1986, 85. Lycurgus and Agesipolis: Plb. xxiii.6.1; L. xxxiii.26.14; cf. Walbank 1979, 224.

10 Sosylus (*FGrHist*. 176): Rawson 1969, 101; Bradford 1977, s.v. Philip-Hannibal alliance: Plb. vii.9 (*SV* III.528); cf. Holleaux 1926, 209–10, 1957, 295–302; Walbank 1967, 42–56. Rome-Aetolia alliance (*SV* III.536): Walbank 1940, 83–4; Holleaux 1957, 302–7; Will 1982, 87–9. Rome and Illyria: Holleaux 1926, 47–66,194–201; Walbank 1940, 12; Badian 1964, 1–33; Errington 1971, 34–40; Harris 1979, 195–7. Romans at Isthmia: Plb. ii.12.4–8; Zon. viii.19.7; cf. Holleaux 1926, 60–1,65; Aymard 1938, 70; Badian 1964, 10 and n.44; Errington 1971, 275n.30.

11 Polybius' version of debate in Sparta, ? spring 210: Walbank 1967, 163, 1985, 255–9. Greek attitudes to Rome, including 'panhellenism': Plb. ix.37.6; L. xxxi.29.12,15; cf. Walbank 1940, 87, 1967, 176; Deininger 1971. Spartan *adscriptio*: L. xxxiv.32.2; cf. Wolters 1897, 144–5; Aymard 1938, 139 and n.23; Badian 1970, 52 and n.79 (meaning of term); Briscoe 1981, 98–9. Nabis-Flamininus debate: below, n.26. Pelops: Aymard 1938, 192n.36; Bradford 1977, s.v. Machanidas: Plb. 11.18.7 etc.; L. xxvii.29.9 etc. ('tyrant'); cf. Freeman 1893, 451; Ehrenberg 1930; Pozzi 1970, 411–14; as Pelops' guardian?: Wolters 1897, 144.

12 Dedication to Eleusia: *IG* v.1,236 = *SIG*³ 551; cf. Walbank 1967, 255. Eleusia/Eileithyia in Sparta (closely associated with Orthia): Dawkins 1929, 51. Machanidas 209–7: Plb. x.41.2, xi.11.2; L. xxviii.5.5, xxxviii.34.8 (with Ehrenberg 1929, 1437).

13 Philopoemen, in general: Errington 1969; at Sellasia: Errington 1969, 20–3; in Crete (*c.*221–211,200–194): ibid., 27–48; army-reforms: Holleaux 1957, 314; Anderson 1967; Errington 1969, 51,62–5. Battle of Mantinea: Plb. xi.11–18; Plut. *Philop*. 10; Paus. viii.50.2; cf. Freeman 1893, 464–5; Holleaux 1957, 314–15; Walbank 1967, 282–94 (map p.284); Errington 1969, 65–7. Aetolia-Philip peace, 206: Plb. xvi.13,3; cf. Walbank 1940, 101; Holleaux 1957, 316–17. Peace of Phoenice: L. xxix.12.13–14; cf. Holleaux 1926, 214–18, 1957, 317–18; Balsdon 1954; Walbank 1967, 516–17 (revising 1940, 103–4n.6); Will 1982, 94–9, especially 96.

14 Nabis as follower of Cleomenes: Ehrenberg 1929, 1437; Hadas 1932, 76; Aymard 1938, 41,138n.19; Holleaux 1957, 330; Mossé 1964, 319; Shimron 1974, 41,44; Forrest 1968, 149; *contra* Mendels 1979; as *aemulus Lycurgi* (L. xxxiv.31.18,32.1): Asheri 1966, 101–5; Jones 1967, 161; *contra* Shimron 1972, 94, 1974; Mendels 1978, 43; as 'socialist' or 'communist': Rostovtzeff 1941, 56; Holleaux 1957, 329–30. See also below, n.32.

15 Nabis' name: Ehrenberg 1935, 1471,1482; Texier 1975, 17. Filiation: Homolle 1896, especially 503–4 (publication of *SIG*³ 584), 512–21. Coinage: Lambros 1891; Wolters 1897, 142; Head 1911, 435; Seltman 1933, 257; Kraay/Hirmer 1966, no.522; Grunauer-von Hoerschelmann 1978, Group IX (but see

Furtwängler 1985, 639, dating IX.1–15 before Nabis). Tile-stamps: *IG* v.1,885; cf. Wace 1906/7, especially 6,20–1. Nabis under Cleomenes: Hadas 1932, 75; Ehrenberg 1935, 1472; Shimron 1972, 96.

16 Doson as 'king': Walbank 1984, 453; cf. Fontana 1980, 928 (comparison with Nabis). Nabis' bodyguard and mercenaries: Plb. xiii.6.5, xvi.37.3; L. xxxii.40.4,xxxiv.27.2,28.8,29.14,35.8,xxxv.27.15,29.1ff.; *IG* v.1,724 (Arcadian Botrichus); cf. Launey 1949, 113,123–4; Walbank 1967, 293; Shimron 1972, 141–2; Welwei 1974, 174; Walbank 1979, 139. Demaratus' Olympic victory: Ste. Croix 1972, 355n.5. Agesilaus II's warhorses: Cartledge 1987, 149. Machanidas' richly caparisoned horse and purple robe: Plb. xi.18.1. Nabis' stable and white horse: Plb. xiii.8.3. Nabis' palace: L. xxxv.36.1. Palatitsa: Andronicos 1984, 38–46. Nabis as 'Hellenistic king': Mossé 1964, 320; Shimron 1972, 86n.21; Texier 1974, 192, 197; 1975, 24 and *passim*. Nabis as 'tyrant': Plb. iv.81.12; L. *passim* (above, n.3); cf. more neutrally Aymard 1938, 34n.12; Mossé 1961, 354,357n.13 (Dionysius' *neopolitai*), 1964, 319–23; Fontana 1980, 921; Walbank 1981, 174.

17 Dionysius: Sanders 1987 (source-critical); cf. briefly Davies 1978, 201–11. Apia/Apēga: Texier 1975, 18–19; Bradford 1977, s.v. Apēga. Pythagoras: Bradford 1977, s.v.

18 Nabis and the 'slaves': Plb. xvi.13.1; L. xxxiv.31.11,14, xxxviii.34.6; Strabo viii.5.4 (trans. Cartledge 1979, 348); Plut. *Philop.* 16.4; cf. Chrimes 1949, 37–42, followed by Robins 1958 (*neodamōdeis*), refuted by Shimron 1966a (perhaps the best account to date); also Mossé 1964, 317–18,322; Texier 1974; Welwei 1974, 169–74; Mendels 1979, 322–4; Ste. Croix 1981, 149–50; Piper 1984–1986, 85–8. Nabis' land-distribution in Sparta: Passerini 1933, 316; Rostovtzeff 1941, 618; Asheri 1966, 98–100; Shimron 1972, 88n.26; Welwei 1974, 174n.56; Mendels 1979, 325n.92. Intermarriage of Spartan women and ex-Helots: Plb. xiii.6.3–4; L. xxxiv.35.7; cf. Piper 1984–1986, 84; see also below, n.28. Dionysius and Kallikyrioi: Mossé 1961, 359; Shimron 1972, 90n.29. Kallikyrioi and Helots: Arist. fr. 586R (trans. Cartledge 1979, 351).

19 Nabis' debt-cancellation at Argos: L. xxxii.38; *not* at Sparta: Asheri 1969, 59. Bottomry papyrus (P. Berl. 5883 + 5853): Wilcken 1925; Bogaert 1965, 146–54; Ste. Croix 1974, 53. Gytheum and trade: L. xxxiv.29.2–3,xxxiv.36.3, xxxviii.30.7; cf. Giannokopoulos 1966; Texier 1975, 76. Nabis as 'pirate' (by land as well as sea): Plb. xiii.6.5,8.2; L. xxxiv.32.18,35.9,36.3,xxxv.12.7; cf. Rostovtzeff 1941, 608; Brulé 1978, 49,159–60. Delian inscription (*SIG*[3] 584, above n.15): Ehrenberg 1935, 1473–4; Aymard 1938, 37n.37; Brulé 1978, 18n.3,49; Baslez/Vial 1987, 296.

20 Sparta's city-wall: Plb. ix.26a.2 (size of circuit); L. xxxiv.34.2–4,38.2,xxxix.37.2; Paus. vii.8.5; cf. Wace 1906/7; Cartledge 1975, 28–9; Piper 1986, 174–6. 'Lycurgan' building regulations: Plut. *Lyc.* 13, *Mor.* 189e,227b,285a. Neopolitae: ch. 4, n.30. Cynosura *hydragos*: Peek 1974 (= App. I, no.1); cf Le Roy 1974, 229–38 (another, more localized board of *hydragoi*, *c.*200). Pottery: Siebert 1978, 83–9. Tombs: Wace/Dickens 1906/7. Sculpture: Wace 1907/8. Grave-reliefs: Tod/Wace 1906, 127 (Cat. 257 + 294) = Bradford 1977, s.v. Paras; contrast ch. 4, n.36 (Echemedes).

21 Cinadon: Cartledge 1987, Index s.v. Nabis' war with Achaea, 204ff.: Plb. xiii.8.3ff., xvi.36–7, xxi.9.1; L. xxxi.25.3; Plut. *Philop.* 13; cf. Aymard 1938, 39–40n.51; Errington 1969, 77–81. Nabis' fleet: L. xxxiv.35.5,36.3, xxxv.12.7,26.2; cf. Ehrenberg 1935, 1473; Aymard 1938, 34–5n.20 (cost). Nabis' allies and (?) possessions on Crete: Plb. xiii.8.2; L. xxxiv.35.9; cf. Aymard 1938, 37n.39; Shimron 1972, 91n.31; Brulé 1978, 28–9,47. 'Iron

Maiden': Plb. xiii.7; cf. Aymard 1938, 36 and n.33. Nabis and Messene, 201: Plb. xvi.13.3,16.17; L. xxxiv.32.16,35.6; Plut. *Philop.* 12.4–6; Paus. iv.29.10; viii.50.5: *SIG*³ 595 (Eumenes); cf. Niese 1899, 566; Ehrenberg 1935, 1474–5; Aymard 1938, 38–41; Walbank 1940, 124; Chrimes 1949, 30–1 (disbelieves); Walbank 1957, 517; Oliva 1971, 283–4. Philopoemen in Laconia. 200: Plb. xvi.36–7; cf. Loring 1895, 57,63.

22 Senate, imperialism and Second Macedonian War: Plb. xvi.27.2 (Philip to make war on no 'Greeks'); cf. Colin 1905, 1–14,53–96; Holleaux 1926 (Rome and Greece 229–05); Walbank 1940, 138–85; Wason 1947, ch. 10; Holleaux 1957, 320–86; Walbank 1967, 537; Errington 1971, 131–55; Briscoe 1973, 39–42; Crawford 1978b, 65–70; Nicolet 1978, 883–920. Harris 1979, especially 21 (triumph), 57,92 (Senate), 212–18; Habicht 1982, 150–8; Will 1982, 131–78; Gruen 1984, especially 8; 343–51 (Plb.); 721–30; Harris 1984.

23 Achaea-Rome alliance: L. xxxii. 19–23; cf. Aymard 1938, x–xi,83–97; Walbank 1940, 163. Nabis, Philip and Argos: Plb. xviii.16–17; L. xxxii.25,38–40; xxxiv.25,40–41.7; *SIG*³ 594 (Mycenae); cf. Freeman 1893, 481n.6; Aymard 1938, 109–11,132–54,185n.3; Walbank 1967, 570; Texier 1975, 45–65; Mendels 1977, 169–71; 1978,39–42; Eckstein 1987, 227–8. Mycenae conference: L. xxxii.39–40; cf. Aymard 1938, 141–9; Walbank 1940, 166 and n.1,323; Texier 1975, 64–6. Roman recognition of Nabis: L. xxxiv. 31.5,12–13; denied by Flamininus (L. xxxiv.32.1); cf. Ehrenberg 1935, 1474,1476.

24 Nabis' 600 Cretans: Oliva 1971, 286–7n.4. Battle of Cynoscephalae: Walbank 1940, 167–72; Holleaux 1957, 359–65 (Macedon's Jena); Badian 1970, 49; Will 1982, 159–60. 'Freedom of the Greeks': Plb. xviii.44–8; L. xxxiii.32–3; cf. Freeman 1893, 473–5; Colin 1905 *passim*, especially 3,81–2,243,253; Ehrenberg 1935, 1477; Aymard 1938, 284–6; Walbank 1940, 178–83; Holleaux 1957, 365–71; Badian 1964, 10, 123–4,130; Errington 1969, 82; Badian 1970, 33–4; Errington 1971, 151–5,180–1; Texier 1976–77, 154; Harris 1979, 140–2; Will 1982, 142,145–6,164–74; Gruen 1984, 132–57.

25 Flamininus' war *vs.* Nabis: L. xxxiii.44.8–45.5, xxxiv.22–4,26ff., 29.4; Just. xxxi.1.5–6; Zon. ix.18.3; *SIG*³ 595; cf. Loring 1895, 64; Niese 1899, 655–65; Aymard 1938, 184–255; Walbank 1940, 187–9; Chrimes 1949, 29; Holleaux 1957, 375–8; Badian 1964, 121–2 and n.43; Oliva 1971, 288–93; Shimron 1972, 92–4; Will 1982, 174–6; Gruen 1984, 450–5.

26 Nabis-Flamininus debate: L. xxxiv.31–2; cf. Aymard 1938, 149–50n.55, 222–6; Shimron 1972, 82; Texier 1975, 69–89, at 77–87; Texier 1976–77; Mendels 1978; Eckstein 1987, especially 216–27, 228–33.

27 Flamininus' 'philhellenism': especially L. xxxiv.48.1–2 (on Sp.); cf. Colin 1905, 97–172, at 133–4; Badian 1970, especially 14, 38, 47, 48, 53, 53–7; Briscoe 1973, 33–4; Will 1982, 153–5, 171. Tarentum as Spartan colony: Plb. viii.33.9; cf. Walbank 1967, 108. Roman-Spartan 'kinship': Rawson 1969, 99–106.

28 195 settlement: L. xxxiv.35.3–11, 43.1–2, 49.2; cf. Colin 1905, 166, 214, 216; Ehrenberg 1935, 1478–9; Aymard 1938, 229–36. Wives of exiles: L. xxxiv.35.7; cf. Aymard 1938, 35n.22; Shimron 1972, 142n.16; Seibert 1979, 191–3nn. 1505–10. Nabis' outlet to sea: Aymard 1938, 234n.27; Cardamyle is my suggestion. Status of 'maritime' Perioeci: L. xxxiv.36.2, xxxv.13.2, xxxviii.31.2; cf. Aymard 1938, 243, 251–5, 333n.10; Briscoe 1981, 164. End of old 'Lakedaimon': Ehrenberg 1929, 1439 = 1935, 1479; Aymard 1938, 234n.25.

29 Gytheum's dedication to Flamininus: *SIG*³ 592 = *SEG* XI.923 (cf. worship of Flamininus in Imperial festival at Gytheum: Ehrenberg/Jones no.102a): Colin 1905, 142 and n.5, 245 and n.3; Aymard 1938, 255 and n.22; Walbank 1987, 382 and n.75. (Note possible pre-195 Spartan harmost at Oetylus: *IG* v.1,

1295.) '*Koinon* of the Lacedaemonians': Strabo viii.5.5, C366; Paus. iii.21.7; *SEG* XI.938 (70s BC?); Le Roy 1974, 222–3, no.2; cf. Costanzi 1908, 56n.1; Accame 1946, 74, 124–9 (post-146); better Gitti 1939, especially 197–8; Giannokopoulos 1966, 79–86; Taïphakos 1973. Aetolia and Nabis: L. xxxiv.12.4–6; cf. Aymard 1938, 189n.25, 296–7, 302n.42; Holleaux 1957, 391–6; Oliva 1971, 296–7n.5; Forrest 1968, 150. Achaea and Nabis: L. xxxv.27–30; Plut. *Philop.* 14; Paus. viii.50.8–9; Just. xxxi.3.2–3. Philopoemen's naval defeat: Walbank 1940, 195; Duggan 1952; Errington 1969, 102–3; Briscoe 1981, 183. Involvement of Eumenes: *SIG*^{3} 605; cf. Aymard 1967, 89n.5; Oliva 1971, 295n.4. Intervention of Flamininus: Plut. *Philop.* 15.3; Paus. viii.50.10; cf. Aymard 1938, 312–13; Walbank 1940, 196; Briscoe 1981, 189–90; Gruen 1984, 463–7.

30 Murder of Nabis: L. xxxv.35–6; cf. Costanzi 1908, especially 53, 57–8; Holleaux 1957, 395–6. Appointment of 'Laconicus' (real name, or L.'s misunderstanding?) as king: L. xxxv.36.8; cf. Aymard 1938, 192n.36; Bradford 1977, s.v. Philopoemen's *coup*: Mahaffy 1892, 189; Loring 1895, 64–6. Incorporation in Achaea: L. xxxv.37.1–3; Plut. *Philop.* 15.4; Paus. viii.51.1; cf. Freeman 1893, 492–3; Aymard 1938, 315–24; Errington 1969, 109–12.

31 Post-incorporation government of Sparta: Plut. *Philop.* 15.3; cf. Errington 1969, 110–1; Shimron 1972, 107,111–12,139n.11; Walbank 1979, 86. Nabis' household effects: Plb. xx.12.7; Plut. *Philop.* 15.4–6; Paus. viii.51.2; cf. Aymard 1938, 337–8; Walbank 1979, 86; Noethlichs 1987, 136, no.8. Nabis' popular support: Plut. *Flam.* 13.3; cf. Mossé 1964, 322 and n.40; Texier 1975, 101–2. Philopoemen's intervention, 191: Plut. *Philop.* 16.1–3; Paus. viii.51.1; cf. Aymard 1938, 330–8; Errington 1969, 121–2; Shimron 1972, 103–4, 143–4; Walbank 1979, 85; Gruen 1984, 467–8 and n.176. Spartan embassy to Rome, 191/0: Plb. xxi.1–4; cf. Aymard 1938, 331n.2,336n.21,355–72; Errington 1969, 133,286–7; Walbank 1979, 88. Spartans attack Las, 189: L. xxxviii.30.6ff.,31; cf. Colin 1905, 215–18; Aymard 1938, 337n.22,359n.7,377–8. Compasium massacre: Plb. xxii.3.1; Plut. *Philop.* 16.3 (80 killed); *contra* the Spartan writer Aristocrates, *FGrHist.* 591F3 (350 killed); cf. Walbank 1979, 177. Philopoemen's settlement, 188: Plb. xxi.32c, xxii.3.1,11.7, xxiii.4.14; L. xxxviii.33–4, xxxix.36.14,37.1,16; Plut. *Philop.* 16; Paus. vii.8.5, viii.51.3; cf. Colin 1905, 218; Aymard 1938, 321n.35; Chrimes 1949, 43ff.; Holleaux 1957, 428–9; Errington 1969, 146–7; Oliva 1971, 300–2; Shimron 1972, 106–7,113; Golan 1974, especially 37–8; Seibert 1979, 199–200. Imposition of Achaean laws confirmed by Plb. xxii.12.3; L. xxxix.37.16; *IG* v.1, 4–5; cf. Jones 1967, 163; Walbank 1979, 138,218; see further ch. 6 and especially ch. 11 in this volume.

32 Nabis as 'revolutionary': Tarn 1923, 139; Aymard 1938, 136–7n.16, 138n.19; Holleaux 1957, 329; Mossé 1964, 323; Jones 1967, 157; Texier 1975, 80,83; Mendels 1979. Achaea unites Peloponnese (minus ex-Perioeci): Paus. viii.30.5; cf. Ehrenberg 1929, 1440; Aymard 1938, 378. Rome and the social order: especially L. xxxiv.51.6; cf. Colin 1905, 651–2; Aymard 1938, xii,190; Holleaux 1957, 382,386; Briscoe 1967; Errington 1971, 162; Briscoe 1981, 124,128; Ste. Croix 1981, 307,523–9. Nabis and the Classical *polis*: Texier 1975, 60–1; Vidal-Naquet 1986, 205.

Chapter 6 Sparta from Achaea to Rome (188–146 BC)

1 Philopomen's 188 settlement: ch. 5 and n.31. Unification of Peloponnese: ch. 5 and n.32. Spartan eccentricity: Larsen 1968, 44. 'Politische Vernichtung' of Greece: Münzer 1925, especially ch. 6 (ending, p. 69, with instructive letter from Bismarck to Ernst Curtius!). 'Nemesis': Toynbee 1965, 458. Polybius' motives for extending *Histories* from 168 to 146: Walbank 1985, 341–3.

2 Embassies of 188/7, 187/6: Plb. xxii.3.1–4, 7.5; cf. Niese 1903, 46–51,56–61 (on diplomacy of 188–79); Larsen 1938, 286–8; Werner 1972, 558–9n.187 (list of known embassies to Rome, 188–71); Briscoe 1967; Walbank 1979, 9 (chronology). Spartan groupings: below, n.6. Rome's *prostasia*: Badian 1958, 91–2n.2; Larsen 1968, 448; Walbank 1979, 177 (important textual note, but different interpretation).

3 Achaean treaty with Rome: Walbank 1979, 219–20; Gruen 1984, 33–4. Lycortas' speech, 184: Walbank 1979, 200.

4 Livy: see ch. 5, n.3.

5 Complaints before Senate: above, n.2; Plb. xxii.11–12; L. xxxix.33.6. On the spot: Plb. xxii.7–10; L. xxxix.35.5–37; cf. Walbank 1979, 200. 'Old exiles': Plb. xxi.1.4,9,11.7; xxiii.4.2,5.18,17.10, 18.2; cf. Walbank 1979, 89. Alcibiades and Areus: Plb. xxii.11.7, xxiii.4.3; L. xxxix.35.5–8,36.1–2; Paus. vii.9.2; cf. Errington 1969, 175–8; Bradford 1977, svv.; Walbank 1979, 195–6,217–18. City-wall: ch. 5 and n.20; Paus. vii.9.5 (suggests rebuilding began 183, but see below, n.10); cf. Ehrenberg 1929, 1441; Walbank 1979, 219.

6 Embassies of 184/3: Plb. xxiii.1.6;4; L. xxxix.48.2–4; cf. Ehrenberg 1929, 1441; Walbank 1940, 238; Errington 1969, 179–83; Shimron 1972, 108–9. Spartan groupings: Errington 1969, 179n.3 ('old exiles'); Shimron 1972, 115–16,146–50 (over-schematic). Senatorial commission (Flamininus, Q. Caecilius Metellus, Ap. Claudius Pulcher): Plb. xxiii.4.7; Paus. vii.9.5; cf. Errington 1969, 181–3. Property-rights: Walbank 1979, 217–18. 'Foreign tribunals' (*dikastēria xenika*): Paus. vii.9.5,12.4.

7 183/2 deputations and senatorial reaction: Plb. xxiii.5.18,6.1–2,9.11–15, especially 9.14; cf. Walbank 1979, 223,228. Serippus and Chaeron: Plb. xxiii.17.6–10; cf. Errington 1969, 188–9. Messene secession and death of Philopoemen: Plb. xxiii.9.8–9; 12–14,17.1–4; L. xxxix.48.5; Paus. viii.52.3; cf. Ehrenberg 1929, 1442; Errington 1969, 189–94. Sparta's readmission to Achaean League, thank-offering to Lycortas: Plb. xxiii.17.5–18.2; Paus. vii.9.5; *SIG*³ 626; cf. De Sanctis 1923, 245–6n.19; Walbank 1979, 250–1.

8 Chaeron's coup: Plb. xxiv.7; cf. Freeman 1893, 507; Ehrenberg 1929, 1442; Benecke 1930, 299; Chrimes 1949, 48 ('socialist agitator'); Oliva 1971, 309; Shimron 1972, 110; Walbank 1979, 259; Piper 1986, 131–2 (preferable). Socio-economic crisis in Greece: Rostovtzeff 1941, 603–32. *Dokimastēres*: Plb. xxiv.7.5, with Walbank 1979, 260.

9 Callicrates in general: Walbank 1979, 559 (collects main Polybius passages); 263 (selection of modern judgements); add Toynbee 1965, 472 (con); Deininger 1971, 135–45 (pro); cf. Will 1982, 245,284; Habicht 1985, 114. Callicrates' embassy to Rome, 180: Plb. xxiv.8–10; cf. Colin 1905, 233–4,236–7; Errington 1969, 202–3; 1971, 190; Walbank 1979, 19 (chronology); Gruen 1984, 497–8.

10 Callicrates' election as *stratēgos*: Plb. xxiv.10.14; cf. Walbank 1979, 19 (chron.). Solution of exile-problem: Plb. xxiv.8–10; L. xl.20.2; Paus. vii.9.6–7; *SIG*³ 634 = Burstein 1985, no.74; cf. Larsen 1968, 459–60; Oliva 1971, 310–11 and fig.59. Restoration of 'Lycurgan' regime?: L. xlv.28.4 (*disciplina, instituta*); cf. Ehrenberg 1929, 1442–3; Piper 1986, 145; *contra* Kennell 1985,

13–19; 1987, 422n.17 (146/5); ch. 14, in this volume. Restored *agōgē*: Plut. *Philop*. 16.6; Paus. viii.51.3; cf. Woodward 1907/8, 94–6, no.47 = Dawkins 1929, 35, fig.19; cf. Chrimes 1949, 46–7. Sussitia: Bradford 1977, s.v. Pasicrates (3) (*SEG* ii.60). Clothing and hairstyle: Paus. vii.14.2; cf. Chrimes 1949, 50. Wall (restored now): Benecke 1930, 300; Shimron 1972, 117; Piper 1986, 134.

11 Third Macedonian War: Colin 1905, 373–446; De Sanctis 1923, 279–333; Larsen 1968, 461–75; Errington 1971, 213–26; Will 1982, 270–85; Gruen 1984, 505–14. Polybius' view of origins: xxii.18.11; but see Walbank 1979, 208–9; cf. 227–8 (references for alleged plans of Philip), 793; also Toynbee 1965, 455–7. Embassy of Eumenes II: Benecke 1930, 256; Walbank 1979, 207. Battle of Pydna: N.G.L. Hammond in Hammond and Walbank, *History of Macedonia* III (forthcoming); as Macedon's Leuctra: Adcock in Adcock/Mosley 1975, 83. Rome's attitude to Greece post-Pydna: Plb. iii.1.9 (original terminal point); cf. De Sanctis 1923, 347; Rostovtzeff 1941, 739,741; Badian 1958, 96; Toynbee 1965, 444–5; Larsen 1968,475; Errington 1971, 226; Adcock/Mosley 1975, 253.

12 Extradition of Achaeans (deportees, hostages): Plb. xxx.6.5–6,13.11; L. xlv.31.4–5; Paus. vii.10.7–11; cf. Freeman 1893, 532–4; Colin 1905, 473–7; Badian 1958, 97; Errington 1971, 224–5 (exaggeration); Gruen 1976, 49–50; Will 1982, 284. Leonidas: L. xlii.51.8 (171 BC); cf. Niese 1903, 104–5; Gruen 1976, 55n.80; Bradford 1977, s.v. Menalcidas in Alexandria: Plb. xxx.16.2; cf. Gruen 1976, 54n.62.

13 Paullus in Sparta: L. xlv.28.4; cf. Plb. xxx.10.3–6; Plut. *Aem*. 28; Benecke 1930, 273; Errington 1971, 223; Will 1982, 282. Jason: *II Macc*. 5.9; cf. Niese 1903, 231n.3; Hadas 1959, ch. 8 (claims of kinship with Greeks); Tcherikover 1970, 160–5,188; Schürer 1973, 184–5n.33; Momigliano 1975, 113–14.

14 Proxeny-decree for Cleoxenus: Woodward/Robert 1927/8, 57–62, no.84; cf. Bradford 1977, s.vv. Damaisidas, Pēdestratus, Peisidamus, Philomachus.

15 Achaean-type institutions: above, n.8 (*dokimastēres*); ch. 5, n.31 *ad fin*. Coinage: Seltman 1933, 257 ('ugly little Pheidonian triobols struck by Sparta as an unwilling member of the Achaean League'). Aegytis, Sciritis, Belminatis: Plb. xxxi.1.7; L. xxxviii.34.8; Paus. vii.11.1–3; *SIG*³ 665; cf. De Sanctis 1964, 128–9; Oliva 1971, 312–13, fig. 61; Gruen 1976, 50–1 and nn.35,37; Walbank 1979, 465; Cartledge 1979, especially 6–7.

16 Sparta, Dōris and Delphic Amphictyony: *SIG*³ 668; cf. Daux 1957, especially 106–7,119n.1; Bradford 1977, s.v. Aristocles. Earlier history: Cartledge 1987, 34 (but Pythii had presumably disappeared with the dual kingship); ch. 1 and nn.21,29. Demise of Aetolia, 189: Plb. xxi.32.2; L. xxxviii.11.1–9; cf. Badian 1958, 85 and n.1; Walbank 1979, 131–2.

17 Menalcidas as Achaean *stratēgos*: Paus. vii.11.7–8,12.2,4–9; Just. xxxiv.1.3ff.; cf. Ehrenberg 1932, 703. Plb.'s *tarakhē kai kinēsis*: Walbank 1985, 325–43, especially 336–7. Liberation of (less than 300 surviving) Achaean hostages: Plb. xxxv.6; Plut. *Cat*. 9.2–3; Paus. vii.10.12; cf. Toynbee 1965, 482–4; Gruen 1976, 48 & n.22; Walbank 1979, 649–50.

18 Pausanias' narrative: vii.11–16; cf. Gruen 1976, 51; Walbank 1979, 698 (?dependence on Polybius); Habicht 1985, 98 (Pausanias usually wrote from memory). Oropus affair: Plb. xxxii.11.5; Paus. vii.11.7–12.3; cf. Freeman 1893, 537–8; Colin 1905, 504–7, 611. Menalcidas' alleged part therein: Walbank 1979, 531–3; Noethlichs 1987, 154, no.29.

19 Menalcidas in Rome, 151/0 or before: Paus. vii.12.2 cf. Gruen 1976, 54n.74; Walbank 1979, 698. 149 embassy: Paus. vii 12.4. Exile of the 24: Paus. vii.12.3–7; cf. Freeman 1893, 539 and n.1; Chrimes 1949, 50–1 (implausible); Oliva 1971, 313–14; Bradford 1977, s.v. Agasisthenes.

20 Revolt of Andriscus: Freeman 1893, 539–40; De Sanctis 1964, 122–6; Walbank 1979, 682–3; Will 1982, 387–9. Third Punic War: Harris 1979, 234–40. Spartan secession: Plb. iii.5.6. Damocritus in Laconia: Paus. vii.13.1–5; cf. De Sanctis 1964,134. 'Cities in a circle round Sparta': Paus. vii.13.5; as Perioecic: Ehrenberg 1929, 1444; Oliva 1971, 314.

21 Iasus: Paus. vii.13.7 (?=Iasaea: Paus. viii.27.3); cf. Cartledge 1979, 188. Mission of Orestes: Plb. xxxviii.9.1; L. Epit. 51; Paus. vii.14.1–3; Dio xxi, fr.72; Just. xxxiv.1; cf. Colin 1905, 615–17; Larsen 1968, 494; Walbank 1979, 48 (chron.); Gruen 1984, 520–1 (mere bluster); contra Walbank 1986, 517.

22 Mission of Caesar: Plb. xxxviii.9; cf. Colin 1905, 618; Harris 1979, 241n.5, 242; Will 1982, 392 (hypocrisy, Machiavellianism). Election of Critolaus: Plb. xxxviii.10.8; Paus. vii.14.3–4. Debt-measures of Critolaus (cf. Aeneas Tact. xiv.1–2, with Ste. Croix 1981, 298: C4 parallel): Plb. xxxviii.11.10; Diod. xxxii.26.3–4 (misrepresentation); cf. Freeman 1893, 544; De Sanctis 1964, 154; Asheri 1969, 68ff.; Fuks 1970, especially 79–81; Walbank 1979, 703–5. Corinth assembly, spring 146: Plb. xxxviii.12.2–11,13.6–7; Diod. xxxii.26.5; Paus. vii.14.4; cf. Freeman 1893, 544–6; Fuks 1970, 84–5.

23 Achaean War: Niese 1903, 337–52. Liberation of slaves: Plb. xxxviii.15.3–5,10; Paus. vii.15.7,16.8; cf. Fuks 1970, 81–2. Sack of Corinth: Freeman 1893, 550; Colin 1905, 634–5 (anachronistic); Benecke 1930, 304; Will 1982, 394, 395–6.

24 Fate of old Achaean League: Paus. vii.16.6–7; cf. Freeman 1893, 550–2; Colin 1905, 628–30, 657–60; Ehrenberg 1929, 1444–5; Larsen 1938, 306–11; Accame 1946, chs 1–2; Larsen 1968, 498–504; Fuks 1970, 79; Schwertfeger 1974, especially ch. 3; Bernhardt 1977 (defending Accame vs. Schwertfeger); Harris 1979, 146, 240–4; Gruen 1984, 523–7. City-constitutions, role of Polybius: Plb. xxxviii.4.7, xxxix.4.1–5.6; Paus.vii.16.6, viii.30.9; cf. Colin 1905, 651–6; Rostovtzeff 1941, 54 and pl.VIII; Accame 1946, 9–10, 33ff.; Fuks 1970, 86; Walbank 1979, 734–5; Ste. Croix 1981, 525; Bernhardt 1985, II.1.B(b).

25 Status of Sparta post-146/5: Strabo viii,365; Pliny, Nat. hist. iv.16; cf. Niese 1903, 351,357; Ehrenberg 1929, 1445; Accame 1946, 14–15,73–4; De Sanctis 1964, 179, 180; Schwertfeger 1974, 51 and n.97; Bernhardt 1977, 71; ch.11 below. 'Lycurgan' restoration: above, n.10. Achaean influence: above, n.15. Lace-daemonian League: ch. 5 and n.29. Recovery of Belminatis now?: Paus. iii.21.3, viii.35.4; cf. Accame 1946, 130; Schwertfeger 1974, 49n.90; but note caution of Ehrenberg 1929, 1445; and see further below, ch. 10. Dentheliatis inscription (Milesian arbitrators decided 584:16 against Sparta in c.138; text carved on base of Paeonius' 300-year-old Nike statue): SIG^3 683 = Burstein 1985, no.80; cf. Colin 1905, 511–12, 636 and n.3, 658 and n.1; Tod 1932, 49–52.

Chapter 7 Sparta between sympolity and municipality

1 Marrou 1965, 60. Historiographical trends: Bowie 1974, 174–88. For the spelling 'Achaia' when the Roman province is meant see Oliver 1983, 152 n.6.

2 Status of Greece after 146 BC: Accame 1946, 2–7; Bernhardt 1977; Gruen 1984, 523–7 (controversial). Lagina: Inschriften von Stratonicea ii.1, no.507 line 30. Thera (c. 100 BC): IG xii.3.1299.25; cf. 1625. Tralles: SEG xi.471.

3 Lodging: IG .v.1.7; 869. Kennell 1985, 23–4. Claudii: Suet. Tib.6; Rawson 1973, 227, 229. Pulcher: ch. 6. Cic. ad fam.xiii.28; Pro Flacc.63; Tusc. Disp.v.27.77 (visit: cf. ch. 14). Rufus: Schwertfeger 1974, 77. Provincial Greek/Roman ties: Bowersock 1965, ch. 1; Quass 1984.

4 Memnon, *FGrHist* 434 F 32. Deininger 1971, 258. Athens: Bernhardt 1985, 39–49. Laconian towns: App. *Mithr*.29.

5 App. *BC*.ii.70; Caes.*BC*.iii.4. Weil 1881, 16. Grunauer-von Hoerschelmann 1978, ch. 2.

6 Plunder: Plut. *Brut*.46.1; App. *BC* iv.11.8. Laconism: Cic. *ad Att*. xv.4. Philippi: Plut. *Brut*.41.4. Mantinea: note Paus.viii.9.6.

7 Businessmen: Le Roy 1978. Painting: Plin.*NH*.xxxv.173; Vitr.ii.8–9; H. Gundel, *RE* 9.A.1, 1961, col.357 (date); Pape 1975, 49–52 (aedilician shows). Gytheum: *IG* v.1.1146 (*SIG*³.748), transl. in Sherk 1984, no.74. Piso: Nisbet 1961, App.2. Pompey: Caes. *BC*.iii.3. Murcus: App. *BC*.iv.74. Decree: *IG* v.1.11. Coins: Grunauer-von Hoerschelmann 1978, 39–40, 51.

8 Messene: *SEG* xxiii.207; Migeotte 1985. Impact: Larsen 1938, 422; Crawford 1977, esp.45–6. Aristocrates: Spawforth 1985, 215–7.

9 Lachares: *SIG*³.786; Plut. *Ant*. 67.1–4; Chrimes 1949, 180 n.5; Baladié 1980, 291. Bowersock 1961, 116.

10 Rhadamanthys: *IG* v.1.141.17; Spawforth 1985, 193–9. Treasure-ship: Plut. *Ant*.67.4.

11 Coins: Grunauer-von Hoerschelmann 1978, 63–72. Strab.viii.5.1, 363; 5,5, 366. Phoebaeum family: Spawforth 1985, 197. Cythera: Cass. Dio liv, 7. Livia: cf. Reynolds 1982, no.13 with commentary. High-priesthood: *IG* v.1.1172. 'Agrippiastae': *CIL* iii.499 (*IG* v.1.374); Spawforth 1978, 256–7 (Deximachus); Roddaz 1984, 445–9.

12 Texts: *IG* v.1.141–2 (*hierothutai*); 206–9 (Phoebaeum: cf. ch. 14); 210–12 ('Taenarii'). *Hierothutai*: Kennell 1987; cf. Carlier 1984, 285–6 (royal prerogatives). Children of Eurycles: *IG* v.1.141.17–18.

13 Actia: Strab.vii.7.6, 325; Sarikakis 1965. Ties with Nicopolis: cf. *IG* v.1.474; 661; *SEG* xi.493.4–5; 828. Laconian towns: Paus.iii.21.6; *IG* v.1.1160; *SEG* xi.923.8. Bernhardt 1971, 116. Military role: note Kjellberg 1921, 52.

14 Jos. *BJ* i.425; 513–31; *Ant.Jud*.300–310; Pani 1984, 123–6.

15 Strab.viii.5.3, 366 with Bowersock 1961 (Piper 1986, 160, failed to give this 'variant reading' its full weight in her account of Eurycles). Plut. *Mor*.207f. Bowersock 1984, 176–8. Gytheum text: *SEG* xi.923. Eleutherolacones: Strab.viii.5, 3, 366 (Bowersock 1965, 92 n.2 for another view).

16 Tac. *Ann*.vi.18.2. Athens: *IG* ii².1069 and *Hesperia* 36, 1967, 68–71, no.13 with Jones 1978b, 227–8. Slave: *CIL* vi.27032. Macer: Bowersock 1984, 178–9.

17 Coins: Grunauer-von Hoerschelmann 1978, 73–77. Inscription: West 1931, no. 67; Bowersock 1961, 117; Pflaum 1960–61 i, 63–5.

18 Livia: *SEG* xi.830. Greek worship of Livia: refs. at *PIR*² L 301.Spartiaticus: West 1931. no.68; Plut. *Mor*.488f. with Groag 1939, cols.7–8 (overlooked by Piper 1986, 165–6). Muson. *ap*.Stob. xl.9. p.750 Hansl; Cass. Dio xlii.14.3.

19 *IG* v.1.970 (Asopus); *BCH* 95, 1971, 88 (Boeae); *SEG* xi. 923–4 (Sasel Kos 1979, no.40); Le Roy 1978 (Gytheum). Epidaurus: *IG* iv².592 + 662 = Peek 1969, no.253; *IG* iv².663. Lycosura/Megalopolis: *IG* v.2.541–2 (Spawforth 1978, 253). Athens: *SIG*³.788; 790. Corinth: West 1931, nos 67–8; cf. Puech 1983, 40.

20 Cythera: Lane 1962.

Chapter 8 Sparta in the Greek renaissance

1 Prosperity: Jones 1971b, 8; Larsen 1938, 482. Vespasian: *IG* v.1.691 (*SEG* xi.848); cf. Suet. *Vesp*.17. Trajan: *IG* v.1.1381. Harmonicus: *IG* v.1.480.

2 Full refs. to Agesilaus and Charixenus: Bradford 1977, s.vv. 'Agesilaos (4)'

and 'Charixenos (6)'. Their patronomates were dated by Chrimes 1949, 464–5, c. 95/6 and 119/20 respectively.

3 Woodward 1950, 630–31. Visit to Sparta: Phil. *VA* iv.31–33. Historicity doubted: Chrimes 1949, 158–9; Tigerstedt 1965–78 ii, 218; Penella 1979, 25. Damis problem: Anderson 1986, ch. 9. Luxury: Muson. *ap.*Stob.xl.9, p.750 Hansl.

4 Archaism: Bowie 1974. Roman dimension: Andrei 1984, ch. 1.

5 Patronomate: Bradford 1986a. Delphi: *FD* iii.4. no. 301 l.5. Visits: *IG* v.1.32a.9–12; 486; *SEG* xi.492; 630. Altars: *IG* v.1.381–404; Evangelidis 1911, 198 nos. 4–5; *SEG* xi.763; Bingen 1953, 642–6. Generally: Price 1984, 112.

6 Caudus: *SEG* xi. 490; Robert 1940a. 'Coronea': *IG* v.1.34 (*SEG* xi.479).11; 36 (*SEG* xi.486).24–5; 44 = *SEG* xi.486.7–8; *SEG* xi.495. Identification with Corone: Kolbe at *IG* v.1.p. 269; Ehrenberg 1929, col.1949; Woodward 1923–5, 186. Kahrstedt 1950a, 239–41 *contra*. Paus. iv.3.4–5.

7 Cephallenia: Cass. Dio lxix.16.1–3. *Ktistēs*: Strubbe 1984–6, 290–91.

8 Nicopolis: *SEG* xi.481. Pannonia: *IG* v.1.37; Millar 1977, 415. Hadrian and Zeus Olympius: Beaujeu 1955, 114–84. Spartan altar: *IG* v.1.406. Paus.iii.14.5. Theophrastus: *SEG* xi.492.2–5; *IG* v.1.167 = *SEG* xi.623.

9 Herculanus: *PIR*² I 302; Halfmann 1979, no.29. Balbilla: *PIR*² 650; Spawforth 1978 (kinship with Herculanus). Vibullii: Spawforth 1980, 208 n.33 with refs.

10 Grunauer-von Hoerschelmann 1978, 81; cf. *IG* v.1.971; 1172.

11 Inscription: Spawforth 1978, 251–2. Cytheran text: *IG* v.1.380. 'Things from Eurycles': *SEG* xi.494.2–3; cf. *IG* v.1.44 = *SEG* xi.486.3–4 (restored). 'Cytherodices': Spawforth 1980, 207; Thuc. iv.53.

12 Paus.ii.3.5; iii.15.6. Heroön: Spawforth 1978, 251. 'Heroic honours': *FD* iii.1.no.466 (a nearly contemporary example from Delphi); generally see Price 1984, 50. Spartan kings: Cartledge 1987, ch. 16; 1988.

13 Helladarchy: Oliver 1983, 110–14 with the reservations of Puech 1983, 20, 32–33. Delphi letter: *FD* iii.4.no.302, lines 1–6; Daux 1976, 73–7. Kahrstedt 1950b, 40.

14 Paus.x.8.4. Panhellenion: Spawforth/Walker 1985, 1986. Plataea: Sheppard 1984–6, 238. Cyrenaean inscription: Reynolds 1978, especially lines 39–40, 42–3; Spawforth/Walker 1986, 96–7; note too the unpublished inscription from Cyrene (ibid. n.81).

15 Atticus: Spawforth 1980. Herodes: ch. 12 in this volume. The evidence for these contacts is collected and discussed at some length in Spawforth/Walker 1986, 88–96, to which the reader is referred; see too Weiss 1984, Strubbe 1984–6 (foundation-legends); Müller 1980, 462–66 (Andragathus); Leschhorn 1984, 60–72 (foundation of Cyrene). Classical Sparta: Plat. *Hipp. Ma.*285d. More literal view of these Spartan ancestries: Woodward 1953 (but note Strubbe 1984–6, 264 n.59). A. Spawforth hopes to return to the subject elsewhere.

16 Altars: *IG* v.1.407–45; *SEG* xi.766–8. Dispute: *IG* v.1.37.7–9.

17 Inscriptions: *IG* v.1.116.17–18; 44 = *SEG* xi.486.4–6; 816; 818 (*dekatarkhēs*: see Mason 1974, 33–4). Enthusiasm: Luc. *Hist. Conscr.*2. Polyaen.i.1; cf. Cartledge 1987, 207.

18 Plague: Gilliam 1961. Thespiae: Jones 1971a. Sparta: *IG* v.1.44 = *SEG* 486.12–13; Woodward 1948, 219–33. Debasement: Grunauer-von Hoerschelmann 1978, 87, 95–6.

19 *Neōterismoi*: *IG* v.1. 44 = *SEG* xi.486.9–10; *SEG* xi.501.7. Woodward 1925–6, 236; 1948, 221–12. Oliver 1970a, 78–80. Pius: *HA, V. Ant. P.*5.4–5. For a well-known, but much earlier, outbreak of this type of *stasis* in Roman Greece see Sherk 1984, no.50 (*SIG*³ 684).

20 *IG* v.1.1361. Coins: Grunauer-von Hoerschelmann 1978, 87–88. Smyrna: Spawforth/Walker 1986, 93–4.
21 Philostratus and the Spartan myth: Tigerstedt 1965–78 ii, 211–19. Militarisation: Campbell 1984, 401–14. Athens: Geagan 1979, 406.
22 Cult: Spawforth 1984, 277–83. Monument: Spawforth 1986, 313–27.
23 Antonine constitution: Spawforth 1984, 264–5; cf. *IG* v.1.599 (Heraclia), 598 (parents). Caracallan contingent: Herodian iv.8.3; 9.4; *IG* v.1.130 (*SEG* xi.603), 817 with Spawforth 1984, 267–9. Cf. Hertzberg 1887–90 iii, 26–7 n.4 (apropos of Hdt.ix.53; Thuc.i.20). 'Moral' army: Cartledge 1987, App.II.
24 Coins: refs. at Spawforth/Walker 1986, 89–90, 95 n.63. Quotation from MacMullen 1976, 41.

Chapter 9 Pagans and Christians: Sparta in Late Antiquity

1 Epithets/titles: e.g. *IG* v.1.501.4; 527.11; 558.1–2; 559.2–3; 534.2; 589.3–4; 590.2–3. Clique: Spawforth 1985. Panthales: *IG* v.1.547; Spawforth 1984, 272–3 (date). Spatalus: *IG* v.1.535.11–12; Spawforth 1984, 285 no.19. 'Divine' patronomates: Spawforth 1985, 210.
2 Compulsion generally: Garnsey 1974. Spawforth 1984, 274–7 (portrait-herms). Catalogues: App.IIA, Table; Spawforth 1984, 285–8. Dedications: Woodward in Dawkins 1929, 293. Coinage: Grunauer-von Hoerschelmann 1978, 92–3; Howgego 1985, 98–9.
3 'Audience': MacMullen 1982, 246. Hoard: Karamesini-Oikonomidou 1966. Syncell. p. 717 (Bonn). Heruli generally: Millar 1969, 26–9; Bengtson 1977, 553–4; Wilkes forthcoming.
4 Devastation: Traquair 1905–6, 428; Woodward 1925–6, 208 (ibid. on the theatre).
5 Tetrarchic dedication: *SEG* xi.850. For later fourth-century repairs to the theatre see *SEG* xi.464–5, 851–2, 892 = xxxii.400. Laconia Survey: *Annual Report of the British School at Athens* 1984–5, 23–4. Boeotia: Bintliff/Snodgrass 1985, 145–7. S. Argolid: Van Andel/Runnels/Pope 1986, esp. 120. Late Roman economy: Whittaker 1986, esp. 7–12.
6 Proconsuls: Groag 1946, 22. Optatianus: *SEG* xi.810; Groag 1946, 25–6. Ampelius: *SEG* xi.464, 465?, 851; Himer. *Ecl.* xiii, ch. 8; Groag 1946, 42–4; Robert 1948. Anatolius: *SEG* xi.773; Groag 1946, 57–8. Zosim. v.6.
7 Lib.*or*.i.23. Amyclaeum: *IG* v.1.455 with Robert 1948, 27–8 n.6. Friends of Libanius: full references in Seeck 1906, 92, 132, 221–2. Tetrarchic notable: *SEG* xi.849 with Spawforth 1984, 280 n.14. Stephanus: *SEG* xi.510; cf.*IG* v.1.596. Panthales: *SEG* xi.464.4: the three letters before the name perhaps can be read as an abbreviation of the *nomen* Pomponius: [*P(omp)]ōn(ios) vel sim*.
8 Letter: Athanassiadi-Fowden 1981, 86. Sozomenus: Jones/Martindale/Morris 1971, s.v.. Lib. *Ep.*1210 (Foerster). Note Tigerstedt 1965–78 ii, 268, 545–6 n.1245, rightly cautious of a modern notion that Julian actually visited Sparta.
9 Ausonius: Lib. *Ep.*1518 (Foerster); Tigerstedt 1965–78 ii, 547–8 n.1264. For the statues in question see Thuc.i.134.4; Paus.iii.17.7. Cults: *IG* v.1.559.15 with Spawforth 1984, 279–80, 282 (Athena); 602.9 with Spawforth 1985, 238 (Aphrodite); chapter 14 (Dioscuri). Attacks on pagan cults: Fowden 1978, esp. 58–61; Gregory 1986, 238.
10 Attack on Sparta: Claudian. *In Rufinum* ii.189; *de IV cos. Hon.* 471; *de bello Poll.*192, 630; Zosim. v.6 (transl. Buchanan and Davis). Roman stage: Dickins 1905–6a, 397–8. Chrimes 1949, 83.

Chapter 10 The Roman city and its territory

1 Bölte 1929, cols. 1350–73 with earlier references; recent treatment in Greek (based on the text of Pausanias): Papachatzis 1974–80 ii, 329–405. For the Roman city Kahrstedt 1954, 192–8 remains important; note too Piper 1986, ch. 10 with the reservations of Spawforth 1987. On Pausanias see now Habicht 1985.

2 Persian Stoa: Paus.iii.11.3; Vitr.i.6; Plommer 1979, 100–101. Greek agoras as cultural centres: Shear 1981, esp.359–62 (Athens); Felten 1983. Imperial shrines: Paus.iii.2.4 with Hänlein-Schäfer 1985, 164,263. *Kaisareia/Sebasteia*: Hänlein-Schäfer 1985, 10–11; nearby examples: *SEG* xiii.258 (Gytheum); xxiii.206.39 (Messene). Site of agora: Dickins 1905–6b, 432–4.

3 Bölte 1929, cols.1365–6. Hellenistic theatre: Woodward 1925–6, 192–3; 1928–30, 152–6, 240. Thoroughfare: Dickins 1905–6a, 398; 1905–6b, 434.

4 Bulle 1937, 5–49; Buckler 1986, 431–6. Augustan and later stage-arrangements: Woodward 1925–6, 187–8 (rubbish-pits), 204–9; 1928–30, 156–60, 198–206. Inscribed epistyle-blocks: *IG* v.1.691 (*SEG* xi.848); *SEG* xi.849 with Spawforth 1984, 280; *SEG* xi.850, 852 = *SEG* xxxii.400.

5 Pers. comm. Susan Walker; cf. Palagia forthcoming.

6 Provincial Greek gymnasia incorporating therms: Delorme 1960, 243–50; Farrington in Macready/Thompson 1987; elsewhere in Achaia note Aupert 1985, 156 (Argos). For an earlier suggestion that the Heracles-herms came from a gymnasium see Wace in Tod/Wace 1906, 129.

7 This evidence was rejected on unconvincing grounds by Delorme 1960, 73.

8 Theophrastus: *SEG* xi.492 with Woodward 1925–6, 227–34. *Thermai*: Ginouvès 1962, 220 with n.5. Greek granaries: see, most recently, Grace 1985, especially 26–30.

9 *Macellum*: de Ruyt 1983, esp.230–35 and 263–4. Laconizing explanations of Roman customs: cf. Varro himself *ap. Servium in Aen.* vii.176; Tigerstedt 1965–78, ii. ch. vi.

10 Spartan bridge: App.I, 5. For examples of these openings in bridges at Rome see Nash 1961–2 ii, s.v. 'Pons Aemilius' (from 179 BC), 'Pons Milvius', 'Pons Fabricius' (62 BC); Blake 1973, 55 (Pons Aelius).

11 For the possible identification of a vast Serapeum at Roman Argos see Aupert 1985.

12 Bosanquet 1905–6, 282–3.

13 Statuary: Wace in Tod/Wace 1906, 128, 130; the group briefly discussed by Spawforth 1985, 231–2, was probably of this type. The sarcophagi from Roman Sparta are largely unpublished: see, briefly, Wace in Tod/Wace 1906, 130; Koch/Sichtermann 1982, 361–2 with the distribution map at 462–3 and, for a local copy apparently using imported Proconnesian marble, Coleman/Walker 1979.

14 Bosanquet 1905–6, 282. Population: Kayser/Thompson 1964, 206 with Cartledge 1979, 23. Intra-mural space: Polyb.ix.26a.2 with Walbank 1957–79 ii.156. Pompeii: Duncan-Jones 1982, 276 with n.7 (citing H. Bloch's population-estimate). Classical settlement: Osborne 1987, 121–3. 'Virgin' soil: Kahrstedt 1954, 194. Little is known of the extent and uses of open land within Greek walled cities; for the well-documented *rus in urbe* at Pompeii see Greene 1986, 94–7.

15 Athens: Shear 1981; Spawforth/Walker 1985, 92–100. Corinth: Wiseman 1979. Classical Sparta: note the remarks on the Persian Stoa of Plommer 1979. Hellenistic theatre: above, n.3.

16 Aqueducts and therms: J. Coulton in Macready/Thompson 1987. For private

use of Roman civic aqueducts see Jones 1940, 214–5.
17 Corinth: Paus.viii.22.3 with Biers 1978. Athens: *ILS* 337 with Travlos 1971,
   242–3. Argos: Spawforth/Walker 1986, 102 with refs. Thebes: Zahrnt 1979 ii,
   104. Entry of aqueducts into Athens and Argos: S. Walker in Macready/
   Thompson 1987.
18 Scenery-store: Woodward 1926–7, 7; 1928–30, 226–31. For the use of
   brickwork at Augustan Athens ('South-west Baths') see Shear 1969, 398–9.
   Peila: *IG* v.1.233 with Spawforth 1985, 203–4; for fresh-water *peilai* at
   Hadrianic Antioch see Malalas, *Chronographia* 278.1 (ref. kindly provided by
   C. Le Roy). Delorme 1960, ch. 8. Garden-sculpture: Wace in Tod/Wace 1906,
   130 (including pieces intended for fountains). For the appearance of Roman
   building-techniques in parts of Asia Minor by the mid-first century BC see M.
   Waelkens in Macready/Thompson 1987.
19 Roman Sparta's frontiers: Bölte 1929, cols.1303–28 *passim*; Chrimes 1949,
   56–72; Kahrstedt 1950a, 227–42 (western frontier); Toynbee 1969, 405–13;
   Cartledge 1979, 5–7 (Classical Sparta). Polybius xvi.17 with Chrimes 1949, 67;
   see Walbank 1972, 17–19 for the different dates of composition of the
   Histories. Boundary-inscription: *IG* v.1.1431.4–6; see further below. Date of
   transfer: Chrimes 1949, 67 (right but for the wrong reason); Bölte 1929,
   col.1309 (favouring Augustus).
20 Eastern frontier: Chrimes 1949, 70–71 with end-map. Croceae: Paus.iii.21.4.
   Priesthoods: *IG* v.1.497; 602; for the families in question see Spawforth 1985,
   229–44. Helos, site and history: *ABSA* 15, 1908–9, 19–21; Bölte *RE* 18.1,
   1912, 200–202; Hope Simpson/Waterhouse 1960, 100–103; Toynbee 1969, 191;
   Baladié 1980, 57–8. Pleiae: *ABSA* 15, 1908–9, 162–3; Bölte *RE* 18.2, 1942,
   cols.2444–5 (denying equation with Palaea) and 21.1,1951, cols.189–91.
   Kahrstedt 1954, 212. Eleusinium: Paus.iii.20.7 with Spawforth 1985, 230, 235.
21 Tacitus, *Ann.* iv.43; Th. Mommsen *ap.* R. Neubauer, *Arch. Zeit.* 34, 1876,
   138 n. 16; Accame 1946, 33; Baladié 1980, 311 n. 59 (preferring 43 BC without
   explanation); *contra*: Kolbe 1904, 376–7; Ehrenberg 1929, col.1446; Kahrstedt
   1950a, 232 with n.2. Productivity: Alcman frg. 92d. Olympia: *IvO* no. 259
   (Meiggs/Lewis 1969, no.74). Messenian text: *IG* v.1.1431 with Kolbe 1904,
   378. Pherae: *IG* v.1.1361 with Kolbe *ad loc.* Toynbee 1969, 412.
22 Pherae: Paus. iv.31.1 with Kolbe 1904, 376–7. Foundation-legend: *IG*
   v.1.1381; *British Museum Catalogue of Greek Coins* 10, 1887, 119–20;
   Kahrstedt 1950a, 235, rightly seeing, contrary to Bölte, *RE* 6A.1, 1936,
   col.637, that this kinship-claim is not evidence for Spartan control.
23 Artificial harbour: Strab.viii.5.2, 363; Baladié 1980, 236 with n.7; cf.242.
   Cardamyle: Kahrstedt 1954, 219; Bölte 1929, col.1340 with refs. (pass). Prusa:
   Dio *or.* xl.30 with Jones 1978a, 2. Sparta-Gytheum route: Bölte 1929,
   cols.1342–3, 1346; Pritchett 1980, ch. 6 esp. 238–9 (*Peutinger Table*).
   Aromation: *IG* v.1.1208 = *SEG* xiii.258 lines 25–38. Euryclids: ch. 7 and *IG*
   v.1.1172 (Eurycles Herculanus). Voluseni: inscription in the Gytheion
   museum discussed by C. Le Roy in an unpublished paper (London 1986).
   Xenarchidas: *IG* v.1.39;505;1174.
24 Eurotas furrow: Cartledge 1979, ch. 2, especially 18–19. Kahrstedt 1954,
   198–203. Laconia Survey: Cavanagh/Crouwel (forthcoming). Note too the
   important work of Hope Simpson/Waterhouse 1960.
25 Depopulation: Larsen 1938, 465–8; Baladié 1980, ch. 12, especially 301–11;
   Davies 1984, 268–9 (on Polyb.xxxvi.17.5–7). Strab.viii.4.11,363 with
   Cartledge 1979, 322. Pharis and Bryseae: Paus.iii.20.3 with Hom.*Il*.ii.582–3;
   Hope Simpson/Lazenby 1970, 75,77. Pellana: Paus.iii.21.2 with Bölte, *RE*
   19.1, 1937, col.352. [Other] settlements: Paus.iii.21.5; 21.4; 19.6; 20.2; 19.9;

10.6; 10.7; 24.8; Baladié 1980, 58 (*khōrion*). Survey: Cavanagh/Crouwel (forthcoming).
26 Villa-definition: Greene 1986, 88–9. Kahrstedt 1954, 200. Psychiko: *Ergon* 1962 (1963), 137–44. Ktirakia: *Ergon* 1963 (1964), 102–15; sarcophagus-type: Koch/Sichtermann 1982, 446–50; Bosanquet 1905–6, 283.

Chapter 11 Local government I: machinery and functions

1 Chrimes 1949, ch. 4. Cic. *Pro Flacco* 63; Cicero's views on Sparta: Tigerstedt 1965–78 ii, 144–60. Roman admiration: Strab. ix.2.39,414; cf. viii.5.5, 365; Dion. Hal.ii.23.1–3, 61; Plut. *Num*.i.3. Roman laconism in general: Rawson 1969, 99–106; Tigerstedt 1965–78 ii, 95–160; Baladié 1980, 290–95. *Rhētrai*: cf. *IG* v.1.20a.2–3. Linguistic archaism: see Bradford 1980, 418 (on *phs(āphismati) b(oulās)*).
2 For a detailed study of Roman Sparta's political institutions see now Kennell 1985. Inscriptions: the great majority are collected in *IG* v.1 and *SEG* xi.455ff. (conveniently gathering together the new finds from the British School excavations of 1924–8 and the emendations to *IG* v.1 of Woodward 1948). Since the war little new relevant material has been published, although note Souris 1981 (*SEG* xxxi.340) and Spawforth 1985, 239–43. A *corpus* of the unpublished inscriptions in the Sparta Museum is being prepared by G. Steinhauer. Coins: Grunauer-von Hoerschelmann 1978, especially 35–62.
3 For the Spartan *sunarkhiai/sunarkhia* see Kennell 1985, ch. 4, with which this chapter is in broad agreement. Davies 1984, 306 with refs. *Sunarkhiai* and the Achaean League: Touloumakos 1967, 12–18; cf.102. Oligarchic overtones: Jones 1940, 164–66; cf. 178. Preambles: *IG* v.1.11.5; 18a.1; *IG* iv².86 = Peek 1969, 29–31, line 1 (decree of consolation). Pherae text: *IG* v.1.1370, which Touloumakos 1967, 105, in spite of its findspot, actually took to be Spartan; for an improved restoration of *[Dogm]a* see Kennell 1985, 119. Colony: Corn. Nep. *Conon* 1 with Kahrstedt 1950a, 237 n.20 (correctly).
4 Other references to *sunarkhia*: *IG* v.1.19.18; *SEG* xiii.256. Its president: *IG* v.1.37.2–3; *SEG* xi.492.17; 495.1–2. Dropping of *sunarkhiai*: Touloumakos 1967, 16–18. Different views of *sunarkhia*: Chrimes 1949, 148–9; Bradford 1980.
5 Bradford 1980, 418. Joint listing: e.g. *IG* v.1.50–72 *passim*; *SEG* xi.523; 533b. Leonidea decree: *IG* v.1.20b.: cf. *SEG* xi.565 (duplicate). Provincial Greek *boulai*: Jones 1940, 176ff.; Bowman 1971 (Roman Egypt). Spartan *boulē* in acclamatory titles: *IG* v.1.589.13–14 and 608.8–9 with Spawforth 1985, 232–5; 541.19–20; 542.12–13 with Spawforth 1984, 70–72 (date) and Veyne 1985 (*prokritos*); *bouleutai*: *IG* v.1.504.5–7 (see ch. 13); 530.4 with Spawforth 1984, 265–6; Moretti 1953 no.18, ll.6–7. Bradford 1980, 419. Secretary of the council: earliest: *IG* v.1.92.11–12 (Augustan); latest: 479 with Spawforth 1986, 329–30 (Severan); cf.97.25 with *SEG* xi.546b; 112.11; *SEG* xi.558.13–14; 563.4; 564.25; 569.24–5; 578.3–4; 585.13–14; xxxi.340. Hadrianic text: *IG* v.1.60 with Kennell 1985, 134. Dedication: *IG* v.1.62. Athens: see the references at Wycherley 1957, 128–37. *Spondophoroi*: *IG* v.1.53; 89 (*SEG* xi.556); 110 (*SEG* xi.587); 112 (called *spondopoioi*); *SEG* xi.550.
6 *Probouleusis* of old *gerousia*: Cartledge 1987, 123–5. Ephors: Chrimes 1949, 155; Touloumakos 1967, 102 with references; Michell 1952, 126–7; Cartledge 1987, 128. *Nomophulakes*: Grunauer-von Hoerschelmann 1978, 42, 54; Christophilopoulou 1968 (generally); Chrimes 1949, 138 citing *SEG* ix.1 line 32; Harding 1985, no.126 (translation). *Nomophulakia* of old *gerousia*:

Cartledge 1987, 123. *Grammatophulax*: e.g. *IG* v.1.65.18; 59 (*SEG* xi.521) 13; 71 *passim*; 86.29.

7 Personification: cf. App.I,39; for the appearance of such statues note Erim 1986, 84–5 (Aphrodisian *Dēmos* in the guise of a young man). *IvO* no.316; note too Peppa-Delmouzou 1980, 434–9 (statue of the Spartan *Dēmos* dedicated on their Acropolis by the Athenians under Augustus). At Roman Athens by contrast dedications by the *dēmos* are somewhat more common: Geagan 1967, 82–3. Scias: Paus.iii.12.10 with Shatzman 1968, 388–9. Provincial Greek city-assemblies: Jones 1940, ch. xi; de Ste. Croix 1981, 300–326 and App. IV esp. 523–9. Leonidea: *IG* v.1.18b.7. Twenty-three *gerontes*: *IG* v.1.93–4; 97 (*SEG* xi.564b); *SEG* xi.564; 585; for a new reading of *IG* v.1.16.9, invalidating Wilhelm's restoration 'of the twenty-eight *gerontes*', see Kennell 1985, 127–8. Ephors and *nomophulakes*: e.g. *SEG* xi.510–56 *passim*. Size of *boulai*: Jones 1940, 176; Bowman 1971, 22.

8 Iterated terms as *gerōn*: e.g. *IG* v.1.254 (Augustan); 97 (*SEG* xi.564b) with *SEG* xi.564a; *SEG* xi.490.7; 495.3; 569.1 and 4.

9 Philostr. *VA* iv.33; Groag 1939, cols.37–8. Possible proconsular letters: *IG* v.1.16; 21, *SEG* xi.466. Remoteness: Burton 1975, esp.105; Hopkins 1980, 120–21. Free status: Strab. viii.5.5, 365; Plin. *NH* iv.16. Privileges of free cities: Jones 1940, 117–120. Absence of a formal treaty: note Gruen 1984, 20–21, denying (controversially) that the *vetustissimum foedus* between Rome and Sparta of Liv.xxxiv.31.5 is evidence of a permanent alliance. Provincial 'plans': bibliography cited by Habicht 1975b, 69 n.22, to which add Reynolds 1982, 114–5. M. Aurelius and Sparta: Oliver 1970a, 8, lines 86–7; cf. Reynolds 1982, no.16 (similar display of formal scruple by Commodus towards Aphrodisias). Cicero *ad fam*.xiii.28a (ch. 7); Plin.*Ep*.vii.24. Embassies: *IG* v.1.36b.28–9; 37.5–7 (successful) (*SEG* xi.481); 485; 508; 545 (successful); 572; *SEG* xi.492.14; 493.15; 501.2–4 with the reading of Groag 1939, col.71 n.291 to be preferred. 'Petition and response': Millar 1977, especially 410–47.

10 *Correctores*: von Premerstein 1901; Groag 1939, cols.125–36 and 162–3; Oliver 1973; 1976. Frequency in the third century: see *SIG*³.877a.6–8. Maximus: *IG* v.1.380.9; Groag 1939, cols.125–8. Iuncus: Follet 1976, 32–4 citing an unpublished inscription from Delphi; Benjamin 1963, 76. Proculus: *IG* v.1. 541.21–2 with Spawforth 1984, 270–73. Paulinus: *IG* v.1.539 with Wilhelm 1913; see Spawforth 1984, 274–7. Letter: Woodward 1927–8, 53–4 no.80.

11 Free cities and *munera*: Bernhardt 1980. Messene: *IG* v.1.1432–3 with Giovannini 1978, 115–22 (date). Import-tax: *IG* v.1.18b.12; cf. Jones 1940, 245. Financial officials: *SEG* xi.778 (cf. Groag 1939, cols.143–4); *ILS* 6953–4; *IG* v.1.501 and 546. Decree: *IG* v.1.11; Touloumakos 1967, 105.

12 Free cities and *viae publicae*: Pekary 1968, 155–9. Laconia and the *Peut. Table*: Pritchett 1980, 252–61; Pikoulas 1984. *IG* v.1.1109; 497 with Spawforth 1985, 231–2.

13 Early Sparta as an exporter of grain: Plut.*Mor*.64b with Cadoux 1938, 80. Early shortages: Theopompus *FGrH* 178 F115; ch. 2. Dietary change: Rathbone 1983, 46–7; cf. Cartledge 1979, 170–71. *Sitōniai* generally: Jones 1940, 217–8. At Sparta: *IG* v.1.44 = *SEG* xi.486.4; 526; 551; *SEG* xi.490.1; 491.1–2, 6–8 with Woodward 1923–5, 180; 492.7–8. Hadrianic shortages and Egyptian grain: Wörrle 1971, 336; Halfmann 1986, 138–9; Garnsey and Saller 1987, 94; Garnsey 1988, 256. A reference to a 'supervisor of the grain-buying fund' conceivably can be restored in an early Antonine text: *IG* v.1.495.3.4: *epimelētēn [tōn sitōnikō]n chrēmatōn*, instead of the *[thematikō]n* of Le Bas. Public honours: *IG* v.1.526 and 551; for the significance of *aiōnios* in the

former, misunderstood by Garnsey 1988, 15, see below. Theophrastus: *SEG* xi.492; Woodward 1925–6, 230–1; Rostovtzeff 1957 ii, 652. *Paraprasis*: Triantaphyllopoulos 1971.

14 Free cities and jurisdiction: Jones 1940, 119,131; cf. Reynolds 1982, 136–9 no.22 (survival of Aphrodisian courts into the third century). Thuriate text: *SEG* xi.974; Bölte, *RE* viA1, 1936, col.637; Kahrstedt 1950a, 236. For the correct reading *kai huper authen[tōn]* see L. Robert *apud* Valmin 1929, 18 n.1; Valmin himself (21 n.2) admitted that this reading would be 'plus géniale et plus habile' than his preferred *huperauthen[tōn]* (followed without comment by the editors of *SEG* xi), a term 'composé lourd et peu connu' – and here, one might add, making no clear sense. His objection that it would have been unseemly in an honorific decree to recall the existence of murderers at Sparta and the efforts of Damocharis on their behalf is hard to follow; these efforts are cited precisely so as to emphasize the extent of the honorand's *eunoia* towards the Thuriates. Free cities and capital jurisidiction: Colin 1965; Millar 1981, 70–71 (more cautiously). Jurisdiction of Classical *gerousia* and ephors: Cartledge 1987, 123 and 128–9. Provincial Greek magistrates as judges: Jones 1940, 123; de Ste Croix 1981, 315–7. Foreign judges: *Klio* 15, 1918, 33–4 no. 54; 18, 1923, 284–5 no.37; Daux 1936, 475–6 and 479 (Delphi); *SEG* xi. 461 (?); 468; 469; 473; *IG* v.1.14 = *SEG* xi.472. *Dikastagōgoi*: Spawforth/Walker 1986, 94–5; see ch. 8.

15 Free city (Alabanda) as an assize-centre: Plin.*NH*.109 with Habicht 1975b, 68–70. Privilege: Dio Chrys. *or*.xxxv.15. Assize-system in Greece: Burton 1975, 97. Jurors: Veyne 1985 citing *IG* v.1.467 (T. Flavius Charixenus) and (with improved readings) 541–2 (P. Memmius Pratolaus *qui et* Aristocles). Appeals: *IG* v.1.21 with Oliver 1970b and 1979, whose attribution of the letter to Hadrian was doubted by Millar 1977, 453 n.45. Brasidas: Spawforth 1985, 228–30 with Gardner 1987. Plin. *Ep*.x.65 with Groag 1939, col.42; Sherwin-White 1966, 650–53. *Sundikoi*: *IG* v.1.36 (*SEG* xi.480); 37 (*SEG* xi.481); 45; 47; 65.20–24; 554; *SEG* xi.501. Athenian *sundikoi* and proconsular jurisdiction: *IG* ii².1100 (*SEG* xv.108) lines 55–7.

16 Civic finance generally: Jones 1940, ch. 17; Migeotte 1984. *Poleitikoi prosodoi*: *SEG* xi.464. *IG* v.1.18b.12 (indirect taxes), 3 (fines); 14–15 with 18a.6 (bank); cf. Bogaert 1968, 99–100,401–2. Coinage: cf. Howgego 1985, ch. 5. Land: *IG* v.1.21 col.i.

17 Euergetism generally: Veyne 1976; de Ste. Croix 1981, 305–10; Gauthier 1985. Pratolaus: *IG* v.1.496.

18 Decree: *IG* v.1.11.8–9. Coins: Grunauer-von Hoerschelmann, 1978, 52–5. *Stēlai*: e.g. *IG* v.1.48; 51; 55; 94; 97. Columns: *SEG* xi.503 with Woodward 1923–5, 225 and 1927, 236; *SEG* xi.499 with Woodward 1927–8, 239. *Anta*-block: *SEG* xi.620 with Woodward 1929, 29–30 no.52. Theatre: Woodward 1923–5, 158–205; 1925–6, 210–236; 1927–8, 2–20. Abbreviation: *SEG* xi.564 and 578 with Bradford 1980, 418. Other architectural blocks: App.I, 11. Chrimes 1949, 150. Beard 1985, esp. 129–40. *Honoraria* and entrance-fees: Jones 1940, 247; Garnsey 1974, 239–40.

19 *Digest* 27.1.6. Agoranomate: *IG* v.1.32.5–6; 40; 1124–7; 128 (*SEG* xi.597); 129; 130 (Spawforth 1984, 267–8); 131–2; 149 (*SEG* xi.600); 150 (*SEG* xi.601); 151 (*SEG* xi.598); 155 (*SEG* xi.599); 473; 482; 497. Kolbe, *IG* v.1, p.48; Chrimes 1949, 138; Jones 1940, 216–7. Panthales: *IG* v.1.547; cf. Spawforth 1984, 272–3 (date); 1985, 239–43 (family).

20 Law: *IG* v.1.20a.5–6; cf. the late Hellenistic gymnasiarchy law from Beroea: Austin 1981, no.118 (translation). *Epimelētēs*: *IG* v.1.133–5. Dedications for gymnasiarchs: *IG* v.1.480 (Flavian: the earliest); 481; 486–7; 492; 494; 505–6;

528–9; 531; 535; 537; 539; 555b; 557; 560–61; *SEG* xi.803. Theophrastus: *SEG* xi.492.9–12 with Woodward 1925–6, 231–2. Gymnasiarchy generally: Jones 1940, ch. 10.

21 *IG* v.1.541.2–3 (hipparch; for the office see ch. 14); 526 (*sitōnēs*); 305; 504; 544; 547; 549; 553–4; 628; *SEG* xi.799; 802 (*agoranomos*); *IG* v.1.468; 528–9; 535; 547; 552; *SEG* xi.799 (gymnasiarch). *Aiōnios*: Jones 1940, 175.

22 Honorific titles and epithets: e.g. *IG* v.1.170.10–11; 464.6–7; 469.3–4; 480.3; 551.14–15; 564.9. 'Incomparable': *IG* v.1.529; *SEG* xi.806a. *Philotimia*: *IG* v.1.531; Panagopoulos 1977, 207–9; Whitehead 1986, 246–52. 'Contest for best citizen': *IG* v.1.65, *SEG* xi.780 (Imperial high-priest); 168 + 603 = Spawforth 1984, 286 lines 15 and 18; 485; 498; 500 (Imperial high-priest); 523; 541–2; 590, *SEG* xi.800 (Imperial high-priests); 849 (Spawforth 1984, 280). 'Perpetual' *aristopoliteutai*: *IG* v.1.504 (Imperial high-priest and 'perpetual' *agoranomos*); 528 (also 'perpetual' gymnasiarch); 537. Wilhelm in Wilhelm/Heberdey 1896, 154. Cf. Schwertfeger 1981 with Puech 1983, 31 with n.64 (Roman Messene).

23. Athens: Geagan 1979, 409–10 with refs. Supernumerary councillors: cf. Bowman 1971, 22–3. Reluctance/compulsion: Jones 1940, ch. 11; Garnsey 1974, esp.230–41; Mitchell 1984.

Chapter 12 Local government II: the social and economic base

1 Letter to the Athenians: Oliver 1970a, 7, lines 64–6 with pp.20–3. *Honestiores*: Jones 1940, 179–80; Garnsey 1970, especially chs. 9–12. Bench: *IG* v.1.254; Dawkins and Woodward in Dawkins 1929, 36 and 355 no.141 respectively; cf. App.I, 38. *Stēlē*: Woodward 1928–30, 221 n.12 (*SEG* xi.855). Theatre-seating generally: Rawson 1987; D. Small in Macready/Thompson 1987 (unsatisfactory).

2 *IG* iv².86 = Peek 1969 no.36 ll.8–9. *Prōtoi/primores viri*: Oliver 1953, 953ff.; Garnsey 1974, 232–5. Senators: Halfmann 1979,nos.29 (Eurycles Herculanus), 111 (Brasidas; see now Spawforth 1985, 226–30). *Equites* (both third century): *IG* v.1.596; Spawforth 1984, 275 (Spartan with the equestrian predicate *ho kratistos*). Theophrastus: cf. Woodward 1925–6, 230–31; for the calculation see Gossage 1951, 238, basing himself on the assumption of one *medimnos* per head for a population of 5000. Arion: *SEG* xi. 501.5–6; L. Robert, *RPh* 1934, 282–3.

3 *IG* v.1.465; 584 + 604 = *SEG* xi.812a (with Kourinou-Pikoula 1986, 68–9). *IG* iv².86 = Peek 1969, no.36 ll. 3–9 with Spawforth 1985, 199–200, 216–19, 251–2. Pedigrees: *IG* v.1. 36.1–3 ('senior Heraclid'); 469 (Tib. Cl. Aristocrates); 471; 477; 488; 495.3; 528.8; 529.4–5 and 530.9–10 (M. A. Aristocrates); 537. 6–7 (P. M. Deximachus); 559.5–6; 562; 615.4 ('kings'); 971 and 1172 (Herculanus); *SEG* xi.847 (Spawforth 1985, 198–201); 849 (Spawforth 1984, 280) (Constantinian high-priest); *IG* iv². 86 = Peek 1969, no. 36 l.8 (Lysander); Plut. *Ages*.35.1–2. Dioscuri: Carlier 1977, 76 n.42. *Eugeneia* as a 'moral quality': Panagopoulos 1977, 203–5.

4 Viritane grants: Sherwin-White 1973, ch. 13; Millar 1977, 479–83. 'Brokerage': Saller 1982, especially ch. 5. Spartan *cives*: Box 1931, 1932. Memmii and Aelii: Spawforth 1985, 198, 246–8. *Gerontes*: *IG* v.1.97 and *SEG* xi. 564; 585; although it is true that *tria nomina* are not consistently recorded in catalogues of magistrates (cf. *IG* v.1.20b.5; Woodward 1923–5, 168 I, C 7, line 7 [C. Iulius Menander]), for what it is worth, neither of the lists in question includes an apparently peregrine Spartan whose Roman citizenship is attested elsewhere.

5 Woodward 1928–30, 222–5. References to pedigrees: n.3. Classical genealogies: Snodgrass 1971, 11–12.
6 Hereditary priesthoods: *IG* v.1.259; 305; 497; 602; 607; *SEG* xi.679. Phoebaeum priesthood: Chrimes 1949, 471–4 *passim*; Spawforth 1985, 195–6, 203–4, 208. 'Iamid' *manteis*: Paus.iii.11. 5–8 and 12.8; *IG* v.1.141.5; 210.42–3; 212.53–4; 599; other lineage ('Scopelids'): 60.1; 209.13; 259 with Woodward in Dawkins 1929, 299 no. 6; 488. Classical Sparta: Rahe 1980, 386. Athens: Clinton 1974 (Eleusinian priesthoods); Garland 1984. For the portrayal in a dynamic light of Greek civic religion in the first three centuries AD see Lane Fox 1986a, chs. 3–5.
7 Architects: *IG* v.1.5.17; 209.17; 168 + 603 = Spawforth 1984, 285–8 l. 16. Gladiator: Robert 1940b, 79 no.12. Free and servile artisans: above all *IG* v.1.208.3–9; 210.18–19. 22–34; 210.55–62; 211.51–4; 212.46.57–66. Spawforth 1985,195–6 (family of Tyndares and Eurybanassa);213–5, 228–31 ('Ageta'); *IG* v.2.542 with *PIR²* I 687 ('Pantimia' as a Euryclid name). Civic slaves: e.g. *IG* v.1.48.18–19; 112.16; 141.7; 149 = *SEG* xi.600.13–15; 151 = *SEG* xi.503.26–7. Thenae: *IG* v.1.153.31–4 with Spawforth 1977. Ctesiphon: *IG* v.1.211.54; Nicocles: *IG* v.1.116.16–18.
8 Strab.viii.5.4, 365; cf. 5.5. Gitti 1939;Shimron 1966a. Bithynia and Egypt: Jones 1940, 172–3.
9 Magistrates: *IG* v.1.129; 148 and *SEG* xi.537b; 585.6; cf. *IG* v.1.151 = *SEG* xi.598.8 (Lycus). Rome: Solin 1982, s.v.. 'Aristocratic' names: Bradford 1977, s.vv.. Aphrodisius: Woodward 1923–5, 222–4 (*SEG* xi.683); cf. too Kourinou-Pikoula 1986, 66–7 no.2. Eurycles: *IG* v.1.287–8; Woodward in Dawkins 1929, 320; Chrimes 1949, 201–2; Bradford 1977, s.v.. Death of Herculanus: Spawforth 1978, 254–5. Athens: Baslez forthcoming.
10 *Sunephēboi*: Woodward in Dawkins 1929, 291; Chrimes 1949, 95–117 (better), 459–60 (catalogue). Athens: Oliver 1971. Corinthas: *IG* v.1.45.7; identification of 'Herodes son of Attikos': Ameling 1983 ii, no.70, superseding Spawforth 1980, 208–10; Oliver 1970a, 54 (Panhellenes). Callicrates: *IG* v.1.259 with Woodward in Dawkins 1929, 299 no.6. Social status of *boagoi*: note the cautionary observations of Woodward 1950, 619.
11 *Kasen*-status: Hesychius s.v. '*kasioi*'; earliest and latest refs. respectively: *IG* v.1.256; Woodward in Dawkins 1929, 297–8 no.2, 330 no. 63 (*SEG* xi.740), dated by the patronomate of Aelius Alcandridas (Spawforth 1984, 279, 284). General discussions: Woodward in Dawkins 1929, 290–92; Chrimes 1949, 95–117, 442–60 (lists). Athens: Baslez forthcoming. 'Good' names: Woodward in Dawkins 1929, 297–8 no.2, 311–2 no. 29, 315–6 no.35 (*IG* v.1.256, 278, 298); cf. Woodward 1950, 619. Antistii: Woodward in Dawkins 1929, 310–11 no.27, 314–5 no.33 (*IG* v.1.278, 281); *SEG* xi.559.4; Chrimes 1949, 113–4 (speculative on origins of *nomen*), 456. Sosicrates: *IG* v.1.65, 19–20 (ch. 14 on *diabetēs*). *Inferiores*: Garnsey 1974, 232–6.
12 Kahrstedt 1954, 192. Coins: Grunauer-von Hoerschelmann 1978, 107–9. Sarcophagi: Koch/Sichtermann 1982, 462–3; Wace in Tod/Wace 1906, 130. Senators: Halfmann 1979, 68.
13 Kahrstedt 1954, 197. *Marmor lacedaemonium*: Strabo viii.5.7, 367; Cartledge 1979, 66–7; cf. Baladié 1980, 197–210, rightly stressing that Strabo's 'in Taygetus' must refer to these quarries (Chrimes 1949, 74 *contra*); Kahrstedt's suggestion, ibid. n.3, that they were once owned by the family of Eurycles, is unsupported by any evidence. Inscription: *CIL* iii.493 with Le Roy 1961, 206–15. Emperors and quarries: Millar 1977, 181–5.
14 Kahrstedt 1954, 197. Middle Ages: Bon 1951, 123–4. Wheat and barley: *IG*

v.1.363.10.15; 364.9–10.14–15. Horses: note Paus.iii.20.4; cf. Baladié 1980, 192–3. Olives: Sid. Ap. *Carm*. v.44. Garnsey 1988, 72–3 (grain-exchange among neighbours). Survey: Cavanagh/Crouwel forthcoming.

15 Wild beasts: Paus. iii.20.5; Claudian, *De Cons. Stilich*. iii.259, 300; Chrimes 1949, 79–80 (speculative); O'Flynn 1983, 33–4 (Stilicho in Peloponnese). Wood: Paus.iii.10.6; Suet.*Tib*.6. Marble: Wace in Tod/Wace 1906, 102; Bölte 1929, col.1347; Chrimes 1949, 72–3. Limestone: Cavanagh/Crouwel forthcoming. Ancient clay-beds: *ABSA* 13, 1906–7, plate I, 19L. Sculpture: Wace in Tod/Wace 1906, 128–30 ('The great majority of the sculpture in the Museum belongs so far as its actual date of execution is concerned to the imperial period'); Woodward 1926–7, 22–36. Quarrying in general: Osborne 1987, 81–92 (Classical period). Stamps: *IG* v.1.850–91; *SEG* xi.873–85; Kahrstedt 1954, 195. Eurycles: *SEG* xi.883a; for the association of tile-kilns with villa-estates: Greene 1986, 10. Rome: Shatzman 1975, 305 no.93; Callicrates: Bradford 1977, s.v.

16 Economic functions of Roman towns: Hopkins 1978b; Millar 1981, 72–3 (town-country exchange). Leonidea: *IG* v.1.18b.11–12 (cf. ch. 14); cf. Dunand 1978, 206. Local imitations of clay lamps (third century): Broneer 1977, 66 n.54. 'Laconian' as trade-mark: Chrimes 1949, 77–8; Kahrstedt 1954, 197 n.1; Bruneau 1976, 27–36; the 'Laconian' horses of *CIL* vi.33937 should probably be understood in this way. 'Souvenir-trade' at Corinth: Bruneau 1977, 262–5; cf. App.I, 62.

17 Slaves: n.7. Marble: Traquair 1905–6, 423; Coleman/Walker 1979. Cyrene: cf. Tod 1948, no. 196. Puteoli: Frederiksen 1980–81. Sicily and Africa: Garnsey 1988, 231–2.

18 Trade-surge: Hopkins 1980. *IG* v.1.741 (Zeuxis); 728 (Troilus). Forgery: Spawforth 1976 (apropos of *IG* v.1.515). Phil. *VA*. iv.32 with Ehrenberg 1929, cols.1451–2; Chrimes 1949, 79, 161; Kahrstedt 1954, 198; Tigerstedt 1965–78 ii, 455 n.54. Commercial interests of Greek provincial élites: Pleket 1983; 1984.

19 Pancratidas: Spawforth 1984, 265–6, 284 (stemma). Skills: *IG* v.1.1145, 1523; *SEG* xi.948.20–21; Forrest 1972. Calamae: *IG* v.1.1369; Kahrstedt 1950a, 236–7 (Smyrnaean dedication: *IG* v.1.662); Kolbe at *IG* v.1.p.258 unaccountably placed Calamae in the territory of Pherae. Menalcidas: *SEG* xi.782; Jameson 1953, 168–70.

20 Decrees: *IG* v.1.961, 112, 1145, 1226, *SEG* xi.974 (cf. chapter 11). Voluseni and Memmii: Spawforth 1985, 193–224. Tisamenis: Spawforth 1980, especially 210–14 (Raepsaet-Charlier 1987, 226–7 no.251, prefers to see her as the aunt of Herodes, without saying why). Spawforth 1978, 258 (Herculanus); 1985, 254–5 (Timocrates).

Chapter 13 High culture and agonistic festivals

1 Decorative arts: cf. Dörig 1987, arguing a Spartan origin for the anonymous master-sculptor of the Olympia pediments. Cartledge 1978 (literacy).

2 Jacoby, *FGrHist* nos. 586–92, 595 (with commentaries); Boring 1979, ch. 3; Tigerstedt 1965–78 ii, 86–94 ('Sparta in Alexandria').

3 Gorgus: *Ind. St. Herc*. (ed. Traversa) col.76; *IG* ii².1938.5; Ferguson 1911, 369. Demetrius: de Falco 1923; cf. *Pap. Herc*. 1014 (dedication to a Nero) with Rawson 1973, 227. Nicocrates: Senec. *Contr*. vii.5.15; *Suas*. ii.22. Greek intellectuals at Rome: Crawford 1978a; Rawson 1985.

4 Herculanus: *Mor.* 539a; Jones 1971, 41. Philopappus: Spawforth 1978; Kleiner 1983, ch. 1.

5 Cleombrotus: Flacelière 1947, 22–6; Ziegler 1951, col.677. Date of *De def. or.*: Ogilvie 1967. *Kasen*: *SEG* xi.513. Zeuxippus and Tyndares: Ziegler 1951, cols.686–7; Flacelière 1952, 18–19. *Nomophulax*: Bradford 1977, s.v. 'Zeuxippos (4)'. *Xenia* at Classical Sparta: Cartledge 1987, 243–45. Priest: *IG* v.1.305; Chrimes 1949, 450 n.88; Wide 1893, 304–32 (cults). Plutarch's marriage: Ziegler 1951, col.648. Florus: Jones 1971b, 49; *PIR*² M 531. 'Academy': Ziegler 1951, cols.662–5. Zeuxippus and Tyndares can probably be recognized in the *kasen*-patrons of *IG* v.1.60,4, and 97 (*SEG* xi.564b). 14; the former may be the *patronomos* of *IG* v.1.81.

6 Phileratidas: *IG* v.1.116.14; the *cognomen* was needlessly emended by Woodward 1948, 238, following Boeckh at *CIG* ii.1253, to 'Philocratidas'; for the kindred name 'Phileratis' see *AP* vi.347. Quintus: *SEG* xi.807 (following Woodward 1927–8, 33–4 no.56), where his *cognomen* has been bizarrely emended into a filiation and his patronymic read as his *cognomen*. Bradford 1977, s.v. saw Quintus as 'undoubtedly not a native of Sparta'; for the recurrence of his distinctive Dorian patronymic in the family of the Memmii see Spawforth 1985, 193–7, 202.

7 Montanus: *IG* v.1.504 with p. 303 *add. et corr..* Pyrrhus: Spawforth 1984, 279 no.9. Mandane: *PIR*² C 1092; cf. Hdt. i.107; Diod. Sic. xi.57. Mithradatids: Reinach 1890, 3–4. Asclepiades: *IG* v.1.525; Spawforth 1985, 235–8 (Spartiaticus). Metrophanes: *IG* v.1.563; Spawforth 1984, 286 line 12, 287 (*hieromnēmōn*). Genealis: *IGB* iii.1573; Apostolides 1937, 80–81 no.17; Seure 1915, 204–8 no.17. On Greek culture in Roman Thrace see Bowie 1980. *Sōphrosunē*: cf. *IG* v.1.466.3–4 (youth); 566.4 (ephebe); 1369.6–7 (*sōphrosunē* and *paideia* of a youth); *IG* iv². 86 = Peek 1969, no.36 lines 11–12 (Timocrates). Sophists called Metrophanes: *Suda* s.vv.; on the Lebadean note *PIR*² C 1303; Bowersock 1969, 54–5. Herodes: Ameling 1983 ii, 139.

8 Eunap. *VS* 482–5 (younger Apsines), 505 (Epigonus); *Suda* s.vv. 'Apsines', 'Onasimos': Jones/Martindale/Morris 1971, s.v. 'Valerius Apsines': Follet 1976, 42 (with earlier references).

9 Julian, *or.*ii.[iii] 119b-c. Libanius: *Ep.*1210 (Foerster). Athens: Millar 1969; cf. Athanassiadi-Fowden 1981, 46–51. Oracles and philosophy: Lane Fox 1986a, ch. 5.

10 Damiadas: *IG* v.1.1174. Others: *IG* v.1.730, 623 (on *arkhiatroi* see Nutton 1977); Forrest 1972 (Cytheran text). 'Nexus': Bowersock 1969, 66. Agathinus: Galen xix. 353; *IGUR* 1349; Korpela 1987, 186 no.181 and 192 no.216 (distinguishing two homonyms). Alexandrian medicine: Longrigg 1981.

11 Games in Achaia: Spawforth forthcoming. Sparta: cf. the remarks of Robert 1966, 104; also Ringwood 1927, 81–6, never very good on Spartan festivals and now outdated.

12 Actors: Loukas 1984; athletes: e.g. Moretti 1957, 653, 702; Bradford 1977 s.vv. Alkidas, Amphiares, Aretippos, Aristokleidas (2), Armonikos (1), Nikodamos and Nikokles (3). Other Achaian festivals for Augustus and his family: e.g. *IG* v.2. 515.31 (Megalopolis); iv². 652. 6–9 (Epidaurus); Clement 1974 (Corinth). Moretti 1953, no.60; cf. no.43 ('Caesarea and Euryclea'); Kolbe at *IG* v.1. p.xvi, 34–6. Imperial festivals generally: Price 1984, ch. 8.

13. Agesilaus: *IG* v.1.667.3–4. 'Uraniads': *IG* v.1.659.4–5; 662.3–4. *Agōnothetēs*: *IG* v.1.32b.8–10. Panegyriarch: *IG* v.1.36a.6–9. Alcman frg.4 (Bergk). Different categories of 'sacred' games: Pleket 1974, 85 no.140.

14 Herodes Atticus: Ameling 1983 ii. no.172 with commentary. Prize-games: Jones 1940, 231–2. Areto: *IG* v.1.666; Woodward 1948, 255; *IvO* no.382;

Moretti 1975, 182–6. Other *agōnothetai*: *IG* v.1.71 col.iii. 53–5; 550 ('ago–nothetic monies'); 168 + 603 = Spawforth 1984, 285–8 line 19.
15 Olympia Commodea: Spawforth 1986. 'Iselastic' status: Jones 1940, 231–2; Robert 1984; Spawforth forthcoming.
16 *Logismos*: Woodward 1923–5, 213–19 (*SEG* xi.838). The (1.7) contest in encomium, *pace* Woodward, could have honoured Zeus Uranius as easily as the memory of Eurycles: cf. *SEG* iii.20–21; xxix.452. 10–12; xxxi. 514. 12 (Musean games, Thespiae). Granianus: lines 9–10; Paus.ii.11.8; Moretti 1957, 163 no.848 ('Cranaus'). Itinerant poets at Greek festivals: Hardie 1983, especially ch. 2.
17 Popularity: Jones 1940, 285–6. Aelii: Spawforth 1984, 272–3; 1985, 246–8. Agonistic titles: *IG* v.1.114.2; 64.12; 539; *SEG* xi.499; *add. et corr.* 803a; Robert 1940b, 252 (on *paradoxos*). Tragic actor: *SEG* xi.838.6. Muscleman: *FD* iii.1 no.216 with Robert 1928, 422–5. Aristides: Lib. *or.* lxiv (Foerster); Behr 1968, 88. Apolaustus: *Inschriften von Ephesos* vii.nos. 2070–71; Robert 1930, 113–4. Cf. Aylen 1985, 325–6.
18 Domesticus: *IG* v.1.669; *IGRR* i.147, 150. Xystarchs: Robert 1966, 100–105; Moretti 1953, no.84; Gasperini 1984.

Chapter 14 The image of tradition

1 Disparaging comments on Spartan archaism: e.g. Bölte 1929, col. 1451; Marrou 1965, 59–60. 'Touchstone': Lane Fox 1986a, 68–9. For the idea of 'invented tradition', coined by modern historians: E. Hobsbawm in Hobsbawm/ Ranger 1983, 1–1-4.
2 Plut. *Mor*.814b; cf. Jones 1971b, 113–4. Roman emperors: Bowersock 1984, 174–6 (Augustus); Lane Fox 1986a, 11–12 (Gordian III). Parthians as *barbaroi* in official Roman documents: e.g. *SEG* xxiii.206.11 (Augustan); Reynolds 1982, no.17 l.10 (Severan). Plataea: Sheppard 1984–6, 238; Strubbe 1984–6, 282–4; Robertson 1986 (dispute). Meed of valour: Plut. *Arist*.20.1. Historical themes in show-oratory: Bowie 1974, 170–3.
3 Monuments: Paus.iii.11; 14.1; 16.6. Artemis Orthia: Plut. *Arist*.17; Xen. *Lac.Pol.* ii.9; cf. H. Rose in Dawkins 1929, 405.
4 Leonidea: *IG* v.1.18–20; Bogaert 1968, 99–100; Connor 1979 (Classical age). Nicippus: *IG* v.1.20b.3; Woodward 1923–5, 168, col.C6/C7, 9 (better). Birth of Herculanus: Spawforth 1978, 254. Minimum age of *gerontes*: Chrimes 1949, 139–40 (advocating fifty). Roman preparations: Baladié 1980, 273–7.
5 Greek paganism under the principate: Lane Fox 1986a, chs. 2–5. Pausanias: the computations are those of Kahrstedt 1954, 192. Christians: Euseb. *Ecc.Hist*.iv.23.1–2; cf. ch. 15 in this volume.
6 Carneonices: *IG* v.1.209.20. Gymnopaediae/Hyacinthia: Paus.iii.11.9; Luc. *de salt*.12; Philostr. *VA*.iii.11.9. *IG* v.1.586–7 (Hyacinthian 'games'); *SEG* ii.88 (*didaskalos*). Earlier contests: Mellink 1943, 22–3. Amyclaeum: Paus.iii.18. 7–19.6; Grunauer-von Hoerschelmann 1978, 97–106 (coins).
7 Inscription: *IG* v.1.213.31–4. Dedications: *IG* v.1.579–80; 581?; 592; 595; 605?; 607; *SEG* xi.676–7 and *add. et corr*.677a-c. Demeter cults: Burkert 1985, 159–61. Eleusinium: Paus.iii.20.5; Cook/Nicholls 1950. Cult: Spawforth 1985, 206–8. Liturgies: *IG* v.1.583; 584 + 604 (*SEG* xi.812a) with Kourinou-Pikoula 1986, 68–9; 594; 596. Reliefs: *IG* v.1.248–9; Spawforth 1985, 230–31 with pl.21a; Walker forthcoming.
8 Dioscuri: Wide 1893, 304–23; Burkert 1985, 212–3. Pedigrees: ch. 12. Sanctuary: Hdt.vi.66; Paus.iii.14.10. Coins: Grunauer-von Hoerschelmann

1978, 38–9, 42–3, 45; 65–6; 100–101. Cult, sanctuary and priesthood: Spawforth 1985, 195–6, 203–4 (building activity), 207–8. *Stēlai*: *IG* v.1.206–9, esp.209.6–10; cf. Bölte *RE* 5.A1, 1934, cols.1190–1 (correctly seeing here a civic cult, not a private association). *Agōnothetēs*: *IG* v.1.559, 6–11; cf. Jones 1940, 175.

9 Priesthood: Hdt.vi.56; *IG* v.1.36a; 40. Titulature: *IG* v.1.667.1–2; cf. I. Opelt in Wlosok 1978, 429–30.

10 Cic.*de div*.i.95. *IG* v.1.1314–5 with Bölte *RE* v.1A, 1934, cols.1190–1 (rejecting the old view of a private *thiasos*). For the patronomates which date the three visits see Chrimes 1949, 464 (Charixenus I), 466 (Memmius Damares); Bradford 1986a (Hadrian). Claros: Lane Fox 1986a, chs. 4–5. Paus.iii.26.1.

11 'Special relationship': Cartledge 1987, 34. Judges: references at ch. 11, n.14. Proxeny-grants: *FD* iii.1.no.487 (*IG* v.1.1566); iii.2.no.160; *SIG*³ 239.iii.30 (*naopoios*); Bradford 1977 s.v. Alkimos. *FD* iii.1.no 543 (Spartiaticus); 215 (Euamerus). Spartan Aurelii: Spawforth 1984, 263–5.

12 Theatre-statue: *SEG* xi.773; 830 (cf. Paus.iii.14.8). Cult and sanctuary: Plut. *Lyc*.31.3; Paus.iii.16.6. Coins: Grunauer-von Hoerschelmann 1978, 40–41 with pl.13. Cf. Richter 1984, 156–7.

13 Magistrates: *IG* v.1.543.11–12; 560; *SEG* xi.626.2. Liv.xxxviii.34; xlv.28.4 (cf. Toynbee 1969, 410 n.3; Tigerstedt 1965–78 ii, 167, 344 n.30); Plut. *Philop*.16.6–7; Paus.vii.8.5; viii.51.3. Modern views: e.g. Ehrenberg 1929, cols.1442–3 (with earlier references); Chrimes 1949, 50; Shimron 1972, 117. The view taken here is also that of Kennell 1985, 13–19; 1987, 422 n.17.

14 *Suda* s.v. 'Dikaiarkhos'. 'Contest': references at ch. 11, n.22; cf. *IG* v.1.467 ('renewal'), 485 (role of assembly). Chrimes 1949, 159 citing Plut. *Lyc*.26.1–3. Messene: Schwertfeger 1981; cf. *IvO* no.465 ('wreath'). Cf. the 'renewal' of the mythical kinship between Aegeae and Argos *c*. 150: Spawforth/Walker 1986, 103–4.

15 List of *ensitoi*: cf. *IG* v.1.1314.3; 1315, 21–2 (mention of a Spartan *protensiteuōn* or 'first on the list of those receiving *sitēsis*'). Cass. Dio liv.7.2; Baladié 1980, 291–2; cf. Grunauer-von Hoerschelmann 1978, 68–9 n.30. Kennell 1987, giving the references at n.8 to dining magistrates, to which add *IG* v.1.149–151, 155 (*SEG* xi.598–601) (*presbus* of *phidition*). Ancient *prutaneia* generally: Miller 1978.

16 **Plut.***Mor***.550b**; 1109c. Philostr. *VA* iv.27. Statues: Tod/Wace 1906, 146, no. **85, 178, no.443** (not yet fully published).

17 **Old licence**: Cartledge 1981. Spawforth 1985, 191–2 (domestic virtues), 206–8 (Xenocratia), 232–4 (Damosthenia). Political significance of civic praise for domestic virtues: van Bremen 1983. Spartan *gunaikonomos*: *IG* v.i. 209.10; other references at App.IIA; for the date of *IG* v.1.170 see Spawforth 1985, 245. Generally: Wehrli 1962; Vatin 1970, 254–61.

18 *Bideoi*: Paus.iii.11.2; Tod/Wace 1906, 18–19; App.IIA (catalogues). Ball-tournament: *IG* v.1.676.2–4; 679.4; 680.5–6 etc. Banquets: *IG* v.1.206.2; 209.6; cf. Spawforth 1985, 196 with n.14. Classical period: Cartledge 1987, 26, 128.

19 Patronomate: Chrimes 1949, 143–54; Schaefer 1949; Bradford 1980. Singular office: *SEG* xi.503; the usual view of modern scholars that the patronomate comprised a board of six magistrates, based on a misunderstanding of *IG* v.1.48, is demolished by Kennell 1985, ch. 3. Pratolaus: *IG* v.1.543–4; Spawforth 1985, 209–10. Combination with gymnasiarchy: *IG* v.1.481; 505; 535; 539; *SEG* xi. 803. *Philotimia*: *IG* v.1.534. *Huperpatronomos/epimelētai*:

IG v.1.275; 311–12, 295 (*SEG* xi.715); 541–2; 683; *SEG* xi.541.

20 *Ephēbia* generally: Jones 1940, ch. 14; Marrou 1965, 280–4.
21 Ephebic dedications: *IG* v.1.255–356 with the improved editions of Woodward in Dawkins 1929, ch. 10; cf. in particular nos. 31, 33 and 41 (Roman-period age-sets). *Paides/ephēboi*: cf. *IG* v.1.493. Agonistic age-class: Robert 1939, 241–2. Greek writers: e.g. Plut. *Lyc.*16.4; Luc. *de salt.* 10; Paus.iii.14.6 (*sphaireis*-teams), 14.9, 16.10. Old *agōgē*: Plut. *Lyc.*16.4. Primary education: Jones 1940, 223.
22 Tribal organization: Chrimes 1949, 163–8. Old *agōgē*: Plut. *Lyc.*17.2–4. Age of *boagoi*: Hesych. s.v.; Spawforth 1980, 209. Change in organization: Woodward 1950, 620. Earliest dedication by a *boagos*: Woodward in Dawkins 1929, no.33 (patronomate dated *c.*89/90 by Chrimes 1949, 464). *Nomophulakes*: *SEG* xi.536. Retention of title: e.g. *IG* v.1.62.6; 64.9–11, 14; 69; 551.16. Athens: Oliver 1971, especially 73–4. Higher education: Clarke 1971, 6. Sixteen-year-olds: Woodward in Dawkins 1929, nos. 36, 42–6, 49–50, 52–4, 56, 58–9, 64, 67–9, 71 (excluding the fragmentary texts). Reappearance of *kasen*-status: Woodward 1950, 629–30; the earliest instance, Woodward in Dawkins 1929, no.310, can be placed late in Nero's reign (for the patronomate of Euclidas see Chrimes 1949, 463).
23 Athletic trainers/*hoplomakhoi*: *IG* v.1.542.2–3, 543.2–4; Spawforth 1984, 270 n.34, 271, n.39; Luc. *de salt.* 10. (?) Hadrianic ephebe: Woodward in Dawkins 1929, no.41; cf. *IG* v.1.663, 668 (boy-athletes). Old songs/dances: Luc. *de salt.* 10–12; Athen. *Deipn.* xiv.33. Artemis Orthia contests: Chrimes 1949, 119–24.
24 Platanistas/*sphaireis*-teams: Cic. *Tusc.Disp.*.v.27.77; Paus.iii.14.6, 8–10; Luc. *Anach.* 38; cf. Woodward 1951, Patrucco 1975, rejecting the view of Chrimes 1949, 132–3 that the *sphaireis*-teams were boxers. 'Endurance-contest': full refs. collected by Trieber 1866, 22–29; note in particular Cic. *Tusc. Disp.*ii.14.34; Plut. *Arist.*17.8; *Lyc* 18.1; Paus.iii.16.9–11; Luc. *Anach.* 38; Hyg. *Fab.* 261. *Bōmonikai*: *IG* v.1.554.1–2; 652–3; 684?; Woodward in Dawkins 1929, nos. 142–44. Modern discussion: H. Rose in Dawkins 1929, 404–5; Chrimes 1949, 262–4. Cheese-ritual: Xen. *Lac.Pol.*ii.9.
25 Caryae: Paus.iii.10.7; Luc. *de salt.*10–12. 'Dionysiades': Paus.iii.13.7; *SEG* xi.610.1–4 (the reference is to some signal achievement connected with the race in this particular year). Sura: *schol.* Iuv.iv.53; Moretti 1953, 168. Victrix: *SEG* xi.830 (honorand's name garbled). Delphi text: Moretti 1953, no.63.
26 Lycurgus: Paus.iii.14.9; 16.10. 'Teachers': *IG* v.1.500.1–2; cf.542.3. Ephebe: *IG* v.1.527. *Ōbai*: e.g. *IG* v.1.674.2; 675.3–4; 676.6–7. Dialect: Woodward in Dawkins 1929, nos. 43–70 *passim*; Bourguet 1927, 25–9. Linguistic archaism elsewhere: e.g. Ameling 1983 ii, no.143; Bernand 1960, nos. 28, 30 ('Aeolic' poems of Balbilla).
27 Chrimes 1949, 124–6; Woodward 1950, 620. Timocrates: Athen. *Deipn.* i.15c. Ball-tournament: *IG* v.1.674, dated by Woodward 1951, 193.
28 Tourism generally: Casson 1974, 229–99. Polemo: Deichgräber 1952, especially cols.1297–8, nos. 7–8. Paus.iii.11.1. Platanistas: Cic. *Tusc. Disp.*v.27.77; 'endurance-contest': Plut. *Arist.*17.8; Lib. *or.*i.23; ball-tournament: *schol. ad Od.*viii.372 (ed. Dindorf), with ref. to the (?) second-century grammarian Pius/Eusebius. Other festivals. Philostr. *VA* vi.20.
29 Romans at Athens: Daly 1950. Laelius: Gow/Page 1968 i, no.xxi, ii 158–9. Pausanias: Habicht 1985, especially 26–7. Lucian in Greece: Hall 1981, 16–44 *passim*. *Exēgētēs*: *IG* v.1.556, dated at Spawforth 1984, 283–4 and variously interpreted by Woodward 1907–8, 116–7, Chrimes 1949, 160, Tigerstedt

1965–78 ii, 452 n.34. For an official guide (*periēgētēs*) at Severan Athens see Oliver 1983, 153 n.10. Philostratus: *VA* vi.20 with Woodward in Dawkins 1929, no.36.

30 Cicero: cf. *Pro Flacco* 63. Philostr. VA iv.31. Favorinus: [Dio Chrys.] *or.* xxxvii.27. Castigation: cf. Bowie 1978, 1664–5. Vianor: *IG* v.1.569; cf. 491.

31 Whole-heartedness: Luc. *Anach.* 38. *Diabetai*: e.g. *IG* v.1.32a.2; 676.4–5; 680.5–9 ('voluntarily'); *SEG* xi.493.2–3. Hipparch: Hesychius, s.v.; *IG* v.1.541.1–3. Memmii: Spawforth 1985, 193–213. 'University-training': Jones 1940, 224. *Sphaireis*-teams: *IG* v.1.675.7–8; 676.9.

Chapter 15 Epilogue: Sparta from Late Antiquity to the Middle Ages

1 Theod. ix, 18–19, p. 126 (Carnivet); cf. Hertzberg 1887–90 iii, 384. Theodosian law: *CTh* xvi.10, 11, 391, 12, 392; Jones 1964b, 938–43. Survival of paganism: Gregory 1986, especially 236.

2 Bishop: Bon 1951, 8–9. Epitaphs: *IG* v.1.820–2; Feissel 1983, 615–7. Athens: Travlos 1960, ch. 7. Byzantium: Rawson 1969, ch. 9.

Bibliography

This bibliography is consciously selective, aiming to list all works cited by author's name and date of publication in the text and notes above. Abbreviations of periodicals follow the conventions of the relevant volume of *L'année philologique*.

Accame, S. (1946), *Il dominio romano in Grecia dalla Guerra Acaica ad Augusto*, Rome.

Adam, J.-P. (1982), *L'architecture militaire grecque*, Paris.

Adams, W.L./Borza, E.N. (1982), eds, *Philip II, Alexander the Great and the Macedonian Heritage*, Washington, D.C.

Adcock, F.E. (1953), 'Greek and Macedonian kingship', *PBA* 39, 163–80.

Adcock, F.E./Mosley, D.J. (1975), *Diplomacy in Ancient Greece*, London and New York.

Africa, T.W. (1961), *Phylarchus and the Spartan Revolution*, Berkeley.

Ameling, W. (1983), *Herodes Atticus*, 2 vols, Hildesheim.

Anderson, G. (1986), *Philostratus. Biography and belles lettres in the second century A.D.*, Beckenham.

Anderson, J.K. (1967), 'Philopoemen's reform of the Achaean army', *CPh* 62, 104–6.

Anderson, J.K. (1970), *Military Theory and Practice in the Age of Xenophon*, Berkeley and Los Angeles.

Andrei, O. (1984), *A. Claudius Charax di Pergamo: interessi antiquari e antichità cittadine nell' età degli Antonini*, Bologna.

Andreotti, R. (1935), 'Sull' origine della patronomia spartana', *Athenaeum* 13, 187–94.

Andronicos, M. (1984), *Vergina. The Royal Tombs*, Athens.

Apostolides, K.M. (1937), 'Syllogē arkhaiōn epigraphōn aneuretheisōn en Traïanēi Augoustēi', *Thrakika* 8, 69–107.

Asheri. D. (1966), *Distribuzioni di Terre nell' antica Grecia*, Turin.

Asheri, D. (1969), 'Leggi greche sul problema dei debiti', *SCO* 18, 5–122.

Athanassiadi-Fowden, P. (1981), *Julian and Hellenism*, Oxford.

Atkinson, J.E. (1980), *A Commentary on Q. Curtius Rufus* Historiae Alexandri Magni, *Books 3 and 4*, Amsterdam.

Aupert, P. (1985), 'Un Sérapieion argien?', *CRAI*, 151–75.

Austin, M.M. (1981), ed., *The Hellenistic World from Alexander to the Roman conquest*, Cambridge.

Aylen, L. (1985), *The Greek Theatre*, Cranbury.

Aymard, A. (1938), *Les premiers rapports de Rome et de la Confédération achaïenne (191–189 av. J.-C.)*, Bordeaux and Paris.

Aymard, A. (1967), *Études d'histoire ancienne*, Paris.
Badian, E. (1958), *Foreign Clientelae (264–70 B.C.)*, Oxford.
Badian, E. (1961), 'Harpalus', *JHS* 81, 16–43.
Badian, E. (1962), 'The Hellenistic World', in Lloyd-Jones 1962, 238–58.
Badian, E. (1964), *Studies in Greek and Roman History*, Oxford.
Badian, E. (1967), 'Agis III', *Hermes* 95, 170–92.
Badian, E. (1970), *Titus Quinctius Flamininus. Philhellenism and* Realpolitik, Cincinnati.
Badian, E. (1981), 'The deification of Alexander the Great', in *Ancient Macedonian Studies in honour of Charles F. Edson*, Thessaloniki, 27–71.
Baladié, R. (1980), *Le Péloponnèse de Strabon. Étude de géographie historique*, Paris.
Balsdon, J.P.V.D. (1950), 'The "deification" of Alexander', *Historia* 1, 363–88.
Balsdon, J.P.V.D. (1954), 'Rome and Macedon, 205–200 B.C.', *JRS* 44, 30–42.
Baslez, M.-F. (forthcoming), 'Citoyens et non-citoyens dans l'Athènes impériale au Ier et au IIe siècles de notre ère', in Cameron/Walker (forthcoming).
Baslez, M.-F./Vial, Cl. (1987), 'La diplomatie de Délos dans le premier tiers du IIe siècle', *BCH* 111, 281–312.
Baynes, N.H. (1955), *Byzantine Studies and Other Essays*, London.
Beard, M. (1985), 'Writing and ritual: a study of diversity and expansion in the Arval Acta', *PBSR* 53, 114–62.
Beard, M./Crawford, M.H. (1985), *Rome in the Late Republic*, London.
Beaujeu, J. (1955), *La religion romaine à l'apogée de l'empire*, Paris.
Behr, C.A. (1968), *Aelius Aristides and the Sacred Tales*, Leiden.
Bellinger, A.R. (1963), *Essays on the Coinage of Alexander the Great*, New York.
Benecke, P.V.M. (1930), 'The fall of the Macedonian monarchy' and 'Rome and the Hellenistic states (188–146)', in *CAH*[1] viii, 241–78, 279–305.
Bengtson, H. (1969), et al., *The Greeks and the Persians from the Sixth to the Fourth centuries*, London.
Bengtson, H. (1975), ed., *Die Staatsverträge des Altertums* ii. *Die Verträge der griechisch-römischen Welt von 700 bis 338 v. Chr.*, 2nd edn, Munich.
Bengtson, H. (1977), *Griechische Geschichte von den Anfängen bis in die römische Kaiserzeit*, 5th edn, Munich.
Benjamin, A. (1963), 'The altars of Hadrian in Athens and Hadrian's Panhellenic program', *Hesperia* 32, 57–90.
Bernal, M. (1987), *Black Athena. The Afroasiatic roots of Classical civilization* i. *The fabrication of Ancient Greece 1785–1985*, London.
Bernand, A./Bernand, E. (1960), *Les inscriptions grecques et latines du Colosse de Memnon*, Paris.
Bernhardt, R. (1971), 'Imperium und Eleutheria. Die römische Politik gegenüber den freien Städten des griechischen Ostens', diss., Hamburg.
Bernhardt, R. (1977), 'Der Status des 146 v. Chr. unterworfenen Teils Griechenlands bis zur Einrichtung der Provinz Achaia', *Historia* 26, 62–73.
Bernhardt, R. (1980), 'Die *immunitas* der Freistädte', *Historia* 29, 190–207.
Bernhardt, R. (1985), *Polis und römische Herrschaft in der späten Republik (149–31 v. Chr.)*, Berlin and New York.
Bernini, U. (1978), 'Studi su Sparta ellenistica. Da Leonida II a Cleomene III', *QUCC* 27, 29–59.
Bernini, U. (1981–1982), 'Archidamo e Cleomene III. Politica interna ed estera a Sparta (241–227 A.C.)', *Athenaeum* n.s. 59, 439–58; 60, 205–23.
Berve, H. (1926), *Das Alexanderreich auf prosopographischer Grundlage*, 2 vols, Munich.

Bichler, R. (1983), *"Hellenismus". Geschichte und Problematik eines Epochen-begriffs*, Munich.

Bickerman, E.J. (1962), *From Ezra to the last of the Maccabees. Foundations of postbiblical Judaism*, New York.

Biers, W.R. (1978), 'Water from Stymphalos?', *Hesperia* 47, 171–84.

Bingen, J. (1953), 'Inscriptions du Péloponnèse', *BCH* 77, 616–47.

Bintliff, J./Snodgrass, A.M. (1985), 'The Cambridge/Bradford Boeotia Expedition: the first four years', *JFA* 12, 123–61.

Blake, M.E. (1973), *Roman Construction in Italy from Nerva through the Antonines*, Philadelphia.

Blouet, A. (1833), ed., *Expédition scientifique de Morée* ii, Paris.

Boardman, J./Vaphopoulou-Richardson, C.E. (1986), eds, *Chios. A conference at the Homereion in Chios*, Oxford.

Bockisch, G. (1974), 'Die sozial-ökonomische und politische Krise der Lakedaimonier und ihrer Symmachie im 4. Jht. v.u.Z.', in Welskopf 1974, i, 199–230.

Bölte, F. (1929), 'Sparta (Geografie)', *RE* iii A2, 1294–1374.

Bogaert, R. (1965), 'Banquiers, courtiers, et prêts maritimes à Athènes et Alexandrie', *CE* 40, 140–56.

Bogaert, R. (1968), *Banques et banquiers dans les cités grecques*, Leiden.

Bon, A. (1951), *Le Péloponnèse byzantin*, Paris.

Boren, H.C. (1961), 'Tiberius Gracchus: the opposition view', *AJPh* 92, 358–69.

Boring, T.A. (1979), *Literacy in Ancient Sparta*, Leiden.

Borza, E.N. (1971), 'The end of Agis' revolt', *CPh* 66, 230–5. See also Adams, W.L.

Bosanquet, R.C. (1905–6), 'Excavations at Sparta, 1906. i. The season's work', *ABSA* 12, 277–84.

Bosworth, A.B. (1975), 'The mission of Amphoterus and the outbreak of Agis' war', *Phoenix* 29, 27–43.

Bosworth, A.B. (1980), *Historical Commentary on Arrian's* History of Alexander. i. *Books I-III*, Oxford.

Bourguet, E. (1927), *Le dialecte laconien*, Paris.

Bowersock, G.W. (1961), 'Eurycles of Sparta', *JRS* 51, 111–18.

Bowersock, G.W. (1965), *Augustus and the Greek World*, Oxford.

Bowersock, G.W. (1969), *Greek Sophists in the Roman Empire*, Oxford.

Bowersock, G.W. (1984), 'Augustus and the East: the problem of the succession', in Millar/Segal 1984, 169–88.

Bowie, E.L. (1974), 'Greeks and their past in the Second Sophistic' (1970), repr. in Finley 1974, 166–209.

Bowie, E.L. (1978), 'Apollonius of Tyana: tradition and reality', *ANRW* ii.2, 1653–99.

Bowie, E.L. (1980), 'Lucian at Philippopolis', *Mitt. des Bulgarischen Forschungs-institutes in Österreich* 3, 53–60.

Bowman, A.K. (1971), *The Town Councils of Roman Egypt*, Toronto.

Box, H. (1931–1932), 'Roman citizenship in Laconia, i-ii', *JRS* 21, 200–14; 22, 165–83.

Bradford, A.S. (1977), *A Prosopography of Lacedaemonians from the death of Alexander the Great, 323 B.C., to the sack of Sparta by Alaric, A.D. 396*, Munich.

Bradford, A.S. (1980), 'The Synarchia of Roman Sparta', *Chiron* 10, 413–25.

Bradford, A.S. (1986a), 'The date Hadrian was eponymous *patronomos* of Sparta', *Horos* 4, 71–4.

Bradford, A.S. (1986b), 'Gynaikokratoumenoi: dĩd Spartan women rule Spartan men?', *AncW* 14.1–2, 13–18. See also Poralla, P.
Brauer, G.C. jr (1986), *Taras. Its history and coinage*, New Rochelle.
Briscoe, J. (1967), 'Rome and the class struggle in the Greek states 200–146 B.C.', *Past & Present* 36, 3–20 (repr. in Finley 1974, 53–73).
Briscoe, J. (1973–1981), *A Commentary on Livy Books xxxi-xxxiii* and *Books xxxiv-xxxvii*, Oxford.
Briscoe, J. (1978), 'The Antigonids and the Greek states, 276–196 B.C.', in Garnsey/Whittaker 1978, 145–57, 314–19.
Broneer, O. (1977), *Isthmia* iii. *Terracotta Lamps*, Princeton.
Browning, R. (1976), rev. of Welskopf 1974, *Philologus* 120, 258–66.
Brulé, P. (1978), *La piraterie crétoise hellénistique*, Paris.
Bruneau, Ph. (1976), 'D'un Lacedaemonius orbis à *l'aes deliacum*', *Fest. A. Plassart*, Paris, 15–45.
Bruneau, Ph. (1977), 'Lampes corinthiennes ii', *BCH* 101, 249–95.
Brunt, P.A. (1976–1983), trans., *Arrian. History of Alexander* and *Indica*, 2 vols, Cambridge, Mass. and London.
Buckler, C. (1986), 'The myth of the movable skenai', *AJA* 90, 431–6.
Buckler, J. (1980), *The Theban Hegemony, 371–362 B.C.*, Cambridge, Mass. and London.
Bulle, H. (1937), *Das Theater zu Sparta*, Munich.
Buraselis, K. (1982), *Das hellenistische Makedonien und die Ägäis. Forschungen zur Politik des Kassandros und der drei ersten Antigoniden im Ägäischen Meer und in Westkleinasien*, Munich.
Burkert, W. (1985), *Greek Religion: Archaic and Classical*, trans. J. Raffan, Oxford (German original 1977).
Burn, A.R. (1952), 'Notes on Alexander's campaigns, 332–330', *JHS* 72, 81–92.
Burstein, S.M. (1985), trans., *The Hellenistic Age from the battle of Ipsus to the death of Kleopatra VII* ('Translated Documents of Greece and Rome' 3), Cambridge.
Burton, G.P. (1975), 'Proconsuls, assizes and the administration of justice under the Empire', *JRS* 65, 92–105.
Bury, J.B. (1898), 'The double city of Megalopolis', *JHS* 18, 15–22.
Bury, J.B. (1923), et al., *The Hellenistic Age*, Cambridge.
Bury, J.B./Meiggs, R. (1975), *A History of Greece*, 4th edn, London. See also Freeman, E.A.
Bux, E. (1925), 'Zwei sozialistische Novellen bei Plutarch', *Klio* 19, 413–31.
Cadoux, C.J. (1938), *Ancient Smyrna*, Oxford.
Cameron, A./Walker, S. (forthcoming), eds, *The Greek Renaissance in the Roman Empire. Proceedings of the Tenth British Museum Colloquium*, London.
Campbell, J.B. (1984), *The Emperor and the Roman Army*, Oxford.
Cardauns, B. (1967), 'Juden und Spartaner. Zur hellenistisch-jüdischen Literatur', *Hermes* 95, 317–24.
Cargill, J. (1981), *The Second Athenian League. Empire or free alliance?*, Berkeley, L.A. and London.
Cargill, J. (1985), 'Demosthenes, Aischines, and the crop of traitors', *AncW* 11.3–4, 75–85.
Carlier, P. (1977), 'La vie politique à Sparte sous le règne de Cléomène Ier: essai d'interprétation', *Ktema* 2, 65–84.
Carlier, P. (1984), *La royauté en Grèce avant Alexandre*, Strasbourg.
Cartledge, P.A. (1975), 'Early Sparta *c.*950–650 B.C.: an archaeological and historical study', diss. Oxford (distributed by G. Bretschneider, Rome 1985/6).

Cartledge, P.A. (1977), 'Hoplites and heroes: Sparta's contribution to the technique of ancient warfare', *JHS* 97, 11–27 (rev. German trans. with add. in K. Christ, ed., *Sparta*, Wege der Forschung 622, Darmstadt 1986, 387–425, 470).

Cartledge, P.A. (1978), 'Literacy in the Spartan oligarchy', *JHS* 98, 25–37.

Cartledge, P.A. (1979), *Sparta and Lakonia. A regional history 1300–362 BC*, London, Henley & Boston ('States and Cities of Ancient Greece') .

Cartledge, P.A. (1981), 'Spartan wives: liberation or licence?', *CQ* n.s. 31, 84–109.

Cartledge, P.A. (1987), *Agesilaos and the Crisis of Sparta*, London and Baltimore.

Casson, L. (1974), *Travel in the Ancient World*, London.

Cavanagh, W.G./Crouwel, J.H. (forthcoming), 'The Laconia Survey 1983–1986', *Lakonikai Spoudai*.

Cawkwell, G.L. (1969), 'The crowning of Demosthenes', *CQ* n.s. 19, 163–80.

Chrimes, K.M.T. (1949), *Ancient Sparta. A re-examination of the evidence*, Manchester.

Christophilopoulou, A.P. (1968), 'Nomophylakes kai Thesmophylakes', *Platon* 20, 135–43 (in Greek).

Clarke, M.L. (1971), *Higher Education in the Ancient World*, London.

Clement, P.A. (1974), 'L. Kornelios Korinthos', in Bradeen, D.W./McGregor, M.F., eds, *PHOROS. Fest. B.D. Meritt*, Locust Valley, 36–9.

Clinton, K. (1974), *The Sacred Officials of the Eleusinian Mysteries (TAPhS 64.3)*, Philadelphia.

Cloché, P. (1943), 'Remarques sur les règnes d'Agis IV et de Cléomène III', *REG* 56, 53–71.

Cloché, P. (1945–46), 'La politique extérieure de Lacédémone depuis la mort d'Agis III jusqu'à celle d'Acrotatos, fils d'Areus Ier', *REA* 47, 219–42; 48, 29–61.

Coleman, M.L./Walker, S. (1979), 'Stable isotope identification of Greek and Turkish marbles', *Archaeometry* 21, 107–12.

Colin, G. (1905), *Rome et la Grèce de 200 à 146 avant Jésus-Christ*, Paris.

Colin, J. (1965), *Les villes libres de l'orient gréco-romain*, Brussels.

Connor, W.R. (1979), 'Pausanias 3.14.1: a sidelight on Spartan history *c*.440 B.C.?', *TAPhA* 109, 21–7.

Cook, J.M./Nicholls, R.V. (1950), 'Laconia', *ABSA* 45, 261–98.

Costanzi, V. (1908), 'La catastrofe di Nabide', *RSA* n.s. 12, 53–8.

Crawford, M.H. (1977), 'Rome and the Greek world: economic relationships', *Econ. Hist. Rev.* 30, 42–51.

Crawford, M.H. (1978a), 'Greek intellectuals and the Roman aristocracy in the first century BC', in Garnsey/Whittaker 1978, 193–207, 330–8.

Crawford, M.H. (1978b), *The Roman Republic*, Hassocks and Glasgow.

Crawford, M.H. (1983), ed., *Sources for Ancient History,* Cambridge. See also Beard, M.

Daly, L.W. (1950), 'Roman study abroad', *AJPh* 71, 40–58.

Daux, G. (1936), *Delphes au IIe et au Ier siècle*, Paris.

Daux, G. (1957), 'Remarques sur la composition du conseil amphictionique', *BCH* 81, 95–120.

Daux, G. (1976), 'L'Amphictyonie delphique sous l'Empire', *Fest. A. Plassart*, Paris, 59–79.

David, E. (1979), 'The pamphlet of Pausanias', *PP* 34, 94–116.

David, E. (1981), *Sparta between Empire and Revolution (404–243 B.C.). Internal problems and their impact on contemporary Greek consciousness*, New York.

David, E. (1982–83), 'Aristotle and Sparta', *AncSoc* 13–14, 67–103.

Davies, J.K. (1978), *Democracy and Classical Greece*, Hassocks and Glasgow.

Davies, J.K. (1984), 'Cultural, social and economic features of the Hellenistic world', *CAH*[2] vii.1, 257–320.

Davis, N./Kraay, C.M. (1967), *Greek Coins and Cities*, London.

Dawkins, R.M. (1929), ed., *Artemis Orthia (JHS* Supp. v), London.

De Falco, V. (1923), *L'Epicureo Demetrio Lacone*, Naples.

Deichgräber, K. (1952), 'Polemon von Ilion', *RE* xxi.2, cols.1288–1320.

Deininger, J. (1971), *Der politische Widerstand gegen Rom in Griechenland, 217–86 v. Chr.*, Berlin.

Delorme, J. (1960), *Gymnasion. Étude sur les monuments consacrés à l'éducation en Grèce (des origines à l'empire romain)*, Paris.

De Sanctis, G. (1923–64), *Storia dei Romani* IV. *La fondazione dell' impero* i. *Dalla battaglia di Naraggara alla battaglia di Pidna*, Turin. ii. *Dalla battaglia di Pidna alla caduta di Numanzia*, ed. M. Zambetti, Florence.

Dickins, G. (1905–6a), 'Excavations at Sparta, 1906. x. The Theatre', *ABSA* 12, 394–405.

Dickins, G. (1905–6b), 'Excavations at Sparta, 1906. Topographical conclusions', *ABSA* 12, 431–9.

Dickins, G. (1907–8), 'The Hieron of Athena Chalkioikos', *ABSA* 14, 142–6. See also Wace, A.J.B.

Dilke, O.A.W. (1950), 'Details and chronology of Greek theatre caveas', *ABSA* 45, 21–62.

Dörig, J. (1987), *The Olympia Master and his Collaborators*, Leiden.

Duggan, M. (1952), 'An ancient battleship', *PCA* 49, 26–7.

Dunand, F. (1978), 'Sens et fonction de la fête dans la Grèce hellénistique', *DHA* 4, 201–13.

Duncan-Jones, R.P. (1982), *The Economy of the Roman Empire. Quantitative Studies*, 2nd edn, Cambridge.

Duncan-Jones, R.P. (1984), 'Problems of the Delphic manumission payments 200–1 B.C.', *ZPE* 57, 203–9.

Eadie, J.W./Ober, J. (1985), eds, *The Craft of the Ancient Historian. Essays in honor of Chester G. Starr*, Lanham and London.

Eckstein, A.M. (1987), 'Nabis and Flamininus on the Argive revolutions of 198 and 197 B.C.', *GRBS* 28, 213–33.

Edmonson, C.N. (1959), 'A graffito from Amyklai', *Hesperia* 28, 162–4.

Ehrenberg, V. (1929), 'Sparta (Geschichte)', *RE* iiiA2, 1373–1453.

Ehrenberg, V. (1930), 'Machanidas', *RE* xiv, 142–3.

Ehrenberg, V. (1932), 'Menalkidas', *RE* xv, 703–4.

Ehrenberg, V. (1935), 'Nabis', *RE* xvi.2, 1471–82.

Ehrenberg, V. (1937), 'Tresantes', *RE* viA, 2292–7.

Ehrenberg, V. (1974), 'The Hellenistic Age' (1964), repr. in *Man, State and Deity*, London, 64–106.

Ellis, J.R. (1976), *Philip II and Macedonian Imperialism*, London and New York.

Erim, K.T. (1986), *Aphrodisias*, London.

Errington, R.M. (1969), *Philopoemen*, Oxford.

Errington, R.M. (1971), *The Dawn of Empire. Rome's rise to world power*, London.

Evangelidis, D. (1911), 'Lakōnikai epigraphai', *AE*, 193–8 (in Greek).

Feissel, D. (1983), 'Notes d'épigraphie chrétienne (vi)', *BCH* 107, 601–18.

Felten, F. (1983), 'Heiligtümer oder Märkte?', *AK* 26, 84–105.

Ferguson, W.S. (1911), *Hellenistic Athens*, London (repr. Chicago 1974).

Figueira, T.J. (1984), 'Mess contributions and subsistence at Sparta', *TAPhA* 114, 87–109.

Figueira, T.J. (1986), 'Population patterns in Late Archaic and Classical Sparta', *TAPhA* 116, 165–213.

Fine, J.V.A. (1940), 'The background of the Social War of 220–217 B.C.', *AJPh* 61, 129–65.

Finley, M.I. (1974), ed., *Studies in Ancient Society*, London and Boston.

Finley, M.I. (1985), *Studies in Land and Credit in Ancient Athens, 500–200 B.C.*, 2nd edn, New Brunswick.

Finley, M.I. (1986), 'Revolution in antiquity', in Porter/Teich 1986, 47–60.

Flacelière, R. (1947), ed., *Plutarque. Sur la disparition des oracles*, Paris.

Flacelière, R. (1952), ed., *Plutarque. Dialogue sur l'amour*, Paris.

Follet, S. (1976), *Athènes au IIe et au IIIe siècle*, Paris.

Fontana, M.J. (1980), 'Nabide tiranno tra Roma e i Greci', in PHILIAS KHARIN. *Fest. E. Manni*, 6 vols, Rome, iii.919–45.

Forrest, W.G. (1968), *A History of Sparta c.950–192 B.C.*, London (repr. with new intro. 1980).

Forrest, W.G. (1972), 'A metrical inscription', in Coldstream, J.N./Huxley, G.L., eds, *Kythera. Excavations and studies*, London, 314.

Fortenbaugh, W.W. (1985), et al., eds, *Theophrastus of Eresus. On his life and work*, New Brunswick and Oxford.

Fowden, G. (1978), 'Bishops and temples in the Eastern Roman Empire AD 320–435', *JThS* n.s. 29, 53–78.

Fowden, G. (1987), 'Nicagoras of Athens and the Lateran Obelisk', *JHS* 107, 51–7.

Frank, T. (1938), ed., *An Economic Survey of Ancient Rome* iv, Baltimore.

Frazer, J.G. (1898), *Pausanias' Description of Greece*, 6 vols, London (repr. New York 1965).

Frederiksen, M.W. (1980–81), 'Puteoli e il commercio di grano in epoca romana', *Puteoli* 4–5, 5–27.

Freeman, E.A. (1893), *History of Federal Government in Greece and Italy*, 2nd edn, ed. J.B. Bury, London and New York.

Fuks, A. (1962a), 'Agis, Cleomenes and equality', *CPh* 57, 161–6 (= Fuks 1984, 250–5).

Fuks, A. (1962b), 'Non-Phylarchean tradition of the programme of Agis IV', *CQ* n.s. 12, 118–21 (= Fuks 1984, 256–9).

Fuks, A. (1962c), 'The Spartan citizen-body in mid-third century B.C. and its proposed enlargement by Agis IV', *Athenaeum* n.s. 40, 244–63 (= Fuks 1984, 230–49).

Fuks, A. (1970), 'The Bellum Achaicum and its social aspect', *JHS* 90, 78–89 (= Fuks 1984, 270–81).

Fuks, A. (1974), 'Patterns and types of social-economic revolution in Greece from the fourth to the second century B.C', *AncSoc* 5, 51–81 (= Fuks 1984, 9–39).

Fuks, A. (1984), *Social Conflict in Ancient Greece*, ed. Stern, M. and Amit, M. (photostatic repr. of articles published 1951–80), Jerusalem and Leiden.

Furtwängler, A. (1985), rev. of Grunauer-von Hoerschelmann 1978, *Gnomon* 57, 637–41.

Fustel de Coulanges, N.D. (1864), *La cité antique*, Paris.

Gabba, E. (1957), 'Studi su Filarco. Le biografie plutarchee di Agide e di Cleomene', *Athenaeum* n.s. 35, 3–55, 193–239.

Gallo, L. (1980), 'Popolosità e scarsità: contributo allo studio di un topos',

*ASNP*³ 10, 1233–70.

Gardner, J.F. (1987), 'Another family and an inheritance: Claudius Brasidas and his ex-wife's will', *LCM* 12, 52–4.

Garlan, Y. (1974), *Recherches de poliorcétique grecque*, Paris.

Garlan, Y. (1988), *Slavery in Ancient Greece*, 2nd edn, Ithaca and London.

Garland, R.S.J. (1984), 'Religious authority in Archaic and Classical Athens', *ABSA* 79, 75–123.

Garnsey, P.D.A. (1970), *Social Status and Legal Privilege in the Roman Empire*, Oxford.

Garnsey, P.D.A. (1974), 'Aspects of the decline of the urban aristocracy in the Empire', *ANRW* ii.1, 229–52.

Garnsey, P.D.A. (1988), *Famine and Food Supply in the Graeco-Roman World*, Cambridge.

Garnsey, P.D.A./Saller, R.P. (1987), *The Roman Empire: economy, society and culture*, London.

Garnsey, P.D.A./Hopkins, K./Whittaker, C.R. (1983), eds, *Trade in the Ancient Economy*, London.

Garnsey, P.D.A./Whittaker, C.R. (1978), eds, *Imperialism in the Ancient World*, Cambridge.

Garnsey, P.D.A./Whittaker, C.R. (1983), *Trade and Famine in Classical Antiquity*, Cambridge.

Garoufalias, P. (1979), *Pyrrhus King of Epirus*, London.

Gasperini, L. (1984), 'Un Buleuta Alessandrino a Taranto', in *Alessandria e il mondo ellenistico-romano. Fest. A. Adriani*, Rome, 476–9.

Gauthier, Ph. (1979), 'EXAGOGE SITOU. Samothrace, Hippomédon et les Lagides', *Historia* 28, 78–89.

Gauthier, Ph. (1985), *Les cités grecques et leurs bienfaiteurs* (*BCH* Supp. xii), Paris.

Geagan, D.J. (1967), *The Athenian Constitution after Sulla* (*Hesperia* Supp. xii), Princeton.

Geagan, D.J. (1979), 'Roman Athens: some aspects of life and culture i. 86 B.C.-A.D.267', *ANRW* ii.7.1, 371–437.

Gehrke, H.-J. (1985), *Stasis. Untersuchungen zu den inneren Kriegen in den griechischen Staaten des 5. und 4. Jhts v. Chr.*, Munich.

Giannokopoulos, P.E. (1966), *To Gytheion*, Athens (in Greek).

Gilliam, J.F. (1961), 'The plague under Marcus Aurelius', *AJPh* 82, 225–51.

Ginouvès, R. (1962), *Balaneutikè. Recherches sur le bain dans l'antiquité grecque*, Paris.

Ginsburg, M.S. (1934), 'Sparta and Judaea', *CPh* 29, 117–24.

Giovannini, A. (1978), *Rome et la circulation monétaire en Grèce au IIe siècle avant J.-C.*, Basle.

Gitti, A. (1939), 'I perieci di Sparta e le origini del KOINON TON LAKEDAIMONION', *RAL*⁶ 15, 189–203.

Golan, D. (1974), 'Philopoemen immodicus and superbus and Sparta', *SCI* 1, 29–39.

Gossage, A.J. (1951), 'The Social and Economic Condition of the Province of Achaia from Augustus to Caracalla', diss., London.

Gow, A.S.F./Page, D.L. (1968), eds, *The Greek Anthology: the Garland of Philip*, 2 vols, Cambridge.

Grace, V.R. (1985), 'The Middle Stoa dated by amphora stamps', *Hesperia* 54, 1–54.

Greene, K. (1986), *The Archaeology of the Roman Economy*, London.

Gregory, T.E. (1982), 'The fortified cities of Byzantine Greece', *Archaeology* 35, 14–21.

Gregory, T.E. (1986), 'The survival of paganism in Christian Greece: a critical essay', *AJPh* 107, 229–42.

Griffith, G.T. (1935), *Mercenaries of the Hellenistic World*, Cambridge (repr. Chicago 1975). See also Hammond, N.G.L.

Groag, E. (1939), *Die römischen Reichsbeamten von Achaia bis auf Diokletian*, Vienna.

Groag, E. (1946), *Die Reichsbeamten von Achaia in spätrömischer Zeit*, Budapest.

Gruen, E.S. (1976), 'The origins of the Achaean War', *JHS* 96, 46–69.

Gruen, E.S. (1984), *The Hellenistic World and the Coming of Rome*, 2 vols, Berkeley, Los Angeles., and London (repr. in 1 vol. 1986).

Gruen, E.S. (1985), 'The crowning of the Diadochi', in Eadie/Ober 1985, 253–71.

Grunauer-von Hoerschelmann, S. (1978), *Die Münzprägung der Lakedaimonier*, Berlin and New York.

Habicht, C. (1975a), 'Der Beitrag Spartas zur Restitution von Samos während des Iamischen Krieges (Ps. Aristoteles, Ökonomik II,2,9)', *Chiron* 5, 45–50.

Habicht, C. (1975b), 'New evidence on the province of Asia', *JRS* 65, 64–91.

Habicht, C. (1982), *Studien zur Geschichte Athens in hellenistischer Zeit*, Göttingen.

Habicht, C. (1985), *Pausanias' Guide to Ancient Greece*, Berkeley, L.A. and London.

Hackens, T. (1968), 'A propos de la circulation monétaire dans le Péloponnèse au IIIe siècle av. J.-C.', in *Antidorum W. Peremans oblatum*, Louvain, 69–95.

Hadas, M. (1932), 'The social revolution in third-century Sparta', *CW* 26.9–10, 65–8, 73–6.

Hadas, M. (1959), *Hellenistic Culture. Fusion and diffusion*, New York and London.

Hänlein-Schäfer, H. (1985), Veneratio Augusti. *Eine Studie zu den Tempeln des ersten römischen Kaisers*, Rome.

Halfmann, H. (1979), *Die Senatoren aus dem östlichen Teils des Imperium Romanum bis zum Ende des 2. Jh. n. Chr.*, Göttingen.

Halfmann, H. (1986), *Itinera Principum. Geschichte und Typologie der Kaiserreisen im römischen Reich*, Stuttgart.

Hall, J. (1981), *Lucian's Satire*, New York.

Hamilton, C.D. (1982a), 'The early career of Archidamus', *EMC* n.s. 1, 5–20.

Hamilton, C.D. (1982b), 'Philip II and Archidamus', in Adams/Borza 1982, 61–83.

Hammond, N.G.L./Griffith, G.T. (1979), *A History of Macedonia* ii. *550–336 B.C.*, Oxford.

Hardie, A. (1983), *Statius and the Silvae*, Liverpool.

Harding, P. (1985), trans., *From the End of the Peloponnesian War to the battle of Ipsus* ('Translated Documents of Greece and Rome' 2), Cambridge.

Harris, W.V. (1979), *War and Imperialism in Republican Rome 327–70 B.C.*, Oxford (repr. with new Preface 1985).

Harris, W.V. (1984), ed., *The Imperialism of Mid-Republican Rome*, Rome.

Hartog, F. (1986), 'Les Grecs égyptologues', *Annales (ESC)* 41, 953–67.

Hasluck, F.W.: see Wace, A.J.B.

Head, B.V. (1911), *Historia Numorum*, 2nd ed., Oxford.

Heberdey, R.: see Wilhelm, A.

Heinen, H. (1972), *Untersuchungen zur hellenistischen Geschichte des 3. Jhts. v.*

Chr. Zur Geschichte der Zeit des Ptolemaios Keraunos und zum Chremonid-eischen Krieg, Wiesbaden.

Herman, G. (1980–1), 'The "friends" of the early hellenistic rulers: servants or officials?', *Talanta* 12–13, 103–49.

Herman, G. (1987), *Ritualised Friendship and the Greek City*, Cambridge.

Hertzberg, G.F. (1887–90), *Histoire de la Grèce sous la domination des Romains*, trans. A. Bouché-Leclercq, 3 vols, Paris (German original Halle 1866–75).

Heuss, A. (1973), 'Das Revolutionsproblem im Spiegel der antiken Geschichte', *HZ* 216, 1–72.

Hobsbawm, E.J./Ranger, T.O. (1983), eds, *The Invention of Tradition*, Cambridge.

Hodkinson, S.J. (1986), 'Land tenure and inheritance in Classical Sparta', *CQ* n.s. 36, 378–406.

Holleaux, M. (1926), 'La politique romaine en Grèce et dans l'orient hellénistique au IIIe siècle. Réponse à M. Th. Walek', *RPh* 50, 46–66, 194–218.

Holleaux, M. (1957), 'Rome, Philippe de Macédoine et Antiochos', in *Études d'épigraphie et d'histoire grecques*, 5 vols, ed. L. Robert, Paris, v.2, 295–432 (v.o. of *CAH*¹ viii [1930], 116–240).

Homolle, Th. (1896), 'Inscriptions de Délos. Le roi Nabis', *BCH* 20, 502–22.

Hope Simpson, R. (1959), 'Antigonus the One-eyed and the Greeks', *Historia* 8, 385–409.

Hope Simpson, R./Lazenby, J.F. (1970), *The Catalogue of Ships in Homer's Iliad*, Oxford.

Hope Simpson, R./Waterhouse, H.E. (1960), 'Prehistoric Laconia, Part I', *ABSA* 55, 67–107.

Hopkins, K. (1978a), *Conquerors and Slaves. Sociological studies in Roman History* i, Cambridge.

Hopkins, K. (1978b), 'Economic growth and towns in Classical Antiquity', in Abrams, P./Wrigley, E.A., eds, *Towns and Societies*, Cambridge, 35–77.

Hopkins, K. (1980), 'Taxes and trade in the Roman Empire (200 B.C.–A.D. 400)', *JRS* 70, 101–25. See also Garnsey, P.D.A.

Hornblower, J. (1981), *Hieronymus of Cardia*, Oxford.

Hornblower, S. (1983), *The Greek World 479–323 B.C.*, London. (corr. repr. 1985).

Howgego, C.J. (1985), *Greek Imperial Countermarks: studies in the provincial coinage of the Roman Empire*, London.

Humphreys, S.C. (1978), *Anthropology and the Greeks*, London, Henley and Boston.

Humphreys, S.C. (1985), 'Lycurgus of Butadae: an Athenian aristocrat', in Eadie/Ober 1985, 199–252.

Huxley, G.L. (1979), *On Aristotle and Greek Society. An essay*, Belfast.

Jacoby, F. (1923–58), ed., *Die Fragmente der griechischen Historiker*, Berlin and Leiden [*FGrHist*].

Jacoby, F. (1950–55), *FGrHist* IIIb (Text, Commentary and Notes), Leiden.

Jameson, M.H. (1953), 'Inscriptions of the Peloponnesos', *Hesperia* 22, 148–71.

Janni, P. (1984), 'Sparta ritrovata. Il modello "spartano" nell' etnografia antica', in Lanzilotta 1984, 29–58.

Jones, A.H.M. (1940), *The Greek City from Alexander to Justinian*, Oxford.

Jones, A.H.M. (1964a), 'The Hellenistic Age', *Past & Present* 27, 3–22.

Jones, A.H.M. (1964b), *The Later Roman Empire 284–602*, 3 vols, Oxford (repr. in 2 vols 1974).

Jones, A.H.M. (1967), *Sparta*, Oxford.

Jones, A.H.M./Martindale, J.R./Morris, J. (1971), *Prosopography of the Later Roman Empire* i, Cambridge.

Jones, C.P. (1970), 'A leading family of Roman Thespiae', *HSPh* 74, 221–55.

Jones, C.P. (1971a), 'The levy at Thespiae under Marcus Aurelius', *GRBS* 12, 45–8.

Jones, C.P. (1971b), *Plutarch and Rome*, Oxford.

Jones, C.P. (1978a), *The Roman World of Dio Chrysostom*, Cambridge, Mass.

Jones, C.P. (1978b), 'Three foreigners in Attica', *Phoenix* 32, 222–34.

Kahrstedt, U. (1950a), 'Zwei Geographica im Peloponnes'. *RhM* 93, 227–42.

Kahrstedt, U. (1950b), 'Zwei Probleme in kaiserzeitlichen Griechenland', *SO* 28, 66–75.

Kahrstedt, U. (1954), *Das wirtschaftliche Gesicht Griechenlands in der Kaiserzeit*, Bern.

Karamesini-Oikonomidou, M. (1966), 'Mia martyria dia ten kathodon ton Heroulon eis ten Sparten to 267 m. Khr. Eurema nomismaton ton Lakedaimonion', *Charisterion. Fest. A.K. Orlandos*, 3 vols, Athens, iii.376–82.

Kayser, B./Thompson, K. (1964), *Economic and Social Atlas of Greece*, Athens.

Kazarow, G. (1907), 'Zur Geschichte der sozialen Revolution in Sparta', *Klio* 7, 45–51.

Kelly, T. (1985), 'The Spartan scytale', in Eadie/Ober 1985, 141–69.

Kennedy, C.R. (1908), trans., *The Orations of Demosthenes* ii. *On the Crown, and On the Embassy*, London.

Kennell, N.M. (1985), 'The Public Institutions of Roman Sparta', diss., Toronto.

Kennell, N.M. (1987), 'Where was Sparta's Prytaneion?', *AJA* 91, 421–2.

King, C.E. (1986), ed., *Imperial Revenue, Expenditure and Monetary Policy in the Fourth Century AD*, Oxford (British Arch. Rep. Int. Ser. Supp. lxxvii).

Kingsley, B.M. (1986), 'Harpalus in the Megarid (333–331 B.C.) and the grain shipments from Cyrene (SEG IX 2+ = Tod, Greek Hist. Inscr. II no.196)', *ZPE* 66, 165–77.

Kjellberg, E. (1921), 'C. Julius Eurykles', *Klio* 17, 49–58.

Kleiner, D. (1983), *The Monument of Philopappus*, Rome.

Koch, G./Sichtermann, H. (1982), *Römische Sarkophage*, Munich.

Kolbe, W. (1904), 'Die Grenzen Messeniens in der ersten Kaiserzeit', *MDAI(A)* 29, 364–78.

Kolbe, W. (1913), ed., *IG* v.1, Berlin.

Korpela, J. (1987), *Das Medizinalpersonal im antiken Rom*, Helsinki.

Kourinou-Pikoula, E. (1986), 'Epigraphes apo tē Spartē', *Horos* 4, 65–9 (in Greek).

Kraay, C.M./Hirmer, M. (1966), *Greek Coins*, London and New York. See also Davis, N.

Kunstler, B.L. (1983), 'Women and the Development of the Spartan Polis: a study of sex roles in Classical Antiquity', diss., Boston.

Lambros, I.P. (1891), 'Anekdoton tetradrakhmon "Nabios" tyrannou tes Spartes', *BCH* 15, 415–18 (in Greek).

Lane, E. (1962), 'An unpublished inscription from Lakonia', *Hesperia* 31, 396–8.

Lane Fox, R. (1986a), *Pagans and Christians*, Harmondsworth and New York.

Lane Fox, R. (1986b), 'Theopompus of Chios and the Greek world 411–322 BC', in Boardman/Vaphopoulou-Richardson 1986, 105–20.

Lanzilotta, E. (1984), ed., *Problemi di storia e cultura spartana*, Rome.

Larsen, J.A.O. (1935), 'Was Greece free between 196 and 146 B.C.?', *CPh* 30, 193–214.

Larsen, J.A.O. (1938), 'Roman Greece', in Frank 1938, 259–498.

Larsen, J.A.O. (1966), 'The Aetolians and the Cleomenic War', *Fest. H. Caplan*, Ithaca, 43–57.

Larsen, J.A.O. (1968), *Greek Federal States. Their institutions and history*, Oxford.

Launey, M. (1949–1950), *Recherches sur les armées hellénistiques*, 2 vols, Paris.

Lazenby, J.F. (1985), *The Spartan Army*, Warminster. See also Hope Simpson, R.

Lepore, E. (1955), 'Leostene e le origini della Guerra Lamiaca', *PP* 10, 161–85.

Le Roy, C. (1974), 'Inscriptions de Laconie inédites ou revues', in *Mélanges hellénistiques offerts à Georges Daux*, Paris, 219–38.

Le Roy, C. (1978), 'Richesse et exploitation en Laconie', *Ktema* 3, 261–6.

Leschhorn, W. (1984), *Gründer der Stadt. Studien zu einem politisch-religiösen Phänomen der griechische Geschichte*, Stuttgart .

Lévêque, P. (1957), *Pyrrhos*, Paris.

Lintott, A.W. (1982), *Violence, Civil Strife and Revolution in the Classical City, 750–330 B.C.*, London and Canberra.

Lloyd-Jones, H. (1962), ed., *The Greeks*, London.

Lock, R.A. (1972), 'The date of Agis III's war in Greece', *Antichthon* 6, 10–27.

Longrigg, J. (1981), 'Superlative achievement and comparative neglect: Alexandrian medical science and modern historical research', *History of Science* 19, 155–200.

Loring, W. (1895), 'Some ancient routes in the Peloponnesc', *JHS* 15, 25–89.

Loukas, I.K. (1983), *La mosaïque hellénistique de Sparte à scènes dionysiaques*, Brussels.

Loukas, I.K. (1984), 'Lakedaimonioi Dionysiakoi tekhnites', *Horos* 2, 149–60 (in Greek).

MacDowell, D.M. (1986), *Spartan Law*, Edinburgh.

MacMullen, R. (1976), *Roman Government's Response to Crisis, AD 235–337*, New Haven.

MacMullen, R. (1982), 'The epigraphic habit in the Roman empire', *AJPh* 103, 233–46.

McQueen, E.I. (1978), 'Some notes on the anti-Macedonian movement in the Peloponnese', *Historia 27*, 40–64.

Macready, S./Thompson, F.H. (1987), eds, *Roman Architecture in the Greek World*, London.

Mahaffy, J.P. (1892), *Problems in Greek History*, London.

Marasco, G. (1978), 'La leggenda di Polidoro e la ridistribuzione di Licurgo nella propaganda spartana del III secolo', *Prometheus* 4, 115–27.

Marasco, G. (1979), 'Cleomene III, i mercenari e gli iloti', *Prometheus* 5, 45–62.

Marasco, G. (1980a), 'La retra di Epitadeo e la situazione soziale di Sparta nel IV secolo', *AC* 49, 131–45.

Marasco, G. (1980b), *Sparta agli inizi dell' età Ellenistica. Il regno di Areo I 309/8–265/4 a.c.*, Florence.

Marasco, G. (1980c), 'Storia e propaganda durante la guerra cleomenica. Un episodio del III sec. A.C.', *RSI* 92, 5–34.

Marasco, G. (1981), *Commento alle biografie plutarchee di Agide e di Cleomene*, 2 vols, Rome (publ. 1983).

Marchetti, P. (1977), 'A propos des comptes de Delphes sous les archontats de Théon (324/3) et de Caphis (327/6)', *BCH* 101, 133–64.

Marek, Ch. (1984), *Die Proxenie*, Frankfurt/Main.

Marrou, H.-I. (1965), *Histoire de l'éducation dans l'antiquité*, 6th edn, Paris.

Martinez-Lacy, J.R. (1983), 'De Cléomene a Nabis', *Nova Tellus* 1, 105–20.

Martinez-Lacy, J.R. (1985), rev. of Marasco 1981, *Nova Tellus* 3, 273–94.

Martinez-Lacy, J.R. (1988), 'Opposition in the Hellenistic World: non-citizen revolts between 323 and 30 B.C.', diss., Cambridge.

Mason, H.J. (1974), *Greek Terms for Roman Institutions*, Toronto.

Meier, Ch. (1984), '"Revolution" in der Antike', in O. Brunner et al., eds, *Geschichtliche Grundbegriffe*, Stuttgart. 656–70.

Meier, Ch. (1986), rev. of M.I. Finley, *Politics in the Ancient World* (Cambridge 1983), *Gnomon* 58, 496–509.

Meiggs, R./Lewis, D.M. (1969), eds, *A Selection of Greek Historical Inscriptions to the End of the Fifth Century B.C.*, Oxford.

Meiggs, R.: see Bury, J.B.

Meister, K. (1984), 'Agathocles', *CAH*² vii.1, 384–411.

Mellink, M.J. (1943), *Hyakinthos*, Utrecht.

Meloni, P. (1950), 'L'intervento di Cleonimo in Magna Grecia', *GIF 3*, 103–21.

Mendels, D. (1977), 'Polybius, Philip V and the socio-economic question in Greece', *AncSoc* 8, 155–74.

Mendels, D. (1978), 'A note on the speeches of Nabis and T. Quinctius Flamininus (195 B.C.)', *SCI* 4, 38–44.

Mendels, D. (1979), 'Polybius, Nabis and equality', *Athenaeum* n.s. 57, 311–33.

Mendels, D. (1981), 'Polybius and the socio-economic reforms of Cleomenes III, reexamined', *GB* 10, 95–104.

Mendels, D. (1982), 'Polybius and the socio-economic revolution in Greece', *AC* . 51, 86–110.

Mendels, D. (1984–86), 'Did Polybius have "another" view of the Aetolian League? A note', *AncSoc* 15–17, 63–73.

Michell, H. (1952), *Sparta*. To krypton tēs politeias tōn Lakedaimoniōn, Cambridge.

Migeotte, L. (1984), *L'emprunt public dans les cités grecques*, Paris.

Migeotte, L. (1985), 'Réparations de monuments publics à Messène au temps d'Auguste', *BCH* 109, 597–607.

Millar, F. (1964), *A Study of Cassius Dio*, Oxford.

Millar, F. (1969), 'P. Herennius Dexippus: Athens, the Greek world and the third-century invasions', *JRS* 59, 12–29.

Millar, F. (1977), *The Emperor in the Roman World (31 B.C.–A.D.337)*, London.

Millar, F. (1981), 'The world of the Golden Ass', *JRS* 71, 63–75.

Millar, F. (1983), 'Epigraphy', in Crawford 1983, 80–136.

Millar, F./Segal, E. (1984), eds, *Caesar Augustus. Seven aspects*, Oxford.

Miller, S.G. (1978), *The Prytaneion: its form and function*, Berkeley.

Miller, S.G. (1982), 'Kleonai, the Nemean Games, and the Lamian War', in *Studies in Athenian Architecture, Sculpture and Topography presented to Homer. A. Thompson (Hesperia* Supp. xx), 100–108.

Mitchell, S. (1984), 'The Greek city in the Roman world: Pontus and Bithynia', in *Praktika of the Eighth International Congress of Greek and Latin Epigraphy* i, Athens, 120–33.

Mitchison, N. (1931), *The Corn King and the Spring Queen*, London (repr. Virago edn, 1983).

Momigliano, A.D. (1975), *Alien Wisdom. The limits of Hellenization*, Cambridge.

Momigliano, A.D. (1977), *Essays in Ancient and Modern Historiography*, Oxford.

Moretti, L. (1953), ed., *Iscrizioni agonistiche greche*, Rome.

Moretti, L. (1957), *Olympionikai: i vincitori negli antichi agoni Olimpici (Atti Accad. Naz. Lincei*⁸ 8.2), Rome, 53–198.

Moretti, L. (1975), 'Epigraphica', *RFIC* 103, 182–6.

Mosley, D.J. (1972), 'Euthycles: one or two Spartan envoys?', *CR* n.s. 22, 167–9. See also Adcock, F.E.

Mossé, C. (1961), 'Le rôle des esclaves dans les troubles politiques du monde grec à la fin de l'époque classique', *CH* 4, 353–69.

Mossé, C. (1964), 'Un tyran grec à l'époque hellénistique: Nabis "roi" de Sparte', *CH* 9, 313–23.

Mossé, C. (1969), *La tyrannie dans la Grèce antique*, Paris.

Müller, H. (1980), 'Claudia Basilo und ihre Verwandtschaft', *Chiron* 10, 457–84.

Münzer, F. (1925), *Die politische Vernichtung des Griechentums*, Leipzig.

Mulgan, R.G. (1977), *Aristotle's Political Theory*, Oxford.

Mundt, J. (1903), *Nabis, König von Sparta (206–192 v. Chr.)*, Köln.

Nash, E. (1961–1962), *Pictorial Dictionary of Ancient Rome*, 2 vols, London.

Nicholls, R.V.: see Cook, J.M.

Nicolet, Cl. (1978), ed., *Rome et la conquête du monde méditerranéen 264–27 avant J.-C.*ii *Genése d'un empire*, Paris.

Niese, B. (1893–1899–1903), *Geschichte der griechischen und makedonischen Staaten*, 3 vols, Gotha.

Nisbet, R.G.M. (1961), ed., *Cicero. In Pisonem*, Oxford (repr. 1987).

Nissen, H. (1863), *Kritische Untersuchungen über die Quellen der vierten und fünften Dekade des Livius*, Berlin.

Noethlichs, K.L. (1987), 'Bestechung, Bestechlichkeit und die Rolle des Geldes in der spartanischen Aussen- und Innenpolitik vom 7.-2. Jh. v. Chr.', *Historia* 36, 129–70.

Nutton, V. (1977), 'Archiatri and the medical profession in Antiquity', *PBSR* 45, 191–226.

Ober, J.: see Eadie, J.W.

O'Flynn, J.M. (1983), *Generalissimos of the Western Roman Empire*, Edmonton.

Ogilvie, R.M. (1967), 'The date of the *de defectu oraculorum*', *Phoenix* 21, 108–19.

Oliva, P. (1968), 'Die Auslandspolitik Kleomenes III', *AAntHung* 16, 179–85.

Oliva, P. (1971), *Sparta and her Social Problems*, Amsterdam and Prague.

Oliva, P. (1984), 'Der Achäische Bund zwischen Makedonien und Sparta', *Eirene* 21, 5–16.

Oliver, J.H. (1953), *The Ruling Power*, Philadelphia.

Oliver, J.H. (1970a), *Marcus Aurelius. Aspects of civic and cultural policy in the East* (*Hesperia* Supp. xiii), Princeton.

Oliver, J. H. (1970b), 'Hadrian's reform of the appeal procedure in Greece', *Hesperia* 39, 332–36.

Oliver, J.H. (1971), 'Athenian lists of Ephebic teams', *AE*, 66–74.

Oliver, J.H. (1973), 'Imperial commissioners in Achaia', *GRBS* 14, 389–405.

Oliver, J.H. (1976), 'Imperial commissioners again', *GRBS* 17, 369–70.

Oliver, J.H. (1979), 'Greek applicants for Roman trials', *AJPh* 100, 543–58.

Oliver, J.H. (1983), *The Civic Tradition and Roman Athens*, Baltimore.

Ollier, F. (1933–1943), *Le mirage spartiate. Étude sur l'idéalisation de Sparte dans l'antiquité grecque* i. *De l'origine jusqu'aux Cyniques* ii. *Du début de l'école cynique jusqu'à la fin de la cité*, Paris (repr. in 1 vol. New York 1973).

Ollier, F. (1936), 'Le philosophe stoïcien Sphairos et l'oeuvre réformatrice des rois de Sparte Agis IV et Cléomène III', *REG* 49, 536–70.

O'Neil, J.L. (1984–86), 'The political elites of the Achaian and Aitolian Leagues', *AncSoc* 15–17, 33–61.

Osborne, R.G. (1987), *Classical Landscape with Figures. The ancient Greek city and its countryside*, London.

Page, D.L.: see Gow, A.S.F.

Palagia, O. (forthcoming), 'Seven pilasters of Herakles from Sparta', in Cameron/Walker (forthcoming).

Panagopoulos, C. (1977), 'Vocabulaire et mentalité dans les *Moralia* de Plutarque', *DHA 3*, 197–235.

Pani, M. (1984), *Roma e il re d'oriente da Augusto a Tiberio*, Bari.

Papachatzis, N. (1974–80), *Pausaniou Hellados Periēgēsis*, Athens, 4 vols.

Papanikolaou. A.D. (1976–77), 'Epitymbion ex arkhaias Sellasias' *Athena* 76, 202–4 (in Greek).

Pape, M. (1975), 'Griechische Kunstwerke aus Kriegsbeute und ihre öffentliche Aufstellung in Rom. Von der Eroberung von Syrakus bis in augusteische Zeit', diss., Hamburg.

Parke, H.W. (1933), *Greek Mercenary Soldiers from the earliest times to the Battle of Ipsus*, Oxford (repr. 1970).

Parke, H.W. (1945), 'The deposing of Spartan kings', *CQ* 39, 106–12.

Passerini, A. (1933), 'Studi di storia ellenistico-romana. vi. I moti politico-sociali della Grecia e i Romani', *Athenaeum* n.s. 11, 309–35.

Patrucco, R. (1975), 'L'attività sportiva di Sparta', *Archaeologica. Fest. A. Neppi Modona*, Florence, 395–412.

Peek, W. (1969), ed., *Inschriften aus dem Asklepieion von Epidauros*, Berlin.

Peek, W. (1974), 'Artemis Eulakia', in *Mélanges hellénistiques offerts à Georges Daux*, Paris, 295–302.

Pékary, Th. (1968), *Untersuchungen zu den römischen Reichsstrassen*, Bonn.

Pékary, Th. (1987), '*Seditio*, Unruhen und Revolten im römischen Reich', *AncSoc* 18, 133–50.

Penella, R. (1979), *The Letters of Apollonius of Tyana*, Leiden.

Peppa-Delmouzou, D. (1980), 'Hypographies kallitekhnōn', in *STELE. Fest. N.M. Kontoleon*, Athens, 430–9 (in Greek).

Pflaum, H.-G. (1960–1961), *Les carrières procuratoriennes équestres sous le haut-empire romain*, 3 vols, Paris.

Pikoulas, G.A. (1984), 'Hē Tabula Peutingeriana kai hē Khersonēsos tou Malea', *Horos* 2, 175–8 (in Greek).

Piper, L.J. (1979), 'Wealthy Spartan women', *CB* 56, 5–8.

Piper, L.J. (1984–86), 'Spartan Helots in the Hellenistic Age', *AncSoc* 15–17, 75–88.

Piper, L.J. (1986), *Spartan Twilight*, New Rochelle.

Pipili, M. (1987), *Laconian Iconography of the Sixth Century B.C.*, Oxford.

Pleket, H.W. (1974), 'Zur Soziologie des antiken Sports', *MNIR* 36, 57–87.

Pleket, H.W. (1983), 'Urban elites and business in the Greek part of the Roman Empire', in Garnsey/Hopkins/Whittaker 1983, 131–44.

Pleket, H.W. (1984), 'Urban elites and the economy in the Greek cities of the Roman empire', *MBAH* 3, 3–35.

Plommer, W.H. (1979), 'Vitruvius and the origin of Caryatids', *JHS* 99, 97–102.

Podlecki, A.J. (1985), 'Theophrastus on history and politics', in Fortenbaugh 1985, 231–49.

Pollitt, J.J. (1972), *Art and Experience in Classical Greece*, Cambridge.

Pollitt, J.J. (1974), *The Ancient View of Greek Art. Criticism, history, and terminology*, New Haven.

Pope, K.O.: see Van Andel, T.H.

Poralla, P./Bradford, A.S. (1985), *Prosopographie der Lakedaimonier bis auf die Zeit Alexanders des Grossen*, 2nd edn, Chicago.

Porter, R./Teich, M. (1986), eds, *Revolution in History*, Cambridge.

Porter, W.H. (1937), ed., *Plutarch's Life of Aratus*, Cork.
Potter, D.S. (1984), 'IG II² 399: evidence for Athenian involvement in the war of Agis III', *ABSA* 79, 229–35.
Pozzi, F. (1968), 'Le riforme economico-sociali e le mire tiranniche di Agide IV e Cleomene III, re di Sparta', *Aevum* 42, 383–402.
Pozzi, F. (1970), 'Sparta e i partiti politici tra Cleomene III e Nabide', *Aevum* 44, 389–414.
Préaux, C. (1965), 'Réflexions sur l'entité hellénistique', *CE* 40, 129–39.
Préaux, C. (1978), *Le monde hellénistique. La Grèce et l'Orient de la mort d'Alexandre à la conquête romaine de la Grèce (323–146 av. J.-C.)*, 2 vols, Paris.
Premerstein, A. von (1901), 'Corrector', *RE* iv.2, 1646–56.
Premerstein, A. von (1911), 'Untersuchungen zur Geschichte des Kaisers Marcus iii. Das lakedaimonische Bundeskontingent', *Klio* 11, 358–66.
Price, S.R.F. (1984), *Rituals and Power. The Roman Imperial Cult in Asia Minor*, Cambridge.
Pritchett, W.K. (1980), *Studies in Ancient Greek Topography* iii. *Roads*, Berkeley, etc.
Puech, B. (1983), 'Grands-prêtres et helladarques d'Achaïe', *REA* 85, 15–43.
Quass, F. (1984), 'Zum Einfluss der römischer Nobilität auf das Honoratioren-regime in den Städten des griechischen Ostens', *Hermes* 112, 199–215.
Raepsaet-Charlier, M.T. (1987), *Prosopographie des femmes de l'ordre sénatorial (Ier-IIe siècle)*, 2 vols, Louvain.
Rahe, P.A. (1980), 'The selection of Ephors at Sparta', *Historia* 29, 385–401.
Rathbone, D.W. (1983), 'The grain trade and grain shortages in the Hellenistic East', in Garnsey/Whittaker 1983, 45–55.
Rawson, E. (1969), *The Spartan Tradition in European Thought*, Oxford.
Rawson, E. (1973), 'The Eastern clientelae of Clodius and the Claudii', *Historia* 22, 219–39.
Rawson, E. (1985), *Intellectual Life at Rome in the Late Republic*, London.
Rawson, E. (1987), '*Discrimina ordinum*: the *Lex Julia Theatralis*', *PBSR* 55, 83–114.
Ray, J.D. (1987), 'Egypt: dependence and independence (425–343 B.C.)', in Sancisi-Weerdenburg 1987, 70–95.
Reinach, T. (1890), *Mithridate Eupator, Roi de Pont*, Paris.
Reynolds, J.M. (1978), 'Hadrian, Antoninus Pius and the Cyrenaican cities', *JRS* 68, 111–21.
Reynolds, J.M. (1982), *Aphrodisias and Rome*, London.
Richter, G.M.A. (1984), *Portraits of the Greeks*, rev. and abridged edn by R.R.R. Smith, Oxford.
Ringwood, I.C. (1927), *Agonistic Features of Local Greek Festivals*, New York.
Robert, L. (1928), 'Études épigraphiques', *BCH* 52, 407–25.
Robert, L. (1930), 'Pantomimen im griechischen Orient', *Hermes* 65, 106–22.
Robert, L. (1939), 'Inscriptions grecques d'Asie mineure', in *Anatolian Studies presented to W.H. Buckler*, Manchester, 227–48.
Robert, L. (1940a), 'EPIMELETES KAUDOU dans une inscription de Sparte', *Hellenica* i, Paris, 109–12.
Robert, L. (1940b), *Les gladiateurs dans l'orient grec*, Paris.
Robert, L. (1948), 'Épigramme d'Égine', *Hellenica* iv, Paris, 5–34.
Robert, L. (1960), 'Recherches épigraphiques', *REA* 62, 276–361.
Robert, L. (1966), *Documents de l'Asie mineure méridionale*, Paris.

Robert, L. (1984), 'Discours d'ouverture', *Praktika of the Eighth International Congress of Greek and Latin Epigraphy* i, 35–45, Athens. See also Woodward, A.M.

Robertson, N. (1986), 'A point of precedence at Plataia. The dispute between Athens and Sparta over leading the procession', *Hesperia* 55, 88–102.

Robins, W.S. (1958), 'The position of the Helots in the time of Nabis, 206–192 B.C.', *Univ. Birmingham Hist. Jnl* 6, 93–8.

Roddaz, J.-M. (1984), *Marcus Agrippa*, Paris.

Roebuck, C.A. (1941), *A History of Messenia from 369 to 146 B.C.*, Chicago.

Roebuck, C.A. (1948), 'The settlements of Philip II in 338 B.C.', *CPh* 43, 73–92 (repr. in his *Economy and Society in the Early Greek World*, Chicago 1979).

Rostovtzeff, M.I. (1941), *The Social and Economic History of the Hellenistic World*, 3 vols, Oxford (corr. impr. 1953).

Rostovtzeff, M.I. (1957), *The Social and Economic History of the Roman Empire*, 2 vols, 2nd edn by P.M. Fraser, Oxford.

Runnels, C.N./Van Andel, T.H. (1987), 'The evolution of settlement in Southern Argolid, Greece: an economic explanation', *Hesperia* 56, 303–34. See also Van Andel, T.H.

Ruyt, C. de (1983), *Macellum, marché alimentaire des Romains*, Louvain-la-Neuve.

Ryder, T.T.B. (1965), *Koine Eirene. General peace and local independence in ancient Greece*, Oxford.

Ste. Croix, G.E.M. de (1972), *The Origins of the Peloponnesian War*, London and Ithaca.

Ste. Croix, G.E.M. de (1974), 'Ancient Greek and Roman maritime loans', in *Debits, Credits, Finance and Profits. Fest. W.T. Baxter*, London, 41–59.

Ste. Croix, G.E.M. de (1981), *The Class Struggle in the Ancient Greek World. From the Archaic age to the Arab conquests*, London and Ithaca (corr. impr. 1983).

Saller, R.P. (1982), *Personal Patronage in the Roman World*, Cambridge. See also Garnsey, P.D.A.

Sancisi-Weerdenburg, H. (1987), ed., *Achaemenid History* i. *Sources, structures and synthesis*, Leiden.

Sanders,L.J. (1987), *Dionysius I of Syracuse and Greek Tyranny*, London, New York and Sydney.

Sarikakis, Th. (1965), 'Aktia ta en Nikopolei', *AE*, 145–62 (in Greek).

Sasel Kos, M. (1979), ed., *Inscriptiones Latinae in Graecia Repertae (Addidamenta ad CIL iii)*, Faenza.

Schaefer, H. (1949), 'Patronomos', *RE* xviii.4, 2295–2306.

Schürer, E. (1973), *The History of the Jewish People in the Age of Jesus Christ (175 B.C.-A.D. 135)* i, 2nd edn, ed. G. Vermes and F. Millar, Edinburgh.

Schwertfeger, T. (1974), *Der Achaïsche Bund von 146 bis 27 v. Chr.*, Munich.

Schwertfeger, T. (1981), 'Die Basis für Tiberius Claudius Calligenes', *Olympiabericht* 10, Berlin, 248–55.

Seeck, O. (1906), *Die Briefe des Libanius zeitlich geordnet*, Leipzig (repr. Hildesheim 1966).

Segal, E.: see Millar, F.

Seibert, J. (1979), *Die politischen Flüchtlinge und Verbannten in der griechischen Geschichte*, 2 vols, Darmstadt.

Seltman, C.T. (1933), *Greek Coins. A history of metallic currency and coinage down to the fall of the Hellenistic kingdoms*, London.

Seure, G. (1915), 'Archéologie thrace. Documents inédits ou peu connus[2] ii.

Inscriptions avec des noms d'Empereurs', *RA*[5] 1 (July–Dec.), 165–208.

Shatzman, I. (1968), 'The meeting place of the Spartan Assembly', *RFIC* 96, 385–9.

Shatzman, I. (1975), *Senatorial Wealth and Roman Politics*, Brussels.

Shaw, B.D. (1985), 'The divine economy: Stoicism as ideology', *Latomus* 44, 16–54.

Shear, T.L. jr (1969), 'The Athenian Agora: excavations of 1968', *Hesperia* 38, 382–417.

Shear, T.L. jr (1981), 'Athens: from city-state to provincial town', *Hesperia* 50, 356–77.

Sheppard, A.R.R. (1984–86), '*Homonoia* in the Greek cities of the Roman Empire', *AncSoc* 15–17, 229–52.

Sherk, R.K. (1984), trans., *Rome and the Greek East to the death* of *Augustus* ('Translated Documents of Greece and Rome' 4), Cambridge.

Sherwin-White, A.N. (1966), *The Letters of Pliny. A social and political commentary*, Oxford.

Sherwin-White, A.N. (1973), *The Roman Citizenship*, 2nd edn, Oxford.

Shimron, B. (1965), 'The original task of the Spartan patronomoi. A suggestion', *Eranos* 63, 155–8.

Shimron, B. (1966a), 'Nabis of Sparta and the Helots', *CPh* 61, 1–7.

Shimron, B. (1966b), 'Some remarks on Phylarchus and Cleomenes III', *RFIC* 94, 452–9.

Shimron, B. (1972), *Late Sparta. The Spartan revolution 243–146 B.C.*, Buffalo.

Shimron, B. (1974), 'Nabis – aemulus Lycurgi', *SCI* 1, 40–6.

Shipley, G. (1987), *A History of Samos 800–188 BC*, Oxford.

Sichtermann, H.: see Koch, G.

Siebert, G. (1978), *Recherches sur les ateliers de bols à reliefs du Péloponnèse à l'époque hellénistique*, Athens and Paris.

Snodgrass, A.M. (1971), *The Dark Age of Greece: an archaeological survey of the eleventh to the eighth centuries B.C.*, Edinburgh.

Snodgrass, A.M. (1983), 'Archaeology', in Crawford 1983, 137–84. See also Bintliff, J.

Solin, H. (1982), *Die griechischen Personennamen in Rom*, 2 vols, Berlin etc.

Souris, G.A. (1981), 'A new list of the Gerousia at Roman Sparta', *ZPE* 41, 171–4.

Spawforth, A.J.S. (1976), '*Fourmontiana*: *IG* v.1.515: another forgery "from Amyklai"', *ABSA* 71, 139–45.

Spawforth, A.J.S. (1977), 'The slave Philodespotos: SYROS POT(E) THĒNATAS', *ZPE* 27, 294.

Spawforth, A.J.S. (1978), 'Balbilla, the Euryclids and memorials for a Greek magnate', *ABSA* 73, 249–60.

Spawforth, A.J.S. (1980), 'Sparta and the family of Herodes Atticus: a reconsideration of the evidence', *ABSA* 75, 203–20.

Spawforth, A.J.S. (1984), 'Notes on the Third Century AD in Spartan epigraphy', *ABSA* 79, 263–88.

Spawforth, A.J.S. (1985), 'Families at Roman Sparta and Epidaurus: some prosopographical notes', *ABSA* 80, 191–258.

Spawforth, A.J.S. (1986), 'A Severan statue-group and an Olympic festival at Sparta', *ABSA* 81, 313–32.

Spawforth, A.J.S. (1987), rev. of Piper 1986, *CR* n.s. 37, 245–6.

Spawforth, A.J.S. (forthcoming), 'Agonistic festivals in Roman Greece', in Cameron/Walker (forthcoming).

Spawforth, A.J.S./Walker, S. (1985–1986), 'The world of the Panhellenion i. Athens and Eleusis', 'ii. Three Dorian cities', *JRS* 75, 78–104; 76, 88–105.

Strubbe, J.H.M. (1984–86), 'Gründer kleinasiatischer Städte. Fiktion und Realität', *AncSoc* 15–17, 253–304.

Taïphakos, I.G. (1972), *Nabis kai Phlamininos. Hē synkrousis tou tyrannou meta tēs Rhōmēs kai tōn en Lakōniai symmakhōn autēs*, Athens (23 pp, in Greek).

Taïphakos, I.G. (1973), 'Hoi Rhomaioi kai to koinon tōn Lakedaimoniōn (*IG* v.1, 1146)', *Hellenikos Logos*, 345–51 (in Greek).

Taïphakos, I.G. (1974), *Rhomaïke Politikē en Lakōniai. Ereunai epi tōn politikōn skheseōn Rhōmes kai Spartēs*, Athens (in Greek).

Taïphakos, I.G. (1984), 'Enas tyrannos ston Tito Livio', *Praktika tou A' Panelleniou Symposiou Latinikon Spoudon*, Ioannina, 125–36 (in Greek).

Tarn, W.W. (1913), *Antigonos Gonatas*, Oxford (repr. 1969).

Tarn, W.W. (1923), 'The social question in the third century', in Bury 1923, 108–40.

Tarn, W.W. (1928), 'The new Hellenistic kingdoms' and 'Macedonia and Greece', *CAH*[1] vii, 75–108, 197–223.

Tazelaar, C.M. (1967), 'PAIDES KAI EPHEBOI: some notes on the Spartan stages of youth', *Mnemosyne*[4] 20, 127–53.

Tcherikover, V. (1970), *Hellenistic Civilization and the Jews*, New York (repr. of 1959 trans. by S. Applebaum).

Texier, J.-G. (1974), 'Nabis et les hilotes', *DHA* 1, 189–205.

Texier, J.-G. (1975), *Nabis*, Paris.

Texier, J.-G. (1976–77), 'Un aspect de l'antagonisme de Rome et de Sparte à l'époque hellénistique: l'entrevue de 195 avant J.C. entre Titus Quinctius Flamininus et Nabis', *REA* 78–79, 145–54.

Thomas, K. (1971), *Religion and the Decline of Magic. Studies in popular beliefs in sixteenth- and seventeenth-century England*, London.

Thompson, F.H.: see Macready, S.

Thompson, K.: see Kayser, B.

Tigerstedt, E.N. (1965–1974–1978), *The Legend of Sparta in Classical Antiquity*, 2 vols + Index vol, Stockholm, Göteborg and Uppsala.

Tod, M.N. (1932), 'Inter-state arbitration in the Greek world', in his *Sidelights on Greek History*, London, 39–68 (repr. Chicago 1974).

Tod, M.N. (1948), *A Selection of Greek Historical Inscriptions* ii. *From 403 B.C. to 323 B.C.*, Oxford.

Tod, M.N./Wace, A.J.B. (1906), *Catalogue of the Sparta Museum*, Oxford.

Tomlinson, R.A. (1972), *Argos and the Argolid* ('States and Cities of Ancient Greece'), London, Henley and Boston.

Toneatto, L. (1974–5), 'La lotta politica e aspetto sociale a Sparta dopo la caduta di Cleomene III', *Index* 5, 179–248 (publ. 1979).

Touloumakos, J. (1967), *Der Einfluss Roms auf die Staatsform der griechischen Stadtstaaten des Festlandes und der Inseln im ersten und zweiten Jhdt. v. Chr.*, Göttingen.

Toynbee, A.J. (1965), *Hannibal's Legacy. The Hannibalic War's effects on Roman life*, 2 vols. ii. *Rome and her neighbours after Hannibal's exit*, Oxford.

Toynbee, A.J. (1969), *Some Problems of Greek History*, Oxford.

Traquair, R. (1905–6), 'Excavations at Sparta, 1906. xii. The Roman Stoa and the later fortifications', *ABSA* 12, 415–29.

Travlos, I. (1960), *Poleodomikē Exelixis tōn Athēnōn*, Athens (in Greek).

Travlos, J. (1971), *Pictorial Dictionary of Ancient Athens*, London and New York.

Triantaphyllopoulos, J. (1971), '*Paraprasis*', *Acta of the Fifth International Congress of Greek and Latin Epigraphy*, Cambridge, 65–9.

Trieber, C. (1866), *Quaestiones Laconicae*, Göttingen.

Urban, R. (1979), *Wachstum und Krise des Achäischen Bundes. Quellenstudien zur Entwicklung des Bundes von 280 bis 222 v. Chr.*, Wiesbaden.

Valmin, N. (1929), 'Inscriptions de la Messénie', *Bull. soc. roy. lett. Lund* 4, 1–48.

Van Andel, T.H./Runnels, C.N./Pope, K.O. (1986), 'Five thousand years of land use and abuse in the southern Argolid', *Hesperia* 55, 103–28. See also Runnels, C.N.

Van Bremen, R. (1983), 'Women and wealth', in Cameron, A./Kuhrt, A., eds, *Images of Women in Antiquity*, London, 223–42.

Vaphopoulou-Richardson, C.E.: see Boardman, J.

Vatai, F.L. (1984), *Intellectuals in Politics in the Greek World. From early times to the Hellenistic Age*, London, etc.

Vatin, Cl. (1970), *Recherches sur le mariage et la condition de la femme mariée à l'époque hellénistique*, Paris.

Veyne, P. (1976), *Le pain et le cirque: sociologie historique d'un pluralisme politique*, Paris.

Veyne, P. (1985), 'PROKRITOS: jurés provinciaux dans les inscriptions de Sparte', *RPh* 59, 21–5.

Vial, Cl.: see Baslez, M.-F.

Vidal-Naquet, P. (1986), *The Black Hunter. Forms of thought and forms of society in the Greek world*, Baltimore (French original Paris 1981, corr. repr. 1983).

Wace, A.J.B. (1906–7), 'The city walls' and 'The stamped tiles', *ABSA* 13, 5–16, 17–43.

Wace, A.J.B. (1907–8), 'Excavations at Sparta, 1908. A hoard of Hellenistic coins', *ABSA* 14, 149–58.

Wace, A.J.B./Dickins, G. (1906–7), 'The Hellenistic tombs', *ABSA* 13, 155–68.

Wace, A.J.B./Hasluck, F.W. (1907–8), 'Laconia. Topography: south-eastern Laconia', *ABSA* 14, 161–82. See also Tod, M.N.

Walbank, F.W. (1933), *Aratos of Sicyon*, Cambridge.

Walbank, F.W. (1940), *Philip V of Macedon*, Cambridge (repr. 1967).

Walbank, F.W. (1957–1967–1979), *A Historical Commentary on Polybius*, 3 vols, Oxford.

Walbank, F.W. (1966), 'The Spartan ancestral constitution in Polybius', in *Ancient Society and Institutions. Fest. V. Ehrenberg*, Oxford, 303–12.

Walbank, F.W. (1971), 'The fourth and fifth decades', in Dorey, T.A., ed., *Livy*, London and Toronto, 47–72.

Walbank, F.W. (1972), *Polybius*, Berkeley, Los Angeles and London.

Walbank, F.W. (1976–7), 'Were there Greek federal states?', *SCI* 3, 27–51 (= Walbank 1985, 20–37.)

Walbank, F.W. (1981), *The Hellenistic World*, Hassocks and Glasgow.

Walbank, F.W. (1984), 'Sources for the period', 'Monarchies and monarchic ideas', and 'Macedonia and Greece', *CAH*² vii.1, 1–22, 62–100, 221–56.

Walbank, F.W. (1985), *Selected Papers. Studies in Greek and Roman history and historiography*, Cambridge.

Walbank, F.W. (1986), rev. of Bernhardt 1985, *Gnomon* 58, 515–18.

Walbank, F.W. (1987), 'Könige als Götter. Überlegungen zum Herrscherkult von Alexander bis Augustus', *Chiron* 17, 365–82.

Walker, S. (forthcoming), 'Two Spartan women and the Eleusinium', in

Cameron/Walker (forthcoming). See also Cameron, A.; Coleman, M.L.; Spawforth, A.J.S.

Wason, M.O. (1947), *Class Struggles in Ancient Greece*, London.

Waterhouse, H.E.: see Hope Simpson, R.

Waywell, S.E. (1979), 'Roman mosaics in Greece', *AJA* 83, 293–321.

Wehrli, C. (1962), 'Les Gynéconomes', *MH* 19, 33–8.

Weil, R. (1881), 'Die Familie des C. Julius Eurykles,' *MDAI(A)* 6, 10–20.

Weiss, P. (1984), 'Lebendiger Mythos. Gründerheroen und städtische Gründungstraditionen im griechisch-römischen Osten', *WJA* n.s. 10, 180–208.

Wells, C.M. (1984), *The Roman Empire*, Hassocks and Glasgow.

Welskopf, E.C. (1974), ed., *Hellenische Poleis. Krise-Wandlung-Wirkung*, 4 vols, Berlin.

Welwei, K.-W. (1974), *Unfreie im antiken Kriegsdienst* i. *Athen und Sparta*, Wiesbaden.

Werner, R. (1972), 'Das Problem des Imperialismus und die römische Ostpolitik im zweiten Jahrhundert v. Chr.', *ANRW* i, 501–63.

West, A.B. (1931), *Corinth* viii.2. *Latin inscriptions 1896–1926*, Cambridge, Mass.

Wheeler, E.L. (1983), 'The hoplomachoi and Vegetius' Spartan drillmasters', *Chiron* 13, 1–20.

Whitehead, D. (1986), *The Demes of Attica 508/7-ca.250 B.C.*, Princeton.

Whittaker, C.R. (1986), 'Inflation and the economy in the fourth century AD', in King 1986, 1–22. See also Garnsey, P.D.A.

Wide, S. (1893), *Lakonische Kulte*, Leipzig.

Wilcken, U. (1925), 'Puntfahrten in der Ptolemäerzeit', *ZAeS* 60, 86–102.

Wilhelm, A. (1913), 'Inschrift zu Ehren des Paulinus aus Sparta', *SDAW*, 858–63.

Wilhelm, A./Heberdey, R. (1896), *Reise in Kilikien*, Vienna.

Wilkes, J.J. (forthcoming), 'Civil defence in third-century Achaea', in Cameron/Walker (forthcoming).

Will, Ed. (1975), *Le monde grec et l'orient* ii. *Le IVe siècle et l'époque hellénistique* (with Cl. Mossé and P. Goukowsky), Paris.

Will, Ed. (1979–1982), *Histoire politique du monde hellénistique (323–30 av. J.-C.)*, 2 vols, 2nd edn, Nancy.

Will, Ed. (1984), 'The succession to Alexander' and 'The formation of the Hellenistic kingdoms', CAH^2 vii.1, 23–61, 101–17.

Wiseman, J. (1979), 'Corinth and Rome i', *ANRW* ii.7.1, 428–540.

Wlosok, A. (1978), *Römischer Kaiserkult*, Darmstadt.

Wörrle, M. (1971), 'Ägyptisches Getreide für Ephesos', *Chiron* 1, 325–40.

Wolters, P. (1897), 'König Nabis', *MDAI*(A) 22, 139–47.

Woodward, A.M. (1907–8), 'Excavations at Sparta, 1908. Inscriptions from the sanctuary of Orthia', *ABSA* 14, 74–141.

Woodward, A.M. (1923–5), 'Excavations at Sparta, 1924–5', *ABSA* 26, 116–276.

Woodward, A.M. (1925–6), 'Excavations at Sparta, 1926. ii. The theatre; iii. The inscriptions', *ABSA* 27, 175–209, 210–54.

Woodward, A.M. (1926–7), 'Excavations at Sparta, 1927. ii. The theatre', *ABSA* 28, 3–36.

Woodward, A.M. (1927–8), 'Excavations at Sparta, 1924–28. The inscriptions, Part I', *ABSA* 29, 2–56.

Woodward, A.M. (1928–30), 'Excavations at Sparta, 1924–28. i. The theatre: architectural remains', *ABSA* 30, 151–240.

Woodward, A.M. (1948), '*Inscriptiones Graecae* v.1: some afterthoughts', *ABSA* 43, 209–59.

Woodward, A.M. (1950), rev. of Chrimes 1949, *Historia* 1, 616–34.
Woodward, A.M. (1951), 'Some notes on the Spartan *sphaireis*', *ABSA* 46, 191–9.
Woodward, A.M. (1953), 'Sparta and Asia Minor under the Roman Empire', in *Studies presented to D.M. Robinson*, 2 vols, St Louis, ii.868–83.
Woodward, A.M./Robert, L. (1927–8), 'Excavations at Sparta, 1924–28. ii. Four Hellenistic decrees', *ABSA* 29, 57–74.
Wycherley, R.E. (1957), *The Athenian Agora* iii. *Literary and Epigraphic Testimonia*, Princeton.
Zahrnt, M. (1979), *Ktistes-Conditor-Restitutor. Untersuchungen zur Städtepolitik des Kaisers Hadrian*, Kiel.
Zeilhofer, G. (1959), 'Sparta, Delphoi und die Amphiktyonen im 5. Jht. v. Chr.', diss., Erlangen.
Ziegler, K. (1951), 'Plutarchos', *RE* xxi.1, 636–92.

Abbreviations

In addition to obvious or easily identified abbreviations of modern works, the following epigraphic abbreviations are used:

CIG	*Corpus Inscriptionum Graecarum*
CIL	*Corpus Inscriptionum Latinarum*
FD	*Fouilles de Delphes*, in progress
IDélos	*Inscriptions de Délos*, vols. by various authors
IG	*Inscriptiones Graecae*
IGB	G. Mihailov, *Inscriptiones Graecae in Bulgaria repertae* (1956–70)
IGRR	R. Cagnat, *Inscriptiones Graecae ad res Romanas pertinentes* (1906–27)
IGUR	*Inscriptiones Graecae Urbis Romae*
ISE	L. Moretti, *Iscrizioni storiche ellenistiche* (1967–75)
IvO	W. Dittenberger and K. Purgold, *Olympia: die Ergebnisse . . . der Ausgrabung. V. Die Inschriften*, 1896
SEG	*Supplementum Epigraphicum Graecum*
SIG³	W. Dittenberger, *Sylloge Inscriptionum Graecarum*, 3rd edition

Index